CW01371182

The future makers

The future makers
Australian wines for the 21st century
Max Allen

hardie grant books
MELBOURNE · LONDON

Published in 2010 by
Hardie Grant Books
85 High Street
Prahran, Victoria 3181, Australia
www.hardiegrant.com.au

All rights reserved. No part of this publication may be reproduced, stored in a retrieval system or transmitted in any form by any means, electronic, mechanical, photocopying, recording or otherwise, without the prior written permission of the publishers and copyright holders.

The moral right of the author has been asserted.

Copyright © Max Allen
Copyright photography © see picture credits

National Library of Australia Cataloguing-in-Publication Data:

Cataloguing-in-Publication data is available from the National Library of Australia.
The Future Makers: Australian wines for the 21st century
ISBN 978 1 74066 661 9

Cover design by Philip Campbell Design
Cover images courtesy of James Boddington and getty images
Map on page 24 by Martin von Wyss, vW Maps
Text design and page layout by Philip Campbell Design
Typeset in Adobe Garamond Pro
Colour reproduction by Splitting Image Colour Studio
Printed and bound in China by 1010

10 9 8 7 6 5 4 3 2 1

Disclaimer

The particularly turbulent nature of the modern Australian wine scene and the long lead times of the publishing industry conspire against anybody trying to write a wine book: the harsh reality is that some of the producers listed within these pages may well have closed down or changed hands by the time you read this. Likewise, I am certain that, in between sending off the manuscript and receiving the first advance copies, I will hear about, taste the gorgeous produce of, and probably visit a dozen or more fantastic vineyards that should have been included. So, for updates, expansions, corrections and the latest views on Australia's alternative wine scene, visit my Real Australian Wines blog: realaustralianwines.blogspot.com

Acknowledgements

The Wine Communicators of Australia Fellowship Grant, which I was awarded in 2003, helped fund some of the necessary travel and research. The good people at Hardie Grant Books (not to mention my family) have displayed saintly forbearance during the agonising gestation of this project: I told you I'd finish it...eventually. My editor Tracy O'Shaughnessy deserves special thanks for working like a demon to pull all the strands together and complete the finished book, as does designer Phil Campbell and the photographers who contributed so much to the look. Thanks also to Martin von Wyss for the map of Australia's wine regions. Some of the material in these pages first appeared in a different form in other publications, including *The Weekend Australian Magazine*, *G Magazine*, *Gourmet Traveller*, *The Wine Magazine* and *Wine & Spirits*: thank you to all the editors for the opportunity to tell these stories. Much of the information about biodynamic viticulture also appears on my web site: www.redwhiteandgreen.com.au

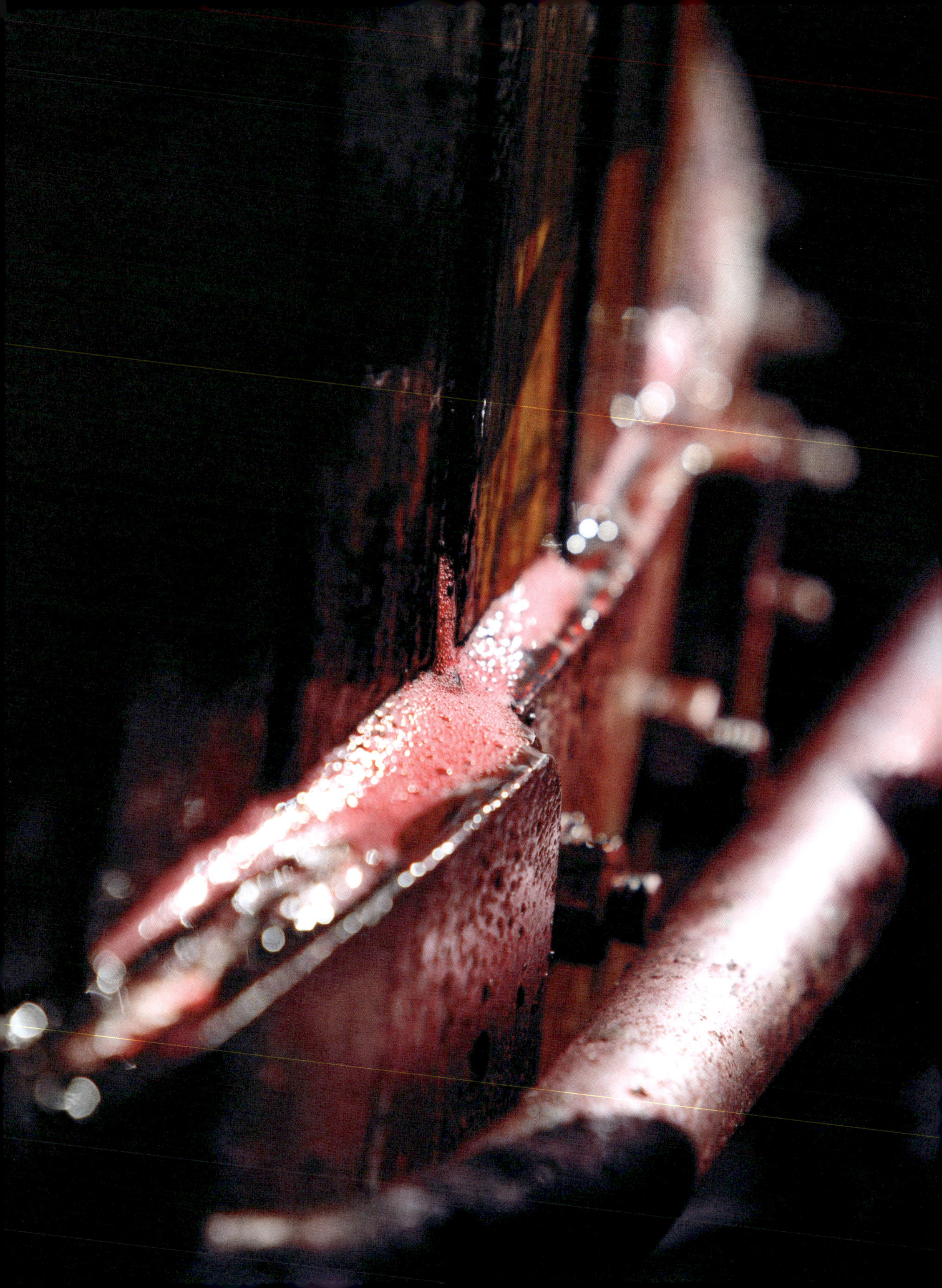

Contents

Aperitif — viii
Introduction: Setting the scene — 2

Part 1: **The big picture**

1 Sunburnt country: The changing climate of Australian wine — 9
2 A sense of belonging: Exploring Australia's terroirs — 17
3 Back to the future: Reviving old traditions in Australia's vineyards and wineries — 31
4 A family affair: Australia's wine industry enters a new phase — 47
5 New tastes, new flavours: Australia's expanding gallery of wine grapes — 55

Part 2: **Vineyards, winemakers, wines**

6 Heart and soul: The Riverland, the Riverina, Murray Darling and Swan Hill — 93
7 Victoria — 113
8 South Australia — 231
9 New South Wales — 319
10 Western Australia — 359
11 Tasmania — 391
12 Queensland — 419

Picture credits — 429
Index — 431

Aperitif

A few years ago, I very nearly opened my own bar. I had this vision of a small, cosy place, crammed with bottles, serving small plates of good food and great wines by the glass. I have also, for a long time, dreamed about planting my own vineyard – again, just a small plot of vines, enough for a few barrels. Thankfully, neither dream has come true: thankfully because I haven't got a business-minded bone in my body and I don't know how to drive a tractor, let alone fix one; the bar would have quickly gone bust and the vines would no doubt have died. I'm much better off sticking to drinking and writing about wine, I've decided, than trying to make it or sell it.

The point is that when you *do* contemplate crossing the line from interested observer to active participant you're suddenly faced with a whole heap of important questions: Where would be the best place for my vineyard? What varieties would I plant? How would I grow my grapes and make my wine? Which wines would I serve in my own bar? And why would I want to go to all that effort when I can buy plenty of lovely wines already?

I soon realised that the answers to these questions came wrapped up in broader considerations, such as the effects of climate change, my aversion to chemically assisted farming and my unashamedly romantic belief that wine should taste of where it's from. I realised that, if I had my own vineyard, it would be planted with varieties suited to a warmer, drier future; it would be farmed biodynamically; I would make the wines with as few additions and as little manipulation as possible; and I would hope to produce something beautiful, which told a story of its place and time.

I also realised that the wines I would want to sell in my mythical bar – the wines I already buy and drink – come from winemakers thinking along the same lines. Winemakers who ask themselves: What's special about where I am? Have I planted the most appropriate varieties? Is this the best way to grow my grapes and make my wine? Why am I doing this?

These are the winemakers who interest and excite me: the ones asking why. Because they are making the most characterful, appropriate and delicious wines sensibly, sustainably and naturally. These people – the larrikins and ratbags, the old and the young, the newbies and the nerds – putting the soul back into Australian wine are the people you'll meet in this book.

Max's Wine Bar

- White
  - Cullen Semillion Blanc, Margaret River, WA
  - Lark Hill Gruner Veltliner, Canberra District, NSW
  - Radford Riesling, Eden Valley, SA
  - Quealy Friulano, Mornington Peninsula, Vic
  - Bindi Quartz Chardonnay, Macedon Ranges, Vic
  - Moondarra Hollys Garden Pinot Gris, Whitlands, Vic
  - Yalumba Organic Viognier, Riverland, SA
  - Mac Forbes Riesling Tradition, Strathbogie Rgs, Vic

- Rose
  - Krinklewood Francesca, Hunter Valley, NSW
  - Spinifex, Barossa Valley, NSW
  - Sutton Grange Estate, Bendigo, Vic

- Red
  - Lucy Margaux Vineyard Pinot Noir, Adel'd H, SA
  - Bass Phillip Gamay, Gippsland, Vic
  - Ngeringa Su..., SA
  - Highbank Me..., SA
  - Boireau Ta...
  - Freeman ...ecco
  - Hewit... O'...
  - ...onda...e Te...
  - Arrivo ...bbioli...

Introduction
Setting the scene

Anton van Klopper makes his wine in the Adelaide Hills. His vineyard is small. Just a few steep, sloping hectares of pinot noir vines. His winery is small, too. A rudimentary shed with a concrete floor. And his approach to growing grapes seems strikingly unconventional to 21st-century eyes.

Most modern Australian vineyards are sprayed with chemical herbicides, fungicides and, in some cases, pesticides. Most modern Australian vineyards are irrigated and have synthetic fertiliser applied to keep them alive and fruitful. Most modern Australian grapevines are trained fast and high, in neat, hedged rows along a wire.

Not here. Instead, Anton lets each vine grow slowly, without supplementary water, allowing the roots to find their own refreshment and nourishment deep in the hillside slopes. And in the few years since the vines were planted, he has never sprayed anything other than homeopathic doses of natural, organic, biodynamic compost preparations to the soil or the plants.

In 2007 Anton picked his first, tiny crop of pinot noir grapes and made just over 100 litres of wine. That's a half-barrel's worth, roughly 130 bottles. I tasted the wine a few months after vintage in the fading light of the makeshift winery at dusk. In the gloom, the small barrel looked like a meagre return for all those years of nurture.

Carefully, Anton eased out the bung, slid in a hose and siphoned off a splash of precious purple liquid into a glass. The wine was gorgeous: full of the scent of ripe autumn plums, plush and velvety across the tongue.

In keeping with his approach to minimal intervention and minimal inputs in the vineyard, Anton made this pinot without adding anything. No cultured yeast, no sulphur, no enzymes, no tannin – all regular additions in other wineries across the country. The crushed grapes fermented naturally. They did their own thing. Anton didn't measure the acid level or sugar content or pH of the grapes or wine either – again, 'standard' winemaking practice – because, he said, he hadn't tasted a problem yet.

And then he told me a story about visiting a small, traditional cellar in Burgundy, where the winemaker, renowned for making wine in the way his father had done and his father before him, was grumbling about his neighbours. They cheat, said the old winemaker. They use chemicals.

❋

Anton van Klopper is about as far removed from the popular image of a modern Australian winemaker as it's possible to be. There's no gleaming stainless steel in the winery, no temperature control, no computer. No reliance, in other words, on powders in bags or hi-tech solutions for when things go wrong.

In many ways, Anton is much more in tune with the wine-drinker's innate sense of what wine is (or should be) than most of his ultra-modern Australian counterparts, with all the latest winemaking toys.

I believe we carry within us an archetypal idea of wine as a natural product of the earth: just grapes, grown naturally, fermented naturally. We like to believe that the wine we drink has not been buggered around with too much. If at all. We carry, too, a little deeper down, a remnant awareness of wine's ancient cultural and spiritual significance. This connection remains vague or subliminal for most wine drinkers who, understandably, are more interested in how much the stuff costs and whether it tastes good or not.

But the cultural and spiritual connection comes bubbling brightly up to the surface whenever we talk about wine's ability to make soil speak through the tastes and textures and flavours it reveals in your mouth.

That's what Anton's trying to do with his little patch of vines: tell the story of his unique crumpled corner of the Adelaide Hills. And he believes that growing his grapes and making his wine as naturally as possible, using biodynamic techniques to encourage soil and vine health, is the best way of articulating the story of his land in all its glorious complexity.

He's not alone. Across Australia's wine regions I am continually meeting grape growers and winemakers thinking along similar lines, sidestepping convention, ignoring their accountants, following their instincts to find a new way of telling the story of their country.

I have seen new vineyards planted like the old vineyards were, without irrigation, as bush vines, tied to single stakes: so much more work, so uneconomic according to the expert consultants, but such *fabulous*-tasting grapes if you get it right. I have walked through tiny pockets of vineyards planted in rambling permaculture gardens, with vines crawling up fruit trees, and met winemakers throwing out modern textbooks and going back to the wisdom found in 19th-century almanacs. And I have listened to winemakers share their burning desire to plant obscure grape varieties that no-one has heard of before.

These people aren't cranks. Most have solid, scientific training in viticulture and winemaking. It's just that they have decided to do things differently. And the results speak for themselves: not only do many of these new wines sell (and sell out) at impressively high prices, but they are also showered with critical acclaim and win trophies in wine shows. The wines are, more often than not, delicious. And people love to drink them.

At this point I can hear the cynic grumble, shuffle uneasily and harumph: 'It's all well and good that a bunch of ratbags and larrikins and hippy boutique operators want to go down the natural warm and fuzzy route and make wine like their grandparents are supposed to have done. But you can't run a modern, vibrant, multi-billion-dollar wine industry using biodynamics and permaculture and 19th-century textbooks, you know.'

Can't you? It may surprise the cynic to learn that these new Australian wine traditions, these new ways of thinking and doing, *aren't* confined to small-scale grape growers and winemakers. I have seen the same spirit of reinvention shining in the most unexpectedly mainstream places.

✢

Tony and Pam Barich grow their grapes at Loxton, in South Australia's hot Riverland wine region. Like hundreds of other growers in the area, they irrigate their 16-hectare vineyard using increasingly expensive and increasingly scarce water from the once-mighty Murray River. Like hundreds of other growers in the area, the Bariches sell their crop to a large wine company – in their case, it's Yalumba. But unlike most of the other vineyards in the area, the Bariches' 16 hectares of vines are certified biodynamic.

Tony is a Vietnam vet. A pig-headed individual, he says. When he started growing grapes, 30 years ago, he pretty quickly took a dislike to the agricultural chemical companies telling him what to do. They'd give him a spray diary at the beginning of each year and he'd immediately think: Why do I have to do this? It's *my* vineyard, not theirs.

He'd look at his neighbours' vineyards, too, where the chemical companies' advice had been followed to the letter, and all he saw were nuked paddocks under the vines, not a single blade of grass left.

So he threw away the chemicals, practised organic viticulture and got certified by the National Association for Sustainable Agriculture Australia in 2001. Got his US organic accreditation in 2007. And in the autumn of the same year started using biodynamic vineyard preparations. He now makes his own biodynamic compost, makes teas from nettles and seaweed, and he times his vineyard activities according to the lunar calendar: applying the biodynamic horn manure soil preparation and horn silica atmospheric spray, for example, when the moon and Saturn are in opposition.

Now, this is no small-scale artisan winemaker in the Adelaide Hills, selling a few dozen bottles of $50 pinot noir. This is a commercial grape grower selling hundreds of tonnes of grapes to one of the country's largest wine companies, to be turned into wine that will end up on shelves in Australian bottle shops and UK supermarkets for an everyday, accessible fifteen bucks or eight quid a bottle.

Tony knows the organic/biodynamic approach has made a difference to the health of his vines. He reckons this approach has the potential to open up a whole new door to the wine industry. And he can't see any reason why in a dry climate like the Riverland, and in other regions across Australia, everyone couldn't adopt it.

It's an attitude that's beginning to gain momentum.

I visited Yalumba's huge, 265-hectare Oxford Landing vineyard, an hour or so's drive from Tony Barich's place, at the height of vintage. It looked like most other large-scale Riverland vineyards: machine harvesters rumbled down vine rows that seemed to stretch away to the horizon. But Oxford Landing's young vineyard manager, Fred Strachan, showed me how he's changing the way he grows his grapes: using much less water, fewer chemicals, chasing lower crops of more intensely flavoured grapes.

Then he drove through the fence into the neighbouring property, a big, bare, red-sandy paddock. The plan, he said, is to put a new vineyard in here, plant obscure new alternative grapes and start from scratch using no chemical herbicide or fertiliser. Just organic methods. Maybe even biodynamics. And you could see the excitement in his eyes, hear it in his voice. The excitement that a Big Australian Wine Company like Yalumba should be investing in all this hippy shit. Who would have thought?

❂

Let me drag this back into perspective. The Australian wine industry is not, *en masse*, embracing organics, ripping out its chardonnay to plant drought-tolerant alternative grape varieties or searching for a unique taste of place in its wild yeast–fermented pinot noir. There are still plenty of head-in-sand winemakers, still plenty of corporate wine business accountants, still plenty of profit-driven grape growers all clinging desperately to business as usual.

But as climate change bites, and as the effects of the financial meltdown continue to ripple through both domestic and export markets, an increasing number of growers and winemakers *have* realised that business as usual simply isn't going to cut it any more. More and more people – including, crucially, people in the largest wine companies as well as the smallest – *are* thinking very deeply about true sustainability; thinking about adapting to and hopefully mitigating the effects of climate change; thinking about growing grape varieties and making wine in a way that better expresses their unique patch of country. These are the people trying to find a way out of the fine mess that the Australian wine industry has got itself into over the last 15 years. These are the people building a new sense of pride in Australian wine.

Part 1 The big picture

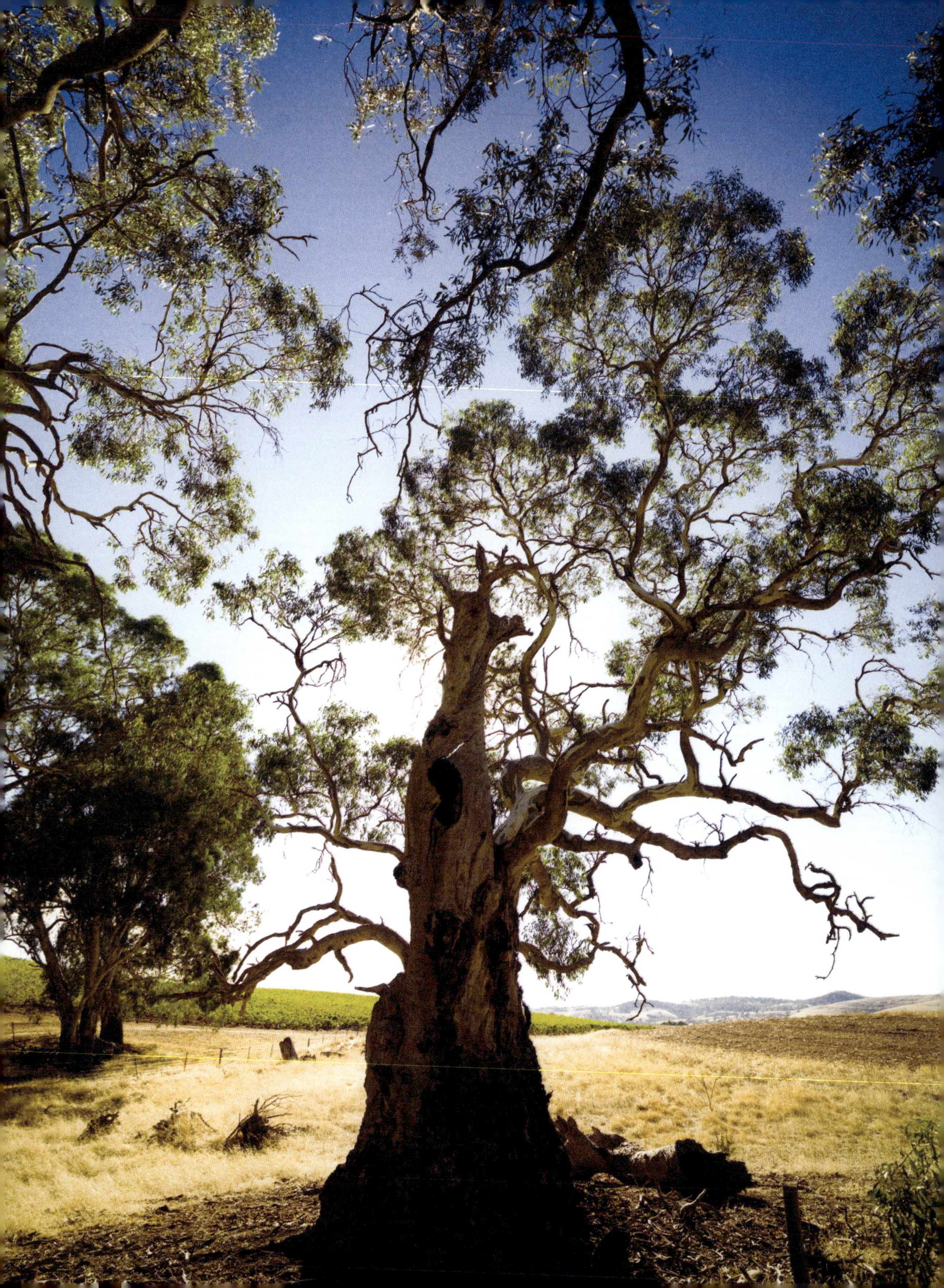

1 Sunburnt country
The changing climate of Australian wine

Professor Snow Barlow walks onto the stage in front of a couple of hundred grape growers and winemakers. He's here today to talk about the threat climate change poses to the Australian wine industry.

As Professor of Horticulture and Viticulture at the University of Melbourne, and as a member of the Australian delegation to the climate change negotiations in Kyoto back in the 1990s, he clearly knows what he's talking about. And what he's talking about is frightening.

'You can run but you can't hide from the effects of greenhouse gases,' the professor says, bluntly. 'Climate change is inevitable, and the wine industry is in a very vulnerable position; because of the infrastructure of your vineyards and wineries, you can't really move. And yet in 50 years' time, thanks to climate change, in Coonawarra, for example, the ripening period will move forward by three weeks, into a warmer part of the year. The wines made there will be in a different style to the wines you make today, will have different flavours, will no longer be "classic" Coonawarra.

'By 2050, there will be 25 per cent less water available than there is today, and it will be much warmer. I don't think you as an industry have any choice but to engage with what is a global problem. You need to establish a clean greenhouse image, and adopt minimisation strategies such as sensible waste treatment, better energy efficiency in design and operation and sequestering carbon where possible. It is crucial that you position yourselves on the side of the angels with this issue.'

This probably all sounds very familiar to you, reading this now, at the end of the first decade of the 21st century. But Snow Barlow's dire warning about climate change was delivered at the First National Wine Industry Environment Conference in November 2000, years before anybody had read Tim Flannery's best-selling book *The Weathermakers*, or watched Al Gore's *An Inconvenient Truth*, years before IPCC and Garnaut and Copenhagen.

Back then, in 2000, the grape growers and winemakers heard the warning but didn't really comprehend – or, worse, chose to ignore – what Snow Barlow had to say. It wasn't the first time the alarm had been raised, either. The effects of climate change on the wine industry have been talked about for at least two decades.

'I first heard about climate change in the 1970s,' says Richard Smart, renowned viticultural consultant and now climate change campaigner. 'I first gave a paper on global warming and the wine industry in 1989 in Luxembourg. At the time the response was totally cynical. Most members of the audience fell about on their chairs laughing when I told them in the future they'd be growing grenache in Bordeaux. But now they concede we may well see that happen by 2050.'

A measure of the low awareness of climate change in the early years of the 21st century is found in a 2002 document called 'Sustaining Success: The Australian Wine Industry's Environment Strategy', published as a result of the conference which Snow Barlow had addressed two years previously. The document listed the then-most important environmental issues facing the industry as 'water quality and use; waste management; and encouraging biodiversity'. 'Ramifications of future greenhouse gas-induced climate change on viticulture' appears at the bottom of the list.

Attitudes began to shift in late 2006 with the publication of a very detailed report on climate change and viticulture by the Commonwealth Scientific and Industrial Research Organisation's Leanne Webb and Penny Whetton (who was also an author of the 2007 IPCC report), and our old friend, Professor Snow Barlow.

This time, the weight of evidence in the report, combined with a growing awareness of climate change in wider society, made more people in the wine industry take notice. It was almost impossible not to see the drought, the fires, and the extreme weather events of the 2007 vintages (followed by even more apocalyptic events in 2008 and 2009) as clear signs that climate change was, all-too-frighteningly, already among us, wreaking havoc.

By the time of the triennial wine industry technical conference in Adelaide in July 2007, global warming and water security were front-and-centre issues. More than 1600 delegates to the conference, all battle-scarred from the vintage they'd just endured, listened as Richard Smart told them that 'climate change is the biggest challenge the Australian wine industry has faced in its history'.

Smart outlined the potential problems; Leanne Webb showed how temperatures are predicted to rise in wine regions across Australia; Penny Whetton told the audience that climate observations are running at the high end of the various modelled predictions; and Snow Barlow once again urged those assembled to make sure they ended up on the side of the angels.

I was sitting in the audience at that conference. All around me winemakers were shaking their heads as the reality of the situation was driven home to them. They were definitely listening now.

※

This is what is predicted to happen.

Temperature rises of up to 2°C by 2030 and up to 6°C by 2050 will have an enormous impact on wine regions across Australia. Grapes will ripen faster, bringing picking dates forward into warmer parts of the year, changing the flavours and styles of the wines produced. Cooler regions will turn into warmer regions. Some warm regions, particularly those inland irrigation areas such as the Riverina in New South Wales, the Murray Valley in Victoria and the Riverland in South Australia – regions which between them currently produce over two-thirds of the country's wine – could well become too hot to grow wine grapes at all. Grape growers will have to contend with more extreme weather events such as heatwaves, flash-floods, frosts and hail, and extended drought will degrade soil quality.

Many Australian winemakers will tell you that global warming not only is already here but also started to make its presence felt well before the consciousness-changing 2007 vintage.

When I visited the huge Angove winery in the Riverland in the middle of that vintage, winemaker Warwick Billings showed me a graph demonstrating how the start of the grape harvest has crept forward by almost a month over the last ten years – and how this has coincided with a steady increase in average temperature throughout the growing season of between 2°C and 4°C.

Paringa Estate sits at the other end of the production and climate spectrum on Victoria's Mornington Peninsula. Winemaker Lindsay McCall has also witnessed a significant advancement of picking dates.

'It's a bit of a worry,' understates Lindsay. 'We *finished* picking our pinot noir in 2006 before the date we *started* picking ten years ago. The question I have in my mind with earlier seasons is the reduced "hang time" for the fruit. Does faster ripening produce big-coloured and -flavoured wines – but reduce some of the delicacy sought after in great pinot?'

A hotter Australia means a drier Australia, and again, many think that we can already see this happening with the drastically reduced inflows to the Murray Darling river system – the same river system that provides the irrigation water for the majority of Australia's vineyards. The 'extreme' conditions of the last few years should perhaps be considered as the new 'normal'.

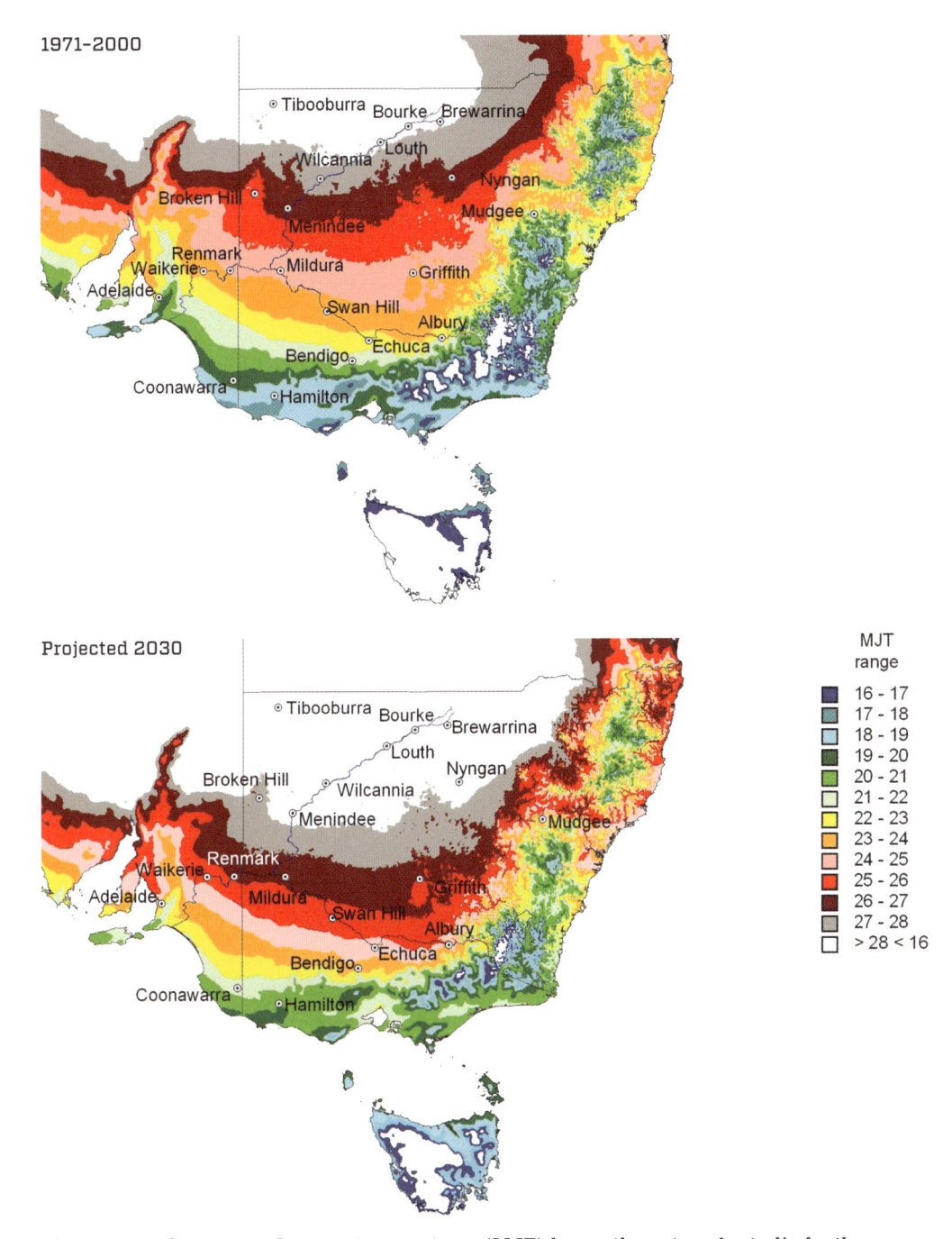

These maps show mean January temperatures (MJT) for south-eastern Australia for the present (1971-2000 data) and with 2°C increases uniformly applied as a first approximation of MJTs for 2030. (Maps courtesy Dr Richard Smart and John Gwalter)

Richard Smart thinks the threat is serious enough to justify the industry shifting both vineyards and wineries. 'People who want to adapt either need to go south or go up, where it's cooler,' he says. 'It's my prediction that the higher altitude of the Great Dividing Range and the lower latitudes of Tasmania will provide a lot of relief for the wine industry. And I think people who are clever will be starting to think about developing irrigation infrastructure further upriver towards the headwaters of the Murray.'

In many of Australia's better wine regions, vineyards were traditionally established on the flatter country or on north-facing slopes to help the vines' exposure to sunlight. In these places, adapting to climate change – in the short term at least – may be as simple as 'going round the back' and planting new vineyards on cooler, south-facing slopes. In the flatter regions such as Coonawarra and along the Murray, though, this isn't an option.

John Angove, managing director of his family's Riverland winery, is determined to stay put for as long as he can. 'The 2007 drought forced a revolution in the way we think,' he says. 'It has brought forward decisions about what grape varieties perhaps to change over to, and how we manage the vineyards, including the adoption of organic viticultural techniques.'

Efficiency is the new buzzword, particularly when it comes to irrigation. The tight water restrictions that have squeezed the regions along the Murray, Darling and Murrumbidgee rivers over the last few years have forced many grape growers to radically restructure their practices, in most cases converting from inefficient overhead spray or furrow irrigation to under-vine drip irrigation. They have realised that it is possible to not only grow grapes but also grow high-quality grapes using half the amount of water as before.

Amazingly, though, a significant minority of vineyards in some of the larger inland regions – up to 40 per cent of vines – is still irrigated by furrow and by overhead sprinklers. It always comes as a shock when you drive past these vineyards in mid-summer and see the sprinklers shooting into the sky, the water evaporating in the oven-hot air before it has a chance to even settle on any vine leaves or the soil.

Winemakers are adapting, too. A decade ago, whenever I visited a winery, I'd usually be shown some fancy new piece of winemaking kit – a computer-controlled pneumatic plunger, perhaps, or a whizz-bang bottling line (or, if I was really lucky, both). These days, I still get to see the pneumatic plunger and the bottling line, but I'm just as likely to be taken out the back to see the environmentally friendly waste management system, or the wind turbine on top of the hill that not only provides enough electricity for the winery but also pumps power back into the grid.

The concept of increasing efficiency and reducing emissions also extends to how the wine is packaged and sold. Many wineries are moving to lightweight glass bottles, even plastic bottles or Tetra Paks. Others are offsetting their carbon emissions either by paying other people to plant trees or, in some cases, by doing the tree planting themselves.

Despite all these positive changes, though, sometimes it feels as though many in the wine industry still don't quite comprehend the enormity of the environmental challenge they're facing. They are making the right noises – doing what they must to comply with an environmental performance checklist that's been forced on them – without thinking too deeply about the true sustainability of their business, or the true impact on the environment in which they work.

Worse still, it feels as though the rush to attain carbon neutral status or to show off environmental credentials is being driven by the marketing department – *not* by the winemaker, or the viticulturist or the owner of the business.

I believe that the best response to climate change should be a polar shift in how we think about growing and making wine in this country. Rather than keep on asking the question 'What does the market want?', Australian grape growers and winemakers need to ask 'What can this country provide?' and work from there.

Thinking this way will probably lead to a reduction in vineyard area, a reduction in grape yields and a reduction in the number of wineries. Can we reasonably expect this fragile, sunburnt country to keep on supporting an industry of 8000 vineyards and 2500-plus producers? Can the Australian wine industry continue to grow all the grapes it is growing now, in all the places it is growing them, using current viticultural and irrigation methods? The answer to both these questions is no. But the result of facing up to these hard truths will be an increase in the quality, integrity, distinctiveness and sustainability of Australian wines.

Samuel de Pury's Vineyard, William Barak, c. 1898

2 A sense of belonging
Exploring Australia's terroirs

'You're talking about the diversity of each of Australia's lands. They are not all the same. And the wines they produce aren't all the same. They don't all produce bloody Yellow Tail.'
Aunty Carolyn Briggs, Aboriginal elder of the Boon wurrung people

Two glasses of white wine sit on the table in front of me. The wines look exactly alike: very pale, with flashes of bright green as I swirl each glass. They were made from the same grape variety, riesling, and come from the same region, South Australia's Clare Valley. The winemaker – Jeffrey Grosset – made them both in the same way. And yet they smell and taste distinctly different.

The first wine, called Springvale, is more perfumed and has a more obvious, eager-to-please, grapefruit-like flavour impact in the mouth. The second wine, Polish Hill, is finer, more introverted, with layers of mineral-like dryness running along the tongue.

As the winemaking is identical, the differences between these two wines must come from the grapes themselves. And those differences must come from where the grapes were grown.

The Springvale riesling was grown in a vineyard in the high, north-eastern corner of the Watervale sub-region of Clare. Here, a thin coating of red loamy topsoil covers a layer of limestone – a combination that produces more vigorous growth in the vines, and slightly larger, more fragrant grapes.

The Polish Hill riesling, by contrast, comes from a vineyard a few kilometres to the east, planted in less fertile soil, full of clay and shale over slate and siltstone. Here the tougher environment produces smaller grapes with a more intense, tart character.

Grosset has been making these two sub-regional rieslings for over a quarter of a century. I have drunk them side by side many, many times over the last 15 years and marvelled at their individuality. Every year when the new vintage is released, I make a point of tasting them blind, to see whether these wines can tell me where they're from through scent and flavour and taste alone. And every year they do.

❋

Wines that taste of where they're from. The French have a word for it: *terroir*. Related to terrain and territory, with roots firmly planted in *terra* (Latin for earth, or country), the word terroir encompasses the unique geological history and soil profile of each vineyard site; how the slope of the land is angled to the sun; the climate and rainfall; human influences such as how the vines are trained, how the vine canopy is managed – and how all these factors produce a specific and recognisable taste in the wine from that vineyard, year after year.

Simply defined, terroir is the combination of country, climate and culture that makes a wine taste unique.

In traditional European wine countries, particularly in France, terroir is prized above grape variety and winemaker: wines should, first and foremost, taste of where they're from. The belief in – and defence of – terroir forms the spiritual core of wine culture to such a profound extent that the hierarchy of individual wine regions and vineyard sites is enshrined in law – France's system of *appellation d'origine contrôlée*, for example, and Italy's *denominazione di origine controllata*.

For the first 200 years of its history, the Australian wine industry has had a more ambivalent attitude towards terroir. Ever since European settlers first poked some fragile young vine cuttings into dusty Australian soil in the late 18th century, grape growers and winemakers have discovered an amazing diversity of terroirs across this wide brown land: Hunter Valley semillon, Coonawarra cabernet, Barossa shiraz, Clare riesling, Rutherglen muscat, etc. Many outstanding single vineyards have also been identified – unique places with the ability to produce unique wines: Henschke's Hill of Grace in Eden Valley; Wendouree in Clare; St Peter's vineyard in Great Western; Yarra Yering in the Yarra Valley – again, the list goes on.

But the concept of terroir hasn't traditionally been embraced here with quite the same universal passion as it has in old European countries. Regional differences have traditionally been explained in broad terms of temperature rather than terrain: Barossa Valley shiraz usually tastes bigger and stronger and richer than shiraz from the neighbouring Eden Valley Hills, for example, because the former region is *warmer* than the latter.

Scientifically minded Australian winemakers and growers have also been reluctant to accept the concept of terroir beyond climate because there is little proof that it even exists. Temperature, rainfall and sunshine can all be accurately measured and directly related to grape ripeness and quality; it's far harder to assess how – or even whether – soil nutrients or structure or trace mineral elements affect wine's subtleties.

Soil scientist Robert White challenged this sceptical view with his 2003 book *Soils for Fine Wines*, a dense, academic analysis of how the vine is influenced by the ground it's anchored in. White is emeritus Professor of Soil Science at the University of Melbourne, and was many years ago attracted both to wine as a drink and viticulture as a science. 'I soon realised that not a lot of thought was being given by Australian viticulturists to the soils,' he says. 'The word terroir was simply not in these people's lexicon. But the impact of terroir is incontrovertible through taste. You only have to drink good wines from specific vineyards to see that. Proving it scientifically, though, is very hard.'

The traditional ambivalence towards terroir also stems from the fact that Australian winemakers have always freely blended grapes from different vineyards, different regions, even different states to produce wines to a consistent *style* – everything from large volumes of commercial brands (think of Jacob's Creek, Nottage Hill, Yellow Tail) to tiny volumes of prestigious, high-quality, so-called 'cellar styles' (think of Australia's most famous red, Penfolds Grange, which has always been a multi-vineyard shiraz blend). And because this tradition – of the winemaker being more important than the place – has been the major driving force in Australian wine for so long, the importance of terroir has historically often been downplayed, devalued and even dismissed.

Indeed, during the export boom of the 1990s and early 2000s, the Australian wine industry – or at least the major commercial wine companies that dominate the industry – appeared to launch a war on terroir: in 2004 I came across a full-page advertisement for Jacob's Creek in a UK Sunday colour magazine that quoted winemaking director Phil Laffer as saying: 'It really ought to be how you make the wine, not where the grapes come from that makes the difference…Wine's like a first-class water: the exact origin is only interesting to a few; to most it's the taste that counts.' With that kind of message being broadcast by the country's most powerful wine producers, it became a struggle for many of Australia's 2500 small producers – most of whom make wines from single vineyards – to tell their terroir story and sell their terroir wines.

Now, though, just a few short years and a string of challenging vintages later, the balance appears to be shifting. The large companies are making a big noise about producing more regionally specific wines (even though, at the same time, they are closing many of their regional wineries and selling off many vineyards). More encouraging is the increasing number of smarter, quality-focused smaller winemakers producing more and more single-vineyard, single-site, terroir-driven wines.

Biodynamic soil from the Paxton Vineyards, South Australia

Drawing the maps
Beyond Australia's geographical indications

Back in 1993, Australia signed a wine trade deal with the European Community, allowing better access to their market in return for tidying up the then-haphazard approach to the naming of wine regions. Australia could boast many established and emerging wine districts, but their names and boundaries weren't protected by law, as European wine regions are.

So, over the ensuing decade, the Australian wine industry went through a long, drawn-out process of defining, debating and describing its viticultural landscapes, and officially registering these as Geographical Indications (GIs) in the Register of Protected Names.

Unlike European wine laws such as France's *appellation contrôlée* system, though, which regulate where vineyards can be planted, which grapes can be grown, when they can be harvested and so on, Australia's GIs only deal with regional boundaries. The idea is that if you buy a bottle of wine with a GI emblazoned across its label, you can be sure that what's inside the bottle comes from that place.

There are now about 100 Australian wine GIs, from the very, *very* large ('South Eastern Australia', which straddles New South Wales, Victoria and South Australia) and the very large (the individual states) to big chunks of country called zones, then down to regions, and finally smaller sub-regions.

It works like this: take the famous Tahbilk vineyard, north of Melbourne. Imagine you're floating a few metres over the vines, and then start zooming out, Google Earth–like: the Tahbilk vineyard is in the Nagambie Lakes sub-region of the Goulburn Valley region, which is in the Central Victoria zone of the state of Victoria, in South Eastern Australia.

The details and boundaries of most of Australia's GIs were drawn up without too much fuss or argument. In some cases, however, the process of deciding exactly where the region stopped and started has been tangled in acrimony and squabbling. Coonawarra's the best-known example: in some people's minds it should have been restricted to the famous 'cigar-shaped' strip of *terra rossa* soil, but in the end, after much shouting and legal challenges, the boundary was drawn over a much larger area that also included the controversial (less prestigious) black soils to the east and west of the *terra rossa* strip. Another is the Strathbogie Ranges and Upper Goulburn regions north of Melbourne: as far as I'm concerned, these two GIs should have both fallen under the one regional umbrella, evocatively called Central Victorian High Country, but petty squabbling over intellectual property (a winery had registered the High Country name) prevented that happening.

Regardless of whether its gestation was trouble-free or fraught, though, the birth of each of Australia's Geographical Indications has focused everyone's attention on what it is that makes their bit of the planet's surface special. This process has, I would argue, been one of the most important factors behind the growth of the terroirist movement.

Now that the frenzy of the first round of GI registration is over, and all of Australia's vineyards are covered by at least one legally protected appellation, many winemakers are registering – or at least thinking about registering – sub-regions.

Over the last few years I've found myself at many regional tastings – in the Yarra Valley, Mornington Peninsula, Tasmania – where the locals have been keen to prove, through the wines they've made, that these sub-regional distinctions are valid. The flavour and taste of the wines themselves usually make a compelling case for the reality of terroir. But the process is not without its problems.

❈

In June 2008, the winemakers of the Barossa gathered together a motley crew of booze hacks, sommeliers, wine-sellers and interested parties, sat them down in a big room at the old Seppeltsfield winery, and poured each expectant taster more than 50 glasses of raw, young shiraz. The wines were arranged in nine groups; we weren't told which group was which, just that each bracket of shirazes came from an area within the greater Barossa zone. Only after we'd studiously sniffed and slurped and spat, staining our tongues, teeth and glass-holding fingers purple, was the provenance of each group revealed.

At the moment, the Barossa zone contains two regions: the Barossa Valley and the cooler, higher Eden Valley. The question was: Should those two regions be further divided into smaller sub-regions? Can you taste, in the wines that are grown there, the individual terroirs that make up this large, diverse Geographical Indication?

Some of the suggested sub-regions were more distinctive than others: I found brighter, perfumed fruit characters in the shirazes from the cooler sands of Lyndoch, in the south of the Barossa Valley; more jubey, plush, purple fruit and roundness in the wines from the red loams of Light Pass and Ebenezer, in the north; even more weight and density and bolder tannins in the shirazes from the ironstone-rich clay soils of Greenock and Seppeltsfield; and a world of difference – more herbal, spicy aromas, morello cherry fruit and graphite tannins – in the wines from the cooler, higher, sandstone and shale of the Eden Valley.

It was a fascinating, thrilling experience tasting these wines, enriched by a detailed explanation of the geological history of the Barossa from David Farmer, former wine retailer, geologist and now local resident. For Farmer – who reckons there are thirteen distinct 'landscapes'

The wine regions of Australia

within the wider district – understanding the Barossa's terroirs is all about developing a deeper identity for the region and its community.

'I think that people who come to the Barossa or drink Barossa wines are hungry for a story,' said Farmer. 'And I don't think that currently we tell our story well enough. There is more detail yet to be found by exploring the different landscapes.'

Not everyone agrees. For a start, a lot of winemakers in the Barossa (echoing the sentiments of many winemakers in other regions) don't *want* to start promoting sub-regions or individual terroirs: they believe it could confuse or dilute the strength of the marketing message of Barossa wine as a whole. There is also a long and noble tradition of blending grapes from various different vineyards within the Barossa to achieve consistency of style from vintage to vintage. Focusing on single-vineyard wines – and potentially suggesting that they have more integrity or value – could undermine that traditional approach.

More politically, while some of the suggestions for the potential sub-regional groupings are legitimate place names and widely used within the local grape-growing community, they are also too closely associated with the intellectual property of established wine companies. It is very hard, for example, to register Seppeltsfield, Kalimna or Ebenezer as official sub-regional GIs, available for anyone to use on their labels, because they are all trademarked brand names.

But some believe passionately that sub-regional, and single site is the way to go. Peter Lehmann is one of the region's winemaking legends and he spoke at the tasting about the cultural importance of the Barossa's viticultural diversity: 'When I started, in 1947, the differences between vineyards in the various sub-regions were already well understood and highly respected by the growers,' he said. 'These people were fifth generation even then: how they pronounced the word shiraz would tell you where they were from – some called it *shee*raz, some called it *shy*raz.'

Lehmann expanded on this cultural aspect of terroir when I interviewed him a few years ago: 'There's a terrific pride and love of the land among these people,' he told me. 'There are blokes in their 40s, 50s, who I remember seeing as kids coming in to the weighbridge at the winery with their grandfathers and then their fathers, and now they're bringing their children in. The ownership, as they see it, is not possessive. They don't really own the land – it's almost Aboriginal, this sense – they look upon themselves as caretakers of their particular vineyard, and their role in life as they see it is to hand it on to their kids in better shape than when they got it from their dad. This is very strong in the Barossa, it's one of the strengths. This feeling of debt and gratitude to the land. It's almost holy.'

The classic Australian tradition of blending between vineyards and regions is still alive and well. But rather than being the *dominant* tradition, it is seen by most of Australia's new wave winemakers as very much a *20th-century* approach. These winemakers are now far more likely to be exploring and promoting their unique vineyards as enthusiastically as their most traditional European counterparts. The terroirists are fighting back.

❃

One of the most articulate of these new wave terroirists is Steve Webber at De Bortoli winery in the Yarra Valley. 'We don't even call ourselves winemakers any more,' says Webber, grinning. 'We call ourselves vignerons. We're winegrowers now.'

Webber says he wants to make wines that taste less of the grape, less of *how* they're made and more of *where* they're from. Not just wines that taste unmistakably Yarra Valley, nor wines that taste like they come from Dixon's Creek, the warmer sub-region of the Yarra where most of De Borts' vineyards are located, but wines that could only come from those individual vineyards.

'We're trying to bypass sub-region and go straight to site-specific wines, because I believe that's what people want,' he says. 'I'm interested in single-site wines because that's where you taste the real highs. Sure, blending gives you consistency, but it can also give you homogeneity. Australia desperately needs more wines with finite-ness, that taste of somewhere. It's the only way forward.'

For many new wave terroirists like Webber, trying to express a sense of place means intervening less in both the vineyard – eschewing chemicals, adopting organic or biodynamic methods – and the winery. Sergio Carlei, who has been using biodynamics at his vineyard just outside Melbourne for ten years, neatly sums up this philosophy in his winemaking manifesto: 'To truly express terroir requires a pure and natural environment free of artificial elements and unnatural interferences. Therefore, vines need to be grown naturally. Like grape growing, winemaking is a natural process too and will express terroir if left to its own elements. No doubt the personality of the winemaker will be imprinted in that win…and that's terroir too!'

Tim Kirk echoes this thinking at his Clonakilla vineyard near Canberra. 'I subscribe to the midwife theory of winemaking,' he says. 'I believe in that very much. I want to capture all that is pure and beautiful and true and good in the fruit we grow.'

Kirk, a devout Catholic, takes the idea further, arguing there is a profound spiritual aspect to making wine from his unique terroir. 'God created the universe out of love,' he says. 'He reveals Himself in acts of creation, transformation. Fermentation is one of those acts. It is the job of the winemaker to capture that love.'

❃

In 2003 Jeffrey Grosset suggested yet another, decidedly non-Western spiritual approach to terroir when he delivered the inaugural New South Wales Wine Press Club lecture in Sydney.

'Terroir is the French word for what some have known in Australia for thousands of years as *pangkarra*,' Grosset said. 'Pangkarra is an Aboriginal word used by the Kaurna people who used to live on the Adelaide Plains. It is a word that, like terroir, represents a concept which has no English translation but encompasses the characteristics of a specific place – the climate, sunshine, rain, geology and the soil–water relations. About the closest we can get in English is to refer to the site, but even that doesn't really cover the major components of terroir – or pangkarra - being the soil and the local topography. In essence, a wine has a certain taste not just because of the variety and vineyard management but because of its place. People who say, "This is my place, I belong here" are more likely to grasp the concept than people who say, "This is my place, this belongs to me".'

Sitting in the audience, I was blown away by this imaginative leap of thought. Australian grape growers and winemakers have often used Aboriginal words to name their vineyards, wineries, regions and brands: Wirra Wirra, Coonawarra, Yattarna, Yangarra. The use of Aboriginal imagery – from 'dot paintings' to Yellow Tail marsupials – is also widespread on wine labels. But here Grosset was travelling beyond the words and the images to engage with an ancient Aboriginal worldview, and by doing so was suggesting a new, profound and unique way of thinking about the concept of terroir in Australia.

'I saw the idea of pangkarra as a valuable tool, to help people come to grips with much broader issues of being here,' Grosset told me recently. 'I thought it might help us come of age. When you go to Burgundy, it looks like those vineyards are part of the landscape. When you get combinations of place and vines like Clare and riesling, those vineyards can also look like part of the landscape. So you have to ask: am I comfortable with this? The answer is yes, I am. I'm comfortable in this country. I am comfortable here. We're not interlopers any more, and neither are the vineyards and what we're doing. It's part of our maturity.'

Grosset also sees pangkarra, and the ancient Aboriginal connection between people and country that the word represents, echoed in James Lovelock's Gaia theory of the earth as a single, interconnected system. It's no coincidence that Grosset named his high-altitude cabernet vineyard Gaia.

'You hear Aboriginal elders talking of "healthy land, healthy people",' he says. 'You can't separate them; you can't have one without the other. Like Gaia, thinking about pangkarra is thinking about true sustainability: it's about the earth, it's not about us.'

Aunty Carolyn Briggs understands precisely what Jeffrey Grosset is talking about.

Aunty Carolyn is an elder of the Boon wurrung people. For thousands of years, long before white settlers arrived in Victoria in the 1830s, the Boon wurrung have been the traditional owners of the country that stretches from Werribee River, just to the west of present-day Melbourne, round the eastern side of Port Phillip Bay, down into the Mornington Peninsula and south to Wilsons Promontory.

Aunty Carolyn owns a restaurant in Melbourne called Tjanabi – it means 'celebration feast' in Boon wurrung language – specialising in indigenous ingredients. She's writing a book of stories and recipes gathered from Boon wurrung culture, stories about the old knowledge of the natural world and the food it produced. These stories resonate with the concept of terroir and the intimate connection between the soil, the food that grows in it, and the people who eat that food.

'Everyone enjoys that feeling, that everything is connected,' she tells me. 'You know, plants can tell us whether they're in the right place or not, whether they're good to eat at certain times. The old people knew that certain flowers would tell them when the fish were spawning, when the eels were running.'

I have come to talk with Aunty Carolyn because the Melbourne suburb I live in is on Boon wurrung country, and I want to find out if there is a word in Boon wurrung language that might be similar to the Kaurna word, *pangkarra*. This to me was the most exciting implication of Grosset's original lecture: that there must be or must have been dozens of different Aboriginal words that might capture or hint at the meaning or spirit of terroir, because Australia's vineyards are planted in regions once inhabited by dozens of discrete Aboriginal language groups. If vineyard owners and winemakers in each region made an effort to find out whether there is or was a local word that comes close to terroir – and then asked the original speakers of that language for permission to use it – it could not only help to foster reconciliation and create a greater joint pride in country, but also help people tell their unique wine stories.

'Yes!' says Aunty Carolyn. 'You're talking about the diversity of each of Australia's lands. They are not all the same. And the wines they produce aren't all the same. They don't all produce bloody Yellow Tail.'

In Boon wurrung language, she tells me, the word *beek* means country. In the same way that the Latin word *terra* means country. But she doesn't know of a Boon wurrung word that comes closer to the spirit of terroir. And she reminds me that, because it was an oral tradition never written down, much of the Boon wurrung language is lost.

'But Boon wurrung language is similar to the language they speak in the Yarra Valley,' she says. 'We share a lot of words with the Wurundjeri people.'

Wurundjeri country covers what is now the city of Melbourne and runs upriver into the land where the Yarra Valley vineyards are now planted. One of the most famous Wurundjeri men was William Barak, a renowned artist and head man of his tribe, who was born ten years before the white settlement of Melbourne in 1835, and who died a couple of years after Federation.

During his later life, William Barak became great friends with the de Pury family, then – as now – winegrowers in the heart of the Yarra Valley. Around 1898, Barak made a drawing of Samuel de Pury's vineyard – an astounding image of orderly vine rows nestled among plunging, tree-covered hillsides.

Barak's great, great niece is Professor Joy Murphy Wandin, a respected Wurundjeri elder. When I visit her at her home in Healesville to discuss Jeffrey Grosset's ideas, she, too, immediately understands. She, too, initially suggests a very similar word, *bik*: 'It means *country*, as in *soil*'. Then she shakes her head and pauses.

'That word terroir,' she says. 'I reckon it also means *belonging to country*: *where the growth comes from*. And that word in our language would be *ngooleek*. Belonging. Sometimes there's not a lot of commonality between English and Aboriginal words. But I think this is close.'

Like her great, great uncle, Aunty Joy has had some associations with the local wine industry: in the early 1990s, Yering Station winery released a wine featuring Barak's name and story, and came to her to ask for permission and help.

'I remember when they were developing the Barak's Bridge label,' she says. 'It was a nice connection – apart from the simple courtesy of asking. Being able to acknowledge the original landowners and the history on a wine label was quite special to me. It was as important as if it was my own project. When I saw that Barak label, it gave me a great enormous pride of belonging.'

Imagine, then, if Yarra Valley grape growers and winemakers were to adopt the word ngooleek as their own, unique local expression of the concept of terroir.

'Oh, it would be so good for my children to be able to buy wine with language on it,' says Aunty Joy. 'Wurundjeri language is so beautiful, and it's not known. Language is the belonging of your culture. It's about who you are. It's the voice of who you are. When I speak language, it's who I am.'

Fermenter, Sutton Grange

3 Back to the future
Reviving old traditions in Australia's vineyards and wineries

When I see Sutton Grange winery's egg-shaped fermenter for the first time, I can't help chuckling. Not that there's anything inherently funny about a big, hollow, thick-shelled concrete egg, standing about the same height as a man, tucked in among more conventional fermentation vessels such as stainless steel tanks and oak barrels. Actually, no, that's not true: it *does* look pretty funny. But what tickles me more is the sheer, fabulous, unexpected eccentricity of it all. Who would have thought that now, in the 21st century, in a wine industry renowned for being at the forefront of cutting-edge wine technology, some mad bugger in central Victoria would be making viognier in a concrete egg? Not only that, but who would have thought that fermenting in an egg would make such a difference to wine quality?

Gilles Lapalus, the French-born winemaker at Sutton Grange, pours two glasses of pale-golden young wine. Each was made from the same batch of viognier grapes: one was fermented in a barrel, the other in the egg. The barrel-fermented wine is creamy, soft, floral. The egg-fermented wine has more depth, more textural interest, more savoury satisfaction.

'The idea of the shape obviously comes from the symbolism of giving birth to the wine,' says Gilles, smiling a faint Gallic smile. 'But you don't have to believe in that. All I know is that the wine fermented very easily in the egg. It kept a perfect steady temperature all the way through, without needing any cooling or heating. It finished its ferment cleanly, with no problems. And I think it tastes better.'

He's not the only one. You'll also find an egg fermenter if you go for a walk in the cellar at Castagna in Beechworth and at Cumulus winery in Orange. It's part of a growing trend in Australia towards what might provocatively be called 'natural' or 'real' winemaking. More and more producers across the country are adopting simple, low-tech innovations in the winery and vineyard, to great effect – although not all are quite as unusual as egg-shaped fermenters.

Back to the future in the vineyard

For decades, Australian vineyards have been planted with mechanisation in mind: vine rows wide enough to get a tractor down, vines trained high to accommodate machine harvesters. This results in great efficiency, but means relatively low numbers of vines per hectare, 2000 or fewer, with big canopies and large crops. By contrast, planting vines much closer together – the 'old-fashioned' way – as many quality-obsessed growers are now doing, results in better-balanced vines, with lower yields of more concentrated grapes.

Brian Croser's new Foggy Hill vineyard on the Southern Fleurieu Peninsula, for example, looks more like a little slice of Burgundy: 4444 vines per hectare, trained low, with fruit hanging just 50 centimetres above the ground. David Freschi's new chardonnay vineyard, Altezza, in the Adelaide Hills, is 8000 vines per hectare. And at Bass Phillip in Gippsland, winemaker Phillip Jones has one hectare planted with a staggering 17,000 vines, a density that manifests in your mouth as the most remarkable tannic complexity in the wine.

The other convention that developed as a result of large-scale mechanised viticulture during the last half of the 20th century is the use of chemical fertilisers, herbicides, fungicides and pesticides. While it is true that most Australian growers are reducing their reliance on these chemicals, particularly the nastier systemic pesticides, their use is still considered conventional practice across the industry. A growing number of vineyards, however, *are* being run along more environmentally friendly lines, using biological, organic and biodynamic practices.

Biological viticulture is a scientific approach to sustainable farming, and employs carefully formulated composts and beneficial fungi and bacteria, usually in the form of compost teas, rather than relying on synthetic chemical fungicides, etc. While this is a huge improvement on 'conventional' viticulture, biological farmers do not necessarily eschew what they consider 'soft' chemicals, such as undervine herbicide.

Growing grapes organically, by contrast, means throwing away all vineyard chemicals except sulphur and copper (both allowable under organic certification guidelines, although in lower doses than in 'conventional' viticulture), and using techniques such as undervine mulching, applications of compost instead of fertiliser, manual weeding instead of herbicide, and spraying whey on the vines instead of chemical fungicide.

Biodynamics is a well-defined system of organic farming. It's also one of the biggest trends in Australian wine right now. In the last five years, the number of wine producers adopting biodynamic techniques has grown from about 20 to well over 150, with some regions such as McLaren Vale and Beechworth now hotbeds of biodynamic activity.

Just say no to GMOs

The biggest, and potentially most controversial technological innovation in grape growing and winemaking is the use of genetically modified organisms.

Research into genetically modified wine has been going on in Australia since the early 1990s, despite the fact that the majority of the population do not want GMOs in their food or drink: in the last couple of years, the AWRI has developed transgenic yeast that produces much lower alcohol than conventional yeast, and the CSIRO is working on genetically modifying grapevines that are resistant to mildew.

At this stage, neither these nor any other GMOs are found outside the lab in real vineyards or wineries because in 2003 the Winemakers' Federation of Australia released a public policy document stating: 'It is the Australian wine industry's position that no genetically modified organisms be used in the production of Australian wine.'

Most small wine producers, particularly those who follow organic and biodynamic methods and philosophies, not only support the WFA position wholeheartedly, but also totally oppose genetic engineering in any way.

'I can't comprehend how anyone in the wine industry would even *want* to adopt this technology,' says Tony Scherer of Frogmore Creek Vineyard in Tasmania, echoing the view of many others. 'Continued industrialisation of our food and drink production will only decrease the public's interest in fine food and wine. It's a very dangerous thing to be fooling around with. The best thing we can do instead is to enhance the culture of natural production and minimise the industrialisation of the whole process.'

Australia's larger wine companies tend to be more equivocal. Publicly, of course, they toe the WFA's party line. 'We have the same policy with respect to the use of GMOs as the rest of the Australian industry,' says Phillip Laffer, director of Viticulture and Winemaking for Pernod Ricard. 'That is, that no GM material enter the entire production chain from vine to bottle. It is an issue we take very seriously.'

But scratch the surface of the large companies' opposition to GMOs and it seems to be based less on deep ethical, environmental or health worries and more on a concern that the consumer isn't ready to accept the use of GMOs in winemaking – *yet*. The industry can see many benefits in GM technology, which is why it has so generously funded the AWRI and CSIRO research. If public opposition to GMOs softens, many of Australia's largest wine companies are fully prepared to use the technology in their vineyards and wineries.

And pressure to adopt GM technology is increasing. Since 2004, genetically modified yeasts have been allowed in wineries in the US. In late 2007, Victoria and New South Wales both lifted their moratoria on the commercial planting of genetically modified canola. At the time, Victoria's chief scientific adviser, Sir Gustav Nossal, said this could result in the door being opened to other crops that could lay claim to being better for the environment. As concern about the green issues continues to grow, supporters of GM are, like Sir Gustav, spruiking the purported environmental benefits of the technology: disease-resistant vines eliminating the need for chemical fungicides, for example, and grapes manipulated to deliver cool-climate flavours or lower alcohol in increasingly hot-climate regions.

I don't think the Australian wine industry should yield to the increasing pressure to adopt GM. I believe the downsides of the technology – including the possible transfer of genes from GM grapes and yeast to other organisms, producing unexpected toxins and allergens and the likelihood of airborne GM pollen or waterborne GM yeast cells contaminating neighbouring vineyards and wineries, compromising any claims other growers and winemakers might want to make about being GM-free – far outweigh the perceived benefits.

Besides, there are plenty of natural solutions to the challenges facing Australian grape growers and winemakers. Drought-tolerant grape varieties, for example, that produce delicious wines with naturally moderate alcohol already exist. And innovative viticultural techniques – many of them organic or biodynamic – have been shown to increase the vine's water efficiency and natural resilience to pests and diseases.

I believe the Winemakers' Federation should strengthen its position on this issue, not weaken it. The WFA public policy statement should be that 'no genetically modified organisms *will* be used or *should* be used in the production of Australian wine'. Individual wine companies – especially commercially powerful ones developing organic labels or converting some of their vineyards to organics – should make an unequivocal stand and publicly guarantee they will not use GMOs. And funding for GM research should be diverted to exploring the potential benefits of alternative grape varieties and organic viticulture.

Just imagine every bottle leaving this country with a little logo on the label proudly claiming 'Australian Wine: GM free.' What a powerful message that would be to send the rest of the world.

Getting the horn: Biodynamics explained

'To our modern way of thinking, this all sounds quite insane.'
Rudolf Steiner, Agriculture, *1924*

In 1924 the controversial Austrian philosopher Rudolf Steiner gave a series of lectures outlining a new agricultural approach to a group of farmers concerned about the dwindling fertility of their crops and declining health of their livestock.

The directions Steiner gave in these lectures regarding specific compost preparations and practices were the foundations of what we now call the biodynamic system of organic farming. Many other people, including Bob Williams and Alex Podolinsky in Australia, developed Steiner's initial ideas over the ensuing decades, and today biodynamics is a complex toolkit of philosophies and techniques available to anybody interested in farming – or growing grapes and making wine – without chemicals.

Steiner was the founder and figurehead of the Anthroposophical Society, a movement dedicated to bridging the gap between the physical and spiritual worlds. He called his 1924 lectures 'Spiritual Foundations for the Renewal of Agriculture' because the methods he proposed worked on many levels: they were not only practical but also energetic and spiritual. *Practical* in that they were intended to increase microbial life, structure and nutrient availability in the soil; *energetic* in that they were intended to synchronise the earth with the cosmic influences of the moon and planets; and *spiritual* in that an anthroposophical approach to agriculture would, Steiner hoped, encourage humans to connect to the spirit world.

Because of these cosmic and spiritual aspects, many people are sceptical or dismissive of biodynamics, accusing it of being 'pseudoscience', 'voodoo' or simply a load of old bollocks.

Most of the 100-plus Australian winegrowers who *have* adopted biodynamic practices don't profess to believe in or even understand the cosmic or spiritual aspects of Steiner's original lectures. But they *do* believe, based on what they've observed in the vineyard, in the winery and in the glass, that BD can help them make better wine, more sustainably.

The biodynamic preparations

The cornerstone of biodynamics is a kind of concentrated compost called preparation 500. This is made by stuffing cow manure into cow horns, burying those horns over winter, then stirring a small amount of the fermented manure in rain water – roughly a handful per bucket – for an hour and spraying the resulting liquid in droplets on your vineyard soil. Preparation 500 is used to improve soil structure and microbiological activity.

Sue Carpenter of Lark Hill vineyard in the Canberra District reckons that spraying the horn manure stimulates soil bacteria, which promotes soil fungi, which in turn enable nutrient exchange between the vine roots and the soil. Lethbridge Wines' Maree Collis, who has a PhD in organic chemistry, also sees 500 as a microbiological inoculation, which explains why the best time to spray it is said to be in the afternoon, when the soil is warmer and its impact is greater. Toby Bekkers of Paxton vineyard in McLaren Vale sees spraying 500 as 'seeding the soil' with life, like adding yeast to a tank of grape juice. The quality of soil in a vineyard that's been managed biodynamically for a long time is undeniable: it's bouncy, like walking across marshmallows, crumbly, full of humus.

Preparation 501 is made by stuffing finely ground quartz (silica) into cow horns, burying those horns over summer, then stirring a very small amount (just a couple of grams) of the powder in rain water for an hour and spraying the resulting liquid in a fine mist over your vines. The purpose of 501 is to complement the earthy forces of the 500 and attract light forces to the plant.

The use of 501 is controversial in Australia. Some BD experts and many grape growers choose not to use it, arguing that the last thing we need here is more sunlight on our vines. Other growers insist that 501 is necessary to 'balance' the 500: Kate Kirkhope of Kiltynane Estate in the Yarra Valley describes 501 as 'an atmospheric umbrella'. Everyone agrees, though, that it is a very powerful prep – even though it is applied in such remarkably low doses.

Sam Statham of Rosnay vineyard in Canowindra, for example, once applied some 501 towards the end of the ripening season because his merlot was ripening too slowly and sugar levels shot up way too far, too fast. 'It's something you definitely need to use with caution,' Statham says.

Tiny amounts – teaspoonfuls – of various other herbal preparations, numbered 502–508, are added to compost to bring a range of benefits to the resulting humus when added to the soil. Preparation 502, for example, is made from yarrow flowers matured in a stag's bladder, hung up in a tree over summer, said to attract light forces and connect the soil to cosmic influences; 503 is chamomile flowers stuffed into cow's intestines and buried over winter, said to help the breakdown of the compost; and 507 is a solution of valerian flowers, sprayed over the compost heap, said to bring warmth to the compost.

Biodynamic practices

Good compost – with preps 500–507 added – spread under the vines and between the rows is a crucial part of building structure and microbial activity in biodynamic soil. Many BD growers also make cow pat pit (CPP), otherwise known as barrel compost or manure concentrate. This is a barrow-load of cow manure, mixed with crushed eggshells, basalt dust and the compost preps, then matured for six weeks, either in a shallow pit or in a half-buried barrel (hence the name). This is then stirred in with the 500 and sprayed onto the soil.

Most BD growers time their vineyard activities to the phases of the moon and positions of the planets. The effect of the moon on the tides – and, arguably, sap flow – is easy to grasp. It's perhaps harder to comprehend, though, that the moon's relative position to distant constellations or planets might also affect what happens on earth. But many biodynamic winegrowers are willing to at least go along with this concept, and follow their Astro Calendar as closely as they can, timing their activities according to whether it's a 'fruit day' (moon in a fire sign such as Leo is good for picking grapes), 'root day' (moon in an earth sign such as Taurus is good for making compost, spraying 500), 'leaf day' (water sign, Scorpio) or 'flower day' (air, Aquarius). Most also avoid agricultural activity (or activity of any kind) during disruptive 'node' times, when the moon's path crosses the path of the sun.

Some people also extend this idea to tasting wine, believing that fruit days will best display the wine's varietal character and quality, and that root days are to be avoided, because the wines will be least expressive.

Steiner wasn't the first person to encourage awareness of the cosmos when farming. Indeed, he described such awareness as 'peasant wisdom' – something which had been lost in his/our materialistic age, and which his 'new' farming methods aimed to recapture. After a biodynamic workshop I co-hosted in the Barossa in July 2006, local winemaker Geoff Schrapel, whose family settled in the area from Silesia in the 1840s, came up to me and said: 'You know, we've always followed the moon when we're planning any work in the vineyard.'

Biodynamic thinking

For me, one of the most important parts of biodynamics is that almost every Australian winemaker who has adopted BD as a method of growing grapes has found their whole approach to life has changed.

'I like the holistic approach of BD,' says leading Margaret River biodynamic winemaker Vanya Cullen. 'It goes right through to all aspects of what we're doing, and fits in with the philosophy of quality and integrity established by my parents. We're all working towards a common goal now. The ego disappears.'

Other winegrowers emphasise how BD makes you pay more attention to the details. 'It gives you a mindset that helps you treat your vineyard as you would your first-born child,' says Rod Windrim of Krinklewood in the Hunter Valley. 'You try to take away the potential for disease to happen – if you know you haven't got the option to drop back on nasty chemicals it keeps you on your game.'

clockwise from top left: cow horns used to make preparation 500; a flowform used to stir the biodynamic preparations before spraying; Barry Morey from Sorrenberg vineyard in Beechworth turning compost

Some biodynamic growers agree with Steiner that the attitude and feelings of the person working the land, making the compost or applying the preps are transmitted to the activity and the energy of the earth. As Liam Anderson of Wild Duck Creek vineyard says: 'I truly believe that the energy you put into making your wine shows in the glass. If you don't care about the vines and the wines, they can taste dull and lifeless. If you show unusual passion, you can taste that in your wine.'

Biodynamics adapted for Australian conditions

Although he was very clear about how and why to make and apply the biodynamic preps, Steiner also says many times throughout his Agriculture lectures that his ideas were *indications*, that more work needed to be done, and people should not be afraid to try variations out for themselves. He even responded to a question about whether stag bladders could be substituted for something else in the yarrow preparation by saying: 'It is entirely possible that somewhere there is another suitable kind of animal, perhaps indigenous to some corner of Australia.'

This again for me is a very exciting part of biodynamics: how the ideas and methods developed in cool, wet Europe can be adapted to (mostly) hotter, drier Australian conditions. Local farmers, for example, have successfully substituted *Casuarina* (she-oak) for the horsetail (*Equisetum*) used in Europe for preparation 508. And others have experimented with making 500 by burying manure in emu eggs instead of cow horns.

There are also many parallels between the holistic approach to nature that Steiner advocated and the interconnectedness at the heart of traditional Australian Aboriginal relationship to country.

'If you're nature-based, you must respect nature,' says Boon wurrung elder, Aunty Carolyn Briggs. 'What's in the heavens is reflected on earth. So many people haven't learned to see that yet.'

There is much to be learned from ancient Australian Aboriginal astronomy, and an understanding of the thoroughly un-European nature of the seasons in most Australian landscapes, all of which could help the evolution of local biodynamic practice and farming in general.

Back to the future in the winery

Some of the most important innovations are the simplest. The theory of the sorting table is incredibly straightforward: pass all the freshly harvested grapes over a slow-moving, gently vibrating conveyor belt so that damaged berries, errant bits of stalk and leaf, and any other undesirables can be picked out and discarded before the fruit is tipped into the fermenting vat. In fact, it's *so* simple, it's slightly surprising the sorting table has only become trendy among winemakers in the last few years. Yes, the process is a little more labour-intensive, but the improvement to wine quality is dramatic. So dramatic, in fact, that it's not only the small, artisan wineries who employ the technique: at De Bortoli, in the Yarra Valley, even the grapes destined for the under-$15 Windy Peak range of wines go across the sorting table.

Another simple concept: letting the grapes ferment spontaneously by not inoculating them with cultured yeasts is also gaining ground, particularly among winemakers who want their wines to be a unique expression of a particular vineyard and who believe that the wild yeasts present in the atmosphere of the vineyard and winery are part of that expression. This really is a case of going back to the future: a few decades ago, all wines fermented like this…naturally. In fact, using cultured yeasts out of a packet is a relatively recent thing: Tyrrell's winery in the Hunter Valley was still fermenting with wild yeasts as a matter of course as late as the 1980s.

Many Australian winemakers are also trying to avoid other additions such as acid and tannin (the latter used to help with colour stabilisation), and many are neither fining nor filtering their wine, believing that something is lost during the clarification process. Others are using electrically powered pumps less and less in the winery, preferring to exploit gravity wherever possible to move juice and wine.

Again, the inspiration behind this minimal intervention movement is two-fold: winemakers believe that doing less produces wines that not only taste better, but are also a more authentic expression of where they're from. These winemakers argue that the flavours and characteristics considered by global wine drinkers to be 'typically' Australian – exaggerated colour, ripe fruit, fresh acidity and bold oak – are in fact often a result of what is added in the winery (tannin, aromatic cultured yeasts, enzymes, oak, acid) rather than what comes from the vineyard. Minimal intervention, therefore, is a plea for honesty and integrity.

'Not having to add acid to your wine is the best indication that you've chosen the right site for your vineyard and planted the right grapes,' says Ron Laughton of Jasper Hill vineyard, a leading advocate of minimal intervention winemaking. 'Flavours are fragile. To get the most out of a grape you need to do as little as possible, because every time you apply energy you knock flavour out.'

What, no sulphur?

Inspired by the sulphur dioxide–free (or very low sulphur) wines of French producers such as Pierre Overnoy, Eric Pfifferling, Thierry Allemand and Jean Foillard, a small but enthusiastic band of adventurous Australian grape-treaders are putting the preservative back in its packet and seeing what happens.

Many, often very good, no-added-preservative wines were made by producers such as Temple Bruer and Botobolar, aimed at drinkers who sought out sulphur-free primarily for allergy or general health reasons. This new wave of winemakers, however, is driven primarily by questions of wine quality: what kind of character, varietal expression and taste of country is revealed if you don't add SO_2?

'Picture the flavour expression of terroir as being like a sine wave,' says Bill Downie, who has made stunning sulphur-free gamay for R Wines. 'The better the terroir, the greater the amplitude of that sine wave. I reckon that as soon as you add sulphur, you reduce the amplitude.'

There are significant challenges involved in sulphur-free winemaking, not least the fact that, once the wine is bottled and sent out into the world, it can easily be stored in too-hot conditions and can rapidly oxidise. But Bill is confident that clean fruit and a fastidious attention to detail in the winery can help reduce this risk. 'The dramatic effects of oxidation are the result of the action of an organism,' he says. 'If you observe everything closely, use a microscope to look at what's in the wine, and make sure you bottle without that organism present, you won't get oxidation. It's like making cheese: you've got to know what's living in your milk; you've got to know what's living in your juice.'

Since 2006, Reid Bosward has been producing small amounts of no-added-sulphur shiraz at his Kaesler vineyard in the Barossa. The first vintage was still drinking beautifully at three years old: pure regional fruit generosity, lifted spice and not a hint of oxidation. Kaesler are also experimenting with organic and biological practices in the vineyard, in an effort to eliminate sulphur sprays.

'The thing is, we're not really changing anything in the winemaking,' says Reid. 'Barossa reds have a natural preservative advantage in having huge tannins in the grapes. But it does put more focus on to how you store the wine: you've got to keep the bottles cool if you want them to keep their freshness. Handle them like cheese, really.'

Down the road at Torbreck, the quality of one particularly good parcel of grenache in 2009 inspired the first Natural Project Wine; no additions at all (no yeast, acid, sulphur – nothing), bottled early, sold quickly. Andrew Guard, who has recently moved on from Torbreck to concentrate on his own imported range of so-called 'natural' wines from Europe, also believes careful handling is crucial.

'We didn't sell the wine through retail stores,' he says. 'We went straight to restaurants where we knew it would be kept cool, be poured by the glass and have a high turnover, reducing the risk of spoilage. Having said that, I've drunk natural, sulphur-free wines in France that are ten years old and they've still been brilliant because they've been stored perfectly. There's no reason why we can't do that here. It just takes a bit more care and effort and education.'

opposite: The deep, purple foaming frenzy of fermenting shiraz

The movement back to minimal intervention is also a conscious, philosophical reaction to the increased availability and employment of extreme manipulation technology such as reverse osmosis (RO), which can alter a wine's character by taking it apart and putting it back together. More worryingly, research is well underway into developing transgenic yeasts and genetically engineering grapes with desirable traits.

This new a dial-a-style approach to winemaking certainly polarises opinion.

Julian Alcorso is a big fan. His company, Winemaking Tasmania, turns grapes into wine under contract for almost one third of the island state's 160 boutique wine labels, and he dangles the magical benefits of RO in front of all his clients.

'A lot of vineyards find their grapes still have green tannins and hard acid at "normal" sugar ripeness,' says Alcorso. 'This technology allows them to pick their grapes fully flavour-ripe without worrying about sugar levels, because we can take out the alcohol after fermentation.' As far as Alcorso is concerned, his job is simply to make better wine – or, rather, a better product. The RO machine is just another tool, along with acid adjustment or tannin addition. 'It's like a camera,' he says. 'It brings everything into focus.'

Mountadam winemaker, Con Moshos, couldn't disagree more. 'Look, I don't want to sound like a technical ignoramus, but I hate this type of "chemical engineering" winemaking,' he says. 'The overuse of the RO machine is one of the big issues of our time.'

Most of the growers and winemakers I have chosen to feature in this book share Moshos' view, and argue that extreme technology is completely at odds with the essence of what wine is – or what wine should be.

'I think there's a reaction building to all the manipulation going on in the industry now,' says Tapanappa winemaker Brian Croser. 'I see this reaction particularly among producers of what I call fine wine. You see, fine wine is – should be – a natural product. The concept of naturalness is an integral part of fine wine. Making fine wine doesn't mean using reverse osmosis, acid addition, tannin addition. It certainly doesn't mean using GMOs. The aim should be to do absolutely nothing to alter the composition of the wine. Naturalness is as important as hedonic quality in fine wine. The consumer needs to believe that the winemaker hasn't mucked around with it.'

Of course, there are still many in the Australian wine industry who dismiss the move towards organic grape growing and 'natural' winemaking as loony hippy shit. For every winemaker letting his ferments occur spontaneously, there are ten who wouldn't dream of using anything but cultured yeasts. For every winemaker who installs a sorting table at the crusher and painstakingly selects only the best berries, there are 50 who are quite content to machine harvest their whole crop. And for every grower converting their vineyard to biodynamics there are plenty more who think that burying cow's horns and picking grapes according to the phases of the moon is sheer lunacy.

Some conventional winemakers, particularly those with a strong scientific background, even feel threatened by the back-to-the-future movement. Robin Day, chairman of the board of the Australian Wine Research Institute (AWRI), summed up this tension when he addressed a wine and environment conference in 2007. 'I suspect,' he said gravely, 'that we are all spectators to an unlearning of knowledge in our industry.'

I'm not sure, though, that this is what's happening. Most of the winemakers and growers I've met who are adopting what look like old-fashioned or arcane methods are not rejecting scientific advances and technology outright. Indeed, if anything characterises the Australian back-to-the-future movement, it's the methodical, cautious, measured approach that its often highly trained practitioners (many with science degrees or PhDs) bring to it. These people are simply saying that relying on reductionist science or conventional wisdom is not the *only* way to make distinctive, delicious wine, imbued with a sense of place. There *are* other ways.

There are signs, too, that the conservative scientific community is beginning to see that there might be something in all this organic business after all. The Australian Society of Viticulture and Oenology's annual seminar in 2009 looked at soil health, and covered topics ranging from mulching and the use of biochar to organics and even biodynamic farming. As one of the organisers, Dr Mark Krstic, told me at the time: 'We need to be quite clear about this: thinking about these things is in the mainstream now. It's on the agenda. The sensible growers out there don't see it as fringe activity any more. They see it as looking after their natural resource base, helping them buffer climate change.'

Justine, Stephen and Johann Henschke, Henschke wines

4 A family affair
Australia's wine industry enters a new phase

'Shareholders work on one-year plans. Governments work on four-year plans. Only families work on long term.'
Kym Tolley, winemaker, Coonawarra

It's tempting to portray the Australian wine industry as a vast collection of wineries all piled onto a huge seesaw, with 20 very large companies churning out 75 per cent of the nation's wine down one end, and 2500 tiny, *tiny* producers crowded far up on the other end, each squirting out a thimbleful of booze.

It's a neatly polarised picture, but it doesn't quite do justice to the messy reality of the business of Australian wine. I like to imagine the country's wine industry more as a big photo, a huge crowd shot, not quite fitting easily into a single frame. Crammed in between the big multinationals selling millions of bottles of cheap booze and the weekend vignerons pottering around among their acre of chardonnay vines, you'll find an incredible diversity of wine producers and wines produced: virtual wineries, where a winemaker buys in grapes, leases winery space and sells wine over the internet; big wineries owned by foreign companies; tiny cellar doors down dirt roads run by fifth generation vignerons; joint ventures between winemakers who live on opposite sides of the globe; new wine empires being built by wealthy businessmen; vineyards established as a tax dodge by investment syndicates; wines made in Europe by Australian winemakers who work vintage in the northern hemisphere every year; small labels established by vineyard owners, sick of dealing with the big companies…you could stare and stare at this picture for hours and always find something new.

Right up in the foreground, though, managing to squeeze out a smile despite the storm clouds in the background, are the large family-owned businesses. Some of the most enlightened thinking about Australia's viticultural and oenological future is taking place in the boardrooms of companies such as Yalumba, Angove and De Bortoli. These families are not only thinking admirably long term, but they're also constantly trying to improve the quality of the wines they produce at every level. And they're doing so on a scale that will make a real difference to the future of the wine industry.

I would even go so far as to say that family-owned companies *are* the future of Australian wine. The huge, publicly listed corporate giants such as Foster's and Constellation have dominated the industry for too long; the result is an ocean of cheap-and-cheerful Brand Australia commodity wines sloshing around the discount bins of supermarkets across the world. That's not sustainable. It never was sustainable.

The big companies clearly realise this: both Foster's and Constellation have spent the last couple of years desperately selling off assets, consolidating their holdings and downsizing their workforce in a bid to survive in a globally depressed world. (In my metaphorical group photo, by the way, I see the corporate giants slinking into the background shadows – one of the reasons you won't find many of their wines in this book.) And while the big corporates panic, the larger family wine companies have been quietly riding out the storm. It was the families who built the foundations of Australia's wine success – the Penfolds, Lindemans, Seppelts, Hardys and Gramps – and it's up to the families to take Australia's wine back to its future.

Wine exists in a very long-term universe. Giant corporate drinks companies are, by definition, driven by shareholder returns to make short-term decisions, not to think long term. Family companies, by contrast, *mostly* think long term and understand every facet of the business literally from the ground up, and as a result can indulge in both solidly cautious and recklessly innovative behaviour.

Winemaker Philip Shaw has seen all sides: he has worked for a large family company (Rosemount), for a corporate giant (Foster's), and is now out on his own. 'The industry has to change,' he says. 'It already is changing. There is no future for big companies. But there is a reasonable future for medium-sized and family companies. The industry needs more leaders with purple hands, rather than blokes in suits.'

❈

Part of the problem with the industry over the last 15 years has been leadership: the wrong kind leading up to and during the boom, and a lack of it during the bust.

During the fat times of the 1990s, the Australian wine industry was like a well-choreographed big-budget Hollywood musical: everything was upbeat, glitzy and full of optimism. In 1996, when renowned wine judge, writer and industry legend Len Evans launched the now famous Strategy 2025 document – the plan to make Australia the most influential and profitable wine country in the world – he was like a vinous Mickey

Rooney: 'Hey kids! Let's put on a show!' And everyone stepped into the chorus line, singing the Brand Australia song.

By the end of the first decade of the 21st century, the Australian wine industry seems to have turned into a disaster movie. Australian wine has grown too big, too fast, driven in part by low-value, multi-regional commodity wines rather than high-value, region-specific premium wines, and in part by Managed Investment Schemes – or Managed Investment Scams as some winemakers contemptuously dub them. Riding on the back of the export wave in the late 1990s and early 2000s, these schemes attracted many investors, lured by the prospect of a nearly 100 per cent tax deduction rather than by the prospect of making the world's best wine, and they planted possibly close to 20,000 hectares, or more than 10 per cent of the total national area under vine. The Australian wine ship was sinking under the weight of too many vineyards, too many wineries and too much booze. It was crippled by the global financial icebergs. And the captain and crew are nowhere to be found.

As Paul Clancy, outspoken chair of the Wine Grape Council of South Australia, wrote in late 2008: 'Now, when wine producers and growers across the industry look up from their bilge pumps and bailing buckets, they see no one on the bridge. We as an industry were noted for our innovation and leadership in the 1990s but there is little visible leadership now, when it is most needed.'

The two main organisations 'running' the wine industry at a national level are the Australian Wine and Brandy Corporation (AWBC), and the Winemakers' Federation of Australia (WFA). The AWBC, a statutory body, funded by a levy on every tonne of grapes crushed and litre of wine exported, is responsible for such things as export regulation, international wine promotion, policing label integrity and defining Australia's Geographic Indications. The WFA is the peak body representing the interests of Australian wine producers on issues such as tax, environmental performance, tourism and technical innovations.

As wine exports fell, and the price-per-litre of those exports dropped over the last few years, many winemakers across the country lost confidence in the AWBC. While some individuals within the corporation, particularly the forthright General Manager of Market Development, Paul Henry, devised new strategies and initiatives to reverse the downward trend, the organisation appeared to be drifting, rudderless: its CEO, Sam Tolley, stepped down in late 2007 and wasn't replaced until mid-2009. That's two whole vintages without anybody in the boss's chair. Similarly, the WFA's Stephen Strachan has been admirably blunt and realistic in his assessment of the challenges facing the industry (the oversupply; the national tax review; the increasingly shrill public debate about alcohol abuse and social responsibility; the need for increased environmental performance, etc.), but the Federation often appears to be so bogged down reacting to these challenges and appeasing its various stakeholders that it has had little time to step back and dream up truly visionary new directions.

In late 2009, long after the reality of the situation had become clear, the AWBC and WFA, along with Wine Grape Growers' Australia and the Grape and Wine Research and Development Corporation, managed to release a joint statement calling for a reduction in the 20 per cent of Australia's vines that are 'surplus to requirements', and virtually urging 'uneconomic' growers and winemakers to seriously consider quitting the industry. To sacrifice themselves so others may survive. It was bleak, blunt and, frankly, about two years too late.

'We are missing the kind of thought leadership that Len Evans provided back in the '90s,' admits Paul Henry. 'In any business, what people most value is clarity, vision and direction. And that's precisely what process-oriented institutions like the AWBC are not good at. It didn't matter so much during the '90s because everyone in the industry was doing okay, and it had its own momentum. Now everyone's not doing okay, there is an assumption that the institutions will be able to provide the leadership. But they can't.'

So who can?

At the height of the doom and gloom in 2008/09, people started whispering about the need for a war cabinet, a think-tank that could dream up new directions and work on the big picture stuff. A council of elders drawn from the country's leading family-owned wine companies, people who can see way beyond annual reports and shareholder dividends and global financial crises. A family intervention, if you like, for these troubled times.

In 2009, just such a group emerged.

Called Australia's First Families of Wine, the group – which includes well-known, well-established family wineries such as Yalumba, Henschke, Brown Brothers, Campbells and Tahbilk – was conceived, according to Yalumba's Robert Hill Smith, to 'put some colour, life and movement from a family perspective back into an Australian wine scene dominated by the big corporates'. A group that could also use its collective experience to help address the massive issues that face the industry – to at least provide some 'thought leadership'.

'We can express a long-term, positive view of the industry,' says Hill Smith. 'We can help influence direction and policy. We need to stop debating the validity of Strategy 2025, stop talking about what has got us here and start talking about what needs to be done right now to fix it. We need to talk about the glass being three-quarters full, rather than a quarter empty. We need to let the world know that Australia still believes in itself.'

Them's fightin' words. And it's reassuring to hear them.

The show must go on
Reinventing Australia's wine judging system

One of the pillars of the Australian wine establishment is the show system, the peculiar 20-point method of judging wines that evolved from the country's 19th-century agricultural societies. And the modernisation of the show system is one of the most visible signs of how Australia's wine establishment is crumbling.

I judged at a conventional, old-fashioned wine show recently and it was like walking into the past. First I was asked to don a white coat, like all the other judges. Then I was given a scoresheet and a clipboard and shuffled into a large room, where huge classes of wine had been lined up on trestle tables. I was given 75 sauvignon blancs for breakfast, poured in small ISO tasting glasses. My heart sank.

I thought we'd all moved on from this fusty way of judging wine. Most of the big shows in Australia – Melbourne, Sydney, Adelaide – and many of the small shows are in the process of reinventing themselves in an effort to make a 150-year-old tradition not only more relevant to winemakers and drinkers, but also fairer and more meaningful. So it was a surprise to be reminded what show judging used to be like.

In most shows, older judges are making way for a new generation of younger judges. The average age of senior winemakers in the country's large wine companies used to be 50-something. Now it's more like 30-something. The old school of white-coated, grey-haired, rusted-on wine show judges are yielding to younger judges who are, in turn, radically redesigning the wine show system. Much for the better. As one judge candidly told me as he stepped down from the senior position he'd held for decades: 'I'm removing a blockage at the top.'

Shows are bringing class sizes down and reducing the total number of wines judged in a day to make the experience more manageable and less daunting. I don't care what any veteran judge might claim, the idea that you can fairly judge each and every wine in a line-up of, say, 100 one-year-old shirazes before lunch is rubbish. The palate and the mind both suffer from fatigue, the quieter, more idiosyncratic wines are lost in the crowd and the big show-pony styles are rewarded simply for standing out. Much fairer to both the wines and the judges to taste no more than 20 or 30 wines at a time, and no more than 100 a day.

A number of specialist shows have been established, such as the Alternative Varieties Show, the Organic Wine Show (I am chief judge of both) and the Canberra International Riesling Challenge, where wines from the rest of the world are judged alongside Australian rieslings, providing some valuable context for exhibitors, judges and public tasters.

Most importantly, conscientious judges are making an effort to reward wines that display subtlety, individuality, finesse and difference. This goes right to the heart of the problem afflicting Australia's show tradition: for too long, the wines that have been given gold medals and trophies have not necessarily been the wines that the judges actually want to drink. I've always found it disheartening when, after a day of handing out gongs to big, dark, over-oaked, technically sound but boring shirazes, Australian judges sit down to dinner and gleefully pour funky, characterful, elegant Rhone wines down their throats; wines that wouldn't have even been awarded a medal earlier in the day. The contradiction – the hypocrisy, even – has always rankled.

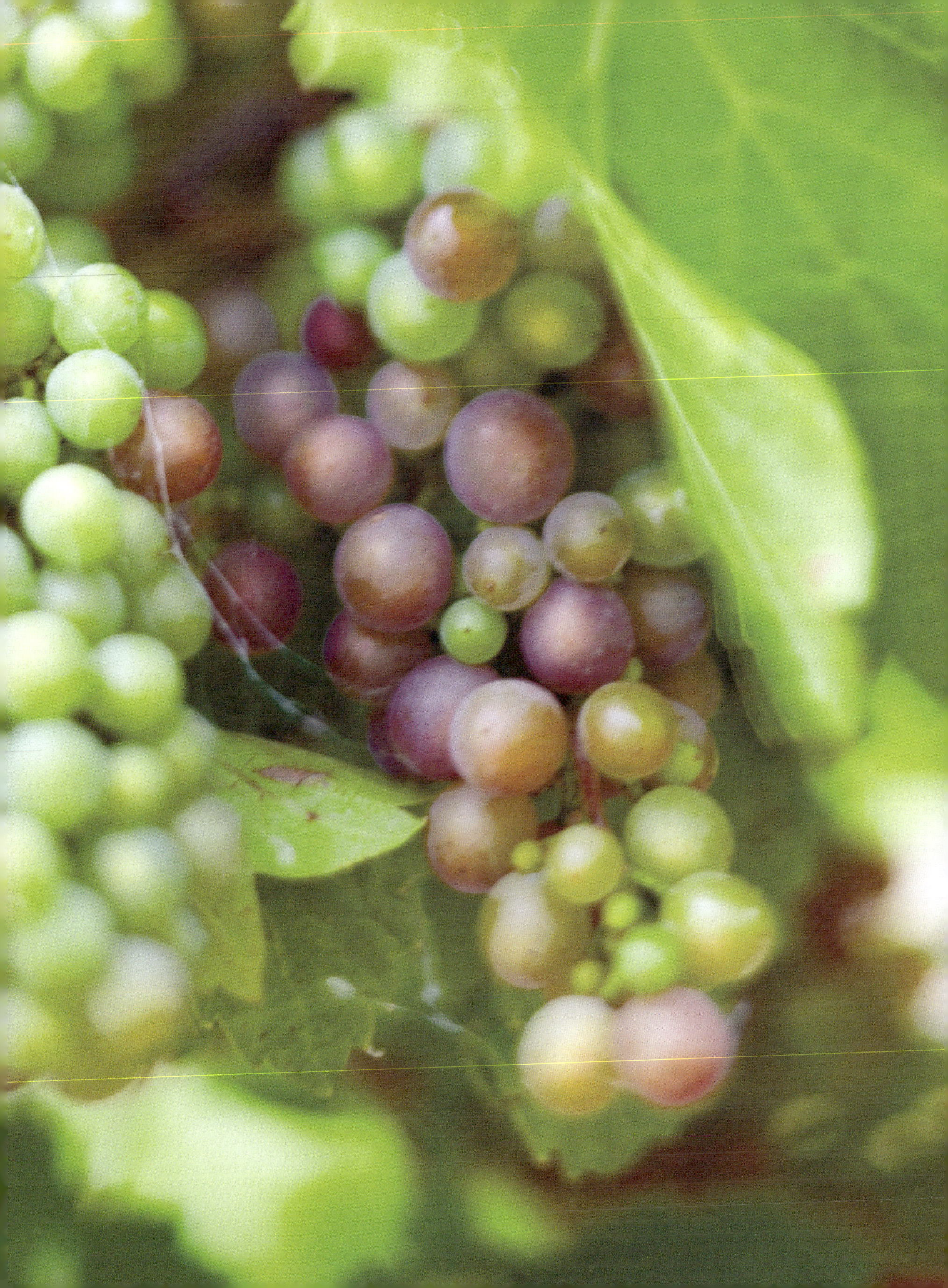

5 New tastes, new flavours
Australia's expanding gallery of wine grapes

On a steep hill just outside Canberra a dozen rows of tender young gruner veltliner vines shelter from the wind. Planted a couple of years ago by David, Sue and Chris Carpenter of Lark Hill winery, this is the first appearance of the Austrian white grape in the Canberra region, and it's one of only a handful of gruner vineyards anywhere in Australia.

The question is: why gruner? Over the last two decades the Carpenters have demonstrated that their cool, high altitude part of the world is well suited to well-known grapes such as pinot noir, chardonnay and riesling. So why plant an obscure variety that hardly any Australian wine drinkers have ever heard of?

The first reason is partly romantic. The Carpenters wanted to expand the vineyard, and liked the look of the hill that crowns the top of their property. The landscape reminds them of the beautiful, vertiginous vineyards of the Wachau, where steep rows of gruner veltliner vines appear to plunge into the Danube. So an experimental patch of gruner felt like the obvious choice for the new planting.

But there's another, more tangible reason why the Carpenters are banking on gruner. Australian wine drinkers are increasingly hankering for white wines with *texture*. Yes, varietal flavour is very important: people still want sauvignon blanc to taste recognisably like sauvignon blanc. Freshness and brightness are desirable attributes, too: drinkers want their white wines to be thirst-quenching and lively. But we also like texture, minerality, savouriness, and complex palate satisfaction. And non-mainstream grapes such as gruner can deliver this texture brilliantly.

The Carpenters' little hilltop patch of gruner vines is just one example of an emerging viticultural resistance movement crackling across the continent, electrifying the mainstream. About bloody time, too.

The country's national vineyard – all 160,000 or so hectares of it – is completely dominated by just six grape varieties: chardonnay, shiraz, cabernet sauvignon, merlot and semillon. These six grapes cover a massive 128,000 hectares, or 80 per cent of the total vineyard area, and produce more than 75 per cent of the annual grape harvest. The next six most widely planted grapes – colombard, riesling, pinot noir, gordo, pinot gris and grenache – account for 15 per cent of the crush. In other words, 90 per cent of Australian wine is made from only a dozen grape varieties.

This viticultural hegemony is partly a result of the export boom of the 1990s. All of a sudden, the world couldn't get enough sunshine-filled golden Aussie chardonnay or ripe, soft Aussie shiraz, so Aussie grape growers rushed to plant as much of those two grape varieties as they could. Some of the other most widely planted grapes are remnants of earlier periods in Australia's wine past: despite being only moderately trendy these days; for example, riesling is still found in many Australian vineyards because a generation ago it was the undisputed king of white grapes. Likewise, many grenache vineyards are less an indication of the grape's current limited popularity and more a reminder of its once-huge role in producing now-unfashionable 'port' style wines.

Don't get me wrong. I'm not against mainstream grapes, per se. Many regions in Australia are extremely well suited to one or more of the top ten varieties, and there are many, increasingly excellent wines being produced from them. Some of the country's most exciting wines are produced by adventurous winemakers challenging accepted wisdom and reinventing traditional wine styles, taking well-known grapes such as chardonnay and shiraz into unfamiliar style territory. Other winemakers are successfully chipping away at the classics, refining, finessing and perfecting them.

But now the export-inspired planting frenzy has died down, many growers and winemakers – the better ones at least – are also asking themselves whether shiraz, chardonnay, cabernet et al are really the best grapes for their particular corner of Australia. They're asking themselves whether, in a hotter, drier future, there might be other varieties among the world's thousands of cultivars better suited to their vineyards. They're questioning the lack of viticultural diversity in a national vineyard dominated by just ten grapes, and they're trying to rectify the situation by experimenting with a whole new host of varieties.

At the moment, many of these new grapes are at the embryonic stage, with only a few hectares here, a couple of hectares there. In the case of some new grapes, there might even be just one solitary grower. But already, very important varieties have emerged from the alternative movement, and are now grown in serious, commercial quantities.

For example, as recently as a decade ago, the white grapes viognier and pinot gris and the red grape tempranillo were decidedly exotic. Now they are so widely planted, and such a fixture on Australian (even international) wine shop shelves that they should perhaps no longer be considered alternative.

Nothing new under the sun

Doctor Alexander Kelly was the founder of the Tintara vineyard and winery in McLaren Vale. In 1862 he wrote *The Vine in Australia*, a classic treatise on growing grapes and making wine. The book is fascinating reading today: Kelly has many things to say about the importance of natural fermentation in winemaking; he exhibits an acute understanding of how Australia's climate and rainfall patterns differ dramatically from classic European wine regions, and urges readers to adopt this understanding in their approach to grape-growing; and he's a big fan of hardy southern French and Iberian varieties such as marsanne, roussanne and mataro, and a grape he calls 'temprana' (probably tempranillo).

In his foreword for the recently re-published edition of the book, Penfolds chief winemaker Peter Gago makes some astute observations about the visionary wisdom contained in the old grape-growing and winemaking manual. 'Equipped with a "back to the future" sensitivity and a willingness to continue this text's earlier teachings,' writes Gago, 'today's winemakers will be well-placed to develop organic and biodynamic grape-growing, improved soil moisture management, canopy control and new varietals, culminating in enhanced sustainable vineyard practice and creation of better wine.' Sounds like a manifesto to me.

It wouldn't be the first time that an 'alternative' grape has crossed over into the mainstream. Now, chardonnay is ubiquitous. We take it for granted, as though it's always been Australia's most popular grape. But it, too, is a relatively recent arrival.

Peter Dry, until recently the Associate Professor of Viticulture at the University of Adelaide, and a long-time advocate of non-mainstream grapes says, 'I'm old enough to remember in the mid-'70s when chardonnay was one of the new varieties. I even predicted then that it would just be a flash in the pan. How wrong can you be?'

If chardonnay was considered an alternative grape variety a generation ago, imagine what varieties we'll be drinking more of in a generation from now.

According to reports from nurseries who propagate and sell grapevine cuttings, and based on the list of new wines entered in the Australian Alternative Varieties Wine Show each year (see breakout), this next wave will be mostly southern Italian, Spanish and Portuguese in origin. Grape growers have been clamouring to plant varieties such as fiano, nero d'avola and sagrantino over the last few growing seasons – all Mediterranean grapes that, not surprisingly, have quickly proved themselves well suited to Australia's warm, dry conditions.

Peter Dry points out these grapes are also 'new' in the wine regions where they've been grown for centuries. 'In their own countries, some of these varieties are also seen as unusual, obscure and alternative because, there, the locals themselves are only now beginning to recognise their potential. If you asked even the educated French, Spanish or Italian wine drinker what tannat or albarino or aglianico were, they probably wouldn't know.'

In their European homelands, these old grapes are often being revived for reasons similar to why they're being introduced in Australia: as a response to climate change and a reaction to the ubiquity of so-called international grapes such as chardonnay, cabernet and, increasingly, shiraz.

There's a similar, positively parochial, revivalist spirit to be found among some Australian winemakers. Rather than go overseas to find viticultural inspiration, these winemakers are looking more closely at the vines that have been growing in their own backyards for, in some cases, well over 100 years. In old, established winegrowing regions such as the Barossa Valley, for example, red grapes such as mourvedre, carignan and cinsault, long considered second-rate varieties, are now sought after both for their savoury flavours and their suitability to hot, dry growing conditions. This resonates strongly with the rediscovery and promotion of heritage fruits and vegetables and rare breed animals championed by the Slow Food and farmers' market movements.

Brand-new grape varieties have also been developed in Australia. Until recently, this has been done by the CSIRO using old-fashioned plant breeding techniques, resulting in generally underwhelming grapes such as tarrango, taminga and tyrian. More and more, though, 'new' varieties will be developed through genetic engineering.

I can see how the promise of drought-tolerant vines, of disease-resistant vines, of vines with flavours genetically manipulated to meet perceived consumer demand might be attractive, especially to winemakers at the commercial end of the industry. But I believe the Australian wine industry should resist pressure to plant GM grapes and collectively agree not to head down this path. The risks of tarnishing what is otherwise an increasingly clean and truly green image are too great. And besides, we just don't need GM vines.

As the swelling ranks of the alternative variety movement testify, the keys to Australia's viticultural future are to be found among the world's rich diversity of existing grapevines, not in a lab or experimental field trial. The future lies, too, in Australia's own diverse and almost forgotten two centuries of viticultural history: many of the questions that grape growers are asking now have already been answered, many times before in the past. McLaren Vale wine pioneer Dr Alexander Kelly, for example, was exhorting his readers to plant heat-loving southern Mediterranean grapes back in the 1860s (see breakout). It's taken 150 years, but Australia's grape growers are finally acting on that advice.

Louisa Rose knows better than most how hard but rewarding it can be to pioneer a new variety in this country: as Yalumba chief winemaker she can take much of the credit for the current popularity of viognier. And she believes that 'real' grapes, rather than 'created' grapes are definitely the way to go: 'You don't get quite the same story with a variety that's been bred out in a paddock as you do with a variety with a history and a provenance.'

The Australian alternative varieties wine show

I should out myself here as an active member of Australia's viticultural resistance movement, not just an interested observer: I've been judging at the annual Australian Alternative Varieties Wine Show held in Mildura in north-west Victoria since its first year in 1999.

The show was conceived by vine nurseryman Bruce Chalmers, vine specialist the late Dr Rod Bonfiglioli (then working for Chalmers) and celebrity chef Stefano de Pieri, whose restaurant in the cellar of the Mildura Grand Hotel is one of Australia's great dining experiences.

Bruce had been encouraged to import dozens of non-mainstream grape varieties by Phil Reedman, the wine buyer for UK supermarket, Tesco. 'You're a boring mob,' Reedman had railed at Australian grape growers in general. 'Why don't you plant more interesting varieties than chardonnay and shiraz?'

For Dr Rod and Stefano, a show judging these varieties seemed like the best way to get the word out. Remembers Stefano: 'I thought that we might be able to initiate a conversation that could push the hot winegrowing areas, in particular, into perhaps doing things differently.'

In that first year, 1999, the judging was restricted to Australian sangioveses – about a dozen of them – before an amazing multi-course Italian long lunch, attended by almost everyone involved in growing and making alternative grapes in Australia. Ten years later, the number of alternative varieties planted had swelled so dramatically that we had over 600 entries in the show.

The purpose of the show was summed up very neatly by a series of speakers at that first long lunch in 1999.

Mornington Peninsula viticulturist and winemaker Garry Crittenden, who had just completed an in-depth study of the potential for Italian grape varieties in Australia, said: 'What we're witnessing in this room is the embryo of how we need to think about wine in this country. It might take a long time to convince the rest of the industry, because people are reluctant to change, they don't often seek change. But that change must come.'

Rod Bonfiglioli agreed, insisting that exotic, alternative grape varieties weren't just for niche players. 'This isn't pie-in-the-sky stuff. These are real opportunities. It's about sustainable regional development.'

Even Australia's former Chief Scientist, Dr John Stocker (who also owns a vineyard in Victoria's Goulburn Valley) was enthusiastic about the very real potential for alternative varieties. 'Regional Australia is entering its renaissance,' he said. 'And it's vital we promote diversity in our regions: diversity in a cultural sense in the community and diversity on our palates.'

Crossing the mainstream: How Australia's traditional grape varieties are evolving

Major mainstream whites
More than 100 hectares planted

Chardonnay 30,000 hectares

Chardonnay is one of the most exciting white grapes in Australia right now. I'm not talking about the ocean of cheap chardonnay flooding out from the hot inland irrigation regions. I'm talking about the increasingly brilliant wines being made in the country's cooler wine regions.

In the last few years, Australia's chardonnay makers have decided – en masse, it seems – to produce wines with lower alcohol, higher acidity, less obvious oak influence and greater textural interest. You can see this shift happening in established regions that already had a good reputation for chardonnay, such as the Yarra Valley, Margaret River and the Adelaide Hills, and you can also find great chardonnay in this fine, subtle mould emerging from newer regions such as high-altitude Tumbarumba in southern New South Wales and Henty in south-west Victoria.

This dramatic leap in quality is due in part to the maturity of the vines – in the Yarra, for example, many of the best chardonnay vineyards are now more than 25 years old – and in part to a concerted effort, encouraged by wine writers and judges at the country's more progressive wine shows, to make chardonnay with more finesse.

Much of Australia's chardonnay crop ends up as sparkling wine (usually blended with pinot noir), and this expression of the grape is particularly exciting in Tasmania at the moment: as the vines mature, the quality of fruit they produce is utterly spectacular. Recent tastings of some long lees-aged, 100 per cent chardonnay, blanc de blancs sparklings from producers such as Bay of Fires and Stefano Lubiana in Tassie leave little doubt that this is a perfect combination of grape and place.

Sauvignon blanc 7000 hectares

Given the extraordinary popularity and skyrocketing sales of sauvignon blanc, it's no surprise to learn that the vineyard area planted to this variety has expanded by more than 50 per cent over the last four years. There is quite a bit of savvy up in the inland river regions, and some producers such as Angove and Westend manage to make acceptably varietal, tropical-fruity quaffing wines from it. But the best sauvignon blanc in Australia comes from very specific, marginal cool spots such as the Adelaide Hills, Orange, Great Southern and – particularly – the truly cool parts of Tasmania such as the Tamar Valley, where the variety's trademark gooseberry, passionfruit and blackcurrant-leaf flavours abound.

An encouraging trend (prevalent in but not limited to the Yarra Valley) is for winemakers to craft their sauvignon blanc more like a chardonnay – wild yeast ferment in older oak barrels, etc. – to emphasise structure and texture rather than exuberant fruit.

Semillon 6700 hectares

Semillon has become a very important grape for Western Australia – particularly Margaret River – where it is almost always blended with sauvignon blanc to make the modern classic, crunchy, grassy, passionfruity thirst-quencher affectionately known as 'sem sav' or SSB (or, indeed, SBS). A similar style of wine is successfully made – albeit with a little more restraint – in cool regions such as the Yarra Valley and the Adelaide Hills. A handful of producers in these areas also give the grape a little more respect and ferment and/or mature it in oak barriques, creating a white wine that has both semillon's snappy green pea–pod freshness and a savoury, creamy undertow.

There is also a resurgence of interest in semillon in the Hunter Valley, the variety's historical and spiritual home, where a younger generation of winemakers are keen to emulate the lean, lemony and eminently ageworthy semillons of the past. Hunter semillon is truly an Australian classic: with careful cellaring, that lemony austerity morphs into the most remarkable, complex and satisfying flavours of lime and buttered toast.

There is also a push to acknowledge the great semillons of the Barossa, with Peter Lehmann, for example, recently launching a bottle-aged reserve semillon as its flagship white alongside the classic reserve riesling from Eden Valley.

Sultana 5000 hectares

No, you're not seeing things. Believe it or not, sultana is the third most-planted white grape in Australia, all of it grown in the hot, inland, irrigated regions along the Murray, Darling and Murrumbidgee rivers. While most of the crop ends up as table grapes or dried fruit, a proportion ends up as 'filler' for generic white wine casks and cheap sparkling wine; especially in drought-affected vintages such as 2007, when there simply weren't enough 'premium' grapes such as chardonnay harvested. Its importance is declining rapidly, though: there were 7300 hectares in 2006, and 15,000 hectares a decade ago.

One of sultana's less talked-about roles in the wine industry is as concentrated grape juice. Australian winemakers are not legally allowed to add cane sugar to either fermenting grapes (to boost the final alcohol content) or to finished wine (to sweeten it). But grape juice concentrate – known in the industry as 'conc' (rhymes with bonk) – *is* allowed.

Riesling 4600 hectares

It was all going so well. At the beginning of this century, it really looked like the much-hyped riesling revival was finally happening. People were buying more riesling, the top wines were gaining critical success, the introduction of screwcaps on almost all riesling bottles in Clare from the 2000 vintage onwards meant that the grape and its unique, spine-tingling brilliant quality was constantly being talked up in the trade and the press. People were obviously desperate to drink unwooded aromatic white wine…but then people discovered New Zealand sauvignon blanc and *it*, not riesling, became the wine of the moment.

Which is a shame, because riesling expresses perhaps better than any other grape Australia's distinct tastes of country: the mineral austerity of Eden Valley; the lime juiciness of Clare; the floral grapeyness of Tasmania; the herbal lift of Great Southern; the steely finesse of Henty.

But in spite of Australian wine drinkers' apparent lack of interest in riesling – perhaps because of it – and encouraged by its acceptance in sophisticated international markets, winemakers are becoming more adventurous with how they treat this noble grape. Some are moving away from the traditional, protective handling (cultured yeast, temperature-controlled stainless steel ferments) towards wild yeast ferments, even in old oak barrels, with encouragingly complex and deep-tasting results. And an increasing number of Australian winemakers are embracing the 'Germanic' style of wine – lower alcohol, higher acidity, more residual sweetness – perhaps unwittingly emulating the sweeter rieslings that made the grape so popular in Australia in the first place, half a century ago.

Colombard 2700 hectares

Yes, that does sound like an *awful* lot of colombard, doesn't it? And yet, you will seldom find a bottle of Australian wine with colombard proudly emblazoned on the label. So where do all the grapes go? Well, the same reason it's widely planted in France and elsewhere around the world applies here, too: it's fairly easy to grow large crops of reasonably alcoholic, nicely tart white wine, making it a good grape (a bit like a slightly posher version of sultana, if you like) to use in generic, cheap white wine. Having said that, some winemakers *do* coax some attractively herbaceous flavours out of it. Primo Estate's La Biondina (admittedly a blend of colombard and sauvignon blanc) is far and away the best example in the country.

Verdelho 1800 hectares

It may just be because I'm getting older, but I'm slowly coming round to verdelho. Until relatively recently, I'd dismissed the grape as boring and characterless, pointing to the rash of sweet, bland commercial verdelhos available in every wine shop around the country as evidence. But recent tastings of some excellent examples

– tangy and apple-fresh in the Swan Valley, rich and satisfying in the Granite Belt, lean and mineral in the Hunter Valley – have forced me to reassess the variety. I still don't think it's well suited to all regions, and made into a sweetish commercial wine it is really quite *un*appealing, but in the right vineyards, with yields kept low, and in the right winemaker's hands (one who wants to make a *dry* style of wine), verdelho can be very pleasant.

Gewurztraminer 850 hectares

Like colombard, most of Australia's gewurz must end up in cask wines and cheap commercial blends because you see very little of it appearing as top-quality wine in varietally labelled bottles. But, unlike colombard, gewurz really doesn't deserve to be so comprehensively overlooked. Viognier seems to have captured the wine drinking public's imagination with its heady, musky perfume and oily, creamy texture – but these are all descriptions that could equally be applied to a good gewurz.

There are some exceptional examples of spicy, complex gewurz dotted around the country: Delatite's biodynamically grown Dead Man's Hill; Chatsfield's newly rejuvenated examples from the Porongorups; luscious late-harvested wine from the Riverina – but they are few and far between. It's time for some bright young thing to come over all passionate about the grape, plant a vineyard on a steep, stony hill somewhere (or buy grapes from the many underrated gewurz vineyards around the country) and get serious about creating a new benchmark for the variety (that someone may well be Gary Mills at Jamsheed in the Yarra Valley).

Chenin blanc 650 hectares

Again, most of the chenin blanc in Australia ends up in casks or cheap blends, but occasionally you come across excellent examples – a beautifully green-apple crisp, refreshing dry style in McLaren Vale, a lovely, toasty bottle-aged example from the Swan Valley, a sweet, late-harvested example from Great Southern – and you wonder why more isn't planted, or, at least, made into top-quality wine. Chenin's high acidity and ability to produce a diverse range of styles make it, you would think, an obvious choice for vineyards in warmer climates.

Trebbiano 200 hectares

Like colombard (see above) this high-cropping, rather bland-tasting grape is a legacy of Australia's cask wine–producing heyday, and the vineyard area is decreasing rapidly.

Marsanne 200 hectares

This *could* be on the list of alternative varieties (see below), because most of the marsanne vineyards in Australia other than the old plantings at Tahbilk in central Victoria were established in the last ten years. Not only that, but many winemakers also view marsanne as one

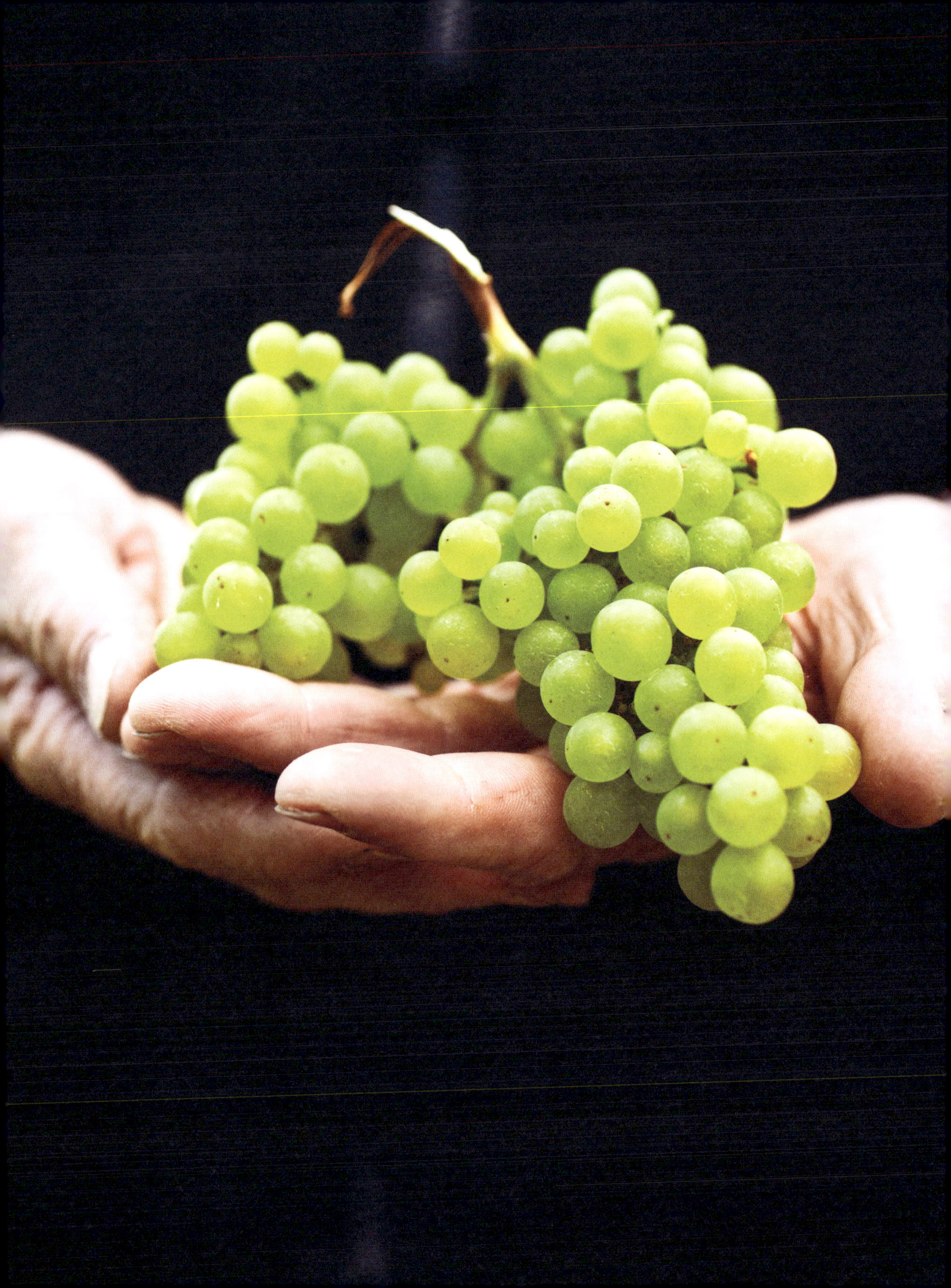

Some alternative white varieties (*left to right*): *1st row*: arneis; fiano; garganega *2nd row*: greco di tufo; malvasia; moscato giallo *3rd row*: picolit; pinot gris; prosecco *4th row*: vermentino; viognier.
opposite: The stalwart: chardonnay

of the three 'Rhone whites' (along with viognier and roussanne) and, therefore, a 'new' grape, rather than seeing it in its true Australian historical context. But its continuous 80-year history at Tahbilk and documented presence in older, now long-gone vineyards means it qualifies as a traditional grape in my eyes. Either way, on its own and unwooded (*à la Tahbilk*) or new-wave oak-matured (often blended with viognier and/or roussanne), marsanne is proving itself capable of producing satisfyingly spicy, honeyed, excitingly full-flavoured whites. A handful of wineries have experimented with it as a dessert wine; Turkey Flat in the Barossa successfully emulate the *vin de paille*, or 'straw wine', of the Rhone, by laying their marsanne grapes on racks to shrivel before fermentation, concentrating the sweetness and flavour.

Minor traditional whites
Less than 100 hectares planted

There are still small patches here and there of white grapes that were once much more important in various Australian wine regions than they are now.

1893
When the Rimfire vineyard was established near Toowoomba in Queensland in the 1990s, an old vine dating back to a late 19th-century vineyard was discovered in a neighbouring property. The still-unidentified variety – dubbed 1893 – was propagated, planted out and now produces crisp, citrusy dry white wine. A curio, perhaps, but a lovely living link to the past.

Crouchen
There are, apparently, just over 100 hectares of crouchen in Australia, but you seldom see the name on a label. Most of the fruit ends up in Brown Brothers' top-selling sweet crouchen riesling blend, and Botobolar produce a deliciously dry white from it in Mudgee. But that's about it.

Chasselas and ondenc
Chasselas and ondenc are Australian historical relics from Switzerland and south-west France, respectively, which found a home in the stony soils of Great Western, in south-west Victoria in the 19th century. Ondenc also made its way to South Australia, incorrectly called sercial (which is in fact a grape from the Atlantic island of Madeira, see below) and used to make fortified sweet white wines. Both these grapes were once – and could again be – used to produce flavoursome, textural dry white wine, but I fear their daggy reputations will scare most winemakers off.

Gouais
This old white grape is so boring it is no longer planted in its homeland of France. It remains in a couple of historic old vineyards in Australia – notably in

Rutherglen – and is remarkable mainly as the ancient genetic parent, with pinot noir, of chardonnay.

Sylvaner
Sylvaner is an old German grape – like a fatter, more spicy riesling – grown in a few pockets in Australia, notably in the Granite Belt in Queensland, where it makes a fabulous late-harvest sweet wine.

White grenache
Some old plantings of so-called white grenache (thought to be in reality the Corsican grape biancone) are hanging on for dear life in South Australia, mainly in the Riverland, where Angove make a surprisingly good, textural dry white from it; and in the Barossa, where the grape plays a minor, freshening role in adventurous grenache and shiraz blends.

Major mainstream reds
More than 100 hectares planted

Shiraz 45,000 hectares
Sometimes it feels as though modern Australian shiraz exists in two parallel universes. On one hand you have shiraz from warmer climate regions such as the Barossa and McLaren Vale, often (but by no means always) picked from low-yielding, dry-grown old vines at extraordinarily high levels of sugar ripeness, then heavily worked in the winery (plenty of vigorous skin contact, whacked into new oak barrels) to produce ink-black, 15-plus per cent alcohol, mouthfilling blockbusters.

And then you have a growing number of shirazes (often labelled syrah) from cooler climates – Beechworth, the Canberra District, the Yarra Valley, Adelaide Hills – usually from younger, but still low-yielding vines, picked slightly less ripe and made in a softer fashion, in many cases co-fermented with a small percentage of viognier, to produce fine, spicy and aromatic, medium-bodied but intense expressions of the grape and the place they were grown.

In some places, these alternate approaches to making shiraz can exist side by side. In the Hunter Valley, for example, some winemakers pursue the former, black and ballsy style, while others exercise restraint and try to let the quieter, but distinctive savoury taste of country speak in the glass. Heathcote is another excellent example of the parallel approach: the soils and climate vary so much from the cool south to the hot north that it's possible to find both spicy and elegant and rich and brawny examples of shiraz carrying Heathcote on the label.

Shiraz has, traditionally, always been a reliable blending grape in Australia, providing good colour, flavour and strength. In the 1970s and '80s, shiraz cabernet blends, often called 'claret', were all the rage; in the early 1990s, shiraz began to find its way into more and more Rhone blends, with grenache and mourvedre; in the early years of this century, the shiraz viognier blend has risen to prominence, the heady aromatic qualities of the white grape adding a very useful lift to the often weak flavours of young vine shiraz.

Encouragingly, I'm tasting ever-more adventurous assemblages, as Australian winemakers try to give new, alternative grapes an Aussie accent by adding shiraz: tempranillo and shiraz, sangiovese and shiraz, malbec and shiraz, lagrein and shiraz, tannat and shiraz. A couple of winemakers have even revived the classic 1940s Hunter blend of shiraz and pinot noir.

Shiraz's once important role as a major grape for 'port' production is now being augmented and in some cases usurped by 'proper' Portuguese grapes such as touriga (in those few wineries who still care about such styles), which is a good thing, as shiraz 'port' often tastes more like blackberry nip, and lacks the complexity of 'port' made from the authentic varieties.

And then there's that other Australian classic wine style, sparkling red. The best examples (made from high-quality, low-yielding shiraz grapes, aged for a long time on lees) are truly wonderful drinks – heady purple foaming brews, perfect for washing down barbecued kangaroo.

Cabernet sauvignon 28,000 hectares

A generation ago, cabernet was all the rage with Australian winemakers and drinkers. Shiraz was so unpopular in the mid-'80s that whole vineyards of it were ripped out of the ground. How times have changed. While plenty of cabernet is still grown and exported and sold and drunk, it's definitely lost out to shiraz in the popularity race.

This is a shame, because Australia makes some completely brilliant cabernet sauvignon, both as a straight varietal and as a blend with shiraz and/or merlot (as well as the other 'Bordeaux' grapes, malbec, cabernet franc and petit verdot). The top wines from top regions such as Coonawarra, Margaret River and the Yarra Valley, where many vineyards are approaching their 40th birthdays, are every bit as impressive as Australia's best shirazes – redolent with fragrant, glossy blackcurrant fruit, firmly structured, ageworthy, complex. But they seldom attract the same level of breathless praise from the wine critics, and only a handful of the top cabernets can command the same kind of serious prices as the latest blockbuster cult shirazes.

Then again, this isn't such a bad thing. It means that good Australian cabernet is relatively affordable – and great Australian cabernet can look like a bargain compared with equally great shiraz.

Merlot 11,000 hectares

I'm buggered if I know why there is so much merlot planted in this country. Most is found in the warmer regions, where it's used, apparently, to 'fill out' or soften cabernet's hard edges. Cabernet merlot blends are very popular and sell well, but this is mostly I think on the back of merlot's perceived reputation for 'softness' rather than the reality of what's in the glass. Because when you taste it on its own, Australian merlot usually turns out to be a rather insipid and gutless red wine. Dilute might be a better word than soft.

To be fair, the majority of the merlot vines in Australia are what we now know to be a poor clone of the variety, and it's hard to make great wine from inferior materials. And, to be fair, there are some notable exceptions to merlot's generally ordinary performance: in places where cabernet is taken seriously (see above), you will also find some merlots that do manage to successfully express the variety's supple but firm black fruit and dried herb characters.

In the last few years, some new, better clones of merlot have also been planted, and the few wines made thus far from those young vines have been very encouraging. Hopefully more winemakers will follow this lead. But in the meantime, most of the examples I taste from the old, dreary clone still remind me of a young winemaker's sardonic observation that 'merlot's not a grape variety: it's an idea'.

Pinot noir 5,100 hectares

Don't get too excited. Even though 4500 hectares looks like a lot of pinot noir, most of the annual crop ends up in sparkling wine, blended with chardonnay. Not that that's a disaster by any means. Pinot juice can bring a lovely nuttiness and strawberry overtone to fizz, and also produces some terrifically full-flavoured *blanc de noirs* style bubblies.

But it's as a red wine that pinot noir shines. Australian pinot is going through two really interesting phases at the moment. At the top end, the best wines from established regions such as Tasmania and southern Victoria are better than ever. A combination of vine maturity, new Burgundian clones, a succession of good, warm vintages and – most importantly – sensitive handling in the winery has seen many winemakers move beyond a deep-coloured, fruit-rich expression of pinot (as seductive as that may be) towards a more ethereal, more complex and ultimately more satisfying style.

At the same time, the quality of 'everyday' pinot noirs – wines that sell for $20 or less – improves with each vintage. Again, this is a result of winemakers consciously doing less in the winery, letting the simple but delicious flavours of the grape speak for themselves.

And pinot is often the grape of choice for a new wave of winemakers who want to produce very dry, pale, savoury rosé – one of the most exciting yet least talked about trends in Australian wine, I think – although almost any red grape can be and has been used to great effect to make this style.

Grenache 2000 hectares

A lot of Australia's large annual crop of grenache grapes still ends up where it has ended up for decades: as 'filler' for cheap red bulk wine blends; or as spicy, slightly sweet rosé; or in barrels, fortified with spirit, as tawny 'port'. But since the early 1990s, grenache has also enjoyed a renaissance in the form of often strong red wine, usually blended with shiraz and mourvedre in various permutations – commonly GSM, but also SMG, GMS, MGS or, rather amusingly, MSG. Some winemakers are now also emulating the Rioja model and blending grenache with tempranillo.

In most cases, blending is necessary because, while it might be able to produce grapes with good spice and sweetness (and, therefore, alcohol), most Australian grenache is straightforward and simple in flavour. There are pockets of old grenache vines – dry-grown, incredibly low-yielding – in traditional warm areas such as the Barossa and McLaren Vale, that produce wines with enough depth and complexity to be bottled as straight varietals. But the best examples of these are few and far between.

Ruby cabernet 1100 hectares

You won't find many bottles with the name of this Californian cross between carignan and cabernet sauvignon displayed on the label. Ruby cabernet's main attribute is that it can crop heavily and still produce red wine with very dark purple colour. As a result, it's mainly used in cheap bulk wines and as an undeclared minor component of a red blend. Remember that Australian winemakers can legally add up to 15 per cent of other varieties to a blend and still label it as a single varietal; so a blend of 86 per cent shiraz and 14 per cent ruby cabernet can still be labelled as a straight shiraz.

Mataro, aka mourvedre, aka monastrell 800 hectares

This is another hangover from the old days. Mataro used to be widely planted because it could be cropped heavily and turned into rough red or port. In many ways mataro's renaissance mirrors that of grenache: the best grapes, from old, low-yielding vines, are now finding their way into some pretty smart red wines, carrying the much posher French name of mourvedre and often blended with shiraz and other grapes. The very best grapes, from the oldest and lowest-yielding vineyards, are also appearing as dark, brooding, deeply earthy and satisfying straight varietal mourvedre wines. A number of winemakers have also cottoned on to mataro's third European incarnation – in Spain, as monastrell – and are successfully blending the grape with tempranillo to produce savoury, structural reds.

Cabernet franc 700 hectares

As it does in Bordeaux, most of Australia's cabernet franc finds its way into blends with cabernet sauvignon, merlot et al, where it adds perfume, freshness and line. A few winemakers in classic cabernet regions such as Margaret River make it a major feature of the blend (*à la*

St Emilion and Pomerol), and produce convincingly leafy, earthy wines. But only a handful of producers bottle their cab franc on its own – with even fewer having the nerve or the nous to keep it away from too much new wood influence, as winemakers do so successfully in the Loire Valley. I think there's huge potential for more cabernet franc in Australia to be made in this fresh, young style, with bright, light purple colour, blackcurrant fruit and juiciness.

Durif 450 hectares

First brought to Australia in 1908, this robust, dark grape spent most of the 20th century in Rutherglen producing robust, dark 'port'. These days, you're more likely to see durif being turned into robust, dark Rutherglen red wine, often with masses of tannin and almost port-like levels of alcohol (15 per cent is normal, 17 per cent or more is not uncommon). Such is the success of Rutherglen durif in this form that the variety has been planted elsewhere, including the Riverina in New South Wales, where it clearly feels at home, producing, um, robust and dark red wines.

Malbec 350 hectares

Here's another grape that I think has massive potential. Indeed, it's a grape that has already indisputably proven its ability to make stunning red wines. The Clare Valley in particular, and Western Australia's Frankland region both make wonderfully black malbec, chock-full of brambly fruit, with alluring violety perfume and firm, grippy, endless tannins. It is a brilliant blending partner for shiraz and cabernet in Clare; it stands tall on its own in Frankland. So why do more people not grow or make it? Traditionally, malbec's fickle performance in the vineyard, where it would crop massively one year then meagrely the next, turned many growers off. But with new, reliable clones sourced from good vineyards in Argentina (arguably the home of malbec) now available, perhaps more growers will get as fired up as I am about the grape.

Tarrango 100 hectares

This is the most widely planted of the grapes bred by the CSIRO in the 1970s, and it is a cross between touriga (see below) and sultana. It produces pale, light red wine like a nondescript gamay (see also below). Other 'created' varieties used to make red wines in Australia include carnelian (a cross between carignan, cabernet and grenache that a few growers in Western Australia mistakenly planted thinking it was sangiovese, which, when you think about it, can sometimes taste like a cross between carignan, cabernet and grenache), cienna and tyrian, both a cross between cabernet and the obscure Spanish grape sumoll. My vote goes to the slightly fleshier, darker, more interesting, herbal-tinged tyrian as a variety with some potential.

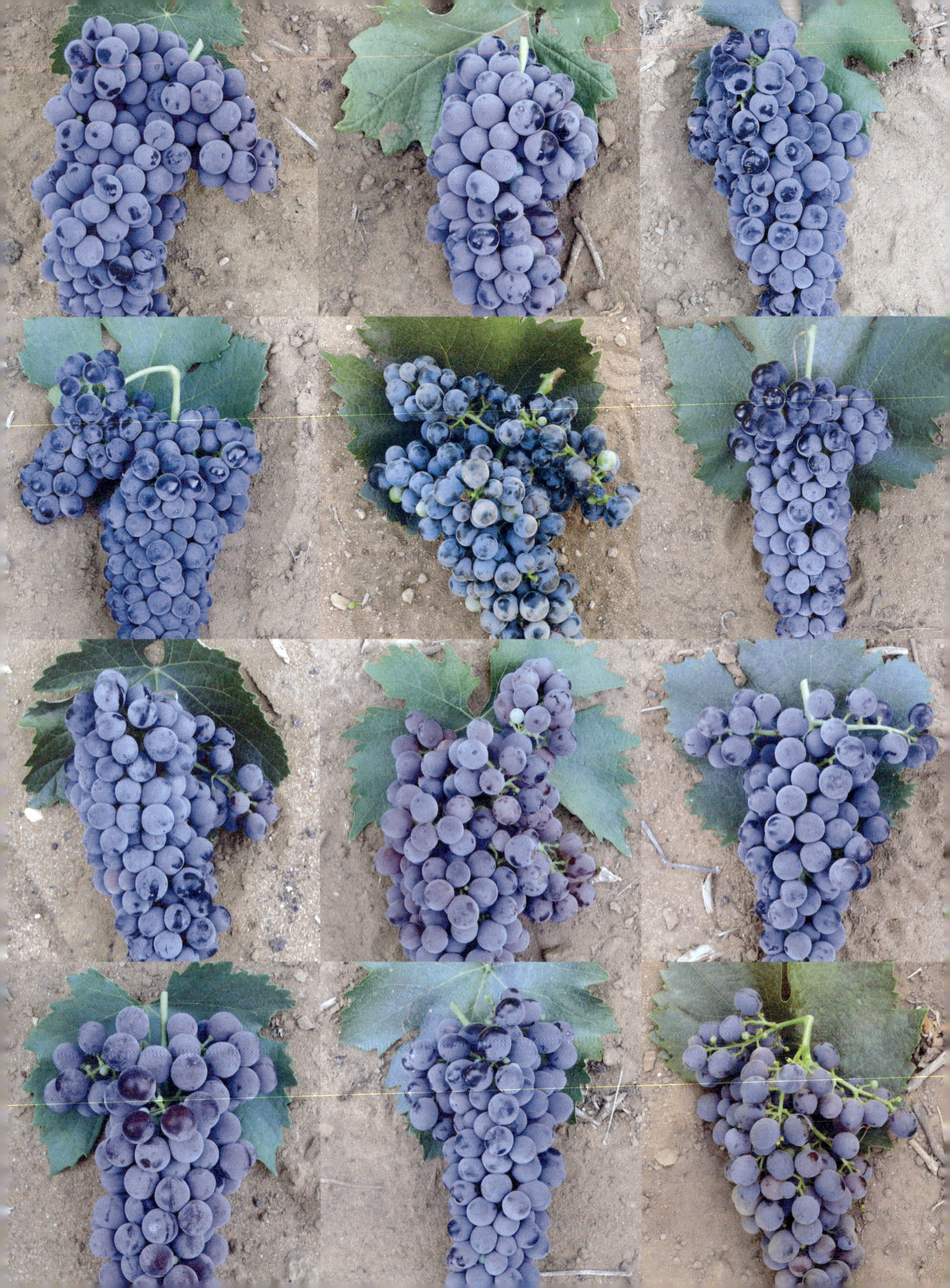

opposite: Some alternative red varieties *(left to right)*: *1st row*: aglianico; barbera; dolcetto *2nd row*: durif; graciano; lagrein *3rd row*: lambrusco maestri; mammolo; marzemino *4th row*: nebbiolo; negroamaro; nero d'avola.

above: Some alternative red varieties *(left to right)*:
1st row: petit verdot; pinotage; sagrantino *2nd row*: sangiovese; saperavi; schioppettino *3rd row*: tannat; tempranillo; zinfandel.

Pinot meunier 100 hectares

Most winemakers use the juice from pinot meunier as a minor component of top-quality sparkling wine. As it does in champagne, meunier adds a soft note of honey to chardonnay's lemony crispness and pinot noir's full dryness. Some winemakers, though, follow a 140-year Australian tradition (it's been grown at Best's in Great Western since the late 1860s) and turn their meunier into a pinot noir–like, light-bodied but often surprisingly earthy and complex red wine.

Minor traditional reds
Less than 100 hectares planted

Despite being grown in Australian vineyards for decades, these red grapes have either fallen out of fashion or have failed to take off in a big way – yet.

Carignan and cinsault

I've lumped these two varieties together because, as in France, they're traditionally grown side by side in Australian vineyards (although the grape we know here as carignan is likely to be the Portuguese bonvedro). In the 19th century, when these grapes first arrived, they had far more exotic names: carignan was Black Prince, and cinsault was Blue Imperial. The grapes are no longer fashionable – indeed, they're almost extinct – because many winemakers believe they lack distinctive flavour or character. A few younger winemakers, though, particularly in the Barossa, are beginning to judiciously blend both varieties into their grenache and shiraz to great effect. Their proven ability to thrive with little or no supplementary irrigation is another plus.

Chambourcin

This hybrid grape (a hybrid is a cross between a *vinifera* – or wine-producing – vine and a non-*vinifera* vine) is planted in quite a few Australian vineyards, particularly in warm, humid regions on the New South Wales coast, because it is strongly resistant to mildew. It produces wine with shockingly intense purple colour and essencey berry fruit flavour but it usually tastes quite coarse and cloying. Sometimes wine made from chambourcin can also smell unnervingly 'foxy'; a typical characteristic of hybrid varieties. As you can tell, I'm not a huge fan.

Dolcetto

While dolcetto is very trendy right now, because it's an Italian grape variety (and Italian grape varieties are very trendy) and because it's great for producing juicy, fruity red wine (and juicy, fruity red wine is also very trendy), it has in fact been grown in Australia for decades; although in many vineyards it was misidentified as malbec. Like cabernet franc, there is great potential for dolcetto in Australia, as the demand grows for lighter, fresher, brighter wines.

Gamay

Gamay is another grape that I love and, again, I can't understand why more isn't planted. Look at how bright and succulent and satisfying it can be when grown in the granite country of Beaujolais. There's plenty of granite country in Australia – all along the Great Dividing Range, in fact – and yet only a couple of those hills have any gamay vines planted on them. As climate change makes it harder to make bright, succulent wines in the warmer, flatter regions, perhaps more growers will explore gamay's possibilities on these stony slopes.

Mondeuse

This obscure French grape, originally from the Savoie region, somehow ended up in Victoria's northeast in the early 20th century. It now produces wonderfully savoury, spicy red wines, particularly blended with shiraz and cabernet by Brown Brothers. It would be fascinating to see it planted in different Australian soils and climates, and blended with other grapes.

Zinfandel

Despite its massive popularity in California (or perhaps because of it), zinfandel has never really taken off in Australia, even though it has produced many compelling, serious, sturdy red wines in regions as diverse as Margaret River, McLaren Vale and the Adelaide Hills. There has, though, been a minor surge of interest in the last couple of years, with the release of particularly wild wines labelled primitivo, the Italian name for the same grape.

Major sweet grapes: Dessert wines and fortifieds
More than 100 hectares planted

Muscat gordo blanco, aka muscat of Alexandria, aka lexia 2500 hectares

Very few grapes have enjoyed the remarkable change of fortune that gordo has experienced in the last decade. For most of the 20th century, this multipurpose white variety (it is also grown for table grapes) was turned into low-value sweet white wine, either sold in cask or very cheap bottles, often labelled 'moselle' or 'spatlese lexia'. But since the craze for low-alcohol, moscato-style, sherbety wines has taken off in the first decade of this century, gordo has been given a whole new lease of life.

Muscat à petit grains blanc and rouge 500 hectares

Many different forms of the finest muscat grape are grown in Australia, including small patches of the rare black muscat and orange muscat. The most widely planted form, though, is the muscat found in Rutherglen, Glenrowan and other traditional warm regions such as the Swan

Valley, where, under the rather prosaic brown muscat name, it has produced incredibly luscious, treacly fortified wines for over a century. A new enthusiasm for classic Australian fortified sweet wines, both among younger winemakers in awe of the heritage and younger wine drinkers in awe of the sheer deliciousness of the wines, has resulted in a surge of interest in both the muscat and muscadelle grapes.

Muscadelle 150 hectares
Muscadelle is the white grape used to make the luscious, golden brown fortified wine traditionally called tokay and now to be called topaque, but it also has a long tradition in Australia of being a component of dry white blends. As in Bordeaux, it's still sometimes blended with semillon and sauvignon blanc – and was even added to shiraz, for acidity and perfume, as far back as the 1950s, years before anyone had even heard of the shiraz viognier blend. A handful of winemakers are reviving these traditions.

Minor sweet grapes: Dessert wines and fortifieds
Less than 100 hectares planted

In most cases, there are very few examples of these grapes – just 5, 10 or 20 hectares perhaps, either concentrated in one region or scattered across the country's wine regions.

Aleatico
First planted by renowned Sydney surgeon Thomas Fiaschi in Mudgee in the 1920s, the bold, spicy, muscatty flavours of the red aleatico grape are good for producing a light, pink-coloured sweet wine.

Alicante bouschet
Limited plantings of this rare, red-fleshed grape still exist, mainly producing very bold, magenta-coloured, sweet pink wine; Rockford in the Barossa is the leading example.

Bastardo
In the past, this strikingly named Portuguese red grape has often been confused with another Portuguese red grape, touriga. In their homeland, both are used to make port, and that is precisely what bastardo is used for in Australia, although a couple of adventurous souls use it to make spicy red and rosé wines.

Flora
Plantings of this aromatic white grape, a cross between semillon and gewurztraminer, are extremely limited; you're likely to find it in just one sweet wine from Brown Brothers, blended with orange muscat.

Mavrodaphne
This red grape is limited to just one vineyard in north-west Victoria, Robinvale, where it makes an unusual, raisined dessert wine, but given the burgeoning

interest in both unusual stickies and Greek varieties, perhaps it has a future in other vineyards.

Palomino and doradillo

One of Australia's great wine tragedies is the dwindling interest in dry 'sherry' style wines. There used to be a lot of the white grape palomino planted along the Murray, and, as in Spain, it was used to make excellent, pale, bone-dry fino and nutty amontillado. Traditionally, another white grape, doradillo, was even more important to the 'sherry' industry, although the wines it produced were not as good. Now, there are barely 50 hectares of palomino left, less than 100 hectares of doradillo, and hardly anybody persists with top-quality fino production any more. The tragedy is that palomino in particular is extremely well suited to a warm, dry climate – both viticulturally and gastronomically.

Pedro ximenez

Like palomino, this white grape's once important role in the production of sweet 'sherry' throughout the 20th century is in danger of being completely forgotten: only a handful of old Australian pedro vineyards have survived. The good news is that the wines they produce can be fabulously rich and seductive.

Sercial

Incorrect name for the white grape ondenc (see above), and almost extinct now in Australian vineyards, but once used to make convincingly Madeira-like fortified sweet wine in South Australia.

Taminga

The white cousin to the CSIRO-bred red tarrango grape variety, and a cross between gewurztraminer and sultana, this grape can produce spicy dry white (like a rather coarse gewurz), but is most successful as a late-harvest dessert wine; although I find its exaggerated musky aroma can be over the top and cloying.

Touriga

Increasingly replacing shiraz, cabernet and grenache in Australian 'port' style wines, along with bastardo (see above) and various other Portuguese red grapes (see below). The result are 'ports' with much more attractive savoury complexity. A number of winemakers are also now making some excitingly vibrant and lively red wines from touriga, sometimes blended with other grapes such as grenache and shiraz. Expect the current 50 or so hectares to increase over the next few years.

An alternative anthology: Australia's new and emerging grape varieties

Major alternative whites
More than 100 hectares planted

Pinot gris, aka pinot grigio
2800 hectares

Yes, I know. With 2800 hectares in the ground, gris is clearly no longer an emerging grape. But I still consider it an alternative, partly because it only really began to be planted seriously from the late-'90s on – the vineyard area increased by over 80 per cent between 2006 and 2007 alone – but mostly because Australian pinot grigio/pinot gris continues to suffer from an identity crisis.

Due to the warm growing conditions in most of the vineyards where the variety is grown, the grapes are often fully ripe when picked, with fat, spicy flavours associated with pinot gris wines from Alsace. But because most winemakers use very clean, protective production techniques, the resulting wine tends towards the light and dry grigio style. So you end up with a wine exhibiting split personality: gris flavours in a grigio body. An increasing number of winemakers are successfully producing true grigio-style wines (light, fresh, crisp), particularly in warmer climates, where the grape ripens faster, and there are a few examples of successfully fat, textural, oily – 'proper' – gris. But, and it's a crucial but, those few examples are good enough to indicate that the variety does have a secure future in Australia. As long as growers pay more attention to where they're planting it and how it grows.

Viognier 1400 hectares

Again, 1400 hectares isn't exactly niche. And although some producers (notably Yalumba and Elgee Park) have more than 20 years' experience with the variety, most of Australia's viognier vineyards are very new. The best Australian examples – from Yalumba, Gary Farr, Castagna and others – have proven that the variety is quite clearly at home in Australian vineyards, and responds well to the heat, to being picked ripe and to winemaking influences such as barrel fermentation and lees-stirring. Unfortunately, though, too many Australian viogniers lack the pedigree of the producers I've just mentioned: they lack the variety's true, entrancing perfume and show clumsy oak handling. Indeed, viognier's most important contribution to Australia's wine culture in recent years hasn't been as a white wine at all, but as a tiny (5 per cent or less) addition to shiraz in the now-ubiquitous shiraz viognier blend. The popularity of this style is out of all proportion to the number of truly exciting examples: too often, the viognier appears to have contributed precisely nothing to the wine (other than being a useful selling point on the label) or it's contributed too much, making the wine taste like tinned apricots. But when it's good – Clonakilla, Castagna, De Bortoli, among others – shiraz viognier can be hauntingly beautiful.

Minor alternative whites
Around 50 hectares or less planted (so far)

Albarino (see savagnin)

Arneis
This very obscure white grape, originally from Piedmont in northern Italy, has produced some deliciously characterful white wines in Australia, particularly in cooler climates such as the King Valley and Yarra Valley. Its characteristic, pear-like flavour and savoury, grainy texture have been easily captured by Australian winemakers.

Assyrtiko
Cuttings of this classic Greek grape have been brought into Australia and will become available to Australian growers in the first years of the millennium's second decade. Which is very exciting. On the island of Santorini, assyrtiko withstands extreme aridity, heat and wind and still produces crisp, aromatic whites with good minerality. Seems like a no-brainer, really, for Australian wine regions facing a hotter, drier future.

Cortese
Like arneis, this northern Italian grape – responsible for the full-flavoured wines of Gavi – seems right at home in the one cool, higher-altitude Australian vineyard where it's been planted so far (Lost Valley in Victoria's Upper Goulburn), producing wine with nutty, savoury texture and satisfying length.

Cygne blanc
Like the 1893 vine (see above), this was propagated from an old cabernet vine in Dorham Mann's vineyard in the Swan Valley; except this particular cabernet vine had mutated to produce white grapes. It's been planted at Mount Benson on South Australia's Limestone Coast and produces a scintillating white wine with delicate perfume and crisp acidity.

Fiano
There has been quite a bit of excitement surrounding the first few Australian examples of this southern Italian white grape. As it does in its homeland, fiano produces deliciously tropical-fruity, full-yet-dry and savoury whites here.

Friulano
This distinctive, delicately aromatic white grape from Friuli in northern Italy has been made into an unusual white varietal called Senza Nome and blended into an even more unusual mélange of grapes called Pobblebonk by innovative winemaker Kathleen Quealy.

Garganega
This is the grape responsible for Italy's white Soave wines, and while only a handful of garganega vines has been planted so far in Australia, the wines produced have the grape-pulpy deliciousness and complexity found in the best Soave.

Greco di tufo
Of all the white grapes originally from Italy's hot south and islands (fiano, vermentino), greco makes wines with the most uncompromisingly savoury, full-flavoured minerality. This makes it perhaps the least obvious commercial proposition, but a brilliant grape for warm-climate growers.

Gruner veltliner
The first vintage in 2009 of the Carpenters' gruner from Lark Hill was absolutely on the money: lean and savoury but with a pretty streak of green melon and grape running through the middle. Austrian gruner continues to be the darling of sommeliers and drinkers in trendy wine bars, so there is a good future for it here.

Kerner
A couple of growers have planted this riesling-like variety, which is a cross between true riesling and the obscure German red grape trollinger. One, Robinvale, produces the most delicious, remarkably long-lived, tropical-fruity white from grapes grown biodynamically in the very warm climate of Victoria's north west.

Malvasia istriana
A very new introduction, this northern Italian grape has so far shown promise in the form of a crisp white with almost top-heavy, spicy floral perfume. In Europe it is often used in blends: it would be fascinating to see what its overt aromatics bring to, say, a pinot grigio – or, for that matter, a red blend.

Melon de bourgogne
Again, I've only ever tasted one example (Crittenden from the Mornington Peninsula), but it was convincingly similar in its green apple tartness and mineral line to good Muscadet to make it memorable.

Pinot blanc
Big potential: frankly, the two or three examples of Australian pinot blanc I've tried – textural, oily, satisfying and complex – have made most of the hundreds of Australian examples of pinot gris I've ever had taste like water. More, please.

Petit manseng
This relatively obscure grape from south-west France has done very well in Victoria's King Valley, producing both dry and sweet white wines with wonderful, creamy, mouth-coating texture. It is beginning to appear in some other regions, too: a recently tasted example from the Riverland in South Australia was also convincingly exotic.

Petit meslier
One producer, Irvine in the Eden Valley, makes a lovely, green-apple-crisp aperitif-style sparkling wine from this obscure old white champagne grape. It's perplexing why more growers haven't planted it.

Prosecco
Prosecco is only planted in a few Australian vineyards, but, just as it does in Italy, it makes wonderfully fruity, lively dry sparkling wine here. Given the growing popularity of fizz in Australia – particularly fizz that is markedly different to the less-fruity chardonnay pinot noir blend – prosecco could have a big future.

Roussanne
The third and perhaps most promising of the three 'Rhone' whites, roussanne (along with marsanne and viognier) makes wine with the most interesting, spicy flavour profile and satisfying, savoury minerality. It needs careful handling in both vineyard and winery, though; it's less forgiving than marsanne and less obviously aromatic than viognier. Winemakers are excited by its potential: there are around 70 hectares planted, mainly in Victoria.

Savagnin (formerly thought to be albarino)
It's not often that an obscure grape variety, new to Australian vineyards, makes the six o'clock TV news. But that's what happened in early 2009 when DNA testing revealed to Australia's small-but-burgeoning band of albarino growers that the vines they had planted were in fact savagnin, the white grape used in France's Jura region to make the sherry-like Vin Jaune. Turns out there was a mix-up 20 years ago when the CSIRO imported some vine cuttings from Spain – and those vines were the source block for almost all Australian plantings. The thing is, though, the savagnin vine has thrived here: from the cool of the King Valley and Orange to the warmth of the Barossa, McLaren Vale and even the Riverland, it has produced good, aromatic, lemony, textural white wines. Perfect for drinking while we wait for real albarino cuttings to be imported, propagated, planted and made into wine.

Shonburger and siegerrebe
These two German varieties, both crosses of aromatic grapes including gewurztraminer and muscat, have found a home in Tasmania, where they produce musky, sometimes quite oily, riesling-like wines.

Verdejo
Early signs are that this could do extremely well in up-and-coming cool regions such as Ballarat in Victoria and New England in northern New South Wales, producing tangy, sauvignon blanc–like wines similar to those in its home of Rueda.

Verduzzo
Although this has been grown in one Yarra Valley vineyard since the 1970s, it has only very recently been planted in other regions, where it produces full-flavoured, savoury white wines.

Vermentino
Another white grape from southern Italy that seems perfectly suited to Australian conditions: even in the dry heat of the Murray Valley where it was initially planted, it produces wines with good crisp acidity and a refreshing chalky dryness. As a result some of Australia's largest wine companies have taken a very keen interest in producing vermentino on a broad scale.

Major alternative reds
More than 100 hectares planted

Petit verdot 1400 hectares
Now here's a strange thing. Petit verdot is a late-ripening red grape, and although it struggles to reach maturity in its homeland of Bordeaux, it does so with ease in warm Australian vineyards, regularly producing deeply coloured, plush-purple wine saturated with black berry fruit and fine, firm tannins. These are all, you would think, attributes that would appeal enormously to Australian wine lovers. A lot of winemakers certainly thought so: almost all Australia's petit verdot was planted in the 1990s, much of it in the inland, irrigated regions. As it turns out, though, wine drinkers *aren't* all that taken with the grape, and sales haven't managed to match the winemakers' initial enthusiasm. I don't know why: I think it can make deliciously dark, polished reds. Perhaps its long-term future will be relegated to its proven minor supporting role in blends of cabernet and merlot.

Sangiovese 500 hectares
This was going to be the great red hope for Australian alternative varieties. Early wines from pioneers such as Montrose in Mudgee and Coriole in McLaren Vale inspired a wave of plantings in the 1990s, with many of the new vineyards established in warm regions. But the results, on the whole, were disappointing: many of these new wave Australian sangioveses turned out to taste like lacklustre lollywater, lacking the fruit weight, the tannic grip and deeply satisfying savoury qualities displayed by the best examples of the grape.

As with merlot, the problem is that most of the sangiovese planted in the '90s was a clone of the vine originally selected in California for high yield, not quality. And many growers duly allowed the vine to do what came naturally to it – crop heavily – resulting in thin, boring wines. Luckily, growers have learned their lesson, and are not only now planting new, much better clones of sangiovese, but also treating the grape with much more serious respect (some are even planting sangio's traditional Chianti blend partners such as mammolo and cannaiolo). The wines made from these new clones are in a different league altogether to the earlier-clone wines. The best examples, particularly from moderate to warm regions such as Heathcote, are really quite exciting: they do have the depth, the complexity and satisfaction this great Italian grape is capable of.

Tempranillo 400 hectares

Tempranillo's rise to alternative stardom has been extraordinary. A decade ago, you could count the number of Australian wines made from this great Spanish grape on one hand. Now, there are at least 250 producers. Like sangiovese, most of the tempranillo vines planted so far have been a pretty ordinary clone, bred at UC Davis in California, yet it appears to be better suited to a broader range of Australian climates and soils than the Italian grape.

Despite its propensity to lose acid towards the end of the growing season (meaning the winemaker has to add more acid than he or she might ideally like), tempranillo often produces convincingly varietal wine: good, juicy red and black cherry fruit, firm but unobtrusive tannins. I have been a big supporter of this grape for years, and I'm very glad to see it not only performing well, but also being embraced by winemakers across the country. I'm even happier whenever I taste really good new examples from central Victoria, from McLaren Vale, from Western Australia, from Queensland. And I can barely contain my excitement when I think that, like sangiovese, the best is yet to come, as the existing vines mature, as winemakers gain more experience, and as new, better clones are planted.

Barbera 150 hectares

At the turn of the century I wrote a book about Australian wine called *Crush*. In it I said that while sangiovese was the grape currently leading the Italian charge in Australia, and nebbiolo was the grape many would like to *see* leading the Italian charge, barbera was the grape that will eventually *end up* leading the Italian charge. Now, having tasted quite a few dozen more examples of Australian barbera I haven't changed my mind in the slightest. I still think that, of the three, barbera can produce wines with the best balance of fleshy purple fruit, juiciness and just enough tannin to let you know you're drinking something serious. It's the wine that full-bodied pinots and elegant shirazes would like to be. I wouldn't be surprised to see the vineyard area at least double in the next few years.

Nebbiolo 100 hectares

It always amazes me when I come across yet another Australian winemaker who has just planted, or is planning to plant nebbiolo vines. Why on earth would you want to do that? I wonder. Nebbiolo is like pinot noir for masochists. It's a bugger to grow, it's a bugger to make, and the wine it produces looks like rusty water, smells like bitumen and tastes like chewing on an old leather satchel. In fact, the better (or rather, more varietally *correct*) nebbiolo is, the drier, more uncompromisingly savoury and more difficult to appreciate it's likely to be. And the more difficult to sell, surely. But what do I know? Just look: over 90 growers, with 100 hectares of nebbiolo, all over the country. That's a lot of masochists. Then again, when you taste a *really* good one – and there are some utterly stunning examples, particularly from Pizzini in the King Valley, and Arrivo and SC Pannell in the Adelaide Hills, all produced by complete nebbiolo nutters – you can understand how people can become so obsessed with this amazing grape.

Minor alternative reds
Less than 50 hectares planted (so far)

Aglianico

I'm very excited by the potential of this southern Italian red grape in Australia. In its hot, dry homeland, it produces red wines of such robust depth and renowned longevity that they are described as the Barolos of the south. But while nebbiolo (the Barolo grape) is fairly picky about which cool slope it will settle on, aglianico is less fussy, and is happy in warmer country. Early Australian examples are encouragingly earthy, tannic and robust.

Carmenere

This grape, originally from Bordeaux, found fame as a varietal wine in Chile, where it produces red wines with pronounced, almost Ribena-like, blackcurrant fruit. It would appear to do the same thing in Australia, if the couple of young examples I've tasted from Olssens in the Clare Valley and Brown Brothers in the King Valley are anything to go by. It also has great potential as a blender, perhaps to flesh out skinny young vine merlot.

Corvina and rondinella

Two of the grapes responsible for Italy's Valpolicella and Amarone red wines. Although they're found in just a couple of vineyards in southern New South Wales, early examples – made using the traditional *apassimento* method of partially drying the grapes before fermentation – are satisfyingly savoury and should inspire others to experiment.

Graciano

Graciano is to tempranillo in Rioja what petit verdot is to cabernet in Bordeaux: it brings good acidity and colour and structure as a minor component of a blend. It has been planted in a few Australian vineyards, and successfully blended with tempranillo, as well as appearing as a bold, vibrant straight varietal wine. It'll be interesting to see how winemakers harness that boldness in other blends.

Lagrein

This intriguing red grape, originally from the Alto Adige region of Italy's north-east, has been planted in Australian regions as diverse as the cold Macedon Ranges and warm Langhorne Creek. In the cooler spots, it makes deep purple wine with mulberry, box hedge and tobacco characters; in warmer vineyards, it makes deep purple wine with riper, more glossy fruit, but still with an underlying herbal note and good acidity. It has been successfully blended with other grapes such as dolcetto and shiraz.

Lambrusco maestri

In its homeland of Emilia, this is one of many similarly named varieties responsible for the famous red, sweet fizzy wines of Lambrusco. It has found an unexpected home, it would seem, in Australia's hot, inland regions: experimental plantings (grown by Chalmers, made by Trentham Estate) have produced a deeply coloured (dry, still) red wine with good natural acidity and plenty of robust fruit flavour.

Marzemino

A northern Italian grape now grown in a few vineyards in Victoria's King Valley. Its rather dull, earthy flavours have never impressed me all that much, and I wonder why people persist when they could be making much more interesting red wines from other, more characterful varieties such as barbera or lagrein.

Montepulciano

This southern Italian red grape is a recent arrival in Australian vineyards, but has already made itself at home in both the hot Riverland, warm Barossa and cool Adelaide Hills, producing bold, dark, solid red wine.

Negroamaro

Like aglianico, nero d'Avola and the other southern Italian varieties, this has huge potential in Australia's warmer climates. Initial vintages made from grapes grown in the hot climate of the Murray Valley have produced wine with a very distinctive, unusual aroma: spicy, but not peppery, more exotic and woody, like fenugreek – and lovely, rustic, grippy tannins.

Nero d'Avola

This Sicilian grape has possibly the broadest appeal of all the warm-climate Italian reds. It, too, has plenty of furry tannin, but it also produces wines with a shiraz-like volume of ripe black fruit in the middle of the tongue. Could prove to be very useful indeed in the hot inland regions in generic red-blended wines.

Sagrantino

Originally from central Italy, early signs are that this could out-sangiovese sangiovese in Australia: it has responded to the warm conditions of its new home by producing wines with great dark cherry fruit and firm but fine tannins.

Saperavi

An unusual grape: as well as having thick, dark skin, it also has deep pink flesh (most red grapes have pale-coloured flesh). The result is dense, black-purple wine with heaps of brambly fruit flavour, high acid and plenty of tannin. In its homeland, Georgia, it makes huge wines that often need to be cellared for many years before they soften. In Australia, saperavi wines also tend to be on the big side, but are approachable younger.

Schioppettino

I have really enjoyed the few examples of Australian schioppettino I've tried, but I'm not sure this Friulian grape will be to everyone's taste. It's a little like a very light cabernet franc, with pale, juicy brightness, but also has pronounced, sappy, spicy herbal notes, like a cool-climate pinot noir. Great for simple, refreshing summer drinking.

Tannat

Described by one Australian grower as tasting like 'dark matter lurking in a pot', tannat makes ferociously black, tannic wines. In a country already so well endowed with grapes capable of producing dense, dry wines (think durif, mataro, shiraz even), do we need a grape renowned for its depth of colour and its dense, chewy tannin? I say yes, based on the brilliant examples of tannat I've tasted from places such as the Granite Belt and the King Valley.

Alternative sweet grapes: Dessert wines and fortifieds
Less than 100 hectares planted

Brachetto

Another Italian grape that could ride the crest of the moscato wave in Australia, brachetto produces wonderfully soft, sherbetty pink wine, with a lovely taste of wild strawberries.

Furmint and harslevelu

These are the two white grapes responsible for Hungary's great, golden Tokaji dessert wines. If the minor trend for adventurous sweet whites continues, perhaps we will soon find them planted in more than a couple of vineyards.

Moscato giallo

A clone used in Piedmont for the production of top-quality moscato. I've tasted a couple of sweet Australian examples, and they have the green apple and candle wax flavours found in the 'real thing'; unlike the floral, muscatty aromas of 'moscato' made from gordo. This fragrant grape has also been used to great effect as a minor component of Friulian-style white blends (along with chardonnay, pinot grigio and gewurztraminer) on the Mornington Peninsula. Expect to see more planted here.

Picolit

In its homeland of Friuli in northern Italy, this white grape is often dried on racks and turned into intense, vin santo–like sweet wine. It meets a similar, delicious fate in the few vineyards it's grown in here, too.

Souzao, tinta amarela, tinta barocca, tinto cao, tinta molle, tinta francesca

All these deeply coloured Portuguese varieties are now found in a few Australian vineyards, sometimes used in spicy, bold red wines, but more often blended with touriga and perhaps bastardo in 'port'. If the winemakers are feeling really fancy, they might also call their tempranillo by its Portuguese name of tinta roriz, and throw that into the vat, too.

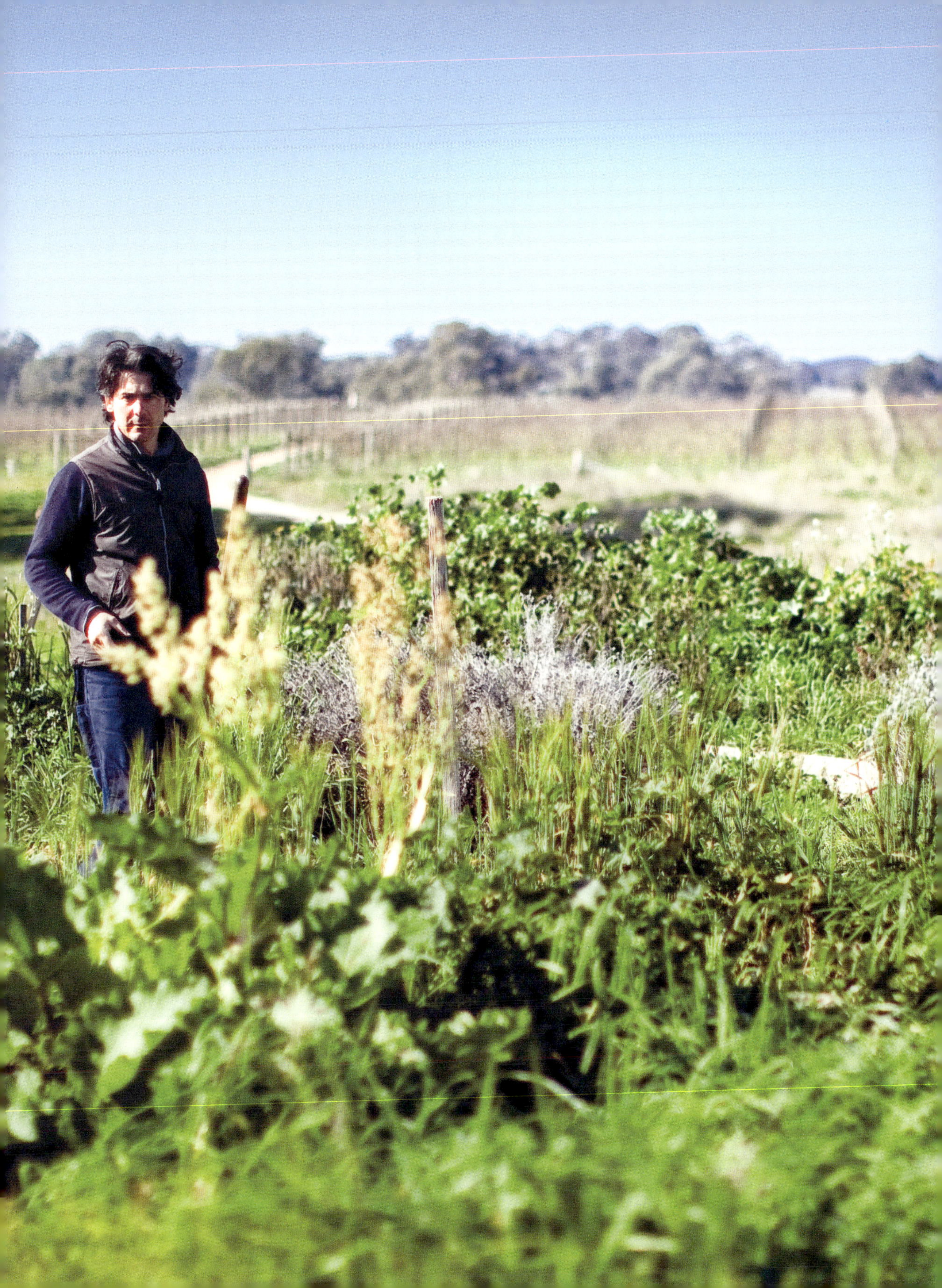

Part 2 Vineyards, winemakers, wines

Vineyards near Whirlpool Corner, River Murray, South Australia

6 Heart and soul
The Riverland, the Riverina, Murray Darling and Swan Hill

Big river regions

I had been writing about Australian wine for almost 15 years before I made my first road trip along the Murray River, through what is in many ways the heart of the country's wine industry. I'd visited vineyards and wineries around Mildura in north-east Victoria and in the Riverland in South Australia before, but these had been brief, fly-in, fly-out affairs. This time, I wanted to see the proper scale of the vineyards, feel the path of the river, bringing water and life to the communities along its banks. And the best way to do that was by car.

So, in the blistering heat of late summer 2007 I travelled from Echuca up to Mildura. The growing season that year was one of the worst – the hottest, the driest – anybody could remember in this part of Australia. To make matters worse, the fierce drought had forced up the price of river water, reducing irrigation allocations to a fraction of normal.

But despite the heat, despite the drought, travelling through Swan Hill, Robinvale and Red Cliffs, I passed endless row after endless row of lush vines: thousands upon thousands of hectares of vineyards, thick bushy stripes of green, marching off across the red sand. Most of these vineyards still appeared to be in remarkably good health, too, because most had been kept alive by the water from the river.

Most. But not all. When I saw the first dead vineyard it came as quite a shock. It was a small paddock, maybe 2 or 3 hectares, with all the strainer posts and wires in place. But instead of the vibrant green canopy that covered the vines on neighbouring properties, the vines on this block were bare-naked, wintery, ashen. The vineyard owner had clearly made the decision to sell his water entitlement, when the prices began to creep up, rather than use the water to irrigate his vines. And because vines can only grow here if they're irrigated, this vineyard had died. It was a stark, mournful sight.

I have flown over and driven through the Murray Valley and Riverina and Riverland regions many times since then. And every time I do, I see more and more dead, dying and abandoned vineyards.

History will record that during the second half of the first decade of this new millennium, the Australian wine industry's prosperous past collided with a nightmare vision of its future – or was slapped by a good, firm dose of reality, depending on your point of view.

For decades, most of the wine produced in Australia has started life as water flowing down the Murray, Darling and Murrumbidgee rivers, because the big inland, irrigated regions located around these rivers have dominated the country's wine industry.

In the middle of the 20th century, vineyard owners in the Riverina, Murray Valley, Swan Hill and Riverland sucked water from the river to grow grapes for 'sherry', 'port' and brandy – the most popular drinks in the country at the time. Then, when the table wine boom took off in Australia in the 1960s and 1970s, and particularly when exports boomed in the 1990s, these river-irrigated vineyard regions sucked up even more water to churn out chardonnay, shiraz, cabernet and, more recently, sauvignon blanc and merlot. Most of it destined for vast quantities of low-value supermarket wine, with cute Australian marsupials and the words 'south-eastern Australia' on the label. And I do mean *vast* quantities: the four big inland regions between them produce over 60 per cent of the country's wine. No wonder they're often collectively, if unglamorously, described as the wine industry's 'engine room'.

As the industry has grown, however, the rivers have been woefully mismanaged. Bickering between state and federal governments over responsibilities and allocations and entitlements; a painfully slow adoption of efficient irrigation practices; rising salinity levels down towards the mouth of the Murray – all these factors and more have resulted in a river system incapable of supporting the 'traditional' level of exploitation. If the big inland wine regions are the engine room, then the rivers provide the fuel. And the fuel's running out.

When the grape glut started to pile up in 2004, it compounded the problems by dramatically forcing prices down: growers couldn't cover their costs, let alone pay for more efficient irrigation systems. Then climate change hit the front page of the newspapers and experts started talking about how global warming will make it simply too hot to grow wine grapes at all in the Riverina, Murray Valley, Swan Hill and the Riverland in 50 years' time. By the time the drought-afflicted 2007 vintage came around, bringing with it stark signs of calamity such as dead and dying vineyards, it seemed like the apocalypse was already upon us.

❖

Things can't go on like this. Whether the extreme heat spikes and ongoing drought constitute a natural cycle, or whether they are a result of climate change, as most people believe, the old ways of growing grapes are clearly unsustainable in Australia's big irrigated inland regions. Even if the market did exist to soak up all the wine.

However, I believe it is possible for a viable – if much reduced – wine industry to continue in these places, and that this wine industry will be able to adapt to climate change (at least in the medium-term). But there will need to be some radical changes.

Quite a few people realised this years ago and started modifying their practices, long before the severity of 2007 and the return to oversupply in 2008 and 2009 forced everybody else to pull their heads out of the bright red sand. Growers and winemakers have been turning the irrigation taps down; chasing lower yields of higher quality grapes; adopting organic methods in the vineyard; planting heat-loving grape varieties and increasing water efficiency in the winery.

The severity of the situation has hastened the adoption of similar thinking among more growers and makers. In fact, I believe that the big irrigated regions could even lead the world in truly sustainable, large-scale organic and even biodynamic viticulture. There are signs that this is beginning to happen right now.

'The Riverland's perfect for organics,' says Brett Munchenberg, who has been growing grapes organically since 1995. 'I don't know why half the growers round here don't go that way. The big winemakers have been screwing them for so many years, why don't they go for lower yields, higher quality, and sell the wines themselves? There's a market for organics now, definitely. If the Riverland got smart, it could punch out a few thousand tonnes of organic grapes no problem, and it would do really well. Chile and Argentina are all over this already, they're potentially way ahead of us. We, the growers, have got to take things into our own hands. We've got to stop the big wineries in this engine room treating us like the coal pile.'

Let's hope they can. Or we may well turn around one day and discover that Australia's irrigated inland regions have disappeared.

And that would be a tragedy. It is easy to be critical of these regions; easy to say, 'Well, grapes shouldn't have been grown there in the first place – the environment simply can't support that kind of industry'; easy to write off the large-scale vineyards; easy to blame the big companies for their lack of foresight.

But there is also, I believe, something remarkable, something precious about the vineyard regions along these big rivers and the extraordinary, multicultural communities that have grown up around them. The landscape is so bold, so big, so uniquely Australian and so far removed from the cool, damp traditions of Europe. If these big inland river regions don't survive, even in a radically reduced form, Australian wine as a whole will have truly lost some of its heart and soul.

Chalmers Wines,
Murray Darling, New South Wales

The 650 hectare (and still expanding) vineyard the Chalmers family planted near Euston on the New South Wales side of the Murray River is one of the most impressive and important viticultural developments in Australia. Impressive because it was established in an incredibly short space of time and in a (relatively) environmentally sensitive way. And important because it proves that large-scale commercial wine production can be sustainable in the big inland irrigated regions.

Bruce and Jenni Chalmers first established a vine nursery here in 1989, and started planting the vineyard in earnest a few years later. The vineyard grew slowly at first, and then incredibly rapidly, when, over ten weeks in late 2005, the Chalmers planted a massive 400 hectares of new vines, mostly pinot grigio to sell to John Casella, to meet demand for Yellow Tail.

To ensure the long-term viability of this vineyard, the Chalmers invested in a cutting-edge pumping station, a state-of-the-art drip irrigation system and sophisticated soil moisture monitoring technology. The pumping station is twice the size it needs to be, so it only needs to run half the time, and only at night. Certified organic composted cow manure is spread undervine across the entire vineyard, both before planting and then every year. Synthetic chemical applications are kept to a bare minimum, often to just two herbicide sprays a year.

According to Bruce Chalmers this combination of smart irrigation technology and increased soil carbon content allows the vineyard to produce 'normal' yields (by regional standards) – even up to 25 tonnes of grapes per hectare – using half the 'normal' amount of water. The regional average for irrigated vineyards in the Murray Darling is between 6 and 8 megalitres of water per hectare. 'In the really hot summer of 2007,' says Bruce, 'we used about three megs. And although everyone else's crops were down by between 30 and 40 per cent, we were only down about 8 per cent.'

What impresses me most, though, about the Chalmers vineyard is not the scale of the place, the emphasis on building soil carbon or the massive reduction in water use – as important as they are. It's the family's commitment to alternative grape varieties and conservation that set this place apart.

When they were building the vine nursery business in the 1990s, the Chalmers started concentrating on Italian grape varieties, importing cuttings of the best new clones from one of Italy's top nurseries. This became a passion, and led to the establishment of the Australian Alternative Varieties Wine Show in Mildura, and to the planting of over 80 new varieties in the Chalmers' own vineyard. While these new and unusual grapes make up less than 10 per cent of the total vineyard area, they are all planted in enough quantity to be made into small batches of wine. Some of this fruit goes to other winemakers to play with, but an increasing amount is made by Sandro Mosele at Kooyong winery on the Mornington Peninsula, and released under the Chalmers Wines label. The whites in this range have been particularly brilliant, I think: the savoury, chalky dryness of the vermentino and the heady, perfumed appeal of the fiano demonstrating how well suited these grapes are to this hot, dry climate.

As part of the vineyard expansion a few years ago, the Chalmers also acquired 1500 hectares of bushland along the Murray River and declared it as a private nature reserve: much of it is old-growth red gum country, breeding ground of the endangered Regent parrot.

Walking through this ancient forest is an unforgettable experience. Some of the big old trees are thought to be well over 500 years old. There are signs of Aboriginal life – canoe trees, burial sites, old campgrounds, middens – that date back at least as far, and probably much, much further. This bend in the river is not that far from Lake Mungo, where archaeologists have unearthed startling evidence of human habitation; including perfectly preserved footprints in an old mudflat, thought to be more than 40,000 years old.

In early 2008, the Chalmers family announced that they had sold this incredible property to the huge Australian financial institution, Macquarie Group. While it seems a shame to see such a visionary development end up in the hands of a faceless corporate giant, there are many encouraging aspects of the deal. Macquarie have agreed to maintain the conservation plan for the bush reserve; and the Chalmers will continue to grow the alternative varieties for their own label on the property. Most importantly, Bruce Chalmers has been contracted as a consultant to the new owners, and will continue to pursue his sustainable viticulture approach, not only at this large property at Euston where Macquarie have established a further 200 hectares of vines, much of it alternative varieties such as moscato giallo and montepulciano, but also at the other vineyards Macquarie will no doubt purchase in the future.

The Chalmers family have also bought land and are planting a vineyard at Heathcote, near the new Greenstone vineyard. They have continued their commitment to Italian varieties by planting negroamaro, lagrein, sangiovese, nero d'avola, aglianico and sagrantino. When the vines mature and the wines appear, they will no doubt re-draw the viticultural map of Heathcote just as dramatically as their extraordinary vineyard at Euston has re-drawn the map of the Big River regions.

919 Wines, Riverland, South Australia

'If you plant the right grape varieties, heat isn't a problem,' says Eric Semmler, standing in the red sandy soil of his vineyard in the middle of a Riverland summer. 'When I travelled to the Douro valley in Portugal in 2001, it was incredibly hot. But I tasted ripe touriga grapes on the vine, and they had such great balance, and the flavours stayed on the palate for 30 minutes. So when I found some touriga rootlings at the Riverland Vine Improvement Committee's vineyard, I thought: I'll have them.'

Before setting up his own small vineyard just outside the town of Berri, Semmler was fortified winemaker for Hardys for ten years, so as well as touriga, he's also planted tinta cao, tinta roriz for 'port'; shiraz and durif for dry red; palomino for an excellent, fine dry 'sherry'; and muscat and muscadelle for sweet fortifieds in his small vineyard.

He uses a fraction of the water most growers put on their vines here – around 2 megalitres per hectare – and only picks about 5 tonnes of grapes per hectare, ridiculously low yields by Riverland standards. When Eric and his wife Jenny were planting their vines and told their neighbour (a big company grape grower) about their plans to use less water and hard prune for low yields, he told them they were mad. 'The vines'll die,' he said. 'You won't get any fruit.'

But the Semmlers are chasing quality, not quantity, and the varieties they've chosen are extremely well suited to dry conditions. The durif, for example, obviously loves it here, producing a bold, vibrant, chocolatey red wine as well as a deeply luscious tawny-style 'port'.

Taking inspiration from Rutherglen, Eric also exploits the region's heat, storing barrels of his fortifieds in a small tin shed – a treasure house – where the strong wines develop amazing, mature flavours. They really are quite delicious, these fortifieds: the 919 Wines 2006 vintage 'port' is particularly spicy, perfumed, bold but fine. Good now, but even better with cellaring.

'I hope people keep rediscovering fortifieds,' says Eric. 'They are so full of complexity, we can make them so well, and they're a really important part of our wine heritage. We need to guard and maintain that.'

Angove Family Winemakers, Riverland, South Australia

Angove is a large, family-owned wine business going through a steady process of reinvention and renewal. Angove winemakers source nearly half the grapes they need for their own wines from just one, massive, 500-hectare vineyard called Nanya, near Renmark. The vineyard, first planted by Tom Angove in the late 1960s, is a fabulous illustration of how the Riverland has changed in the last four decades.

A few hectares of the original plantings have survived from the 1960s and reflect the prevailing tastes of the time: palomino for 'sherry', carignan for bulk red, and white grenache for god knows what (these days, Angove make it into a spicy, textural white sold exclusively through the *Sunday Times* Wine Club in the UK). But the majority of the vineyard reflects more modern tastes: chardonnay, cabernet, shiraz and, more recently, sauvignon blanc and petit verdot.

Since 2001, the old overhead sprinkler system has been slowly replaced by a drip-irrigation system, which has slashed water use from up to 10 megalitres per hectare to less than 5. And according to winemaker Tony Ingle, the forced reduction in irrigation has led to an unexpected leap in grape quality.

'Because they're not exactly popular, the carignan and palomino went right down our list of irrigation priorities, and got virtually no water in 2007 and 2008,' says Ingle as we drive over the red sand down one of Nanya's 5 kilometre–long vine rows. 'But the carignan, which normally gives huge crops of ordinary grapes, produced some lovely low yields and very good wine.' He stops the car and points out some old but healthy-looking vines. 'And we thought we'd kill the palomino if we took the water away, but look: it's fine, and it's given us a great crop. Just shows you can make do with a lot less water here, especially on these older varieties.'

In early 2008, Angove converted a discrete 40-hectare block of Nanya, closest to the river, to organic viticultural practices with a view to expanding organics to a much larger portion of the whole vineyard. And a saltbush cover-crop was established between the rows to help combat rising salinity levels. Later that year, they purchased a 10-hectare vineyard in McLaren Vale and are now running that biodynamically. 'In the long run,' says Tony Ingle, 'I believe organically managed vines, grown without chemical support, will have a better ability to withstand pressures of climate and drought.'

Angove have launched an organic range using grapes bought from local growers, people such as Sue and Bruce Armstrong. The Armstrong's 11-hectare vineyard near Waikerie has been NASAA-certified organic since 1999, and is part of a mixed farm that also includes goats, vegies and fruit. As far as the Armstrongs are concerned, farming organically in the Riverland makes sense from both an environmental and an economic point of view.

'I'm not a closet hippy,' says Bruce. 'We saw an opening for organics in the market in the late 1990s. If the industry started to go down, we thought, we might have an option.'

'Also, I just didn't want to be handling chemicals,' says Sue. 'You really don't need to here. We haven't even sprayed with copper or sulphur [both allowable under organic certification rules] for the last four years. Unfortunately, there are still guys up here who just stick to the spray calendar, because the chemical companies tell them to.'

'My dad says that his generation of growers never used to spray as many chemicals as they do today,' adds Bruce. 'The plant's a living thing, like a human being. Once you keep spraying it, it's like a person who keeps taking pills. They become reliant on the drug, and their natural resistance weakens.'

Back Verandah, Riverland, South Australia

You won't find Back Verandah Wines at your local bottle shop. There's no web site, no email address, no contact phone number. Owner Andrew Duncan, a dentist by profession, does have a producer's licence, and he makes a few barrels each year from his small vineyard just outside the Riverland town of Berri. He even had some labels printed, once, a few years ago. 'But you know what?' says Andrew. 'I just can't be bothered with the hassle of selling the stuff. My joy is in the vineyard, in creating the wine. It's more fun than golf!'

So why am I telling you about Andrew Duncan's vineyard – more a crazy hobby than a business? Because it is so deliciously the opposite of what you might expect to find in the Riverland, dominated as it is by vast, mechanised vineyards and huge, refinery-like wineries. Back Verandah is run along biodynamic permaculture lines, and it looks and feels more like a secluded Tuscan farmhouse than an Australian vineyard.

Dusk was beginning to fall when I first visited Andrew's place in late summer, and the thick violet twilight lent an other-worldly air to the scene. I opened a small gate off the vegie patch and walked into the most remarkable sight: short rows of vines trained between large paulownia trees, their floppy leaves providing shade during the height of summer, frost cover during spring and autumn, and a good source of carbon for the soil when they fall and rot. Apples, oranges, figs – natives, too. A host of other trees, many with vines growing up into their canopies, create a diverse range of mini-environments.

Andrew has planted the usual Riverland grapes between the trees: shiraz, chardonnay, cabernet; as well as some unusual varieties, viognier, tannat and baroque, a large-berried white grape originally from hot south-west France. And there doesn't appear to be any sense of order to this vineyard: 'When the agricultural census people ask me how many vines I've got, I like to say, oh, 20 of this, 30 of that, a few metres of this, enough to make a barrel of that. It really stuffs them up,' chuckles the winemaker.

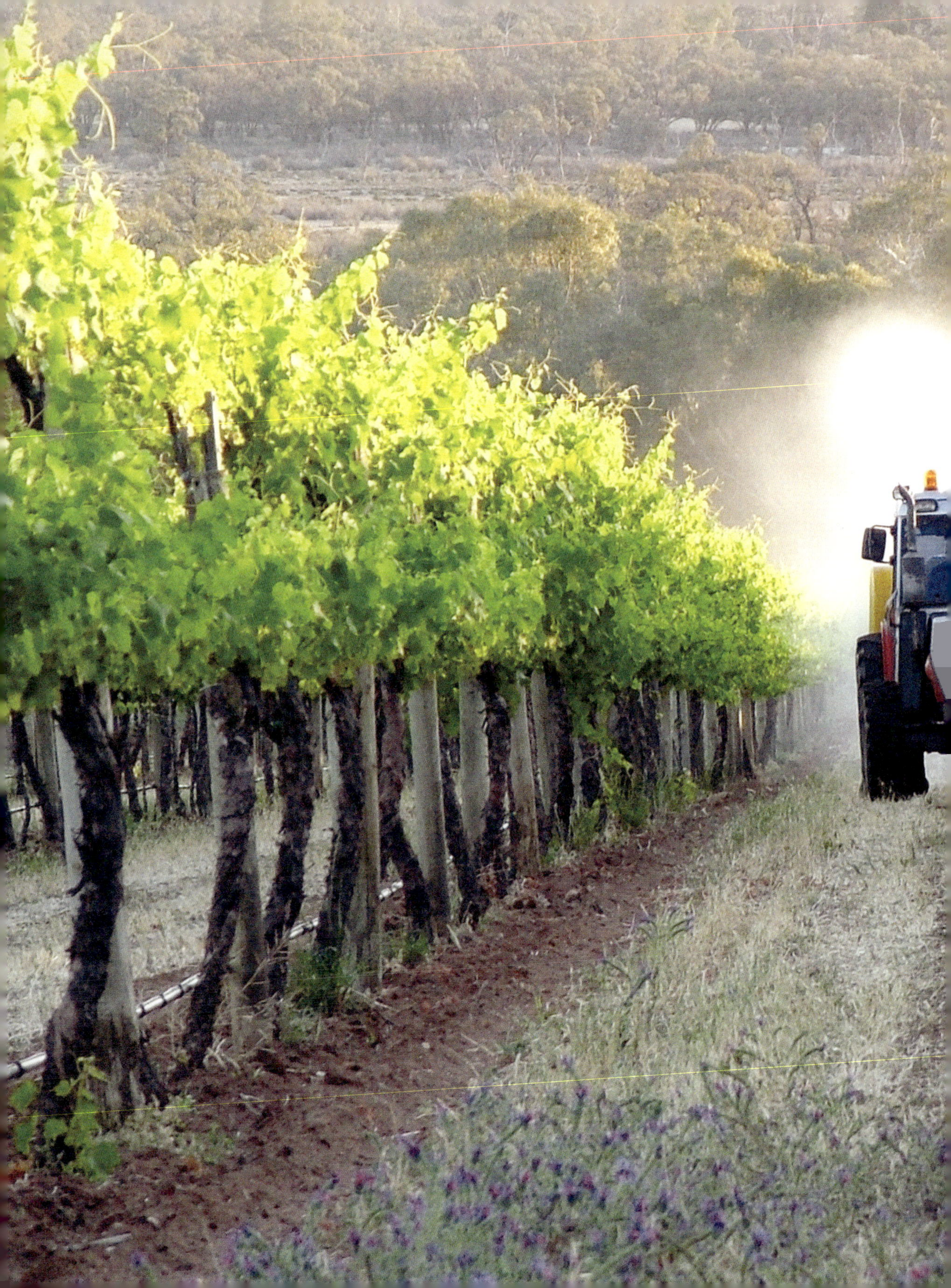

Spraying biodynamic preparation 501 at dawn, Barich Vineyard, Riverland

He started spraying biodynamic compost preps on his vineyard in 2006. 'Even though I have an orthodox science background, I've always run the vineyard organically, so I thought I'd give BD a whirl,' he says. 'It was like flicking a switch. The colour of weeds and the vines changed immediately. I've always struggled to get enough nitrogen into the system using organics, but since using the BD, I've had no problems. My wild ferments go through more easily, too. I'm very happy with the results.'

So am I: one of those wild-fermented wines, a viognier, tasted from barrel in Andrew's shed/winery was brilliant – all furry apricots and satisfying creamy texture and lingering finish. A shiraz viognier was incredibly vibrant, full of life and juicy. And a petit manseng (made using grapes from the biodynamic Barich vineyard we visited in the Introduction) was fantastically rich, golden and true to type.

Yes, it is a shame that you and I can't buy these wines in our local bottle shop. It's a shame that Andrew Duncan hasn't even bottled them. But it's great to know that such wines, such vineyards, such quiet renegades exist. There are even signs that others in the region are beginning to pay attention to what Andrew has achieved: Pennyfield vineyard near Berri is in the process of adopting permaculture techniques, as well as planting grape varieties specifically for fortified wine production.

De Bortoli, Riverina, New South Wales

De Bortoli has been one of the Riverina's leading wineries for a long time. It was the pioneer – and is still, in my opinion, the best – producer of botrytis semillon in the region: the Noble One gets better and better with each vintage, is less cloying, more intense, shows better integration of oak. The Deen de Bortoli range of vat-numbered wines is consistently good value and high quality (I particularly like the rugged durif and slinky petit verdot reds), and De Bortoli's fortified wines challenge all but the best from Rutherglen.

But until Rob Glastonbury started work as operations manager – and, by default, environmental officer – at De Bortoli in 2004, the company had been, it's fair to say, neglectful of its environmental responsibility. Rob has turned the place into a paragon of green virtue and a showcase for the environmental initiatives being adopted across the Riverina.

Prior to Rob's arrival, for example, the winery waste water would end up in huge holding dams. 'It was irresponsible to leave water hanging around like that,' he says. 'And besides, it smelled bloody awful.' So now, the water is pH-adjusted, aerated and used to irrigate the cereal crops on the 65-hectare farm De Bortoli bought just up the road.

As well as turning waste water into profit, the new treatment system has also resulted in massive energy savings. 'Before we set up the farm, the old waste-water system used 400 kW of power a year. Now we use 4 kW.'

Glastonbury also went to the local Catchment Management Authority for advice on what he should be planting around the farm to help control salinity and a rising water table, and as a result the place has been seeded with native grasses and plants such as saltbush. And he is also conducting trials on the farm with heavy mulching and seed drilling 'to increase carbon content, encourage worms and bacteria and make micro-nutrients available', with a view to expanding the techniques to the vineyards.

'It's not about being into hair-shirt organics,' he says. 'It's about stewardship.'

Glastonbury is also acutely aware of the commercial benefits of adopting this new, greener image. 'If Tesco supermarket in the UK ring up and ask about our environmental credentials,' he says, 'we can turn around and say: Look, here you go.'

Organic One, Riverina, New South Wales

The Bonic family were ploughing the green furrow at their vineyard just outside Jerilderie, in the far south of the Riverina district, long before natural grape-growing became trendy.

The vineyard was established on the banks of Billabong Creek by Croatian migrants, Jure and Eva Bonic, in the late 1970s, and has been managed without synthetic chemicals from the beginning. The Bonic's sons, Frank and John, expanded the vineyard to its present-day 110 hectares, and since 1998 the family have been farming the property using biodynamic principles. As well as applying the biodynamic preps, which includes making and spreading 1000 tonnes of biodynamic compost each year, the Bonics run sheep through the vineyard to help control undervine growth, and have established a wildlife sanctuary around a lake on the property.

Yields are kept very low by regional standards, around 5 tonnes of grapes per hectare, but this is enough to produce a fairly sizeable 30,000 cases of certified organic wine a year. Frank Bonic makes the wine on-site and although much of it ends up under other people's labels – Tesco organic chardonnay in the UK, for example, and 1-litre Tetra Paks of Green Path organic chardonnay in the US – a couple of wines are also sold under the Bonic family's own Organic One label: a very soft, candied-fruity chardonnay and a floral, oaky, medium-bodied shiraz.

As far as I'm aware, Organic One is the largest certified biodynamic vineyard in Australia, and one of the largest in the world. And yet very few people know about the place. What's more, of all the Australian grape growers and winemakers I've met who have embraced biodynamics, Frank Bonic seems to have the most instinctive spiritual connection with the ideas and philosophies Rudolf Steiner talked about in his 1924 agriculture lectures, which became the foundation of the biodynamic movement. Bonic talks freely about the spiritual calmness of the old gum trees that fringe the lake; about the power of intent and of positive thinking; about working with the etheric forces of the cosmos.

Beyond the sticky
A new wave of sweet wines

I'm standing in a cellar door in the Riverina having a chat with the winemaker about his latest vintages when in walks a young bloke in a singlet and sunnies and his blonde girlfriend. He's obviously pretty keen on his wines, this bloke, and wants to taste all the various styles on offer, especially the rich, sticky botrytis-affected semillon that the Riverina has become so famous for. She, on the other hand, is no wine buff: when the winemaker behind the tasting bench asks her if she'd like to try the botrytis semillon, a regional speciality, she replies: 'Oh, no, thank you. I only drink moscato.'

I only drink moscato

What a fabulous line. And what a transformation. In less than ten years, the moscato style, with its low alcohol and gently fizzy, grapey flavours, has gone from relative obscurity, made by one or two innovative producers (notably Brown Brothers), to a mainstream fixture in bottle shops and cellar door fridges around the country. Every Australian winery, it seems, now has a moscato in its portfolio.

Some see the moscato craze as nothing more than déjà vu: a worrying renaissance of the sweet, fizzy wines such as Barossa Pearl that were so insanely popular in the 1960s. I see it as part of a broader and very welcome move to expand Australia's sweet wine repertoire beyond casks of bland 'fruity lexia' and half-bottles of deep golden botrytis semillon. The great thing is that, when it's good, a well-made moscato (particularly one of the increasing number of pink versions, such as the little beauty from Innocent Bystander in the Yarra Valley) is not only a crowd-pleaser but can also bring a smile to the tight lips of even the most curmudgeonly wine connoisseur.

Inspired by Germany

One of the most delicious trends to have emerged in recent years is the low-ish alcohol, slightly sweet, high-acid riesling style modelled on the scintillating rieslings of the Mosel and Rheingau regions of Germany. Again, say the critics, haven't we seen it all before? Sweet rieslings, often labelled spatlese, or even, erroneously, moselle, were all the rage in the 1960s and '70s. Aren't today's winemakers simply reinventing the wheel?

The answer is: not really. Thirty years ago spatlese rieslings were made from later-picked, riper grapes and while they were sweet, they also had higher alcohol. Today's styles are made from earlier picked grapes; they have higher acidity, lower alcohol, more balanced freshness.

The best examples, from producers such as Frogmore Creek, KT and the Falcon, Lethbridge and Mac Forbes, are stunning, complex, completely valid expressions of the riesling grape. Indeed, the success of Frogmore's wine – cheekily labelled FGR (officially it stands for 'forty grams residual' sugar; unofficially it means '*fucking* good riesling') – has led to the approved adoption of the 'FGR' designation by other Tasmanian wineries, including neighbouring Meadowbank Estate.

Dried grape wines

Given Australia's tendency to be bloody hot and sunny during summer, it's a surprise more people haven't cottoned on to the dried-grape methods of making sweet wine. There are exceptions – Stephanie Toole's fantastically intense Mount Horrocks Cordon Cut Clare Valley riesling, for example, which is made from grapes partially dried while still hanging on the vine, has a long track record – but few others have tried. That's changing: fabulous vin santo-like wines such as Charlie Melton's Sotto di Ferro from the Barossa (made from pedro and muscadelle grapes hung up to dry under the iron roof of the winery, hence the name), di Lusso's Apassimento in Mudgee (picolit and chardonnay grapes laid out on racks to dry), and Turkey Flat's Last Straw, also from the Barossa (made from sun-dried marsanne, a la Vin de Paille from the Rhone) are all exceptionally complex sweet wines that should inspire many other winemakers to explore this style.

Ice wines

Some obsessive-compulsive winemakers such as Stephen Doyle at Bloodwood in Orange have attempted – and occasionally managed – to produce proper ice wine, from grapes frozen on the vine, by letting the fruit hang as long as possible, even into July, hoping for frosts and snow. But very few wine regions in Australia enjoy the right climate to do this on a regular basis, so winemakers keen on the ice wine style tend to simply pick late-harvested grapes and bung 'em in a freezer before crushing them. Not quite as romantic, perhaps, but the results can be spectacular with the right grapes in the right hands – riesling at Frogmore Creek in Tasmania, for example, and viognier at Oakridge in the Yarra.

Liqueured up

Again, given Australia's rich history of adding alcohol, in the form of grape spirit, to fortify sweet wines such as muscat and 'port', it's slightly surprising that there hasn't been more experimentation with the 'vin doux naturel' style as found in southern France. But, again, this is slowly changing. A few winemakers, inspired by wines such as Muscat Beaumes de Venise, are adding clean grape spirit to fresh young muscat and bottling early, to capture the lift and cut and perfume. A good example of this style is Torbreck's The Bothie in the Barossa.

Which is perhaps the last thing you expect to hear when you talk to a producer of wines destined for supermarket shelves on the other side of the globe.

Tom's Drop, Riverland, South Australia

By any objective measure, the red wines from Michael O'Donohoe's 4-hectare vineyard just outside Berri are some of the most successful in the entire region. Adelaide wine writer Phillip White called the 2002 Tom's Drop mourvedre shiraz the best red he'd ever tasted from the Riverland, and O'Donohoe's wines – which sell for $30 a bottle, more than twice the regional average price – have been poured by the glass at Bilson's, one of Sydney's poshest restaurants.

Not bad for a certified organic vineyard whose owner talks about 'wild farming'; of growing his grapes as though they were bush tucker, like quandongs ('bugger-all water, 1 tonne to the acre yields'); and, unexpectedly, given his initially reticent, even prickly manner, of the power of meditation and the infinite love of the universe.

Mick is clearly proud of his achievements. As he throws a couple of huge steaks onto the barbecue – 'Mick's rough-as-guts cookin'' – I sit on the verandah of his old sandstone house overlooking the vineyard, drink some of his dark, earthy, warm-hearted red wine, and browse through his 'boasting book' full of press clippings, the Bilson's wine list and more accolades.

Mick stopped using synthetic chemicals on his orchards (oranges, apricots, pears, olives) in 1986. The vineyard's never been sprayed with anything but a little copper or sulphur. It certainly looks wild: the undervine area is positively shaggy, and wild olives, even the odd apricot tree, grow up here and there in the middle of the row. But this farmer's not concerned about his vines being robbed of water by competing plants: he'd much rather there was a good, self-mulching array of biodiversity, to keep the soil cool and to provide too comfortable a habitat for potential pests.

'Everything's living down there in the weeds rather than up in the vines,' he says. 'Snails couldn't find their way out. They'd get lost.'

Like many other growers in 2002, Mick was offered a pitiful price for his intensely coloured, low-yielding, powerfully flavoured grapes, so decided to make them into wine himself, in some hastily scrounged old gherkin barrels. The result was the mourvedre shiraz that made Phillip White swoon.

Mick O'Donohoe wants to take his wild farming ideas even further. He plans to plant some more mourvedre, as bush vines, and to see how little irrigation he can get away with. He also wants to plant Mallee trees – 'the best bloody carbon sinks on the planet' – around the edges of the vineyard.

'I'm trying to prove a point,' he says. 'By relying on nature, I'm trying to prove to the big industrial wineries around here that there is another way of doing things.'

Then he goes inside and returns with another book, a thick academic journal with the rather dry title of *Advances in Public Interest Accounting*. Mick finds the page he's looking for and hands the book to me: a long, dense article called 'Gandhian-Vedic Emancipatory Accounting: Engendering a Spiritual Revolution in the Interest of Sustainable Development'.

The author is Dr Kala Saravanamuthu from the University of Newcastle, and her thesis is deceptively simple: replace the Christian, Calvinist philosophy underpinning western capitalism (man has dominion over nature) with the ancient, eastern, holistic view of man as an integral part of nature, and then fuse that to social environmental accounting practice.

A few years ago, when Dr Saravanamuthu was working with a group of farmers in the Riverland on a sustainability project, she interviewed Mick O'Donohoe and found a living, breathing example of the Ghandian-Vedic philosophy of interconnectedness. Mick's chuffed that she's quoted him in her article. He told her, and he told me, that when he's walking in the bush down by the river, when he's working in the vineyard or the orchard, when he's standing over the fermenting vat, he will meditate, breathing in the infinite cosmos, and project that positive energy into the vines and the fermenting must.

Funny to think that beneath this Berri farmer's 'rough-as-guts' exterior might lurk a spiritual revolutionary.

Trentham Estate, Murray Darling, New South Wales

The Murphy family runs one of the region's most pleasant and popular cellar door restaurants on the New South Wales bank of the Murray at Trentham. The winery has a loyal clientele of locals and tourists, who've been coming here to eat and drink on the beautiful lawns overlooking the river for 20 years. It's also an unlikely crucible of alternative winemaking activity.

As well as the standard range of Murray Darling varietals and blends – robust shiraz cabernet, fruity chardonnay, disappointing merlot, etc. – Trentham's viticulturist and winemaker brothers, Patrick and Anthony Murphy, produce a burgeoning range of at times truly exciting wines from new and unusual grapes. They appear to have a particular affinity for Italian varieties, many of which are sold under the La Famiglia label: the moscato is very good, the vermentino properly dry and chalky, the pinot grigio fresh and crisp, and the sangiovese rosé has good savoury grip.

The most impressive of Trentham's forays into alternative varieties, though, comes in the unlikely form of a grape called maestri. In its homeland of Emilia Romagna in Italy, this is one of many clones responsible for the internationally renowned sweet, fizzy red wine, Lambrusco. In the Murray Darling region, the grape was first grown by Chalmers, who passed the initial crop on to the Murphy brothers. According to both grower and winemaker, maestri ripens perfectly, retaining great natural acidity despite the heat of the growing season and despite minimal irrigation. The result is a deep-purple wine with heaps of dark fruit flavour, good bold chocolatey structure and a juicy freshness.

The first release of this wine caused quite a stir: I awarded it the rather pompously named trophy for Chairman's Wine to Watch at the Alternative Varieties Wine Show in 2006, and many other growers have shown interest in planting it. Look out for more maestri appearing on bottle shop shelves soon.

Angove Family Winemakers, Riverland, South Australia

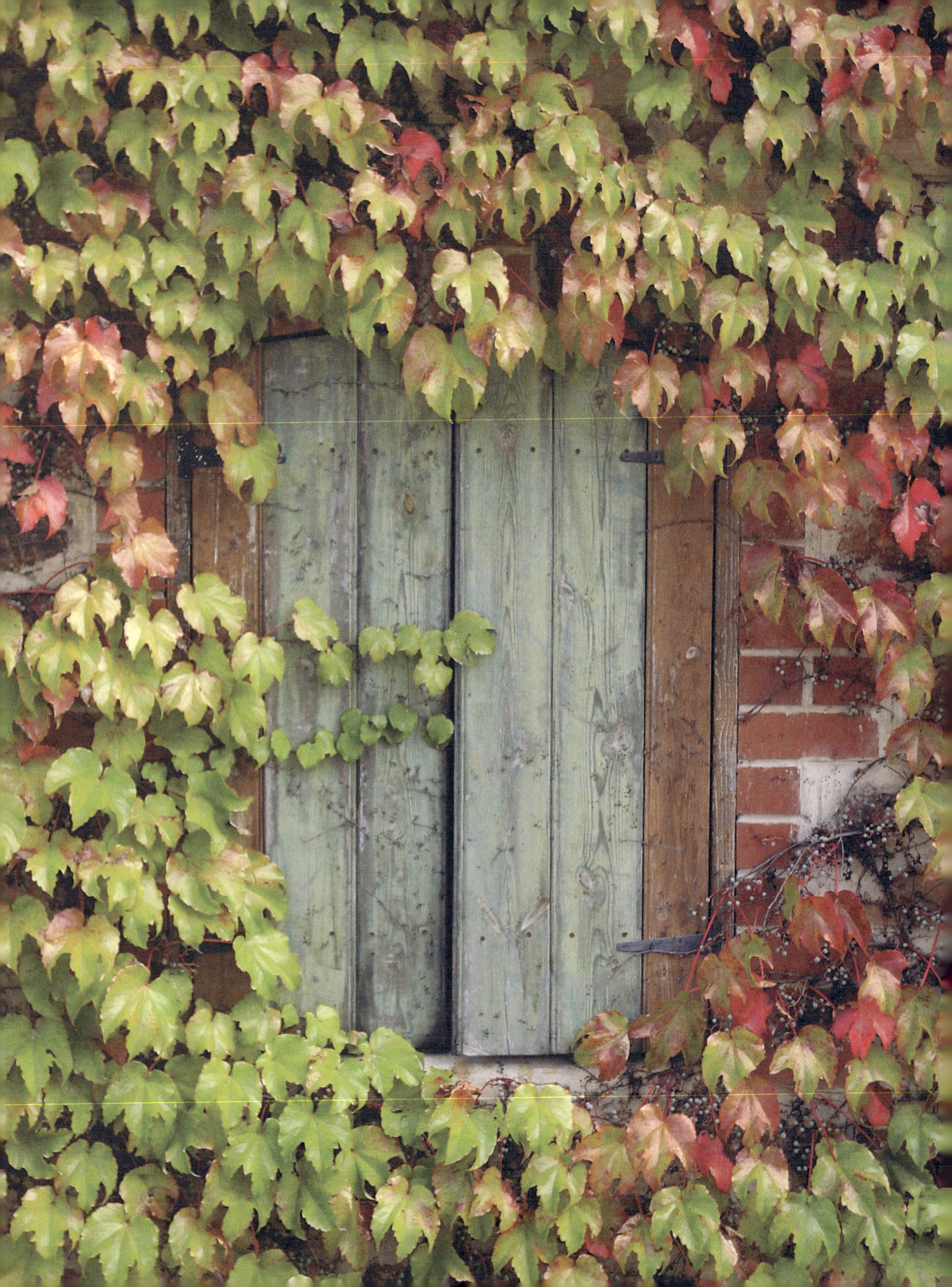

7 Victoria

Melbourne and surrounds

A vineyard is the last thing you expect to see when you're cycling along the Yarra River just a couple of kilometres from the centre of Melbourne. But there it is: 1 acre of neatly tended cabernet sauvignon vines planted in a little patch of old flood plain on a bend in the river in Kew, tall gum trees and the lazy ping of Studley Park bellbirds on one side, old Edwardian houses on the other.

It's an amazing little viticultural oasis, this place. And a piece of living history: it was a market garden for a century before Melbourne lawyer Geoff Pryor planted cabernet here in the mid-1990s, and some straggly old 19th-century grapevines remain, snaking their way wildly up equally ancient fig trees.

Drinking the Studley Park cabernet, with its pure blackcurrant fruit flavours and firm but elegant tannic grip, you imagine the wine that once flowed from Melbourne's early urban vineyards. In the middle- and late-19th century, the city boasted many wine labels, some as close as the perfect north-facing Punt Road hill, now covered in run-down apartment buildings and choked lanes of traffic.

Today, the vineyards are returning: Melbourne's sprawling metropolis is fringed with wineries, in the ranges south of the Yarra Valley, on the volcanic plains north of Tullamarine airport, and down at Werribee, half way from Melbourne to Geelong.

Sergio Carlei Carlei Wines and The Green Vineyards

I have an appointment to meet Sergio Carlei at his vineyard/winery/house at Beaconsfield in the hilly green southeastern outskirts of Melbourne. But when I arrive, I can't find him amid all the end-of-vintage chaos. I bump into Pascal Marchand drawing a sample of raw purple wine from a barrel. Pascal is the big, bearded biodynamic wine consultant from Burgundy who flies out to Australia to advise Carlei each year. I find Steve Kapolice, a local biodynamic farming consultant, mixing up a batch of preparation 500 in his mobile copper stirring machine to spray on the vineyard. But Serge is nowhere to be seen.

I'm not surprised. The man runs at a million miles a minute, his head full of plans, ideas, winemaking schemes, wild theories and experiments. He's meant to have calmed down in recent years, since dropping a number of his winemaking contract clients (Serge has a problem saying no to exciting new opportunities), but it doesn't look like it. The winery is still stuffed with barrels of wine from all over: sauvignon and cabernet from the Yarra, shiraz from Heathcote, pinot from here at Beaconsfield, chardonnay from the Mornington Peninsula.

But when I do find him, and we open some bottles and taste from the barrel, it's clear that things are changing here: Serge is focusing his energy on finessing his wines, and is exploring how biodynamics can improve the complexity and texture of those wines even further. You can taste the change in the chardonnays he's making for the biodynamically run Prancing Horse vineyard on the Mornington Peninsula (Prancing Horse's Tony Hancey, a Burgundy nut, is a part-owner of Carlei Wines). Recent vintages of this chardonnay have so much more clarity, precision and linear acidity than before. You can taste the finesse in the exquisite powdery acidity of the sauvignon blanc from Streamville vineyard in the Yarra, which Steve Kapolice has been managing biodynamically for years. And you can taste the exciting spirit of experimentation in a winemaking trial Serge and Pascal Marchand undertook in 2007, exploring the influence of the moon on picking times.

A lot of biodynamic farmers time

their activities according to lunar cycles, believing, for example, that when the moon is passing through a 'fire' constellation such as Leo, the fruity aspects of a plant are favoured, and when the moon is in an 'earth' constellation such as Virgo, the rooty aspects are enhanced.

Carlei and Marchand tested this theory by picking alternate rows from a shiraz vineyard in Heathcote at different times: the first half when it was a 'fruit day', and others 24 hours later, when the moon had shifted and it had changed to being a 'root day'.

The two wines were fermented, pressed and aged in identical ways. I have tasted them on a number of occasions now, without knowing which was which, and found that there really is an amazing difference: the 'root day' wine is firm and savoury, while the 'fruit day' wine is brighter, juicier and, well, fruitier.

Sergio Carlei isn't amazed in the slightest. Just over a decade ago, he managed to cure himself of a rare form of leukaemia by fasting, meditating and then eating a healthy diet of organic and biodynamic food. He believes in the power of positive energy. 'It's all about energy,' he says, 'My view of the vine is that I see it like a human. I knew cancer was caused by toxicity in the blood, and that taking stress out of the body is a form of detoxification. Blood to a human is like soil to a vine. Toxic soils produce unhealthy vines. Healthy soils produce healthy vines.'

Hence the biodynamic practices in the vineyard and winery. 'Adopting BD was easy,' he says. 'I never questioned it because I was living proof of what happens when you get the energy right.'

Many people find Serge's talk of energy and universal truths and cleansing himself in old Aboriginal spiritual waterholes rather confronting. But the inescapable fact is that he's making some of the best wines in Australia right now, and they're getting better all the time.

Craiglee

Young winemakers, especially the ones producing alcoholic fruit bombs designed to garner 90-plus points from international wine critics, run the risk of believing their own bullshit. They can become arrogant and pompous, swinging their extra-heavy bottles full of turbo-charged shiraz like pendulous trophies. When this happens, these cocky grape-treaders need to be sent to Craiglee, to spend some time in the calm company of Pat Carmody, the most humble winemaker I've ever met.

The thing is, Pat has a lot not to be humble about. Craiglee vineyard and its fabulous old bluestone winery were established in a gully just outside the town of Sunbury, north of Melbourne, in 1863. A legendary shiraz made here in 1872 was still drinking superbly well over a century later. Pat sees this gift of heritage as both a great responsibility and an endless source of inspiration and comfort. The 19th-century vignerons clearly chose a good site, and 19th-century winemaking techniques were clearly good enough to produce an extraordinarily long-lived wine from that site. Why muck around with that formula?

Pat comes from the keep-it-simple school of winemaking. 'I had a wine supplies salesman here the other day,' he told me once, 'trying to sell me bags of acid and tannin and other powders and potions. I just looked at him and said: Why would I need any of that?'

He worries about the alcohol levels in his precious shiraz when they creep up over 13 per cent. And he worries about Australia's cheap-and-cheerful image overseas. 'I wonder whether the horse has bolted,' he says. 'It might be too late to get back our reputation for producing good wine. My agent in London keeps telling me to drop my prices, because I'm Australian, and Australian shiraz doesn't sell for more than ten quid a bottle, don't I know that? But I tell them: I'm half the price of the Rhone wines that aren't any better than mine. It's you blokes who need to get your head around what *I'm* trying to do.'

He's right. Finding a Cornas or Hermitage with the same finesse and complexity as a good Craiglee shiraz would be a frighteningly expensive exercise. Pat's wines are effortless, honest and often breathtakingly beautiful. And great value.

His chardonnay is a deeply underrated wine, with lovely minerality and a twist of lemon pith to the finish. His pinot is a reflection of the site more than the grape: a plum-stone firmness underneath earthy red fruit. His cabernet is classic, taut, violet-perfumed Victorian elegance. And the shiraz is, as I say, exceptional: focused, balanced, pure, with floral spice and red fruit and perfect, tucked-in tannins.

These are not modern wines. They're not flashy wines. They're not wines that pay the slightest attention to trends or influential wine critics or wine shows. Which is precisely why they are inspirational.

Jinks Creek

Andrew Clarke is one of Australia's great ratbag non-conformist winemakers. His grandfather was a wine merchant in Melbourne, and although he trained as a chef, he's spent much of the last quarter century planting vineyards for other people across southern Victoria, and working with other single-minded winemakers such as Rick Kinzbrunner (when he was at Brown Brothers) and Brian Fletcher (when he was at St Huberts).

Andrew makes wine from grapes sourced from a variety of regions: from his own 30-year-old vineyard at Tonimbuk, tucked away in the Bunyip state forest on Melbourne's fringe; from Heathcote and the Yarra; and from as far away as Longford in East Gippsland.

He likes to work slowly in the winery, making sure everything's done well and right. There's an element of the famous Rockford philosophy here: buckets are used to transfer must and wine, the reds are pressed at a gentle 1 tonne per hour. Each batch, each barrel, is given special attention, and treated like a potter would his pots: Andrew plays with different yeasts for different vineyards, as though he were adding glazes and layers to the texture of the raw materials. As a result, there are quite a few wines produced under the wild, painterly Jinks Creek label, and the range can vary from year to year.

The whites from Andrew's own forest-fringed vineyard at Tonimbuk – a pinot gris and a sauvignon blanc – share a lovely refreshing purity (although I'm not so sure about the rather minty pinot noir from this site), and his marsanne/viognier blend from Heathcote is terrifically honeyed and textural.

And while he makes wine from a number of other varieties – Heathcote merlot, Yarra cab franc, King Valley sangiovese – Andrew is best with shiraz: whether it's fine and nervy from Yarra Glen, powerful and majestic from Heathcote, or gravelly and wild from Longford.

These are really exciting, satisfying wines. Jinks Creek deserves to be much better known than it is.

Limbic Wines

Michael Pullar is a neurosurgeon. This goes some way to explaining the fastidious precision with which the Limbic vineyard and winery have been established in bushland at Pakenham Upper, a couple of kilometres from Serge Carlei's place. It could also explain why Michael has enthusiastically embraced the seemingly wondrous practices of biodynamic farming: slicing through a person's brain must only increase the sense of wonder at how such spongy grey matter can contain the thoughts, memories and soul of that person.

The Limbic vineyard feels like a special place, especially at dusk. Fading rays of watery sunlight seep through the trees as a nearly full moon rises in the east. Under my feet the soil is cool, fine and powder grey. Over the last ten years, the 6 hectares of vines have easily worked their roots deep into this country, through clay and pockets of red rock, searching for water, for sustenance, and now produce exquisite-tasting grapes.

Michael started applying biodynamic preps in 2004, encouraged by his down-to-earth brother-in-law and vineyard manager, Rob Norris ('as in Chuck…'). Compost is made on-site using manure from a few Dexter cows. Michael says that botrytis had been a problem here, but, thanks to the application of 501 (the horn silica preparation) and 508 (the horsetail preparation), used to increase light energy and help build up natural plat resistance in the vine, botrytis is no longer an issue.

All the hand-picked grapes go across a sorting table and additions are virtually non-existent: there's certainly no need for acidification in this cool site. As a result, the Limbic wines are a perfect reflection of their site.

The sauvignon blanc is wonderfully reserved, with delicate smells of herbs and flowers, subtle, not showy, and with the most delicious, mouth-watering fine, powdery dryness. The chardonnay is all grilled nuts and savoury dryness and spicy, almost smoky complexity. And the pinot noir is pale in colour, almost rosé-like, with quiet aromas of red plums and autumn forests that don't prepare you for the mouthful of structure to come – that powdery dryness again, and some fine-grained juiciness and grip.

These wines won't appeal to everyone. If you like pungent, fruity sav blanc or dark, concentrated pinot, you probably won't like these. But if restraint, clarity, crispness and elegance are your thing, I urge you to seek out the wines from this brilliant vineyard. It deserves to be much better known.

Shadowfax Wines

Shadowfax has been an impressive operation from the day it opened in 1999. Winemaker Matt Harrop, simmering with laconic Kiwi energy, seemed perfectly at home in the architecturally striking winery, looking for all the world like a big rusted iron tent rising out of the Werribee bush. He soon made his mark with multi-vineyard Victorian chardonnay, Adelaide Hills sauvignon, and some extraordinarily subtle and complex Geelong pinot noir, but the wines that cemented Shadowfax's – and Matt's – reputation, were the single-site shirazes from some old vineyards the company bought in Heathcote in 2000. Here were wines that sang of their terroir: the One Eye shiraz, for example, from 40 year-old vines planted in a block of Cambrian rock overlaid by clay loam has marvellous succulent fruit and dense chewy tannin, while the Pink Cliffs shiraz, from a rockier site a few hundred metres away, has sappier fruit, spikier tannins, firmer structure.

Since 2007 Matt has been moving the company-owned vineyards to more organic viticultural practices: kelp foliar sprays, deep undervine mulching, applications of the biodynamic 500 manure spray, running sheep through the vines during winter. This shift to greener ways was primarily inspired by a desire to minimise and hopefully eliminate chemical inputs, and get the winemaking team out into the vineyard more often, observing, tasting, thinking. It was also inspired by the exceptional quality of the grapes Matt has been buying over the last few years from biodynamically farmed vineyards such as Limbic in Pakenham and Staindl on the Mornington Peninsula. 'There's something different about that fruit,' he says. 'Something really beautiful and trippy.'

Shadowfax winery

Yarra Valley

Don't expect to find any Yarra Valley winemakers in their wineries just before vintage each year. They're far more likely, at least the better ones are, to be out in the vineyards, either their own estate plantings or one of the dozens of small patches of vines spread over the folds and gullies and slopes and flatlands that abound across the region's undulating country. Understanding this diversity is the key to understanding the Yarra Valley, and that's precisely what the region's better winemakers are doing.

'The easy way to explain the terroirs of valley is by pointing to the three highways,' says Dave Bicknell of Oakridge. 'The warmer, gently sloping country along the Melba Highway, up through Dixons Creek; the grey soils of the valley floor, along the Maroondah Highway, where most of the vineyards are; and the cooler, higher country and red soils down the Warburton Highway to the south east. There is a broad difference between the valley floor and the Upper Yarra: it's easy to see the fineness in the wines from the Upper Yarra's red soils, and the richness of the wines from down on the grey soils, thanks to the greater heat loads during summer.'

But there's more to it than just soil types and climate: once you get away from the highways and begin to explore the nooks and crannies of this ancient river valley, says Dave Bicknell, you find pockets of vineyard that defy the overall logic. South-facing slopes that should be too cold, but manage to ripen chardonnay and pinot beautifully; places that should be warm enough to ripen cabernet that struggle to produce good sauvignon blanc.

And there's more. 'John Middleton [of pioneering Yarra vineyard, Mount Mary] used to point out that there are two vintages each year here. Once we're in March, and the grapes have started coming off the valley floor vineyards but before they've ripened in the Upper Yarra, the prevailing weather often shifts from hot northerly winds to cool south-westerlies. We go from being a continental to a maritime region. And this increases the differences between the wine styles coming from those two broader sub-regions.'

Steve Webber De Bortoli

Steve Webber is so excited he's literally jumping up and down with glee. It's not the exquisite new wines he and his team are making that are ringing his bells. It's not even the salami he makes each year from Berkshire Duroc pigs reared on the estate. Webber is jiggling at the sight of his new compost-turning machine in action on thousands of tonnes of beautiful black compost, laid out in huge great windrows in the bottom paddock.

'Look at it!' he says, grinning from ear to ear. 'Is that not the most beautiful thing you've ever seen in your life?'

The compost, which will be spread undervine to improve soil structure, carbon content and moisture retention, is part of a concerted effort to move De Bortoli's Yarra vineyards to sustainable viticultural practices.

'As well as spreading compost, we're using compost teas and other biological farming techniques developed by Elaine Ingham of Soil FoodWeb. In the end we want to be using no chemical herbicides, fungicides or pesticides.'

As we get in the car and head back up to the winery, I ask why he feels there's a need to invest so heavily and change viticultural practices so dramatically. '*That's* why,' he says, pointing out the window to a near-empty dam. 'We just haven't got the moisture in the soil that we used to have when we first came here 20 years ago. We need to do more – a lot more – to keep our soil healthy, so we can keep on making wine.'

It would certainly be a tragedy if Steve and his winemaking team weren't able to continue nudging the style boundaries in the exciting and compelling way they are at the moment. Steve's philosophy is simple: make wines with detail that people actually want to drink; wines that taste more of site and seasons than variety or winemaking.

'We've lost so much detail in Australian wine over the last few decades by mechanising everything,' he says. 'Especially in the winery: once you've crushed and de-stemmed and pumped your must, you've mashed and minced the grapes and lost the detail. So we've gone back to careful sorting, lots of whole bunch, lots of stems. Many of the vineyards we're taking fruit from were planted in the 1980s and early '90s and they're really just starting to hit their straps now. I want to make the most of that maturity.'

The De Borts' Yarra whites are increasingly extraordinary: wines of thrilling purity, leanness and minerality. The sauvignon is all tightly bound, nettle-wrapped stones; the chardonnay is all wheatmeal subtlety and lingering intensity; the viognier has just a whisper of creaminess, with a latent energy that could snap at any moment. And the reds set new standards for the region: deeply foresty but transparent, ethereal pinot noir; supple, fragrant, very, *very* sexy syrah; and cabernet that captures the Yarra's perfect balancing act between herbal lightness and berry concentration.

As well as being an inspiration to (and former employer of) many of the Yarra's new wave of young winemakers, Steve has also influenced winemaking thinking in other parts of the De Bortoli range. The most recent and impressive examples of this are his duo of multi-regional wines: a classic dry white and 'syrah carbonique', released under the budget-priced Windy Peak label. The former is a perfect illustration of his (not so) tongue-in-cheek obsession with anti-varietal 'flavourlessness': it's a super-refreshing, ultra-crisp blend of sav blanc, grigio, semillon and vermentino. And the latter is, as the name suggests, pitched perfectly between the juiciness of the Beaujolais and the spiciness of the Northern Rhone.

Let's face it: you don't hear many Australian producers of hundreds of thousands of cases of red wine that will be sold for twelve bucks in supermarkets citing Jean Foillard Morgon and Maxime Graillot Equinoxe as inspiration.

Kiltynane

A few days after the horrific Black Saturday Victorian bushfires in February 2009, I drove out to the Yarra Valley. Along the Maroondah Highway between Lilydale and Healesville, there was little indication that the region had been attacked by a firestorm just a few days before. Most of the vineyards, wineries and restaurants on the main tourist strip were untouched. It was only when I drove up along the Healesville – Yarra Glen Road that I could trace, in the blackened paddocks and charcoal trees, the frantic course of the fire on that dreadful day.

As I turned a bend in the road I realised that the sooty smudge across the landscape was leading directly to Kate Kirkhope's biodynamically farmed Kiltynane pinot noir vineyard near Tarrawarra. In all the many news reports that had crackled out about the tragedy, I hadn't heard anything about this little slice of the world. On entering the drive I could see the vines had taken the full brunt of a raging grassfire.

Kate was putting on a brave face. She said she was one of the lucky ones. She had had a good vintage in 2008, too, she said, so there was wine in the cellar, waiting to be sold. But there would be no 2009 vintage.

We walked through the small stables-cum-winery (Kate had also lost some of her precious horses in the fire) and stood, looking at scorched leaves, melted black irrigation pipes, charred end-posts, and at where the flames had licked at the winery doors.

The vine is an amazingly resilient plant: most of the vines will bounce back in time, green leaves will shoot and bunches will set, although the lower block, the vines that felt the full force of the fire as it came in from the south-west, may have to be bulldozed.

Like the plants they grow, wine producers can also be remarkably tough people: I'm not sure I could cope with the trials Kate Kirkhope has been through. In 2000, she lost two-thirds of her newly established pinot noir vineyard due to water stress and other complications, and had to re-plant – only to see those vines engulfed in flames and smoke a few years later.

The Kiltynane wines have impressed since the first vintages emerged in the middle of the decade and I think they deserve wider acclaim but I understand why they haven't: they're not glossy, up-front, commercial styles. The Preliminaire Blanc de Noir, for example, inspired by Kate's friendship with Alsace producer Frederick Blanck and made using free-run juice from estate-grown pinot noir grapes, wild-fermented and matured in older barrels, is a pale bronze-coloured wine with tangy, slightly volatile aromas of feral honey and quince and nuts, and with a deliciously creamy, mouthcoating texture. I've seen quite a few people simply not know where to place the wine in their carefully compartmentalised mental-style library. It's not a rosé, it's not sparkling ('but I thought blanc de noir was champagne?'), it's not quite a white – what do I *do* with it?

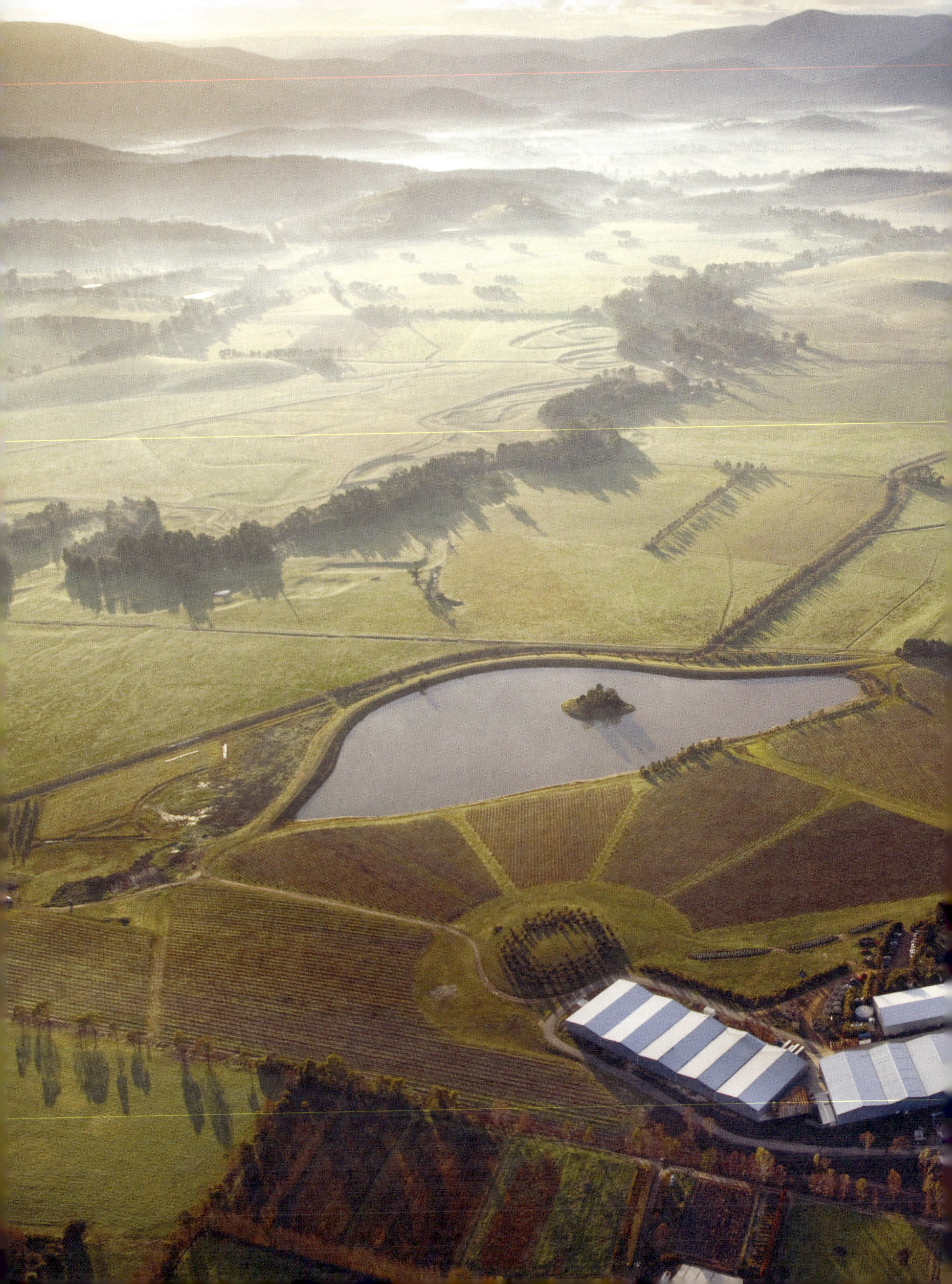

Yarra Valley

Kate's pinot noir is also quite different from the robust, plum-and-beetroot purpleness of many Yarra Valley pinots such as those from the nearby TarraWarra vineyard: pale in colour, it has autumnal aromas of hedgerow berries and damp leaf litter, and a sinewy, earthy texture, like supple entwined twigs.

Like many vineyards in the central valley floor, Kiltynane is planted on ancient weathered Silurian grey loam overlying hard yellowy clay. Unlike many other vineyards on the central valley floor, the low-yielding vines are grown biodynamically, and this pinot is made with minimal additions. As a result, I think it accurately and evocatively expresses a true sense of place.

'Biodynamics is more than just trying to grow grapes that taste of where they're from,' Kate told me a couple of years ago. 'For me, using biodynamics is a survival technique: a positive way of making it through the difficult seasons.'

Oakridge

David Bicknell's nickname is Carlos. As in Jackal. He earned this slightly menacing moniker working at the De Bortoli winery in the 1990s; not because he has the cold, hart heart of a trained assassin, but because he is extraordinarily focused on the job at hand. (At least I *think* that's the explanation.)

Since moving across the valley from De Borts a few years ago, he has applied that focus to the increasingly brilliant wines at Oakridge. He also drew on his reserves of jackal-like determination by snatching back the farm from the jaws of the corporate crocodile: when the flailing Evans and Tate group, who'd bought Oakridge five years before, put the Yarra winery on the market in 2006, Dave managed to put a management team together to buy the place. An inspirational vote of confidence not only in his own winemaking abilities and the viability of the winery in a depressed marketplace, but also in the quality of the vineyards and growers he's been working with.

Unusually – but entirely appropriately – Dave proudly names the places that grow the grapes that make the wines. Many producers might tell you that the fruit for their chardonnay, say, was grown in the cooler high country of the Upper Yarra, but they'll refrain from naming names for fear of a competitor winery swooping in and making the grower a better offer. Not Dave. His gorgeously ethereal, floral 2008 pinot noir, for example, was sourced predominantly from the Killara Park vineyard in the red volcanic soils of Seville; the 2006 cabernet sauvignon, with its classic, grey-loam, valley-floor, elegant cedary-cassis fruit characters, is a blend of two neighbouring vineyards, Pemberley and Whitsend, in Coldstream; and the stunning 864 chardonnay, the wine that has placed Dave right at the forefront of the New Chardonnay vanguard – winemakers crafting superbly refined, elegant, lean and citrusy expressions of the grape – came from the Tibooburra vineyard, up in the steep hills of the Upper Yarra, near Yellingbo.

Allied to this keen understanding of the climate and terroirs of the Yarra is Dave's sensitivity in the winery. He knows, for example, that the region seldom produces sauvignon blanc, with exaggerated perfume, so he aims for and achieves a more textural, subtle, savoury style by fermenting in old barrels, and working the lees to add a slick of cream to the fruit's natural crisp acidity. He also knows how best to coax fine, powdery tannins from Yarra cabernet. 'A lot of people press the wine too early, because of the tannin load,' he says. 'They get scared. But I've learned you've got to ride through it, wait till that first build-up of tannin subsides, then wait again as it builds and subsides once more, and then press the wine.' The result is cabernet with exceptional elegance and finesse.

Dave applies just as much care to Oakridge's $20 'second label' wines, called, somewhat bizarrely, Over the Shoulder: the mineral-laden, cool and crisp pinot grigio (Upper Yarra fruit, wild-fermentation, lees contact) is one of the best Australian examples of the style I have tasted; and the exceptionally vibrant, perfumed and silky 2007 shiraz viognier was a multi-trophy winner. Bicknell is also making excellent wines for other vineyards – notably pristine, focused arneis and chardonnay for YarraLoch.

Dave Bicknell's confidence shines most clearly, though, in his response to the apocalyptic events that have beset the Yarra Valley in the last few years: the disastrous frosts and the outbreak of the vine louse phylloxera in the heart of the region leading up to the 2007 vintage; the bushfire-derived smoke taint that afflicted wines from that vintage; and the deadly bushfires of Black Saturday 2009.

'These things bring the wine community together,' he says. 'Particularly the re-planting that will happen because of the phylloxera. It gives us the opportunity to take stock, think about what we really want to be doing here in the Yarra Valley, and to correct the mistakes we've made over the last few decades.'

South Pack: the Yarra Valley's next generation of winemakers

The future of Yarra Valley wine appears to be in very good hands. The region is home to an energetic, sociable network of innovative, like-minded winemaking souls, constantly in each others' wineries, stickybeaking through each others' vineyards (observing all the appropriate phylloxera protocols, obviously), sharing information and, most importantly, regularly getting together to drink a shed-load of top booze from around the world – often at Phil Sexton's buzzing Giant Steps/Innocent Bystander cellar door, which manages better than any other in Australia to mix breezy, youthful fun with deeply serious winemaking intent.

clockwise from top left: Adam Foster, Syrahmi; Luke Lambert; Timo Mayer; Gary Mills, Jamsheed; Barney Flanders, Allies; Mac Forbes

garagiste
chardonnay

allies
MORNINGTON PENINSULA PINOT NOIR
2009   The Wine Alliance 15 Hume Road Somers 3927
Preservative (220) added. Product of Australia
Approximately 8.0 standard drinks.
750ml
13.6% alc/vol

JAMSHEED
2008
YARRA VALLEY
SILVAN
SYRAH

SYRAHMI
climat
2009
HEATHCOTE SHIRAZ

reserve
syrah
LUKE LAMBERT
2008
YARRA VALLEY   750ML . 12.5% ALC/VOL

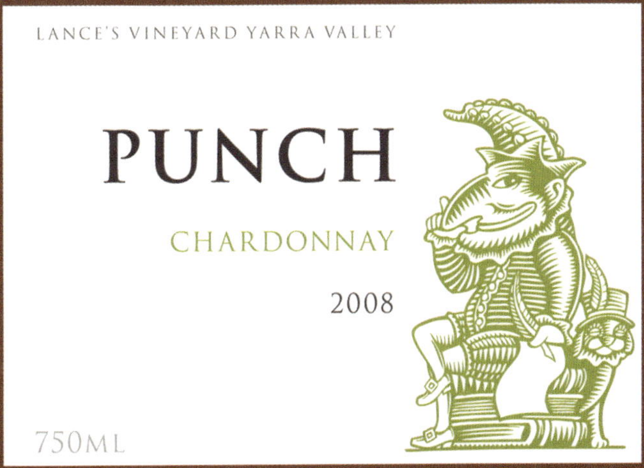

LANCE'S VINEYARD YARRA VALLEY
PUNCH
CHARDONNAY
2008
750ML

Some of them – winemakers Paul Bridgeman, Bill Downie and Mark O'Callaghan, and viticulturist Stuart Proud – have even formed a band called The Yeastie Boys. (For the record, other possible names included Thirsty Marc, The Veuve, Wolf Blass Mother, Powderyfinger, Bungs 'n' Hoses, AOC/DOC and, my fave, Flagon.)

In many ways this group is similar to the networks of young(ish) winemakers I've also written about in McLaren Vale, the Barossa and the Hunter and elsewhere, but this mob is particularly intent on making wines with more finesse, by bringing alcohols down, and by 'natural' grape-growing and winemaking.

Some of these new-wave Yarra winemakers have formed a loose alliance called South Pack. An excuse, some may say, for boozy road-trips thinly disguised as marketing. Formed by erstwhile Yarra Valley grape-treader, William Downie, the group includes Luke Lambert, Gary Mills at Jamsheed, Mac Forbes and Timo Mayer.

After stints in some of the region's bigger wineries, including Coldstream Hills and De Bortoli, Luke Lambert started making wine for himself in his garage in Yarra Glen in 2005: just a few barrels of exquisitely fine, satiny syrah sourced from the mature Rising vineyard at St Andrews, high in the valley's north-west corner; and some thrillingly perfumed, tannic nebbiolo sourced from the Shelmerdine vineyard in Heathcote. He has since been hired as the winemaker for Maddens Rise vineyard on the Maroondah Highway in the heart of the valley, but continues to make increasingly brilliant wines under his own label.

Luke also worked in Piedmont for Giacomo Brezza, and puts the experience to good use in making his nebbiolo: rough, wild ferment, frequently plunged, 40-day maceration, basket pressed, gravity-fed into old oak, no fining, no filtration. The results are stunning: Luke's reserve nebbiolo, in particular, has the most remarkable, ethereal quality, a dancing, elusive aroma of spice and rose petals, and then a tongue-grabbing tannic finish.

Luke's syrah is, if anything, even more impressive, especially the reserve, which is 100 per cent whole bunch, wild yeast ferment, macerated for six weeks. Tightly structured and brooding, it's a seriously deep and dark wine with fine but persistent tannin and exceptional concentration and length. And it's 12.5 per cent alcohol.

'The moderate alcohol is all down to that vineyard,' says Luke. 'Up in St Andrews, 100 metres above the valley floor, it's on this tough Silurian mudstone: it's the most depleted old rocky soil in the valley. It's very windy, too, and this helps to devigorate the vines, so they have less canopy and more dappled light. And it's funny, if you pick the shiraz at about 12, 13 baumé you don't get any green characters, but pick a little later and you do. There's a window of green. Bailey Carrodus [at Yarra Yering] thought that you needed to pick Yarra shiraz either early or late to avoid that green pippiness.'

Luke has planted and grafted two small patches of nebbiolo in St Andrews and at Maddens Rise. It will be fascinating to see how these sites express themselves through the hands of this incredibly talented winemaker.

Gary Mills also sources fruit from the Rising vineyard and elsewhere for his Jamsheed wines. Gary spent two years working for Paul Draper at Ridge in California in the late '90s, and was heavily influenced by the veteran American's approach to single-vineyard, minimal intervention wines. He also evokes the name of French natural wine guru, Jules Chauvet when he talks about his own methods.

'You could describe it as winemaking by negligence,' smiles Gary. 'I try to do as little as possible to the wine. I try not to panic, and just let it go. The results may not be technically perfect but they're wines that, I hope, are full of character.'

They certainly are. The Jamsheed gewurztraminer, sourced from the stony Rising vineyard, is whole bunch pressed into large, 800-litre old barrels, wild-fermented with no acid additions, and left on lees for seven months. The result is a thoroughly unusual but thoroughly drinkable, minerally expression of grape and place. In 2008 Gary tried the Chauvet approach with one batch of pinot noir: whole berries, no additions, five weeks maceration on skins, six months in barrel, bottled unfined and unfiltered, and no sulphur throughout the process except for a little at bottling. Again, the wine was fabulously different: lively, bouncy, full of autumn red fruit and juiciness.

The most impressive Jamsheed wines, though, are the single-vineyard shirazes, sourced from an array of sites in the Yarra and the Grampians. Tasting through them, from the prickly pepper and spice and latticework tannins of the shiraz from a vineyard in the cool red soils of Silvan in the southern Yarra to the dark black composty complexity and firm, bony tannins of the shiraz from a 40-year-old vineyard in Great Western, is a fascinating exercise.

Mac Forbes is possibly the most ambitious of the South Pack winemakers, certainly as far as the sheer number of different bottlings is concerned. Mac produces small batches of wonderfully wheatmealy single-vineyard chardonnay from Woori Yallock in the south of the valley; no fewer than five single-vineyard Yarra pinots; nervy, spicy shiraz from Gruyere; and superbly elegant, 12.5 per cent alcohol cabernet modelled, says Mac, on the classic old-fashioned Yarra cabernets of the '70s and early '80s. Although he doesn't (yet) own any of his own vineyards, he works closely with a number of growers, most of whom farm without irrigation, and he is encouraging them to move towards organic and biodynamic techniques in their vineyards.

His five single-vineyard pinot noirs speak eloquently of their provenance: woody and strawberryish from the warm, east-facing, most northerly Dixons Creek site, savoury and tannic from the more exposed Yarra Glen site, intense and tangy from the north-facing

Coldstream site, perfumed and plush from north-facing Gruyere, and ethereal and juicy from the coolest, highest, most southerly Woori Yallock site.

'What I see in these wines is an increased volume of flavour and an increase in vinosity as you move from warm to cool,' says Mac. 'And I think, for me, that makes wine interesting. Those elements just below the fruit.'

Mac has worked a few vintages in Austria in recent years, and sells a very good white gruner veltliner and juicy red blaufrankisch under his own label that he made over there. He has also imported cuttings of both these quintessentially Austrian vines to plant in Australian soil – in particular, the high country of the southern Yarra and the Strathbogie Ranges in central Victoria.

He already makes a selection of excellent rieslings from a 25-year-old, dry-grown vineyard in the Strathbogies. The RS9 ('RS' stands for residual sugar in grams per litre) has a lick of lovely, grapey sweetness but the mouthwatering acidity and gentle grip (some of the wine was fermented in old barrels) balance the sugar to produce a dry finish. The RS37 has delicious apple- and lime-flavoured sweetness running through it, perfectly balanced zesty natural acidity. The Tradition was fermented wild, had no acid added, spent three months on skins and a further seven months in barrel, and has the most unusual but alluring perfume of spiced ginger, and a gorgeously long, grapefruit-grippy finish. And the Auslese, also fermented with no additions in old oak barrels, has the most wonderful, grapey, musky fragrance. Like all of Mac Forbes' wines, they're thrillingly adventurous.

As well as making exceptionally good, textural, complex wines at Gembrook Hill, right on the southern fringe of the Yarra Valley, Timo Mayer also produces lovely wines under his own label from his 2.5-hectare hillside vineyard opposite the winery where Gary Mills and Mac Forbes are based. Timo's catch-cry, one that he is wont to yell out, grinning, in the middle of a tasting, is 'Bring back the funk!' A philosophy that he lives up to in the superb, creamy, barrel-fermented Gembrook Hill sauvignon blanc, and his own gloriously spicy, unfiltered Mayer pinot noir, its label shamelessly modelled on those of Armand Rousseau in Burgundy.

Timo's close-planted vines struggle to hold on to the incredibly steep, gravelly sandstone slope that he, characteristically, has christened Bloody Hill, but they eke out some intense, refined wine. When it was released in 2005, Timo's Big Betty shiraz was the first of the new wave, spicy, slinky artisan expressions of this grape to make me sit up and take notice of what was happening with this South Pack group of winemakers.

The South Pack group also includes some excellent non-Yarra winemakers that share the same fascinations. Barney Flanders and David Chapman make lovely wines from the Mornington Peninsula and Heathcote under the Allies and Garagiste labels, including a brilliantly thoughtful, lemon- and honey-flavoured blend of Peninsula viognier with a

Phoenix rising
A new lease of life for old Yarra wineries

A decade ago I interviewed the irascible Doctor Bailey Carrodus at his Yarra Yering winery. I was intrigued. Here was a man who had spent decades establishing one of the country's most revered wine estates; a man who was light years ahead of everybody else in planting viognier and blending it with shiraz; a man who had helped to kick-start the Yarra Valley's wine renaissance. And yet he had no family to inherit his remarkable achievement after he was gone. Did it concern him?

'Oh no,' he said, in his characteristically chirpy-but-exasperated voice. 'It doesn't matter, because I won't be here to see it, will I? One only hopes one dies with one's boots on, and then someone else can clear up the mess.'

In September 2008, the good doctor got his wish when he died suddenly at the vineyard. Old friends took over as executors and soon quietly started looking for a potential purchaser. Eventually, in June 2009, a buyer was announced: a syndicate of offshore investors, long-time customers and lovers of Yarra Yering wines, who also have interests in Kaesler winery in the Barossa, and Chateau Maris in the Languedoc in France.

It looks like it could be the perfect fit. Yarra Yering winemaker Paul Bridgeman, who moved across the valley from De Bortoli just before Bailey Carrodus died, is keen to adopt the greener, biological farming practices that Kaesler have been exploring for a few years. 'The doctor liked his chemicals and his plough,' he says. 'I think that if we can unlock some of the things that have been bound up in the soil for so long, we'll amplify the Yarra Yering character in the wines even more.' And Kaesler winemaker, Reid Bosward, is keen to learn more about the unique, 700 kg small-batch fermentation techniques that Bailey Carrodus designed.

The concept of succession is just as fraught in the wine industry as in any other agricultural sector. Older wine companies always worry that the next generation won't want to enter the family firm, thus forcing a sale to some faceless drinks multinational. And the pioneers of the boutique wine boom of the '70s and '80s, now heading towards (or way past) 'retirement' age, worry that the kids (if there even are any) might not share their parents' dream of being a vigneron. Indeed, growing up on the vineyard every weekend, pruning in the chill of early winter, picking in the heat of late summer, may well have turned them off wine for life.

Luckily, succession seems to be occurring relatively painlessly in the Yarra. James Lance is the second generation of his family to make wine at St Andrews: his parents, David and Cathy, planted Diamond Valley Vineyards in 1976.

'The tricky bit with changing over,'

says James, 'is that the older generation needs to extract enough money from the company to live on in their retirement. And that's hard after only one generation of making wine.'

The Lances' solution to that problem came in 2005 when Graeme Rathbone (brother of Yering Station owner Doug Rathbone) bought their well-known Diamond Valley label – but not the vines and winery – and son James, with his wife Claire, leased the vineyard from his parents. It meant losing the name that the family had spent 30 years establishing but presented the opportunity of starting afresh with now-mature vines.

The result is some seriously sensational wines under the striking Punch label (also part of the South Pack group), particularly the magnificent close-planted pinot noir, with its glossy dark plum fruit, its concentrated flavours of blackcurrants and compost, and its firm, dense finish.

Elsewhere, fourth generation Sandra de Pury and brother David have helped parents Guill and Katherine de Pury expand the small Yeringberg vineyard from 2 to 20 hectares, returning this historic property to some of its 19th-century glory. Second generation David Church is making brilliantly regional examples of Yarra cabernet, shiraz and riesling at the dry-grown Warramate vineyard his parents established next door to Yarra Yering in 1970. Second and third generations of the Middleton family are now running the iconic Mount Mary vineyard near Coldstream, and are implementing a series of environmental improvements including an extensive native revegetation program and alternative energy use in the winery. And although Seville Estate, founded by Peter and Margaret McMahon and one of the Yarra's pioneering 1970s vineyards, passed through through a number of hands before ending up with the current owners, Graham and Margaret Van Der Meulen, the McMahon's grandson, Dylan, is now employed as the winemaker.

splash of chardonnay called Saone, and a wild, rippling 50 per cent whole bunch, old-oak-matured Heathcote syrah. And sommelier Adam Foster, now at the fantastic Lake House restaurant in Daylesford, produces characterful, multi-layered wild yeast shiraz from low-yielding vineyards on the deep red Cambrian soil in Heathcote under his Syrahmi label, as well as a terrific sangiovese rosé with fellow sommelier Lincoln Riley, and even, in 2008, some red wine in Banyuls, in south-west France.

Although it's not officially part of the South Pack, I'd also nominate Hoddles Creek Estate as an honorary member. Hoddles Creek winemaker Franco d'Anna has been producing sensationally focused, pristine and great-value wines at his family's 35-hectare vineyard in the cool hills of the southern valley for a few years now, but in 2008 he stepped up to another level again with, of all things, a pinot blanc. The first wine to be released under the vineyard's faux-French reserve label, 1er Yarra Valley, the wine sang a sweet song of delicate white flowers, intensely flavoured grape-pulpy texture and a clean, light (12.8 per cent alcohol) grapefruity finish.

Wedgetail Estate

As well as Kiltynane, other biodynamic activity is erupting across the Yarra Valley. Judy's Farm in Yarra Glen produces a little pinot noir as well as growing some extraordinarily flavoursome biodynamic vegies, and Naked Range up in the thickly wooded hills around Smiths Gully is converting to certified organic practices, and uses some BD preps.

Guy Lamothe is taking a cautious approach at his steep, sloping Wedgetail Estate vineyard in Cottlesbridge, in the north-west of the region. Guy stopped using herbicide and started using the BD sprays on some of his blocks in 2007, and is gradually applying the methods across all 5 hectares of vines. 'Now, instead of spraying, I pay someone to come and weed the vineyard by hand,' says Guy. 'We also now hoe and after 14 years of chemicals, this is opening the soil up beautifully, and encouraging deeper root penetration. Yes, it costs more, but it makes me feel rich without having to drive an expensive car.'

The country up here has the same underlying yellow clay as you find 100 metres further down in the valley floor, but there's more gravel and orange mudstone running through the loamy top soil, and a harder rocky base. Guy chose to emphasise the cool climate of his site even more by planting some of his vines — the chardonnay — on a south-facing slope, and it's this block, I think, that produces Wedgetail's best wine: lean, taut and singing a beautiful, pure, lemon-zesty song.

As Steve Webber from De Bortoli points out, 'When everybody started here in the Yarra, they thought the north-facing slopes were the best, the ones that faced the sun. Now we reckon that the east- and south-facing slopes are the ones to go for: wines from south-facing slopes don't taste like the sun, they taste like the soil they're grown in.'

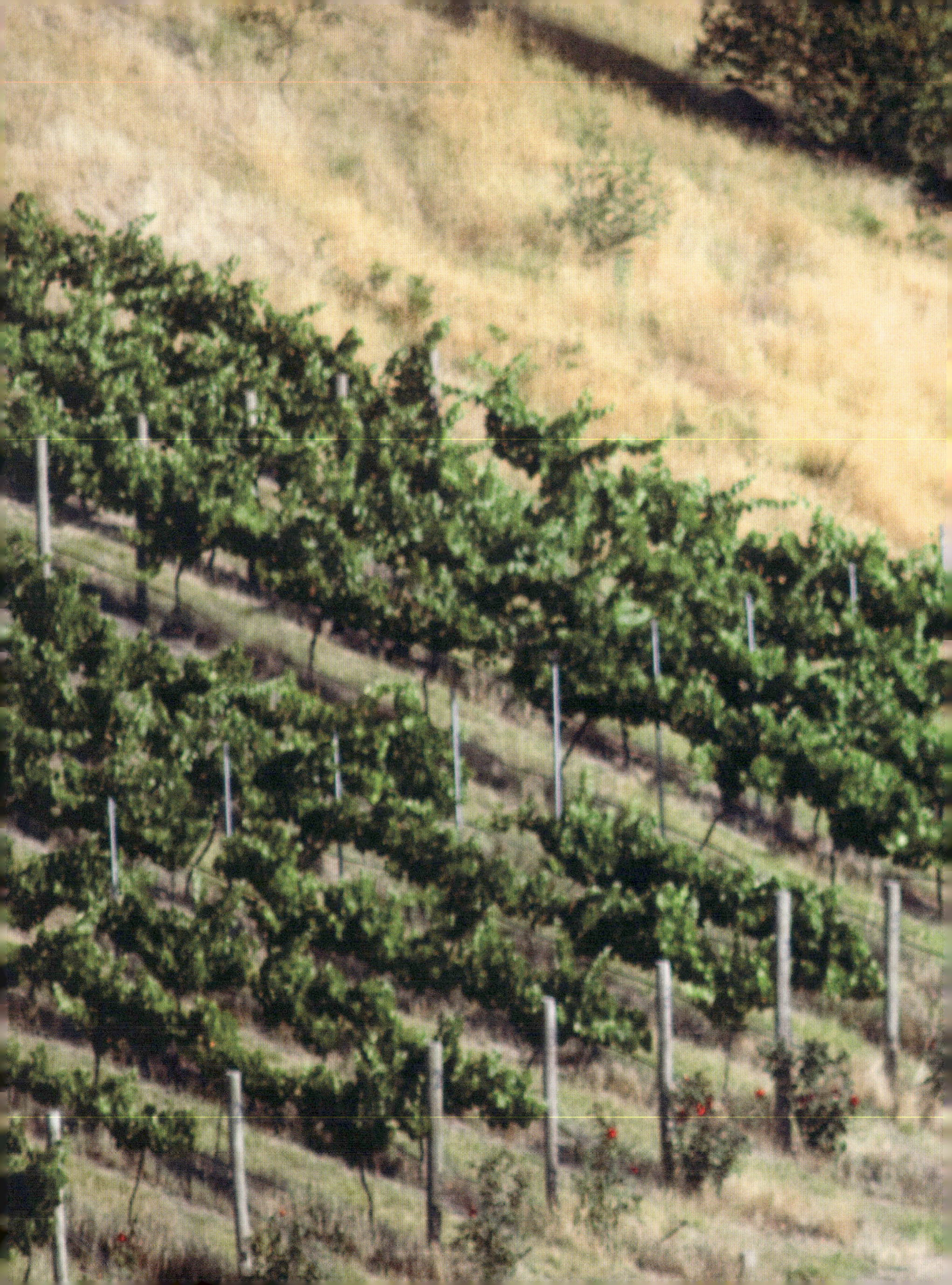

Wedgetail Estate, Yarra Valley

Mornington Peninsula

If any Australian wine region is crying out to be mentally sliced up into sub-regions it's the Mornington Peninsula. The tongue of land curling down the eastern flank of Port Phillip Bay south of Melbourne looks like it has been moulded by some winemaking creator spirit fascinated by the potential of terroir: the sandy flatlands of Moorooduc and Tuerong in the north; the pale brown alluvial soils of Dromana on the northern coastline; the deep russet volcanic soils up in the crumpled country of Red Hill and Main Ridge, and sloping down around Merricks and Balnarring to the southern coast, facing Western Port. The combinations of aspect, altitude, terroir and sea breezes are almost endless – and endlessly fascinating.

The differences between the flavour and character of the wines from these broad sub-regions are clear, especially when you shine the terroirs through the prism of the pinot noir grape. Try a pinot from Red Hill next to a pinot from Merricks, for example, made by the same producer, and although the soil types may be similar the altitude and proximity to the sea make a world of difference: the former wine is lighter, more elegant, spicy, with floral, herbal lift, while the latter is plummy, firmer, more tannic.

Some of the region's winemakers are wary about promoting these sub-regional differences: they would rather not detract from the important job of selling the Mornington Peninsula region as a single cool-climate wine region, which is in itself hard enough for some wine drinkers, especially in export markets, to grasp. But I believe some of the most distinctive wines emerging from the Mornington Peninsula right now come from single vineyards – and specific blocks within vineyards.

Sandro Mosele Kooyong

Nat White, winemaker at pioneering Peninsula vineyard, Main Ridge Estate, cast the mould for single-vineyard wines in the early 1990s when he bottled pinot from one half-acre patch of his small vineyard separately. Planted on shallower, meaner soil, the wine from this block has more sinewy, powdery, lingering tannin and more delicate floral aroma than the rest of the vineyard, and is, I think, the benchmark for Red Hill/Main Ridge high country/red soil Peninsula pinot.

Ten Minutes by Tractor release chardonnays and pinots from the company's three single vineyards – Wallis, McCutcheon and Judd – all within ten minutes' drive of each other in Main Ridge. The wines, made by the supremely talented Rick McIntyre at Moorooduc Estate, are totally distinctive: even though the Wallis and McCutcheon chardonnay vines, for example, are the same age, picked at the same time and the grapes are fermented in the same types of barrels, the former is more elegant, wheatmealy and citrusy, while the latter is more deeply savoury, more concentrated, and has a longer finish.

The most compelling Mornington Peninsula wines of terroir, though, are made by Sandro Mosele at Kooyong.

Sandro is much in demand as a winemaker. As well as the Kooyong range (which includes a brilliant second label collection comprising a wheatmealy Clonale chardonnay, juicy Massale pinot noir and mouthfilling, gorgeously oily Beurrot pinot gris), he makes the wines for a number of Peninsula vineyards including sister company Port Phillip Estate in Red Hill, Scorpo in Merricks North and Dunn's Creek in Red Hill. He is also winemaker for Chalmers Wines and Greenstone in Heathcote.

Sandro's approach to winemaking is minimalist, laid-back and influenced far more by European tradition than the winemaking course he did at Charles Sturt Uni in the late 1990s.

'Australian winemakers have been concentrating for too long on making wine according to the 20 tenets of Croser they learned at wine school,' he says. 'They're obsessed with clean juice, using cultured yeasts, chasing varietal expression. I'm not. I like the way Henri

Jayer makes wine in Burgundy. Wild yeasts, lots of solids in chardonnay, getting good texture and tannin into the wine. I like the reticence of pinot noir, not the fruit expression. I want to make wines that taste of the soil where the grapes are grown. I want to make wines at Kooyong that taste of our property and are wines that can cellar.'

This approach – allowing the fruit to express its site – results in some of the most understated, savoury and impressive wines on the Peninsula. Compare the prickly, juicy, white pepper spice wafting through the high country Port Phillip Estate shiraz, for example, with the darker, bolder black pepper and bramble rippling through the Scorpo shiraz.

Sandro's greatest wines, though, are the amazing single-block pinots from the Kooyong Vineyard itself. Made in almost identical fashion, they are wines with great clarity – flavour snapshots of very precise points on the surface of the earth: Meres, from a patch of vines surrounded by small dams, which act as a moderating influence on the mesoclimate, is the prettiest, lightest of the pinots, with simple red fruit; Ferrous, from a block of ironstone soil, which reduces plant vigour and results in smaller, more concentrated grapes, is darker, more black-fruity, more chewy; and Haven, from the most sheltered patch of vines, is the most complex, floral and fruity, hedgerow-berry-flavoured, more structured. What's more, these three wines repeatedly display these differences from one vintage to the next.

These are exactly the kinds of wines that pinot-tragics go ga-ga about.

Crittenden

Garry Crittenden is stalking me. Ever since he and winemaker son Rollo decided to convert their 25-year-old vineyard at Dromana to organic viticulture in early 2008, Garry has been enthusiastically emailing pictures of his compost piles, his cover crops and his undervine mulching; as well as detailed letters about the incredible quality of the vegies he's now growing chemical-free in his own garden, and the tentative application of the biodynamic sprays. He knows that I write a lot about organic and biodynamic wines, so it's understandable he'd want to keep me informed. But high-resolution photos of compost piles? It does seem a bit over the top.

I'm being paranoid, of course. Garry isn't just stalking *me* with his new green evangelism. He's broadcasting the good word through his mailing list newsletters and articles in the local tourist magazines, too. He's like a kid with a new toy: he just can't stop playing with it and telling everyone he bumps into how brilliant it is.

Cynics (and there are plenty of them in the wine game) will see this as pure marketing, something that Garry showed rather a flair for when he established his previous wine business, Dromana Estate, in the early 1980s. His critics will accuse him, no doubt, of jumping on the green bandwagon, trying to make a buck with a bit of greenwashing.

Rubbish. Sure, there is a marketing (or, rather, a public relations) advantage to bathing yourself in an eco-friendly light. But you only have to talk to Garry to see that he is clearly quite astounded by the benefits he's already seen in terms of soil health, vine resilience and flavour, and increasingly convinced that it's the right way to go. Remember, this is someone who enthusiastically followed a conventional, chemically dependent viticultural regime for decades, and was highly sceptical about the vineyard's ability to cope without those chemicals in what traditionally is a cool, humid environment.

Then again, the Crittendens have always been innovative. Garry was a very early advocate of Italian varietals in Australia, making wines from Fred Pizzini's nebbiolo and barbera grapes back in the early 1990s, and co-authoring a guide to planting Italian grapes in this country at the end of the decade. Rollo has inherited his father's love of non-mainstream wines: as well as working in Piedmont and developing a love of Piedmontese red grapes, Rollo has also introduced a Spanish theme at Crittenden Estate with a juicy, vibrant joven-style tempranillo and a zesty, grape-pulpy 'albarino' under the Los Hermanos label.

As well as using some biodynamic techniques such as spraying preparation 500 and following the lunar calendar in the vineyard, Gary and Rollo are working with a biological farming company to make large amounts of compost.

'I find that these two approaches, biodynamic and biological, are quite compatible,' says Garry. 'Neither group uses practices that are inimical to one another: both abjure the

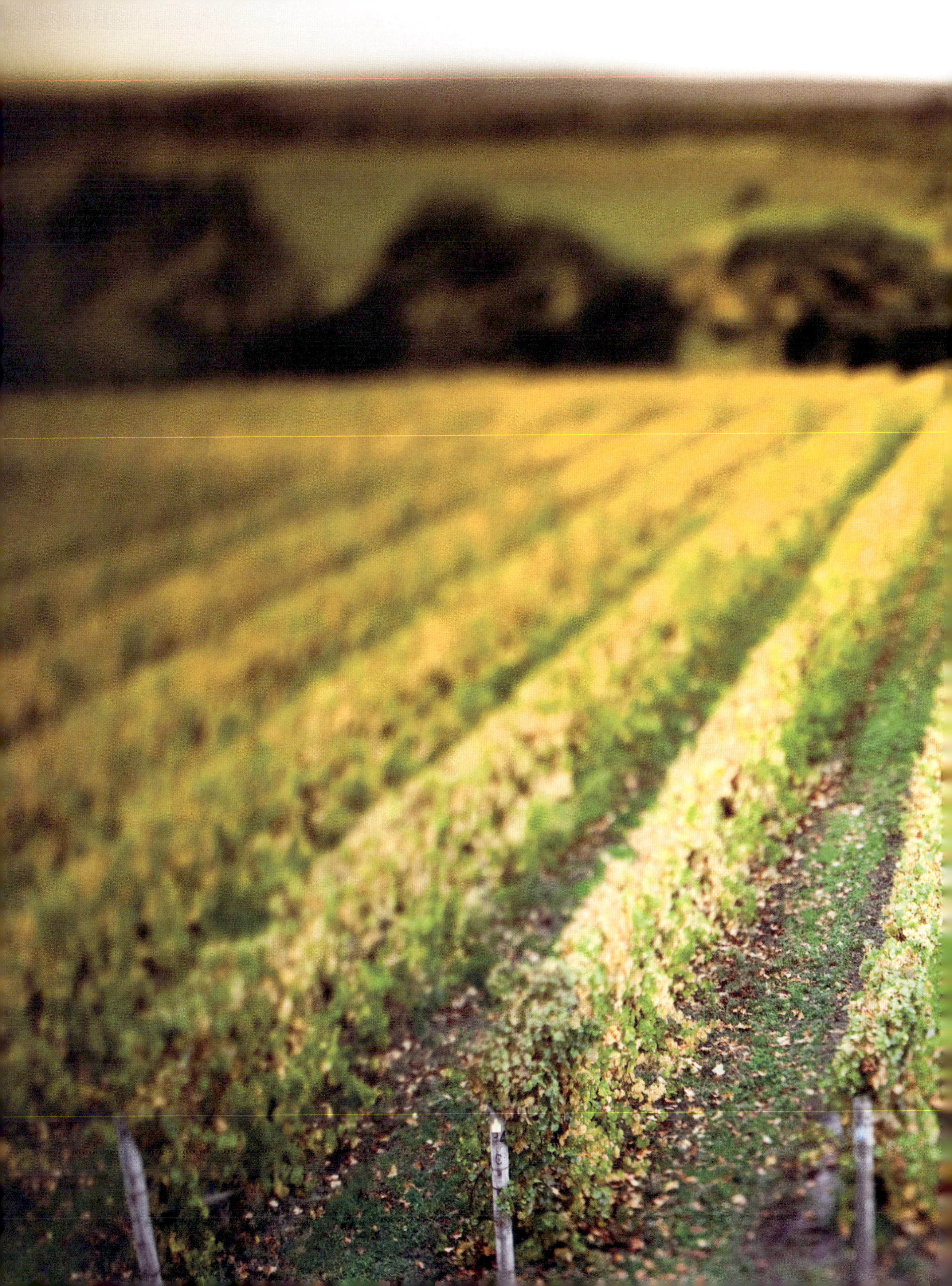

Moorooduc Estate, Mornington Peninsula

use of chemicals and artificial fertilisers. They even talk to one another! So we're evolving our own combination of the two streams; although I find it funny that "biological" requires the use of a microscope and "biodynamic" requires an understanding of planetary alignments and the cosmos. Microscopic and macroscopic in tandem, really.'

Kathleen Quealy and Kevin McCarthy

Kathleen Quealy's Balnarring winery is a wonderfully scatty microcosm of what's happening on the Mornington Peninsula right now. When you walk into the place, there's a palpable sense of the excitement and confidence that comes with re-invention.

I visited the winery just after Kathleen had moved into the place a couple of vintages ago. The shed was chock-a-block with barrels and bits of winemaking equipment. The lab was being given a hasty paint-job to make it presentable as a sales area. In the meantime, cellar door was a trestle table and a few glasses in a corner of the barrel shed. It was about as far as you could get from the slick, modern cellar doors elsewhere in the region, but that's just as you'd want it to be. Here, it's all about the wine.

Kathleen lined up a succession of fascinating wines on the trestle. A deliciously crazy white blend of pinot gris, riesling, gewurztraminer, chardonnay and the rare friulano with an equally delicious name of Pobblebonk (and a tiny label image of two frogs fucking). A juicy red called Rageous, blended from sangiovese, shiraz, pinot and merlot. A luscious fresh young muscat (who would have thought, on the cool Peninsula?).

It was truly thrilling to see a winemaker pushing boundaries like this, but it was also good to see there is substance behind the novelty.

The pinot noir vineyard surrounding the winery here at Balnarring is now a mature 25 years old, and while it produced some cracking wines in the 1990s, it's stepped up a notch or two recently.

And Kathleen herself is, of course, no newcomer to the area: she established T'Gallant Winemakers in the early 1990s with husband Kevin McCarthy, finally selling to Foster's a decade later (McCarthy still works for the larger company). Now she's started again by buying Balnarring and launching her eponymous label.

T'Gallant pioneered revolutionary styles such as pinot grigio (and gris) and minerally unwooded chardonnay on the Peninsula. Kathleen has, if anything, become even more adventurous as she's got older.

Since that first visit, I've been blown away by subsequent releases. She rightly describes her Independence Pinot Gris as 'a luxury model', with its rich, peach-fuzzy texture; her Senza Nome, by contrast, the country's first varietal friulano wine, is fabulously lean and green-apple crisp at first sip, revealing extraordinary fleshy aromas of hand cream (Nivea, to be precise) with time and air; the pretty, pink Earl's Muscat is like musk-scented raisin juice; and the Seventeen Rows Pinot Noir from that mature Balnarring vineyard is an un-reconstructed, dark, brawny old vine wine. In Kathleen's words: 'It's punk rock, not some puny fashionista.'

The Quealy turn of phrase is legendary. She talks about the grapes in Pobblebonk like a painter talks about colours, or a perfumer scents. 'Pobblebonk is only made from free-run juice,' she says. 'This encourages that dewy freshness that is so attractive in white wine…Traminer can be frumpy on its own but contributes deep floral notes as a very small proportion of the blend…Friulano can be big and chesty in Italy as well as delicate, but always with a cool, creamy middle palate, rich and filmy in texture.'

Indeed, Kathleen is so obsessed with the incredibly unusual acid structure and flavour of the friulano variety, she recently opened a bunch of northern Italian and Slovenian examples of the grape and invited various wine people to come and have a taste and a natter. (Most winemakers like to do benchmark tastings with Burgundy. Kathleen prefers Brda.)

'My poor mind is like crumbling sandstone sometimes,' she said, smiling her exasperated smile. 'But I reckon friulano tastes like chicken soup. Don't you?'

You had to smile, take a sniff and a sip and agree that there was indeed a kind of salty, savoury character to many of the wines. Especially those that had been made with extended skin contact – a technique traditional to northern Italy and Slovenia, but anathema to a conventionally trained Australian winemaker.

On one hand, Kathleen says she is tempted to try more skin contact with her friulano in the future: 'In its homeland, friulano is a working-class drink, the kind of thing you see at every bar, being poured alongside bar food. It needs to have that bitterness, that texture, that phenolic grip to handle the food.'

But a few minutes later: 'I don't think we should be using skin contact in Australia. It's culturally an Italian thing to be doing. It's not culturally Australian.'

Over at T'Gallant, Kevin McCarthy is a big fan of skin contact. His Volante is, like Kathleen's Pobblebonk, inspired by the marvellously textural whites of Friuli in Italy's north-east: a gorgeously creamy, floral-perfumed, co-fermented, wild yeast blend of chardonnay pinot gris and viognier. And his Claudius – a white wine made more like a red, with extended skin contact – is one of the most revolutionary wines ever produced in this country.

A truly wild white inspired by the maverick northern Italian winemaker Josko Gravner, Claudius is made from chardonnay, gewurztraminer and moscato giallo grapes. Both the juice and the skins of the grapes were fermented together, and the wine was left on skins for four months before being pressed off into large barrels for a few months' further maturation before bottling without filtration.

Biodynamics on the Mornington Peninsula

Crittenden Estate is just one eddying wisp of the green haze beginning to settle over the region.

Winemaker Tony Lee has started down the biodynamic path at his family's small Foxeys Hangout winery in Red Hill. Tony is making some great wine at Foxeys, from really textural, satisfying chardonnay to intensely nectarine-fuzzy late-harvest pinot gris; and for the last couple of years he's been running his youngest 2-hectare vineyard without chemicals, applying the BD preps. He's also slowly converting his older small vineyards, and hopes to convince his growers to at least move to organic viticulture.

One of the motivations to convert was a belief that chemical viticulture poisons soil. 'The oldest vineyard I take fruit from I inherited and it has the poorest soil: hard and not friable, with moss growing under the vines, and a serious problem with powdery mildew after years of herbicide and fungicide abuse. This is the vineyard that has caused me to go BD: I don't want my two younger vineyards to end up like this.'

Tony's greater inspiration, though, was wine quality: 'I'm not trying to save the world, I'm just trying to make good wine. That's why I've been fermenting with native yeasts for years: I don't like packet yeast estery characters. More than just good, clean wine, I want to make wine that speaks of a paddock's soil and climate. Organic/BD viticulture I think will help with that obsession.'

Melbourne lawyer Paul Staindl has also taken up the organic challenge. Soon after buying a small (just over a hectare), 20-year-old dry-grown vineyard on Red Hill in 2003, he added another hectare or so of vines and started converting to biodynamic practices. He and vineyard manager Adam Irish are convinced that this intensive form of organic farming has taken the mature vineyard up to the next level of quality. The wines are made by Phillip Jones of Bass Phillip, and they are wonderfully idiosyncratic. I particularly like the riesling and pinot noir, the former because of its almost Wachau-like, gritty pear and mineral style; the latter typically Jonesian in its forest fruit and leaf litter aromas and translucent, wild beauty.

Phillip Jones also consults to Shashi and Devendra Singh's north-facing 3-hectare Wildcroft Estate vineyard at the top of Red Hill: managed biodynamically since 2006, this site produces an exceptional, spicy, super-aromatic, Cornas-like shiraz.

I think it's a stunning wine. What strikes me most is how the extended skin contact process doesn't diminish the delicate aromas of the aromatic grapes in the blend, but instead seems to intensify the perfume. And, contrary to all expectation, it also results in a remarkably un-phenolic wine; yes, there's plenty of grip and minerality and texture there, but it's balanced by the extra weight of grapey flavour.

Other winemakers, judges and critics have derided these experimental styles – the Pobblebonk, the Volante, the Claudius – as being too blowsy, lacking acidity, being too lactic, too flabby, not clean. I think they're wrong. I think these wines are hugely important and brave and inspirational, and more people in the Australian wine industry need to open their minds to styles like this that don't fit easily into neat little compartments.

Macedon Ranges

You could drive right through the cold, high, windy Macedon Ranges north of Melbourne and be forgiven for thinking that there was no wine produced here at all. Most of the well-scattered vineyards are tucked away in shallow gullies, sheltering from the bone-chilling south-westerlies in winter and the searing northerlies in summer; or they're half-way up mountainsides, or round corners or off remote bush tracks. A lot of this region is marginal grape-growing country: high altitude (400 metres rising to 900), some of the coldest winemaking spots on mainland Australia, and, in places, really skinny, tough, granite sand soil washed down from the Great Dividing Range. You'd have to be slightly obsessive (or mad) to want to grow grapes here. Luckily, enough crazy people have made the trek up into the hills, and are making wines with the kind of intensity that marginal viticulture brings.

The same can't, unfortunately, be said for the wine tourists. There are no beaches up here like there are down on the Peninsula; no large, glamorous cellar door restaurants owned by interstate or international wine companies like there are in the Yarra. There are, however, pockets of extreme gastronomic endeavour in the mist-covered hills of Daylesford (the marvellous Lake House restaurant), Kyneton (the newly resurgent Royal George Hotel) and Woodend (the brilliant Holgate Brewery). In other words, there is a strong food and wine culture here, but you have to go searching for it.

I can't help feeling that it's this sense of quiet isolation, of contemplation and solitude, an almost-hidden quality that informs the best wines emerging from Macedon right now: all the winegrowers profiled here are fiercely single-minded in their pursuit of excellence, and they don't need a constant stream of cellar door visitors to distract them from their mission.

Michael Dhillon Bindi

As I turn in to the driveway at Bindi and the early morning mist clears a little, two multi-coloured Rosellas burst out from a tree by the side of the road and shoot off up towards the winery. I drive slowly past the rows of naked, mid-winter chardonnay vines trooping away across the paddock into the fog, and a black cockatoo glides over the car, heading in the same direction as the parrots. Then a kangaroo lollops past, also winery bound. And I have to try very hard to suppress the sudden feeling that I'm in a Disney movie, where animal welcoming parties are a perfectly natural occurrence; a movie set in a vineyard where the winegrowers are enthusiastically trying to do the right thing by nature.

Bindi is rightly considered the leading vineyard in the Macedon Ranges, and Michael Dhillon is one of the best winemakers in the country. This is a special site: the soils on this part of the north-facing ridge 500 metres up on the slightly warmer, southern edge of the region lie over a rich vein of quartz; you can see the shimmering crystal chunks scattered throughout the brown loam as you walk through the 6 hectares of 20-year-old vines. And Michael has travelled and worked extensively in Champagne, Tuscany, Burgundy and elsewhere, picking up tips, philosophies and an approach to winemaking that is deeply informed by a European sensibility.

'I'd just come back from Champagne in the early 1990s and was walking through the chardonnay block with Bill [Michael's father and founder of Bindi]. We were tasting the grapes as we went and I noticed that the flavours began to change as we went down the row. I looked at the ground and saw that the amount of quartz in the soil differed between the top half of the vineyard and the bottom half. And when we walked back up the row, it was obvious that where the flavours changed coincided with where the quartz changed. I realised I was experiencing exactly the same subtle differences in terroir that I'd seen in Europe. And I've been trying to capture those differences in the wines we make here ever since.'

Michael receives the greatest praise for his pinot noirs, particularly the Original Vineyard with its suppler, succulent fruit and lifted raspberry/cherry/spice perfume;

and the Block 5, a more sinewy, more deeply fruited wine with persistent tannin from a patch of the vineyard more heavily laced with quartz. They are brilliant wines. But I think the chardonnay – especially the Quartz, an exceptionally concentrated, focused expression of lemon pith and powdery minerality – is not only their equal, but is also one of the best examples of the variety in Australia.

Michael also produces one of the country's best, most elegant and refined shirazes from a vineyard on the deep-red Pre-Cambrian earth at Colbinabbin, up on the Mount Camel Range north of Heathcote. Fermented in 1-tonne vats and treated to just 20 per cent new oak during maturation, the wine, called Pyrette, is slinky, svelte and medium-bodied, with a tantalising tension between black pepper, purple plums and brown woody spices. The key to the lighter style is the picking date. 'Many Heathcote winemakers leave their grapes to hang well into autumn,' he says. 'They're seeking ultra ripeness and high alcohol. But the grapes for Pyrette are picked a couple of weeks earlier; I think it makes a better balanced wine.'

After establishing the vineyard along 'conventional' (chemically assisted) lines, over the last decade or so, Michael and Bill have moved the entire 170-hectare property to a more sustainable farming model. As well as reviving patches of rare remnant indigenous grassland and planting forests of gums, the Dhillons now run the vineyard using a combination of biological and biodynamic methods, and Michael believes that both soil and vine health have improved markedly.

'Perhaps the best thing about thinking in a Bio D way is that it leads you to care more, to think more,' he says. 'To look at what the broader options are. To test things out. To be more attentive and focused on the importance of timing rather than just action. We used to do things out of a desire to control, from a perspective of fear. We didn't want the project to fail, to be compromised, to be anything less than the best, so we felt we needed to kill all the bad things that could diminish our endeavor. Then [about ten years ago] we started to think: do we really need to do this – whatever it was? Do we really need to *control* the problem? *Is* it really a problem? Can we do something else to alleviate the likelihood or severity of that issue? What will happen if we promote life instead of inflicting death? What if we aid the life in the soil and the health of the plants rather than attend to the death of potential diseases?

'I believe it's all about still being here in 60 years' time, and making better wine then than we do now. We are still closer to the start of that journey than the end, but we have come a long way from where we were. And interestingly – and pleasingly – we are growing better fruit than ever; the vines are in as good a condition as ever [I actually feel they're even healthier]; and by not beating up on our land and plants we will have a healthier, safer future.'

Cobaw Ridge

I'm crunching across the granite sands of the Cooper family's 5-hectare Cobaw Ridge vineyard, 600 metres up the Great Divide, when it suddenly hits me: the soil here looks and feels like coarsely ground white and black peppercorns – which is exactly the fine, prickly aromatics that so often permeate the wines grown here. Yes, this is a completely unscientific, utterly romantic association between place and taste, but take a sniff and a sip of the Cobaw Shiraz Viognier and you'll see exactly what I mean: the wine walks a fine ridgeline between spiky spice and peppercorns and floral perfume on one side, and taut, nervy acidity and sappy twigginess on the other. You can taste this clear, cool sense of place in the mineral acidity of the Cobaw chardonnay, a clean brace of tartness clamped around concentrated candied citron fruit; and you can taste it in the Cobaw lagrein, a marvellously juicy, purple, angular wine that, not surprisingly, bears more than a passing resemblance to lagrein from its northern Italian high-country homeland of the Sudtirol. These are, simply, brilliant wines of terroir.

Alan and Nelly Cooper first planted vines at Cobaw in 1985, releasing the first commercial Australian lagrein in 1999. There has been a renewed sense of energy and enthusiasm here in the last couple of years: the Coopers have converted the vineyard to certified organic viticulture, and their son, Joshua, has started the oenology course at Adelaide Uni, as well as working for Dean Hewitson in the Barossa. 'It gives Nelly and I a great feeling to think that what we have put our blood, sweat and a few tears into will be in good hands in the long term,' says Alan.

At Joshua's urging, the Coopers have started applying the biodynamic preparations to the vineyard, and from the 2007 vintage, they renamed the shiraz viognier, preferring to call it 'syrah' – a much more accurate representation of the style. Alan is increasingly interested in the charter of quality devised by Nicolas Joly's association of biodynamic vineyards, 'Return to Terroir'. The Cobaw Ridge estate-grown wines already satisfy almost all of the criteria – no synthetic chemicals, hand-pruned, hand-harvested, no acid, yeast or enzyme additions, etc. – and from the 2010 vintage are also biodynamically grown.

Curly Flat Vineyard

Growing up on a farm, Phillip Moraghan says he struggled with the use of chemicals. 'I never understood how you could walk a sheep through an arsenic footbath one day and then a week later knock it over and eat it.' He always grappled with his conscience whenever he used chemicals such as herbicide on his 14-hectare vineyard near Lancefield. So, in 2005, he stopped. In 2008 he even managed to get by without using copper and sulphur. Now, slowly and thoughtfully, he's adopting biodynamic practice and philosophy: conducting moon planting trials, for example, and measuring how ferments change according to the astro calendar.

'I've noticed over the years that our ferments can be erratic,' he says. 'Sometimes they take longer to start; sometimes you need to put a handbrake on them. Our native yeasts can go pretty hard: they can make the ferments bubble up like blancmange, producing massive CO_2, which may account for the lower alcohol levels, higher glycerol and softer mouthfeel you find in our wines. I'd love to know if there's a pattern to it.'

The Curly Flat wines do have gorgeous texture, it's true. The chardonnays exhibit a soft, powdery minerality, a lemon/chalk quality sitting underneath round waxy citrus fruit. The pinot gris is spot-on stylistically: lots of fat, slightly oily grape pulp coats the tongue, finishing with plenty of apricot fuzz. And the pinot noirs, fermented with a proportion of whole bunches, and lots of whole berries, are all about sinewy forest fruit and sappy, lingering complexity on the finish.

While Phil places some of the credit for the complex qualities of these wines on the wild yeasts and his playful experimentation (each vintage he might have 30 or more separate ferments on the go, trialling this technique, sussing out that clone), he also admits that he's very lucky to have a lovely site: gentle slopes of really deep, free-draining red basalt-derived soils.

'There's something about soil that I love,' he says. 'The smell of it, the feel of it, it's imprinted on me, the soil. We are custodians of our place, we really are. We have an obligation to improve it.'

Hanging Rock Winery

Hanging Rock is Macedon's biggest winery, producing a whopping 30,000 cases or more of wine a year, plus doing lots of contract winemaking work for other vineyards. Yes, everything's relative: this isn't, by national industry standards, all that much booze, but by regional standards, it's massive. Fruit comes from all over to fill the vats and barrels, from across Macedon and Heathcote and further afield in Victoria. But the best wines that John Ellis and his team make are grown very close to home, on the Jim Jim vineyard next to the winery, looking out to the imposing outcrop of the infamous Rock itself.

The relatively close-planted (4500 vines/hectare), low-trained vineyard on this cold, exposed, windy volcanic mound 700 metres above sea level produces edgy, intensely flavoured wines with exceptional natural acidity. The Jim Jim sauvignon blanc is consistently powdery, nettley and bracing; the Jim Jim RS Fifty Riesling (the RS refers to grams per litre of residual sweetness) has a lovely core of ripe grapey fruit, balanced by a super-tangy zestiness and a light (9 per cent alcohol), clean finish; the Petit Noir, a fresh, 11 per cent alcohol red made from Jim Jim–grown pinot noir and bottled under Hanging Rock's

Hanging Rock Winery, Macedon Ranges

quirky Odd One Out label, has sappy, strawberry-fruity perfume leading onto a juicy, fresh and lively mouthful of cranberry and cherry.

The real stars of the Jim Jim vineyard, though, are the sparkling wines, made with extraordinary passion and patience. John Ellis started making and putting aside reserve wines, the juice of pinot noir and chardonnay fermented and aged on gross lees in barrel, for Hanging Rock's Macedon Cuvée in the mid-'80s. This stock of increasingly nutty, rich, complex, aldehydic blending components gives each release of the Cuvée (an amalgam of roughly half current vintage and half reserve wines, aged on lees in bottle for at least three years) an amazing depth of flavour and personality. Not to everyone's taste, perhaps, but I love its tangy yeastiness and sherry-like overtones.

In 2006, Hanging Rock took this already take-no-prisoners style to another level with the first release of a late-disgorged version of the Macedon Cuvée. This wine – and subsequent releases, all disgorged after spending nine years on lees – is startlingly complex, with aromas of wholemeal bread, creamy ripe brie and truffle, and amazingly full-bodied but dry in the mouth, with a minerally, satisfying finish that lasts for ages. Exactly the kind of powerfully flavoursome bubbly that makes for heavenly drinking with fat, creamy, freshly shucked oysters. And I don't even *like* oysters.

Geelong

The story of the tiny Prince Albert vineyard, perched on a hillside just south of the city of Geelong, is a perfect metaphor for the region as a whole.

A century and a half ago, Swiss settlers recognised that this north-facing slope of red loam over limestone was perfect for growing grapes and planted what was to become one of the new colony's most famous vineyards. The same happened right across the region: Geelong soon became renowned for its fine, European-style 'burgundy', 'hermitage' and 'claret', until, in the 1870s, phylloxera reared its vicious little head and the vineyards disappeared.

Then, in the late 1960s and early 1970s, a small, passionate band of viticultural pioneers planted the first vineyards of the modern era, many on the old sites, including, in 1975, Bruce Hyett, who re-established Prince Albert as a pure pinot vineyard. The wines soon won widespread acclaim, thanks to their intense black cherry concentration, great clarity, edgy, sappy tannins and refreshing poise.

In the past few years, though, the huge potential of this gorgeous site has not been fully realised, due to a succession of difficult seasons and the failing health of the vineyard's founder. There is a parallel here with the sprawling region as a whole: while there are undoubtedly some great, internationally renowned vineyards, the region hasn't quite captured the imagination or loyalty of wine drinkers in its closest market, Melbourne.

In 2008, David Yates, a long-time fan of Prince Albert wines, bought the vineyard and started the long, slow process of rejuvenation, replacing the old, inefficient irrigation, for example, in an attempt to bring the drought-ravaged vines back to full production. Despite his day job as an industrial chemist, Yates has maintained the certified organic status of Prince Albert: he grew up on a farm and sees 'modern' organic methods as 'not too different to how we farmed when I was a kid'.

Hopefully, with a bit more committed organic love Prince Albert – and Geelong in general – can regain some of the glorious heights of the past.

Ray Nadeson and Maree Collis Lethbridge

It seems pretty obvious to me. Ray Nadeson is a frighteningly talented winemaker with an ever-deepening understanding of Geelong's varied terroirs. And since he and partner Maree Collis embraced biodynamic viticulture on their own 6-hectare vineyard, employing some serious non-interventionist philosophies in their straw-bale winery, the wines they make continue to get better and better.

And yet Ray remains sceptical about some of the wackier aspects of biodynamics, despite the fact that the methods have clearly improved the quality and health of his soil and vines. He credits the constantly improving quality of his wines to the increasing age of those vines rather than his increasing skill, even though he makes blindingly good booze from other people's often very young vines.

It's the scientist in him, I think, that compels Ray to cling to a veneer of self-deprecation and doubt. Both he and Maree have solid science backgrounds: he was a neuroscientist, she has a PhD in organic chemistry and has worked with the Environmental Protection Agency. Their analytical approach is applied to everything they do at Lethbridge, thinking deeply about why things are working (or not working) rather than just trusting on instinct and emotion.

Ray and Maree planted their vineyard in gritty black clay over honeycomb basalt and porous bluestone in the dry, windy northern reaches of the Geelong GI, in 1996. It's a challenging site, with the tough soils and sometimes harsh conditions having a stern devigorating effect on the vines and the yields. As a result, Ray and Maree soon started sourcing grapes from other Geelong vineyards to complement their meagre crop, and building long-term relationships with the owners of some outstanding sites: Ken and Joy Campbell's 40-year-old Rebenberg vineyard (formerly known as Mount Duneed), planted on a north-facing rise on the road down to Torquay, south of Geelong; and the Pindari pinot noir vineyard on red clay over limestone marl 25 kilometres north-west of the city.

As well as adopting organic and then biodynamic methods on their own vineyard, Ray and Maree also encourage the growers on their contracted vineyards to move towards greener viticulture; more successfully in some cases than others. Partly this is about environmental improvement – 'It really makes a difference,' says Ray. 'You can see that the vines are healthier, the leaves are thicker, the grape skins are thicker, more resistant to disease.' – but mostly it's about emphasising the terroir. 'Farming this way you can taste the differences that the soil brings in each bit of our own vineyard, especially when you compare it to the other vineyards we source fruit from,' he says. 'It's all about capturing those differences in the wines, and it's why we allow things to ferment naturally, using indigenous yeasts.'

One of the most impressive things about Ray Nadeson's winemaking is the clear knack he has with every variety he touches. (What's the wine equivalent of a green thumb, purple hands?) His sauvignon blancs – sourced usually from the southerly Rebenberg vineyard and either made simply, or given the whole wild-yeast, old barrel-ferment treatment – have exceptional floral perfume and lively acidity thanks to their coastal provenance. The sangiovese and shiraz, made from the stony, shallow soils of the Lethbridge site, have stunning depth and tannin concentration, brooding aromas and tightly wound structure. The Vin Gris, a blanc de noir made from free-run pinot juice, has fantastic texture and richness, with apricot skin fuzziness and a lingering, spicy, dry finish. The top wines in the Lethbridge stable – the Allegra chardonnay, Mietta pinot noir, Indra shiraz and Hugo George merlot cabernet (all named after Ray and Maree's children) – are simply some of the best examples of their respective varieties coming out of the Geelong region right now.

For the last few years, Ray has also managed to secure a parcel of riesling grapes from Rod and Sandra Barrett's 25-year-old, painfully low-yielding vineyard located in the cold climate of far south-west Victoria. The first year Ray took delivery of the grapes, he cautiously attempted a 'kabinett' style wine. 'I decided to go the whole hog and do what the Germans do,' he says. 'So I put most of the juice into big old barrels, three-year-old puncheons rather than stainless steel tanks, and let it ferment spontaneously. Because the natural acidity in the juice was so high, the wild yeasts found it hard going, and they really slowed up in some barrels. But when I tasted them, I found that, with about 60 grams of residual sugar, the wine tasted great, so I stopped most of the ferment [by cooling the must right down] and bottled that batch.'

Ray left the rest of the must in barrel to see what would happen. Eventually it stopped fermenting at about 12 grams of sugar, with a slightly higher alcohol (about 10 per cent, as opposed to the kabinett's 8 per cent). Even more cheekily, this second wine's name is a nod to Dr Loosen, the Mosel estate whose wines have inspired many Australian producers to delve into the Germanic style: he called it Dr Nadeson.

The two wines were so successful – and so different, despite sharing the same fine acidity and a similar intensity of flavour, thanks to the climate and soil of where they were grown – that Ray has repeated the exercise every year since.

Having the guts and faith to let something slip out of your control, and then having enough brains and talent not only to understand why it worked and employ the method the following year, but also to improve on it. Could this be some kind of definition of great winemaking?

Amietta

Nicholas Clark and Janet Cockbill's ten-year-old, 2.5-hectare vineyard is perched on a north-facing slope overlooking the Moorabool Valley. It's not far, as the crow flies, from Lethbridge Vineyard, but the terroir is quite different: dark, basalt-strewn rocky clay sitting over limestone. This marly undertow gives the meticulously fashioned wines a sensational purity and piercing cut: the Amietta riesling, for example, is an ultra-steely regional classic, with bracing lime zest and great freshness.

Nick and Janet have also, adventurously, planted about half a hectare of the northern Italian red grape, lagrein, and a little less of the Chilean/Bordeaux red grape, carmenere. They blend the former with shiraz: 'We feel the lagrein [about a third of the blend] brings lovely savoury, tobacco overtones, and a lift of violets on the nose. It gives the shiraz more depth and complexity,' says Janet. And the latter they blend with cabernets sauvignon and franc: the carmenere adds exuberant blackcurrant juiciness to the elegant minerality of the cabernets grown in this limestone-rich soil.

Following a stint working at the biodynamic Chapoutier winery in the Rhone, Nick and Janet try to organise the pruning, spraying and (where possible) picking in accordance with the lunar calendar. And since winter 2009, they have run the vineyard using what Nick calls 'facultative biodynamics', combining BD preparations such as the 500 horn manure and 501 horn silica (which he sees as microbiological 'starter cultures') with canola-based fungicide and liquid seaweed. With an annual production of just a few hundred cases and a loyal mailing list customer base, these gorgeous, sensitively grown, exquisitely labelled wines are not as well known outside of the region as they deserve to be.

The Bannockburn legacy: Bannockburn Vineyards, By Farr and Farr Rising

Okay, yes, it is just a *bit* mischievous to list these two wineries together: original Bannockburn Vineyards winemaker Gary Farr split acrimoniously with his former employer when he left a few years ago, leaving rather large and well-worn shoes for current Bannockburn Vineyards winemaker, Michael Glover, to fill. But the fact remains that these two extremely high-quality producers are located next to each other and while Gary Farr – and son Nick – have carried their winemaking philosophy down the lane with them to the new winery (whose design is eerily similar to the old winery), Michael Glover is taking the Farr legacy and tweaking it, finessing it, moulding it in his own image. In other words, while they might not like to admit it, you simply can't have one without the other.

Gary Farr is a model for many of the winemakers featured in this book: he was riding the whole low-input, minimal intervention, it's-all-about-the-terroir train long before it

By Farr and Farr Rising, Geelong

was trendy. Informed by a decade of vintages working at Domaine Dujac in Burgundy, Gary introduced close-planted vineyards (7000 vines or more per hectare) and wild yeast ferments back in the 1980s. Inspired by the new-wave Rhone wines of Alain Graillot in the early 1990s he radically changed the Bannockburn shiraz into a lighter, more peppery, spicy style, and went on to explore viognier, as a voluptuous, stand-alone varietal and co-fermented with his shiraz, at By Farr.

Son Nick has inherited his father's approach to winemaking ('I've been drinking wine since I was 16, eating smoked salmon, visiting Dujac and DRC. I didn't really have any choice,' he says), and employs similar techniques; although I find that the Farr Rising wines tend to be a little more elegant and restrained than the By Farrs. Recent vintages of Gary's wines have been brooding, lavishly textured wines: the viognier is one of the best in the country, with layers of honeysuckle-infused cream; the shiraz is an almost painfully intense amalgam of exotic spice and slinky purple fruit; the pinots are muscular, finely tannic, sweet-composty. By contrast, the Farr Rising chardonnay is savoury, wheatmealy, needing time to evolve in the bottle; the pale bronze-coloured saignée is rose-hippy, spicy; and the two regional pinot noirs have distinct, subtle character: the Mornington Peninsula is sappy, floral and the Geelong is drier, more earthy.

Over the road at Bannockburn, Michael Glover has made quite a few changes to the old regime. Since starting at the winery in 2005 he has turned off the irrigation (reducing the yield by a third), introduced earlier picking times (the chardonnay and pinot noir are now picked below 13 baumé), and no longer adds acid to the ferment (Gary Farr believes it's important to acidify early to compensate for the fruit's tendency to lose acid rapidly towards the end of the growing season). The idea, says Michael, is to refine the Bannockburn style, and allow more of the site to shine: 'In my opinion, a winemaker that routinely uses supplementary irrigation, acidification, packets of yeast, packets of enzyme, packets of tannin, packets of god knows what, betrays and denies any concept of terroir.'

The first few Bannockburn vintages under this new regime have been very impressive. The chardonnay is super-fine, still intense and concentrated, but with a lightness of touch and powdery acidity; and the pinot is exceptional, especially the 'reserve' level Stuart pinot (30-year-old vineyard, 100 per cent whole bunches in the ferment), with its deceptively pale colour, restrained perfume and tight, grippy hedgerow berry-like brightness of flavour.

Paradise IV

After an extended stint working in the winery at Giaconda in Beechworth and with his ongoing sideline as the Australian agent for Bordeaux-coopered Bossuet barrels, it was only natural for Doug Neal to eventually end up making his own wine. Paradise IV is the perfect place for him to flex his winemaking muscles, too: planted in the late 1980s by Graham and Ruth Bonney (still partners in the business) on the site of one of the original and best-known 19th-century Swiss vineyards north-west of the city, the two-hectare vineyard is rich in history and potential.

The soil is gravelly granite, washed down from the nearby Dog Rocks outcrop, over limestone and basalt. Apart from adding acid to the red must ('These warmer parts of the Geelong region are notoriously bad for retaining acidity,' says Doug), the winemaking is hands-off: alcoholic ferment and malo are both spontaneous, a proportion of whole bunches is included in all the red vats, gravity is used to rack the wines, and the reds are neither fined not filtered.

The result is some of the best new wines to have emerged from the region in recent years. The chardonnay is picked at around 12 baumé, fermented in big oak and spends its entire life before bottling a few months later on lees, no stirring, 100 per cent malo: it's a very fine, lemon-puff-like, lean and elegant expression of the grape. The Batesford shiraz (with a splash of cabernet and a drop of viognier blended in) is gorgeously pretty, supple, fine and approachable red wine; the Dardel (shiraz with a touch of cabernet), named after the founder of the original Paradise in the 1840s, James Dardel, is a wild and earthy red wine that tastes strongly of the granite sands it was grown in; and the Chaumont, a classical blend of cabernet, shiraz, cab franc and merlot, tastes a little as you imagine 19th-century Bordeaux might have tasted (back in the days when a little syrah from Hermitage was routinely added for backbone and depth): spice and wild bramble fruit come charging through the firmly wrought, dusty herbal tannins.

Gippsland

Gippsland is a slumbering giant of a wine zone. The vineyards on its western rump are 300 kilometres or so from those on its eastern tip. And all manner of soils, mesoclimates, rainfall patterns and landscapes are laid out in between. As a result, locating the heart of Gippsland wine has always been difficult. But the vastness of the zone could well turn out to be its greatest asset in the years ahead.

As climate change bites, rain will become an increasingly precious asset. And there is rain here, especially in the south-west, in the heart of dairy country – 1200 millimetres throughout a good year, half of that falling in the growing season – more rain and humidity certainly than many regions to the north and west. There are hills here, too: gorgeous slopes galore, with amazingly diverse pockets of mineral-rich silt and fat black loams and red clay. As the weather warms and vignerons escape the drying country further north, seeking to plant in cooler, moister spots, they will find sanctuary here.

A handful of truly outstanding producers already have.

Phillip Jones Bass Phillip

The personal and professional renaissance of Phillip Jones is one of Australian wine's great comeback stories.

At the end of the last century, for various reasons, some business-related, some private, the already famously cantankerous winemaker lost the plot a bit. His legendary, if inconsistent, wines went into a prolonged slump. The cork-dorks continued to rave about their annual allocations, but in truth, the wines were really quite disappointing. The little girl with the curl (when they were good, they were very, very good, but when they were bad…) had turned into the empress with no clothes.

Signs that Phillip was back on track began with the 2004 vintage: suddenly here were wines that once again possessed the unique robustness of spirit that had characterised the best Bass Phillip pinots from previous decades. By 2006, the revolution was in full swing: 'We chucked out 30 old barrels that year,' says Phillip. 'We waged a war on VA [volatile acidity] in the cellar.'

Since the 2007 vintage, the quality of the Bass Phillip wines has been as good as, or better and, crucially, more consistent than, ever before. The greater attention to detail in the winery is clearly paying off. But adopting biodynamic principles in the vineyard is also a contributing factor.

On a trip to Burgundy in 2006, Phillip had tasted many wines made using biodynamic techniques and was converted: 'Here were wines from people I'd been buying for 20 years, but they were different, because of the BD; I was blown away by how good they were, even Michel Lafarge's lowly little aligoté was fantastic.'

So from spring 2006, Phillip started applying biodynamic compost preparations to his already virtually organic vineyards. And he has been enormously impressed by the results. 'In just a couple of years I've seen the vines come into balance,' he says. 'In one vineyard we've always had trouble getting the juice and wine to fall bright; since going BD, I've had no problems. The use of biodynamic processes imparts energy to the end result. So, to me, biodynamic wines, if they're well done, are more energetic, they're more vibrant. And I see, in white wines sometimes, there's a luminescence. I also think you can taste the terroir more clearly now.'

And what terroir! Or rather: terroirs. Jones has five vineyard sites, mostly planted to pinot noir ('mostly MV6, too: clones don't matter when you're cropping as low as I am, and you can't taste the difference after a few years in bottle anyway') but also a dribble of chardonnay, gewurztraminer and gamay.

There are four hectares of vines on the oldest, Estate vineyard (also known, in characteristic Jones fashion as 'Head Office'), first planted in 1979 around the winery near Leongatha, plus one extremely close-planted pinot noir vineyard (17,000 plants squeezed into one hectare) across the road. Both these blocks are on deep, silty, grey ferrous loam with some buckshot running through it.

Twelve kilometres to the north, at Leongatha, the 10-hectare Village vineyard is on fine grey silt again, but has a more northerly aspect. Issan, 17 kilometres to the east of the winery, is just under 3 hectares on even finer, siltier, hungry soil, resulting in less vigorous vines and truculent cropping (five worthwhile vintages in 14 years, says Phillip). And the Belrose vineyard, 25 kilometres to the north, is 3 hectares on heavy mudstone.

Bass Phillip viticulture and winemaking is uncompromising: all the vines are dry-grown, low-yielding (as little as 120 grams of grapes per vine in some cases), with the fruiting wire at knee height. 'The closer you get to disaster the closer you get to the best solution,' he says. 'And the closer you get to serious fungal disease problems the closer you get to the finest, most complex aromatics in wine, I reckon. That's why we've got grapes so low off the ground: because the humidity there is double what most Australian growers have them at.'

The pinots are crushed and destemmed and given a few days cold soak (waiting for natural yeasts to kick in) before a week-long fermentation, then straight to barrel (mostly Allier) and bottling by hand after about 15 months. Wherever possible, Jones will avoid pumps, believing that the wine can be 'torn' by the process; buckets are used to transfer the newly fermented wine from vat to press. Fining and filtration get short shrift in this winery, too: a wine might be passed through a 'mothcatcher' – 150 micron steel mesh – before bottling if it's lucky.

The Bass Phillip whites are better than ever. The gewurztraminer ('my hobby wine' says Phillip) is all steely cut and mineral and puckering dryness. The 'standard' Estate chardonnay has flashes of opulent golden richness and luscious fat, while the Premium chardonnay, which spends longer on lees, is tighter, leaner and more wheatmealy.

The rosé is a delight, juicy rosehips, summer flowers and dried herbs, as is the gorgeously succulent and ripe gamay. There is a similar succulence and richness to the Belrose pinot noir, and while I adore its heady dark raspberry fruit, Phillip is typically dismissive: 'Yes, it has the deepest fruit of all my pinots, but that mudstone soil gives it the shortest finish.'

There is outstanding definition in Phillip's other pinots now. The Issan reflects its tough site: pale, tart and spicy, with an underlying autumnal woodiness. The Crown Prince, made from the Village vineyard, is earthy, open, textured, forward. The Estate is upright, rich and layered. The Premium, mostly made from the oldest vines on the original property, is tighter, with more powdery tannins and finesse. And the Reserve – a single barrel's worth made from a small block of vines that exhibit what Phillip calls 'bunchus erectus', where the grape clusters literally point upwards instead of hanging down – is rich in brawn and flavour.

And then there's the pinot made from that single, crazy close-planted hectare. This is the wine I'd choose if I wanted to prove to any sceptic, anywhere, that Australia is capable of producing jaw-dropping pinot noir: as well as the vigorous intensity of wild forest fruit that characterises the best of Phillip's other pinots, there is a profound, assertive quality to the tannins and the lingering finish that takes your breath away. And as Phillip points out, the plants are yet to reach their tenth birthday; it is slightly scary to imagine how good the wine from this special site will be when the biodynamically grown vines are mature.

Moondarra

I've known Neil Prentice since he worked as Donlevy Fitzpatrick's irrepressible, big-dreaming, right-hand wine man at the groundbreaking George Hotel in St Kilda in the early 1990s. I was working on the now-defunct *Divine* magazine in an office upstairs but spent quite a bit of time in the bar downstairs, listening to – and relishing the results of – Neil's crazy schemes. Single-vineyard Mornington Peninsula pinots bottled under The George's own label; crisp white pinot grigio from the King Valley, years ahead of its time; and eventually, from Neil's family farm at Moondarra, heading up into Gippsland's northern mountain country, his very own pinot and some of the most incredible, pasture-raised Wagyu beef I've ever tasted.

'There's a synergy between Wagyu cattle and pinot noir,' says Neil, smiling cheekily as he leads to the punchline. 'They're both more difficult to grow than other varieties. You have to keep crops low; they need to be grown properly – which means naturally; and they've both got more complexity of flavour than sauvignon blanc.'

You can taste the spirit of place in both meat and wine from Moondarra: the hard volcanic country in the foothills of the Victorian Alps gives a strong ferrous minerality to the farm's produce: a tang behind the sweet Wagyu fat, and a backbone to the pinot's dark cherry fruit.

'Many years ago I was strongly of the opinion that the concept of finding the flavour of soil in wine was a crock of shit,' says Neil. 'Now that I can see it happening in my own vineyard, I believe it's *all* about the soil.'

The 2-hectare pinot noir Moondarra vineyard produces two quite different wines: Samba Side is made with about 70 per cent whole bunch inclusion, and is bolder, chunkier, firmer; while Conception has only 50 per cent whole bunches, and is spicier, more taut. Both have a firm core to them, like a dark, central supporting stalk, as well as intense, almost dried currant concentration. They're not pretty, charming pinots. They're serious, savoury drinks.

Neil produces a much more approachable pinot gris under the Holly's Garden label from a vineyard at Whitlands, 700 metres up in the high reaches of the King Valley. For the number-crunchers, the stats on this wine are incredible: in recent vintages, it has carried around 16 per cent alcohol, 3.2 pH, 9 grams of acid, and 7 grams of residual sugar, which goes some way to explaining why it tastes so fabulously rich and honeyed and yet so fresh and balanced.

And he is experimenting with more adventurous styles such as his Ramato, a mostly gris (with a little chardonnay, pinot noir juice or riesling blended in depending on whether the gris needs extra weight, juiciness or more crispness), pale bronze-coloured wine made with plenty of oxidative juice handling, natural ferment and lots of lees in old oak.

Both Moondarra and Holly's Garden are farmed along biodynamic principles. 'Years ago I got into BD after hearing they were using it at DRC and Leflaive [in Burgundy],' says Neil. 'Seeing the cow horns reminded me of an incident from childhood at my uncle's farm at Garfield in Gippsland. I got into terrible trouble for digging up a pile of cow horns filled with cow shit. He was always doing things by the moon and had lots of lunar calendars around the place. So I asked him about biodynamics and he didn't know what I was on about. It was just the stuff his father, my grandfather, taught him about farming, lots of old methods that weren't mentioned in public for fear of ridicule or being burnt as a witch.

'Moondarra is biodynamic because I believe in that piece of dirt passionately and I want it to be sustainable for my kids to farm; although the second I kick the bucket they'll probably sell it. But that's okay, because if I've made it successful biodynamically someone who does love it will buy it and love it and will kiss my cows and talk to the vines.'

William Downie

Bill Downie arrived in a whirlwind of media hype a few years ago when he was working at De Bortoli in the Yarra Valley. Encouraged by De Borts' chief grape-treader, Steve Webber, this mostly self-taught young winemaker applied an uncompromising, Burgundian-inspired artisan approach to great effect, both in De Borts' own wines and in the fine, subtle pinots he soon started producing under his own, eponymous label (designed, in a stroke of marketing genius, by Reg Mombassa).

He appeared confident almost to the point of arrogance. He was disarmingly serious and articulate.

'It's only wine,' he once told me when I asked about his techniques. 'It's not that fucking hard. The less you do, the better. Getting the grapes right is the hard bit. Remington Norman's book on Burgundy is the best textbook I ever had. I'd read about how the top domaines made their wine, I'd buy the wine, drink it and figure out for myself what to do and what not to do.'

Life working for a big company (even one as progressive as De Bortoli) was never going to satisfy young Bill, though, and he has now set out on his own, purchasing, with his partner Rachel Needoba (a trained cheesemaker), a 40-hectare farm on a north-sloping hill just outside Yarragon in west Gippsland. The back-to-the-future approach is being taken to its logical conclusion in this lovely slope of red soil and ironstone gravel: the farm is run along biological principles, without synthetic chemicals, as a self-contained unit, with vegies, chooks and rare breed pigs feeding (eventually) on estate-grown hazelnuts, acorns and chestnuts (oooh, just *think* of the ham); and, of course, a close-planted (12,000 vines per hectare), dry-grown pinot noir vineyard, which will be cultivated when it's fully established using a draught horse.

While early vintages of William Downie pinot (from other people's vineyards) were good, the 2008 vintage wines, from three single vineyards and all fermented wild in big open-top *cuves* (wooden vats), really delivered on the promise of greatness. The Mornington Peninsula pinot, from the cool volcanic soil of Merricks, was all spice and florals; the Yarra Valley pinot, from the grey loam of the central valley, was svelte, cherry-juicy; and the Gippsland pinot, from a low-yielding vineyard in the volcanic clay of Leongatha, was solid, chewy and syrah-like.

Given all this marvellously earthy naturalness and Bill's passion for refined pinot noir, perfumed by the spirit of place, I found it slightly surprising when, in 2008, he left De Bortoli and started working for R Wines, the bold brash brand developed by Dan Philips of the US import business, Grateful Palate, and Barossa winemaker Chris Ringland. The R Wines portfolio includes labels such as Bitch grenache and Suxx shiraz and Evil cabernet. The wines are as in-your-face and unsubtle as their packaging. How would Downie go making 16 per cent alcohol McLaren Vale bruisers? I wondered.

Turns out, though, that R Wines was embarking on some new, very earthy, natural and terroir-driven projects: pinot from Oregon and Victoria; no-additions, wild-ferment gamay from Geelong-grown fruit; minimal intervention, single-vineyard grenaches from the Barossa. Over a glass of that Geelong-grown, unsulphured gamay, and amid talk of natural wine gurus, Pierre Overnoy and Jules Chauvet, Bill told me why he'd been attracted to the job: 'No other winery in Australia would allow me to make wine this way, on this scale. And I think it's important someone has a crack at making natural wines that are also commercial.'

William Downie, Gippsland

Bendigo

This is a region of two halves.

The wines, mostly red, mostly shiraz and cabernet, from the warm, flat plains to the north and west of the city of Bendigo, with their sun-baked red volcanic soils and russet-brown alluvial loams around Bridgewater-on-Loddon, tend to be big-boned and brawny, with inky black fruit and substantial, solid tannin, often wrapped up in sweet American oak.

The story is quite different south of Bendigo. Here, around Harcourt, Sutton Grange and Mt Alexander, and over towards Castlemaine and Maldon, the country is more akin to that of the south-western end of the Heathcote GI, and the north-western slopes of the Macedon Ranges, as are the newer wines produced here: spicy, syrah-styled shiraz, lean and savoury Italian varietals, and textural perfumed whites.

It's not soft and easy country here in southern Bendigo, though, by any means. Those Mt Alexander granite sands can be unforgivingly harsh and infertile if treated poorly: Adam Marks from Bress described the soil on parts of his property as 'Harcourt concrete' when he bought the vineyard in a fairly dilapidated state in 2005. And while it's cooler here, thanks to the altitude, it's not as wet as some other cool-climate wine regions. Still, given the increasing hardship associated with growing grapes in the north as it gets even warmer and drier, I believe that Bendigo's ultimate future rests down here rather than up there.

Gilles Lapalus
Sutton Grange Winery

Sutton Grange is the leading new winery in the cooler southern Bendigo region, and one of the most impressive new wineries in the country.

French-born, Burgundy-trained winemaker Gilles Lapalus arrived here in 2001 and quickly converted the three-year-old, 12-hectare vineyard to chemical-free, biodynamic viticulture. Gilles happens to be the son-in-law of Stuart Anderson, the visionary who established Balgownie vineyard in the late 1960s and consulted to Sutton Grange during its establishment. At 300 metres above sea level and planted in a mix of granite sand and clay, with some pockets of red basalt-derived loam, this is classic southern Bendigo terroir. It took a while for him to get a feel for the place, and for the effects of the biodynamics to become apparent, but Gilles is now capturing the soul of Sutton Grange exquisitely in the wines he makes.

All the wines – the 'second' Fairbank label (which might include fruit bought from other central Victorian growers) or the Estate label – are made using natural wine techniques such as wild fermentation in barrel, plenty of oxidative handling and solids/skin/lees contact for the beautifully layered, harmonious viognier and the absurdly good, Provençal-style rosé. (Incidentally, this rosé is best drunk with a dense, fudgy cheese called La Luna, produced by the outstanding Holy Goat artisan dairy next door to Sutton Grange.

The standout red here is the Estate syrah, a thrilling mouthful of vibrant spice, refined black cherry fruit and grainy, finely engraved tannins: you can really taste the essence of the terroir in this wine. But hot on its heels is Giove, a magnificent blend of sangiovese, cabernet and merlot with more cherries (red this time and glossier), a lick of polished wood and some deep rumblings of dark humus. Sangiovese is not the only Italian varietal here: the two great southern grapes fiano and aglianico were planted in 2004, and early trial wines show great promise. I'm particularly excited about the potential of the aglianico: once the vines are mature, it will be fascinating to see how this grape's notoriously mouth-gripping tannins are moulded by Sutton Grange's granite soils and Gilles Lapalus' sensitive handling.

Bress Wine, Cider & Produce

The first time I pulled up in the car park at Bress vineyard near Harcourt a couple of years ago, winemaker Adam Marks dragged me off to help him make some 'cow pat pit', one of the biodynamic compost preparations. I thought I'd come to taste some wines and have some lunch cooked in Adam's wood-fired pizza oven, but I soon found myself up to my elbows in fresh, sloppy, steaming manure, mixing in some crushed eggshells, basalt dust and a few sprinklings of chamomile, stinging nettle, oak bark and valerian.

Adam Marks has enthusiastically embraced biodynamics and other organic techniques such as undervine mulching as a way of improving the condition of the 'crappy granite gravel' soil he inherited when he and wife Lynne bought the place a few years ago. Then again, he does everything with an enthusiasm that borders on the manic: as well as the 11 hectares of vines, he breeds chickens (luxuriously accommodated in a large pen dubbed the Henndorf Hilton; his chook fetish is also the inspiration for the majestic rooster which graces the Bress labels), has guinea fowl, ducks, a productive market garden and an orchard full of cider apples and perry pears.

Grapes grown on the property make their way into three wines: a lovely, crisp, dry rosé with faded petal aromas and a light, savoury palate; an off-dry, grapey riesling; and, occasionally, a barrel's worth of intensely flavoured shiraz cheekily called Le Grand Coq Noir. Adam also sources fruit from far and wide for his other wines, all of which are well-made and frequently exceptional quality: grassy sem sav from Margaret River; fine and elegant Macedon chardonnay and pinot noir; deeply sexy, svelte Heathcote shiraz; and The Kindest Cut, a delicate, complex dessert wine produced from fruit left on the vine to dessicate after the canes have been snipped late in the season.

Pondalowie

When they first planted vines just outside the town of Bridgewater in 1996, young winemakers Dominic and Kristina Morris chose shiraz, cabernet and malbec, grapes that had already proven themselves in the Bendigo region. Not just any old clones, though: they sourced cuttings from classic vineyards in South Australia, including Wendouree in Clare and an ancient shiraz vineyard in the Stonewell sub-region of the Barossa.

This careful clonal selection, the dry red soils and warm climate, and fairly extractive winemaking techniques – fermentation in small, half-tonne pots, plenty of plunging, drain-and-return, and some extended maceration – produce pitch-black/purple wines with exceptional sturdiness of character, intensity of aroma and firmness of spirit. The cabernet malbec in particular is, I think, a modern classic: dark iodine and pitch perfume, not dissimilar to Wendouree, with concentrated little glossy currants and sensational grip.

In 1997, keen to expand, and inspired by Dominic's experience making red wine and port each northern hemisphere vintage at Quinta do Crasto in Portugal, the winemaking couple also took a punt on tempranillo, planting a third of their new 4-hectare vineyard to the Iberian grape. This was well before the current tempranillo trend took off; at the time it was a risk for a small producer.

The risk paid off. Even in the hot northern Bendigo summers, the tempranillo seldom ripens to more than about 13.5 baumé, at which point it can be left to develop richer flavour, more mature tannins. The early vintages of Pondalowie's unwooded tempranillo, called MT, or 'minha terra', Portuguese for 'my land', were a revelation: spot-on varietal characters of black cherry, leather, cinnamon spice and succulence, overlaid with that characteristic northern Bendigo menthol twang. This was the wine that first validated my pet theory (formulated on a trip to Spain in the mid-'90s) that central Victoria is a perfect place to grow this classic Spanish red grape.

Yandoit Hill

Colin and Rosa Mitchell's small, 20-year-old Yandoit Hill vineyard on the shallow red slopes of a volcanic hill is tucked away in the very southern end of the Bendigo region, just this side of the border from the Macedon Ranges GI.

This stark, volcanic country north of Daylesford was home to a thriving gold rush community in the middle of the 19th century: in its heyday in the 1860s, Yandoit boasted 2000 residents and seven pubs. Today you can see some evidence of that prosperous past in the few large stone houses, mostly abandoned, standing proudly in bare paddocks.

The Mitchells have long been active members of Melbourne's Slow Food community: Colin is a past president of the local convivium and Rosa cooks brilliantly simple, heartfelt southern Italian dishes at inner-city foodie haunt, Journal Canteen. It made sense, given this background and Yandoit's Italian heritage, to continue the theme at their vineyard, where early, pioneering plantings of nebbiolo and barbera were joined in the mid-1990s by the Piedmontese white grape, arneis.

Colin soon found the grape lived up to its Italian nickname of 'the little rascal'. 'It's a bastard of a thing to grow,' he says. 'It crops very poorly, but I kind of like it, because it's so quirky.'

I love it. Colin makes his arneis into a nervy, bone-dry white, with typically varietal pear-skin roughness of texture and a long, mineral-laden finish. It's not polished, clean or pristine, but it's a lovely, characterful drink. His simply made reds, the Italian varietals and a cabernet blend, are similarly savoury and lean and cry out for Rosa's food.

When establishing their vineyard, the Mitchells became very close to an elderly neighbour, Vince, whose family had settled in Yandoit in those early, heady days. He died a couple of years ago, and much to their surprise, Vince left Colin and Rosa a substantial

Sutton Grange Winery, Bendigo

part of his property. For it contained treasures: as well as a collection of ramshackle stone buildings, the land boasts two small, run-down vineyards that were planted by Vince's ancestors sometime in the middle of the 19th century.

One patch of dry-grown shiraz bush vines, on a steep hillside behind Vince's house, although horribly neglected, is, amazingly, alive. The old man would often take a chain-saw to the gnarly plants over the years because he couldn't be bothered maintaining them, but the vines kept shooting, refusing to die. Colin is in the process of rejuvenating the vines, and will eventually make a single-site wine from them.

The other vineyard is further down the hill, in the middle of a paddock leading down to the creek. Here the vines were originally inter-planted with an orchard, the traditional Italian way, and many have grown wild, winding their way up equally feral olive and fruit trees. Colin's not absolutely sure what varieties they are: some of the vines have been identified as shiraz, mourvedre and cinsault, but there are others, white and red, that have eluded identification.

In 2008, Colin dragged out some tall ladders (wild vines develop bunches high off the ground), picked as many of the grapes as he could reach and made wine from these old plants. The wine, called Giupponi, in honour of Vince, is a spine-tingling taste of history: just 12 per cent alcohol, and with no acid addition required, it's a wild, rustic and earthy red with more concentration and fruit weight than you'd expect from completely untended vines. Remarkably close, you can't help feeling, to the taste of the wines drunk in Yandoit 160 years ago.

Heathcote

This is personal. I've said this a few times before in various magazine articles and books, and I'm sure I've bored friends witless with my frustrated ramblings over the years, but I'm going to say it again because it's true: if I ever yield to that deep, lingering, totally mad urge to plant a vineyard, Heathcote is where I'd go.

I still have a dream to make my own wine. I have this image of a sturdy but supple, dark and concentrated but elegant red wine, a blend, perhaps, of the grapes I love the most: tempranillo and carignan, maybe with a little shiraz for oomph and malbec for perfumed lift…Made from dry-grown, biodynamically farmed vines in Heathcote.

Why Heathcote? Because it has that north-of-the-Great-Divide warmth. Not much water, it's true. But I'm in no hurry. I'm not chasing big crops. Just intense flavour. And because Heathcote is amazing country. You can see it when you walk through or drive past the best vineyards. You can even see it from 30,000 feet as you fly past on your way from or to Sydney: the Mount Camel Range, where the famous red Pre-Cambrian soil and greenstone bursts from the ground and on whose slopes many of the region's vineyards are planted, rises from the surrounding flat land like a giant, fat earth serpent. Or (more accurately, perhaps, if less romantically) a gargantuan geological scab.

The regional winegrowers association's own description of their terroir explains it best: 'The Heathcote area can be considered as two slabs of rolling, folded, eroded sedimentary rocks separated by a strip of super complex minerals formed by volcanoes, igneous intrusion and metamorphosed sediments with all sorts of mineral lying around in the rubble. However there is another complication. Press on along the road to Eppalock Bridge 6 kilometres from town and you run into the residues of those ice sheets that grooved the rocks south of Tooborac. The rolling country here is made up of gravel dropped from the toe of an ice sheet or glacier flowing north and west, off the Dividing Range.'

See what I mean? Exciting stuff, isn't it? Why *wouldn't* you want to plant a vineyard there?

Ron and Emily Laughton
Jasper Hill

The web of influence that the Laughton family and Jasper Hill have woven across the Australian wine landscape extends from their nuggety 35-year-old hillside vineyards and winery right in the heart of Heathcote to the distant shimmering horizon and beyond.

Locally, in Heathcote, Jasper Hill wines are the touchstone, the beacon, the *ne plus ultra*: the Georgia's and Emily's Paddock shirazes are the region's wine royalty, the two reds that first proved how incontrovertibly exceptional this place is for growing grapes. They are the models, in many ways, for all Heathcote red wines; the ones that many other winemakers try to emulate, and the ones against which all others are ultimately judged. The Laughtons' long-term, uncompromising commitment to minimal intervention winegrowing – absolutely no irrigation; organic and biodynamic farming; meticulous fruit sorting at harvest; spontaneous ferment and malo; minimal acid addition – has emboldened many other Australian winemakers to head down a similar path. And their commitment to their terroir, making wines that are true expressions of place and time, has brought them fame around the globe.

The Laughtons have also had a big influence on the way I think about Heathcote wines, about Australian wines, about biodynamic wines and about wine in general.

Jasper Hill founders Ron and Elva Laughton have a firm view of why they do what they do. 'We make our living from the soil, so we must keep our soil living,' is Elva's catchcry, a deceptively simple philosophy that should be enshrined at the core of a national wine industry strategy.

The 2004 vintage of Jasper Hill's amazingly good and often overlooked riesling was one of the wines that flicked a switch in my mind connecting biodynamic viticulture with quality. While previous vintages of this wine were very good, this particular vintage – the first to benefit from the full effects of the use of BD preps in the Jasper Hill vineyards – had an extra layer of taste, an added dimension in the mouth, a deeper satisfaction on the finish.

Visiting the Jasper Hill vineyard at the height of a hot Heathcote summer and seeing the low-trained, dry-grown vines cowering from the glare, a covering of small leaves barely shading straggly bunches of tiny grapes, I am in awe at the resilience (some would say foolhardiness) of the plants, and the people who choose to grow them without supplementary watering. Tasting the produce of that difficult season in bottle years later, the awe is rekindled: here is a glowing black purple wine, oozing sophisticated scents of sandalwood and glossy currants, full of life and vitality and slinky firm tannin on the tongue. From such ancient red earth, and from such scorching sun, the vines can coax such wondrous tastes.

And such *different* tastes. The remarkable ancient geological history of the Heathcote region lends itself to an extensive, educational exploration of terroir, on both a micro and macro scale. Georgia's Paddock and Emily's Paddock vineyards are on that ancient, glowing red Pre-Cambrian soil just a couple of kilometres apart. The former, from slightly deeper soil, is more robust and fleshy, and the latter, from skinnier soil, is more concentrated and elegant. Both wines are in stark contrast to daughter Emily Laughton's own Occam's Razor shiraz, made from grapes grown on a vineyard to the west of the Pre-Cambrian ridge, on hungrier, more granite-sandy soils, and showing dustier perfume and leaner, more savoury tannin.

The Occam's Razor project and Emily's increasing involvement in the day-to-day running of Jasper Hill are just two of many developments here over the last decade or so. At the turn of this century, in conjunction with biodynamic winemaker Michel Chapoutier from the Rhone Valley, Ron planted a new vineyard called Cambrien, next to Georgia's Paddock, using a combination of shiraz cuttings from the Laughtons' own vines and cuttings from Chapoutier vines in the Rhone. The wine from this vineyard, called La Pleiade, is a stunningly dense, firm and brooding expression of both grape and region. The pair of winemakers get on so well they also co-own a vineyard in Roussillon, in France's hot south, and make a gutsy, wild red called Agly Brothers.

The Laughtons pioneered nebbiolo in Heathcote, producing a wine that is both fiercely regional (that alluring sandalwood perfume comes barrelling through when you take a sniff) and unmistakably varietal (a massive blanket of dryness drapes itself across the back of your tongue when you sip). The 'new' vineyard, Cornella, planted in 1998 on the north-east facing deep Pre-Cambrian slopes of the Mount Camel Range – a vineyard the Laughtons like to call their 'rockery garden' – has yielded a powerful, brooding grenache, with surprisingly delicate spice perfume wrapped in a stone lattice of tannin.

Greenstone

If you wish to establish a vineyard in Heathcote, you are obliged to plant shiraz. It's not official policy, of course; there's nothing written in stone. The Heathcote Winegrowers Association won't come along and inspect your vineyard to make sure you do. But it's compulsory, nonetheless: there is just an assumption that you will. After all, shiraz *is* the grape that made the region's reputation.

The group of highly experienced wine men behind Greenstone, one of the region's newest and most impressive ventures, planted shiraz when they established the vineyard in 2003. Eighteen hectares of shiraz, to be precise. Well, they'd be mad not to, wouldn't they? But because of who they are, they also planted smaller blocks of tempranillo, monastrell (aka mataro or mourvedre) and sangiovese. And it's these latter varieties, I think, that will make Greenstone's reputation.

The credentials are impeccable. The vineyard is a collaboration between UK wine importer and merchant, David Gleave, Australian viticulturist Mark Walpole and Italian consultant winemaker Alberto Antonini. Gleave specialises in wines from Italy and the New World through his company, Liberty Wines. During his 20-year tenure as viticulturist for Brown Brothers in the King Valley, Walpole introduced many new alternative grape varieties; he also has his own small vineyard in Beechworth, where he grows tempranillo. Antonini works with vineyards in Italy, Spain, California and Argentina, as well as Australia. And the wines are made by Sandro Mosele at Kooyong on the Mornington Peninsula. If anyone has an instinctive affinity for savoury-tasting Mediterranean grapes, it's Sandro.

Alternative varieties are nothing new in Heathcote, of course. Jasper Hill has nebbiolo and grenache; the Wanted Man vineyard produces an excellent, textural marsanne blend, as well as a little juicy dolcetto in their complex shiraz; Ian 'Bomber' Rathjen makes a very good, lithe and lean sangiovese as well as burly shiraz at the Whistling Eagle vineyard; and the Heathcote Winery was one of Australia's first producers of viognier back in the 1980s.

Sandro Mosele is also making the wines for the brand new Chalmers vineyard, planted a little north along the ridge from Greenstone. This vineyard boasts a remarkable selection of Italian red grapes, including negroamaro, lagrein, sangiovese, nero d'avola, aglianico and sagrantino, and when these vines mature and the wines appear over the next couple of years they will redraw the map of expectation and assumption in the region. In the meantime, Greenstone's sangiovese provides a glimpse of that new, different future.

Until then, Italian varieties remain a niche proposition in Heathcote. And an Italian winemaker is the last person you expect to hear supporting regional styles and terroir in Australian wine. But Alberto Antonini is no ordinary Italian winemaker.

'I hear people in Europe say that New World countries have no terroir,' he says. 'This is wrong, absolutely. It is nothing more than oenological racism. When Mark was still working for Brown Brothers and took me to see their vineyards in Heathcote, I liked very much the soil, the greenstone rocks in it. And I liked very much the flavour this terroir gave the grapes.'

Under Antonini's guidance, the Greenstone vineyard is relatively close-planted (4500 vines per hectare) in an east–west orientation, running up and down the hill (rather than the north–south, along-the-ridge orientation favoured by many other growers), to minimise the debilitating effects of the burning afternoon mid-summer sun on the exposed berries.

The shiraz, blended with around 10 per cent monastrell, is a complex, elegant beast, with autumnal perfume, medium body and a dense, grainy texture. All classic expressions of that greenstone-rich Pre-Cambrian soil.

The sangiovese, produced from new Tuscan clones of the variety, is a heavenly mix of Heathcote sandalwood aromatics and the most amazing, fine, powdery tannic grip that gently hugs your tongue and refuses to let go. It's a new benchmark for sangiovese in Australia.

Red Edge

Back in 1999, I got a call from winemaker Peter Dredge, who a couple of years before had bought an old, dry-grown vineyard on the Pre-Cambrian soil to the south-west of Heathcote. 'I hear you're looking to buy some land up here,' he said. It was true: I'd travelled through the region the previous year, and was seriously excited about the potential of it. 'I think you should have a look at a block for sale not far from my place: 20 acres, gentle north-facing slope, same soil. I can't afford it right now, otherwise I'd buy it myself.'

So I went and had a look. Kicked the red dirt. Dreamed a little dream. And let the opportunity pass. In one way I'm kicking myself: even if I'd just bought the land (which at the time seemed a little expensive but now, thanks to Heathcote's booming popularity, looks like a bargain), not planted a vine and simply sold it off a few years later I would have made a bundle. But in another way I'm glad I didn't give in to my romantic urges, because Peter Dredge eventually bought the block, and did pretty much what I would have done: planted dry-grown shiraz, cabernet and tempranillo, the latter a variety that I think is eminently suitable to this dry, warm part of the world. And I have a sneaking feeling he's done a much better job with 'my' vineyard than I ever would have.

Peter's a very talented winemaker and the Red Edge shiraz (sourced from his old vineyard) is one of the region's best: opulent and deeply concentrated black fruit, so typical of the unirrigated Pre-Cambrian soil vineyards, reined in by a firm seam of tannin and a brooding, lingering undertow of woody spices. He also makes a sensational, gluggable red called Degree: a juicy, brambly blend of young-vine shiraz (from 'my' vineyard on Jacksons Lane), mourvedre (aka monastrell) and a splash of perfumed riesling from the Red Edge vineyard. But the wine I – predictably, perhaps – have the most sentimental attachment to is his tempranillo monastrell, a gorgeously rustic red with glossy cherry fruit from the tempranillo backed up by that wild, hedgerow tannic roughness you can get from mourvedre.

Vinea Marson

The wines that inspired Heathcote's boom period during the late-'90s and early-2000s were fairly opulent reds. Wines such as Wild Duck Creek's uniquely, extravagantly alcoholic Duck Muck shiraz and Jasper Hill's dense single-vineyard expressions had been lavished with high scores by Robert Parker and other influential American wine critics, and many wannabe vignerons flocked to Heathcote hoping to emulate the high-octane style. But the newcomers tended to copy the methods (pick the grapes really late, use lots of new oak, etc.) without understanding the methodology. And as a result, a succession of overblown, over-priced Heathcote shirazes beached themselves on fancy wine lists and bottle shop shelves. Big, charmless wines that lacked the sinewy, restrained integrity found at the heart of the original Heathcote classics.

Once that initial flush of overexcitement cooled down in the second half of the decade, wine drinkers went searching for a more subtle expression of Heathcote shiraz. They found that quieter taste in the lean, spicy wines of the cool granite country in the region's south-west corner from producers such as McIvor Estate and Redesdale Estate, and in earlier-picked wines from producers located outside the region, such as Bindi in Macedon (who bottle a gorgeously seductive, medium-bodied Heathcote shiraz called Pyrette) and peripatetic sommelier/winemaker Adam Foster (whose Heathcote label is called Syrahmi).

Some of the best examples of this third wave of savoury, subtle Heathcote wines are made by Mario Marson, who worked at Mount Mary in the Yarra Valley and at Jasper Hill before establishing his own Vinea Marson vineyard on the gentle slopes at the southern end of the Mount Camel Range.

Like many Heathcote shirazes, the Vinea Marson Syrah can carry fairly high alcohol (nudging 15 per cent), but is a velvety-textured, pepper-perfumed wine, thanks in part to the addition of a handful of viognier grapes at fermentation, and also to the use of a few different clones of shiraz to add complexity.

Clonal diversity is also the key to Marson's fantastic sangiovese and nebbiolo. 'My sangiovese clones include Mudgee clone [taken from the Montrose vineyard, originally imported by Carlo Corino], which is light and floral, as well as a Brunello clone from

Banfi and a Ruffina clone from Frescobaldi [both leading estates in Tuscany], which makes firmer, more tannic, darker wine.'

The resulting blend is brilliant: savoury and tightly structured sangiovese with the grape's classic cherry fruit and a hint of typical Heathcote mint and sandalwood aromatics. I also love Mario's pale, savoury, spicy rosé; a mostly sangiovese blend (with dollops of nebbiolo and cabernet) that sits at the top of the dry pink Australian wine pyramid.

Wild Duck Creek

For 30 years, David 'Duck' Anderson has been Heathcote's resident larrikin ratbag outsider. While most of the region's winemakers agree that the best reds are grown in the red Pre-Cambrian soil, the Duck reckons 'that's bullshit – aspect and climate and water are much more important to quality'. He would say that, of course, sourcing grapes as he does from a variety of sites on everything from deep red dirt up in the hot north of the region to the gritty clay and orange sandstone of his original estate vineyard, west of town.

He's been fiercely critical of the rush of planting that Heathcote experienced over the last decade, especially the investor-driven, broadacre vineyards in the north, past Colbinabbin. 'A lot of what's going on up there just reeks of money,' he told me during the middle of the boom. 'There are newcomers in it for the wrong reasons. They're barking up the marketing tree, arguing about logos and corporate identity, before they've even made anything. I reckon you have to go through ten or twelve years of just drinking what you make before you can start understanding what you're doing or selling it to anyone else. You need time in the saddle before you can say you really know how to ride a horse.'

His winemaking is often intuitive, seat-of-the-pants stuff, pushing flavour boundaries and richness to bursting point: his notorious Duck Muck shiraz can top 16 per cent alcohol, and all the Wild Duck Creek reds have plenty of power, drive and structure. It's no surprise to find he used to be a painter before he built his cellar, but he says, 'I've never touched a canvas since I started winemaking; the button that made me want to paint then makes me want to make wine now. I look at flavour and colour and creativity as all being part of the same impulse.'

It's no surprise either to find that Duck's son, Liam, has embraced his father's attitude to life and wine. As well as converting the family's 14 hectares of vineyards to biodynamic farming, Liam has also planted a small patch of bush vine tempranillo on his own property a couple of kilometres from the winery.

'I love the whole ethos behind biodynamics,' says Liam. 'The idea that there's something extra out there that we haven't been tapping into. I'm trying to highlight the differences between the sites we get fruit from across Heathcote. The sub-regional differences are so stark, we're mad not to celebrate that tremendous variation.'

Vinea Marson, Heathcote

Central Victorian High Country: Upper Goulburn and Strathbogie Ranges

There isn't a wine region called Central Victorian High Country. But there should be.

It was on the cards for a while. Or a version of it was. When the process of defining and registering Australia's Geographical Indications began in the mid-1990s, the winemakers of the Strathbogie Ranges north of Melbourne and the steep country of the Great Dividing Range to the east of Strathbogie talked about forming a big GI together called Central Victorian High Country. But a wine producer up in the King Valley went and trademarked a brand called High Country, which quashed any possibility of the evocative description being used as a GI. So the Strathbogie Ranges vignerons formed their own region. And the vignerons next door ended up, for some bizarre reason, going for the rather anodyne name of Upper Goulburn for their GI.

I think this is a shame, for a few reasons. While the Strathbogie Ranges as a name *almost* does justice to the hilly topography that lies within its GI boundaries, the name Upper Goulburn doesn't even *begin* to capture the spirit of the dramatic landscapes and ancient geology that form the country around Yea, Yarck, Murrundindi and Mansfield, all the way up to the snowfields of Mt Buller.

More importantly, the Strathbogies and Upper Goulburn regions are compellingly similar in many ways. The same sandy loam soils (mostly granite-based, but also derived from sandstone, ironstone and granodiorite), altitude (most of the best vineyards are above 300 metres) and climate (unequivocally cool) characterise both regions. I think it would have made much more sense, and would have been *much* more romantic, to group the two together under the name of Central Victorian High Country and allowed sub-regional identities to work themselves out over time. So, cheekily, that's precisely what I've done on these pages.

There's plenty to get excited about up here in the High Country. (See what I mean? Sounds good, doesn't it?). As well as producing some thrillingly spicy cool-climate shiraz – few are better than that from Plunkett Fowles, whose super-intense reserve shiraz is a distilled essence of the high plateau where the grapes were grown – and steely, perfumed rieslings and traminers, a number of High Country vineyards have found a niche for non-mainstream grapes. Kinloch Wines produce a superbly earthy, herbal and fine red wine from pinot meunier; and Lost Valley Winery pioneered the northern Italian grape cortese, and does such a good job with it – bone-dry, grainy pear skin texture, chalk and granite to finish – it amazes me more haven't planted the grape up here or elsewhere.

Will de Castella
Jean Paul's Vineyard

Like most grape growers, when Will de Castella encounters problems in his vineyard, he consults a textbook for advice. But instead of turning to the latest cutting-edge viticultural research, he browses through a precious collection of 19th-century volumes that once belonged to his grandfather, Francois de Castella, Victoria's early 20th-century state viticulturist and son of Yarra Valley wine pioneer, Hubert de Castella.

I'm grateful to Francois for 'sandalwood', one of the most accurate tasting descriptions I've heard for the haunting perfume you find in many central Victorian red wines: a perfume that's not quite mint and not quite eucalypt, but tends more towards some exotic, oily rainforest timber. In his role as Victorian state viticulturist, Francois was famous as the man who introduced the durif vine to Rutherglen. Today three members of the de Castella family are involved once again in the state's wine industry: Will de Castella at his tiny Jean Paul's Vineyard near Yea; Damien de Castella, Foster's Victorian regional vineyard manager; and Louis de Castella, whose eponymous winery is in Heathcote.

Like the other de Castellas, Will was brought up fully aware of his heritage. There was always wine on the dinner table, and he remembers as a kid masking the bottles for his dad's Beefsteak and Burgundy group tastings. Since 1994, when Will and his wife Heather established the 3-hectare Jean Paul's Vineyard in the rugged hills north of Melbourne, he's looked to those old books for inspiration. He planted shiraz and cabernet 'because grandfather recommended those for central Victoria', and is slowly establishing a couple of rows of the Austrian white grape, gruner veltliner, propagated from a clone that no longer exists in any Australian collection.

Will has never sprayed any chemicals on his vines, and adds nothing but minimal amounts of sulphur dioxide to his wine just before bottling. The vineyard was certified organic ten years ago; since 2002, Will has also been applying biodynamic compost preparations, and the vineyard is now certified BD.

The passion for biodynamics runs in

the family: Will's brother Lou de Castella has also converted the tiny, half-hectare, 35-year-old Heathcote vineyard he bought in 2004 to certified BD status. As well as buying in some grapes to produce a regional Heathcote shiraz, Lou bottles his spicy, deeply earthy estate-grown shiraz – which exhibits a subtle, persistent streak of sandalwood – separately.

'When we started,' says Will, 'people told us we were mad to go organic, that it'd be a breeding ground for pests and diseases that would destroy the vineyard.'

A decade and a half later, despite being ravaged by bushfire in 2006, the vineyard is not only still very much alive, but it's a picture of lovingly hand-tended health and is producing trophy-winning wines: the taut, elegant and spicy 2005 Jean Paul's Shiraz was named best under-$25 wine at the 2007 Great Australian Shiraz Challenge.

What amazes me about Will's wines is that, despite their low sulphur and lack of tannin or acid additions (both commonly used to make wines more 'stable' in the cellar), they are remarkably robust; indeed, the cabernet (appropriately labelled Bold Colonial Red) needs to breathe for a day at least before its firm, dusty tannins relinquish the scent of violets and iodine lurking within.

In that respect, they're wines that both speak very much of the hard, hilly country they're from, but they're also resolutely, proudly old-fashioned.

Grandfather Francois would be proud fit to bursting.

Baddaginnie Run

'My folks bought this land 130 years ago,' says Winsome McCaughey, standing on the northern foothills of the Strathbogie Ranges, looking out across her vineyard to the hot plains of the Goulburn Valley. 'They were astute Scots, and had to clear 10 acres of trees a year if they wanted to keep it. My mother remembered as a child when there was black wattle and red gum right across here. Remembers having to ride to Benalla along the creek lines, because there were so many trees. It wasn't like that when I was growing up here.'

The tree clearing continued, and eventually the property began to show signs of salt creeping up to the surface. 'We were in our 30s when it dawned on my generation that the land was dying,' she says. As a result, Winsome became active in the conservation movement, eventually becoming chief executive of Greening Australia in the 1990s. And back home at Baddaginnie she and her partner Snow Barlow embarked on a massive regeneration program comprising the planting of 100,000 trees and 24 hectares of grapevines.

We met Snow Barlow, Melbourne University viticulture professor, in the first part of this book, speaking in his role as one of Australia's foremost experts on the impact of climate change on the wine industry. Initially, says Snow, the vineyard was established as a high-value cropping venture (i.e., the grapes would all be sold to large wineries), but falling grape prices soon forced their hand.

'We started making wine under our own label earlier than expected,' he says. 'And I won't pretend it's been easy, having to sell it all. But it's worked out well: if you're only a grower you can be at the bottom of the heap in discussions with wineries, but winemakers tend to take you more seriously if you make wine from your own grapes, too. And at wine conferences it helps me spread the message about climate change when I am introduced as a fellow grape grower and producer.'

Moving from being growers to producers is not the only unexpected modification to the Baddaginnie Run business plan. When they first planted the grapes in 1996, says Winsome, 'It was so wet the bottom paddocks would get boggy. Now it's much warmer and drier.'

Luckily, the main two grapes at Baddaginnie, verdelho and shiraz, are able to cope quite well with the new conditions: the verdelho, in particular, seems to like it here, producing a flavoursome dry white full of corn and nectarine and wheat characters.

In 2006, Snow Barlow helped develop the Strathbogie Ranges Terroir Research Project, an ongoing analysis of the viticultural landscape of the region and how it might adapt to climate change. 'What this does is mimic the process of natural selection,' says Snow. 'We want to find out what we do best here by looking at the soils, water availability, varieties and clones, all the viticultural details, and then feed that data into climate change modelling. We're doing it first in the Strathbogie region, and we'll then go national.'

When I last visited, then-vineyard manager Leonie Stevens said: 'It's knowledge that will help you best manage your place. The landscape will express itself in the fruit if you're managing the vineyard in accordance with that landscape.'

She took the idea further, explaining why she was moving towards organic practices in the vineyard: 'If you're just quiet and watchful, the environment will often solve problems by itself. I've learned not to panic. Learned that I don't always need to reach for the silver bullet. We've all got to slow down and stop tripping up over ourselves all the time.'

Delatite

The 40-year-old Delatite vineyard near Mansfield, right up in the cool eastern edge of the High Country, built its reputation on ultra-steely, crisp dry whites – riesling and gewurztraminer in the early years, with pinot gris joining the gang in the new millennium. David Ritchie, who bought the winery from his parents in 2007, also produces plenty of other wines: rather minty reds; the obligatory sauvignon blanc; some interesting sweeter styles of riesling and gewurz inspired by Germany and Alsace. But it's the three characterful, aromatic dry whites – the riesling with its great purity and line, the gewurz with its old-rose perfume, the gris with its exotic spices – that still make Delatite, for me, one of the region's best producers. Not only that, but the wines have been steadily improving, I think, since 2002 when David started adopting biodynamic techniques in the vineyard, and treating the gris and gewurz to extended post-ferment lees contact.

The first bit of the Delatite property to have the biodynamic preps applied and herbicide taken away was the unforgettably named Dead Man's Hill vineyard, planted in an infertile, rocky outcrop 100 metres higher than the main vineyards and grown without irrigation for much of its 35 years. Soon after converting to BD, David noticed an improvement in the soil structure in this vineyard, and felt a certain resilience, a stiffness in the vine leaves. From the 2005 vintage, before I even knew Delatite was using BD preps, I noticed a clear improvement in the quality of the Dead Man's Hill gewurztraminer: the wine had extra complexity, vibrancy of fruit, length.

'Better fruit composition follows from healthy vines, and healthy vines tend to follow on from healthy soil,' says David. 'Simple, really.'

Rees Miller Estate

It was inevitable, really, that Sylke Rees and David Miller would end up running a small certified biodynamic vineyard. She studied astrology in the 1990s; he was one of the founders in the early 1970s of *Grass Roots* magazine, the self-sufficiency bible. So when they settled on their 60-hectare farm just outside Yea and planted 7 hectares of red grapes – pinot, shiraz, merlot, cabernet – in 1998, it made perfect sense to run the place using BD principles.

It's cool here, but it's tough, dry country, and while that dryness helps keep disease pressure low (a good thing for organic and biodynamic growers) it means that the vines struggle in low-rainfall years, like the last ten or twelve have been in southern Victoria.

The mudstone soil the vines are planted in contains lots of iron and manganese – good for colour in red grapes, according to David. When I went for a walk through the vineyard here, the undervine weeder had just been through the rows, and the soil had been churned up a little: it was cloddy, stoney and bitty. You can taste this textural quality in the Rees Miller wines, especially in the Thousand Hills shiraz, with its pitch-black purple hue, dense aroma of woody spices crushed between rocks, and grainy, tongue-hugging, brooding tannins.

'I think we're lucky we found this place,' says David. 'There is real flavour here, real terroir here. And because we keep the yields low, you can taste that terroir in the wines.'

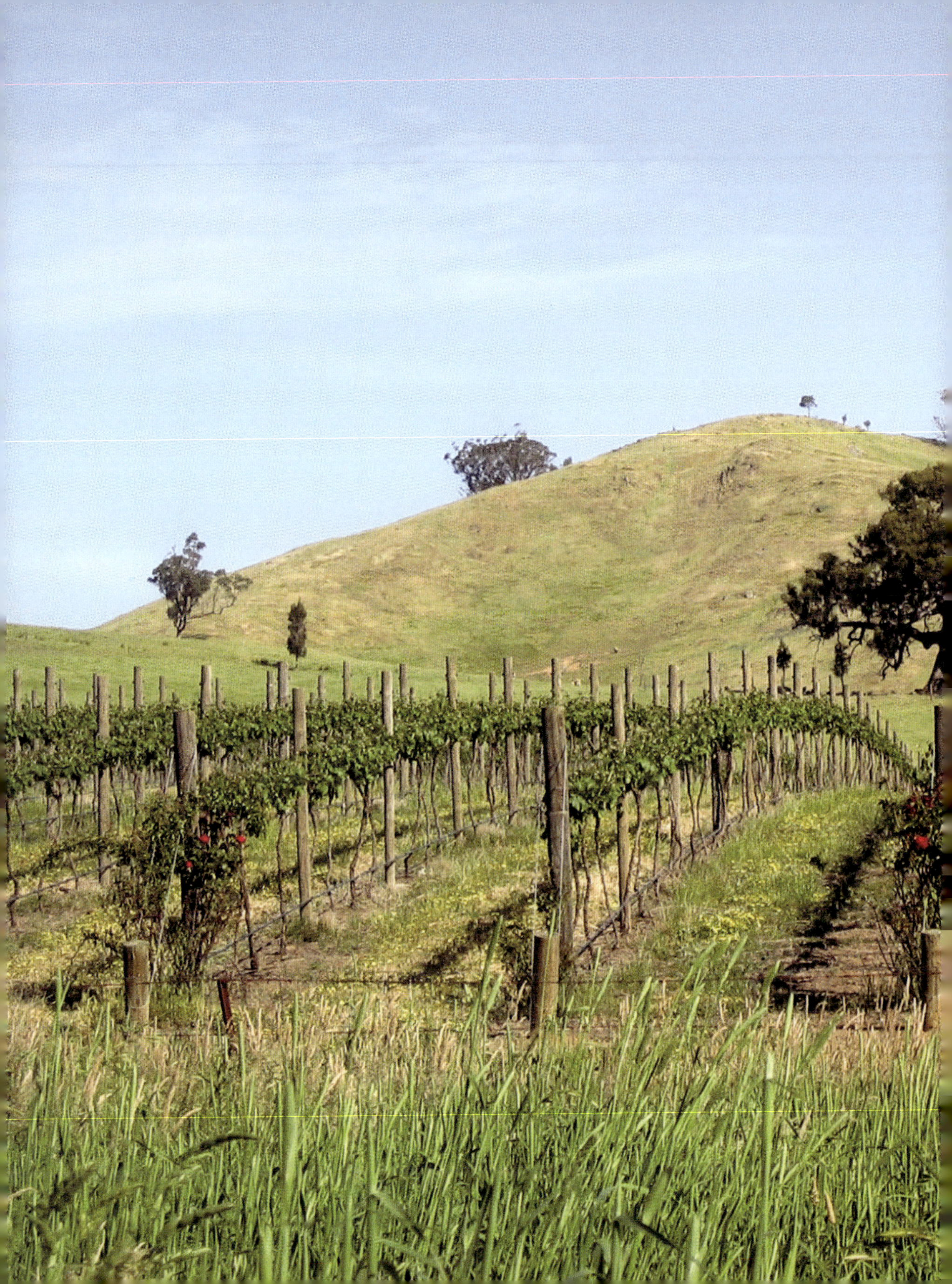

Rees Miller Estate, Central Victorian High Country

King Valley

Culture. In some regions it's the most important prong of terroir – the unique combination of country, climate and culture I have described throughout this book. The King Valley, for example, is a region defined just as much by the winegrowers who live there as by the incredible diversity of climates and soils that influence the wines grown there.

Hundreds of Italian migrants settled in the valley in the middle years of the 20th century. These settlers grew tobacco, fruit and nuts in country that reminded them of the northern Italian landscape they had left behind. Initially, this community helped support a local trade in table wine from well-established producers such as Brown Brothers, at a time when most Australians drank fortifieds. When the demand for tobacco waned and the demand for wine grapes grew in the 1980s, these Italian families readily adapted and planted vines. And over the last decade or so, as Australian interest in Italian varietal wines has grown, the families, now into their second and third generations, have embraced the change and planted everything from prosecco to nebbiolo, proud that their heritage is now valued. As a result, these people have forged a vibrant and thoroughly regional wine culture: plenty of chardonnay and shiraz and merlot is grown here (much of it ending up in multi-regional blends produced by wineries located outside the King Valley), but it's the alternative, Italian and Med-inspired wines that the King Valley does best.

Fred Pizzini
and the Italian tradition

Fred Pizzini picks up his glass of pale, orange-coloured liquid and takes a sniff. 'Plums,' he says finally. 'Plums and star anise.' Another sniff, a knot in the brow. A slow, thoughtful sip. 'And asphalt. Plums, star anise and asphalt. That's what good nebbiolo should taste like.'

Fred should know: he and his family have been growing and making nebbiolo for longer than almost anyone else in Australia. And their early success was a catalyst for many other growers of Italian heritage in the King Valley to also set up their own wineries.

'Back in the early '80s, when I first became interested in nebbiolo, there were maybe only three vineyards in the country who had any planted,' says Fred. 'I was encouraged by Peter Brown [at Brown Brothers], and I talked to Carlo Corino at Montrose in Mudgee, who was making some nebbiolo. Eventually I found some vines, and Brian Freeman at Charles Sturt Uni in Wagga propagated them up for us. By 1991, we were able to produce our first barrel. It took a long time to do things differently then. You've got to have a lot of love and passion to stick with it.'

I remember visiting Fred and Katrina Pizzini in the late '90s and tasting that first wine: it was spectacularly good, truly savoury, restrained, and with exactly the kind of growling asphalty tannic grip that Fred talks about. So different from the fruity, minty, juicy and soft red wines being made at the time in the King Valley from shiraz and cabernet and merlot grapes.

The Pizzinis have gone on to plant a host of other Italian varieties – sangiovese, arneis, verduzzo, pinot grigio, picolit and brachetto. And, thanks in part to advice from Brown Brothers viticulturist Mark Walpole and Italian consultant Alberto Antonini (both now involved in Greenstone vineyard in Heathcote) and, in the last few years, thanks to the involvement of Fred and Katrina's son, Joel, in the winery, they now produce some of this country's best Australian–Italian varietals.

The three dry whites are totally correct examples of variety, all reflecting the upper King Valley's remarkable climatic similarity to north-east Italy: the grigio is fresh, crisp, lean and minerally; the arneis is also crunchy, like a green pear; the verduzzo is riper, richer, broader. The reds are also right in their respective stylistic grooves: the sangiovese walks a delicious line between black morello cherry juiciness and fine, supple but grippy tannins, while the nebbiolo (the Pizzinis' best wine) is indeed redolent of plums – slightly dried, warm, dusty – and spices and is asphalt-like in its tarry grip. The two more obscure grapes, brachetto and picolit, have been used, respectively, to produce a pale, wild strawberry–flavoured, gently frizzante style and an intensely citrus-fruity dessert-style wine.

Emboldened by the critical success of these Italian varietal wines, the Pizzinis have also released 'reserva' expressions of their two top reds: Coronamento nebbiolo and Rubacouri sangiovese. The wines are expensive – both more than $100 a bottle, which is what you pay for a great Barolo or Super Tuscan – and I realise this is a bold statement of pride and confidence, but frankly, I don't think they're worth the money. Yes, they are impressive, big, stern, serious wines, and I may well change my opinion once they've matured a little in bottle, relinquishing more of their varietal, regional personalities, but on release they were both so overwhelmingly dominated by oak that I felt the point had been lost somewhat. Much more successful, I think, is the Pizzinis' other 'reserva' red, Il Barone, a bold, rich, multi-layered, better-value ($45-ish) blend of shiraz, cabernet, sangiovese and nebbiolo.

Pizzini is just one of many Italian-roots wine producers in the King Valley, all sharing a similar career progression from 1950s/'60s migrants to 1980s 'conventional' growers (planting shiraz, riesling, etc. to sell to big wineries), to champions of their culture and heritage in the 1990s and beyond.

Fred Pizzini's cousin, Arnie, runs the Chrismont vineyard a little further up the valley at Cheshunt, where winemaker Warren Proft produces excellent Italian varietals under the La Zona label, including superbly savoury arneis and fleshy, snappy barbera.

The Dal Zotto family pioneered the prosecco grape in the King Valley, producing the first example of this light, apple-crisp dry sparkling wine in 2004. Dal Zotto now make two versions, a simple, fresh, youthful, tank-fermented expression of the grape called Pucino, and a much more characterful, powdery, slightly cheesy, 'methode champenoise' expression called L'Immigrante, as well as a number of other very good Italian varietals such as a particularly citrusy, savoury arneis; a grape that, I would argue, produces much more interesting whites than the more widely planted pinot grigio.

And visiting the Corsini family's La Cantina is like stumbling across a rustic Tuscan farmhouse in the middle of the Australian bush, with its chunky stone winery building and no-added-preservative sangiovese or barbera.

Brown Brothers

It's a conundrum, Brown Brothers. On one hand you have a very traditional, conservative family company, producing vast quantities of reliable, popular and populist wines, traditionally labelled, unremarkable in style, and found in every drive-through bottle shop in the country. On the other hand Brown Brothers is, and has been for a long time, one of the most innovative wine companies in the country, willing to take what often look like massive risks, launching grape varieties that no-one's ever heard of, pioneering vineyards in regions everyone else thinks are way too cold for grapes and completely upsetting expectations of what a large family-owned wine company should be.

The company has 40 grape varieties planted across Victoria: traditional reds such as shiraz and cabernet at its Milawa property on the warmer flat lands of the King Valley; spicier-tasting shiraz and pinot grigio at its Banksdale vineyard, 450 metres up in the higher reaches of the valley; pinot and chardonnay for sparkling at Whitlands, 800 metres above sea level; newer plantings of Mediterranean reds such as tempranillo and sangiovese at the Patricia vineyard in the very warm and dry climate of northern Heathcote; crouchen, gordo and a host of others at its Mystic Park site on the Murray. Hundreds of hectares, in other words, of enormous diversity.

The company was way ahead of many in Australia in planting (and, crucially, encouraging contract growers in the King Valley to plant) Italian grapes such as sangiovese, barbera and nebbiolo in the 1980s; the first Australian examples of tempranillo and graciano I ever tasted were from Browns; and recent exciting additions to the line-up have included a delightfully crisp and crunchy vermentino, super-juicy, Ribena-like carmenere, and stunningly vibrant schioppettino.

Not every innovation has taken off. When I worked in a Melbourne drive-through bottle shop in the early 1990s, we had a few unusual stray Brown Brothers wines lurking in the bottom of the fridge, but unlike the Brown Brothers Spatlese Lexia that flew out the door, no-one wanted to buy these unloved 500 millilitre bottles of gorgeously complex Alsace-style gewurztraminer from the family's then new, ultra-cool Whitlands vineyard. If a wine like this was introduced today – quirky bottle size, extreme viticulture, aromatic variety – it'd be fashionably hip. Two decades ago it was sorely ahead of its time.

Brown Brothers also eagerly jumped on the organic bandwagon with an excellent low-preservative chardonnay in the mid-'90s when it looked like green wines were about to become mainstream. Again: great idea, bad timing.

But for every fizzer, there's a fabulous success, and few have been more fabulous for Brown Brothers than moscato. Browns was the first large winery to release a proper commercial moscato in Australia just over a decade ago, and the enormous popularity of the light, sherbetty wine has not only encouraged many other producers to make their own, but also inspired Brown Brothers to up the ante and release a white and pink zibibbo (a glorious synonym for muscat).

Sam Miranda/Symphonia

It's not all Italian action in the King Valley. The broad diversity of climates and sites suits a mob of other Mediterranean grape varieties, too. And the winemaker most successfully herding this mob is Sam Miranda.

Sam comes from an old Griffith winemaking family, up in the hot New South Wales Riverina region, and fell in love with the cooler King Valley in the early 1990s, during grape-buying trips to north-east Victoria. He established his own winery there in the late '90s, moved to the valley in 2003, and the following year bought Peter Read's Symphonia vineyard at Myrrhee. Peter Read was ahead of his time when he planted thoroughly exotic grapes such as tempranillo, tannat and petit manseng over a decade before. Peter had fallen in love with the wines from both the French and Spanish sides of the Pyrenees, and felt that his cool vineyard spot at Myrrhee would suit these varieties and styles.

He was right: I think the best wines Sam Miranda now makes are those sourced from Peter's old vineyard and released under the Symphonia label. The assertively grippy tannat in particular has fantastic depth of black berry fruit, and the tempranillo is beautifully medium-bodied, with bright wild strawberry fruit backed up by layers of persuasive tannin.

King River Estate

The 20 year-old, 20-hectare King River vineyard, right in the heart of the valley, is unusual in a number of ways. For a start, the vines here are dry-grown, and yields are low – in contrast to most of the irrigated, higher-yielding properties in the region. And since 2006 winegrower Trevor Knaggs has been slowly moving the estate away from chemically assisted viticulture: in that year he stopped using weedicide and started to manage his vineyard using mulch, sheep and an undervine slasher, following in 2007 with the biodynamic field sprays 500 and 501.

The low yields and lack of irrigation, says Trevor, result in small berries with a high skin-to-juice ratio: this gives the King River red wines – particularly the dense, taut reserve cabernet and juicy-rich, deeply purple lagrein – an impressive, sturdy, powdery quality. His viognier, released after a couple of years bottle age (unlike most other Australian examples of this grape variety), also has uncommon concentration, haunting and subtle honeysuckle perfume, and a great, mouthcoating, creamy texture; his 'cuvée sauvage' chardonnay (wild yeast, natural acid, lots of lees stirring) is similarly multi-layered and satisfying.

Sam Miranda, King Valley

Beechworth

Beechworth is swarming with top winemakers, all crowded up on the high ground at the heart of the state's north east. An awful lot of these people have made it known they're out to make the best wine in Australia. Some already are. From a distance, late at night, you can hear the clangs and see the sparks as the winemaking egos glance off each other in the darkness.

Why have they come, this band of super-ambitious grape-treaders? Could it be the climate? It is, after all, much chillier up here than even just down the road. A few minutes' drive south-west from the centre of Beechworth town, and you're down on the sun-bleached plains around Milawa; a few minutes' drive to the north and you're in the hot vineyards of Rutherglen up along the Murray, watching muscat grapes shrivel under the sun's relentless onslaught.

Could it be the country – the folds and slopes and gullies and exposed ridges that provide plenty of different possible aspects for vineyards? Could it be the soils – the marvellous mix of dusty red loams, sandstone gravel and granite sands over clay?

It's all of the above, of course. But there's another reason why so many successful winemakers have been drawn to Beechworth: since the first wines from here started appearing in the late 1980s and early '90s – wines made by unusually talented winemakers in unusually favourable terroirs – the region has always been associated with high quality. The first success bred further success. And because the country here is marginal, crumpled and difficult, the more commercially minded larger companies haven't been able to plant big vineyards, hoping some of the Beechworth magic will rub off on them. Which means that the Beechworth magic has retained much of its initial purity.

Julian Castagna Castagna

Few Australian winemakers are prepared to publicly stir the possum, to really have a spray at the things that irk them. Plenty of grape-treaders will happily bitch – in private, and with a few drinks inside them – about the powers that be, or the bloody politicians or other winemakers. But convincing them to go 'on the record', or reading their inflammatory views in print is a rare occurrence: most Australian winemakers prefer to maintain at least a semblance of industry unity at all times.

A notable, deliciously irascible exception to this rule was the late Dr John Middleton, of Mount Mary vineyard in the Yarra Valley, who was famous for sticking the boot into whatever target took his fancy in his annual mailing list newsletter: taxation, the Australian Wine and Brandy Corporation, high-alcohol fruit-bombs, wine journalists (a pet hate) – all these topics and more came in for an extended, entertaining shellacking whenever they got under the good doctor's skin. Which was often.

Now it appears that Julian Castagna has hoisted Middleton's mantle onto his own, wombat-like frame. In a recent newsletter, Julian told his mailing-list customers precisely what he thought of the parlous state of Australia's international reputation: 'As I travel around the world,' he wrote, 'I am constantly amazed by the reception our [Castagna] wines are accorded. Amazed, not because [people] like the wines – why wouldn't they? – but totally amazed and saddened by the perception held by many who think Australia is incapable of making anything other than non-gastronomic, sweet, high-alcohol wine. Amazed, also, because when I tell them of the very many other wonderful small producers making wine that is real, how it used to be, they are surprised at our industry's lack of communication in that regard.'

He railed against 'the exaggerated influence of some powerful but myopic journalists in Australia's main overseas markets', an 'official wine body ruled by a South Australian–centric view of wine to the detriment of the rest of Australia', and a 'self-appointed club' of wine show judges and opinion formers who 'put self-interest before what this country needs

'Peppers' which are scattered on biodynamic vineyards to keep unwanted critters at bay

[to promote]: individual, high-quality, terroir-driven wines made by people who eat, breathe and live their land in pursuit of something special.'

But wait, there was more. Julian was only getting started.

'It is time Australia had a revolution from the ground up, one that shakes our industry's mixture of self-satisfied smugness and corporate neglect…If ever there was a time for the small, serious producers to take matters into their own hands, it is now. If we leave it to those who seek to lead us, Australian wine will continue its slide into sameness and consistent mediocrity.'

Blimey. But I would expect nothing less from Julian. He is a man of extraordinary self-belief, conviction and passion. And not averse to confrontation: when the Australian Wine and Brandy Corporation's export approval tasting panel rejected one of his critically acclaimed wines a couple of years ago, he didn't just re-submit it (as most winemakers would have done), he threatened to have the wine assessed by various eminent expert tasters in the UK – in front of a television film crew.

Julian's consuming passion is biodynamics. When he and his wife Carolann bought a ridgetop property in Beechworth in the mid-'90s to plant a vineyard on the north-facing slope, they were told the land was stuffed: the shitty granite-laced clay loams contained no organic matter, apparently, and would never amount to anything. After setting the vineyard up 'conventionally', donning the full-body protective armour to spray various chemicals, the Castagnas had an epiphany and set about converting the place to biodynamics. To prove, in part, the sceptics wrong.

By 2004, Julian was so utterly convinced that BD was the right way to go, he organised an International Biodynamic Wine Forum in Beechworth, and invited French BD guru, Nicolas Joly, as keynote speaker. In his introduction to the event, Julian made a bold prediction: that in the near future, most of Australia's, and the world's, top wines would come from biodynamically managed vineyards. At the time it was easy to dismiss this as evangelical enthusiasm. Now, less than a decade later, the rate at which top producers are adopting BD, many inspired by the forum in Beechworth, makes me think he could be right.

Julian Castagna is just as convinced that the way he makes wine is the best way: picking, racking, bottling, etc. according to the lunar calendar wherever possible ('I never make any major decisions with regard to our wine on root days,' he says, 'indeed, I try not to even taste wine on those days; my palate simply lies to me'); his ferments have always started naturally ('I've never had packets of yeast in the winery') and he's recently started fermenting in larger vessels such as man-sized egg-shaped concrete tanks and 900-litre barrels from Bordeaux.

Like Nicolas Joly (Castagna is one of only four members of Joly's *Return to Terroir* group), Julian talks about making wines that are true because they are beautiful; wines that are beautiful because they are true. He is also completely up-front about how good he thinks his wines are: phrases like 'this is the best wine I've made' pepper his conversation when you taste with him.

Extraordinary arrogance? Well, perhaps. But he's right. His wines *are* beautiful – and they get better with each vintage, as the biodynamics build up the vineyard's ability to transmit its terroir through the grapes, and as he understands how best to let that taste of country shine in the glass.

The Allegro rosé is a model for the pale, super-dry, savoury and multi-layered style that I adore; the Ingenue viognier takes the emphasis away from fat, exotic perfume and places it on your tongue in a perfect balance of soft cream, grilled nuts and a sprinkling of honeysuckle nectar; the Chiave sangiovese has both density of black cherry fruit and dark, earthy, grippy tannins and transparency of acidity that adds a fresh, light, elegance; and the Segreto sangiovese/syrah sees bright peppery syrah spice and an extra layer of bramble compote depth added to the fine grippiness of the sangio.

Julian is deeply, sentimentally attached to these last two red wines, and believes the Chiave to be the best expression of his vineyard. I don't agree. For me, the outstanding wine produced here is the Genesis syrah: exquisitely scented with wild hedgerow berries and prickly white pepper, it is an exercise in subtle but persistent black fruit intensity, perfect balance, long anise-saturated tannins and a haunting finish.

These wines are incendiary devices in Julian Castagna's revolution.

Giaconda

Wine with a postcode. That's how one speaker at Giaconda's 20th-anniversary celebration in 2005 described Rick Kinzbrunner's entrancing, multi-layered, gob-smacking chardonnay. And he's right: it's a wine that could only come from the cold, south-facing slope in Beechworth that Rick planted in the mid-'80s. It's *the* wine that first proved to the rest of the world how special Beechworth is – and how talented this deeply thoughtful winemaker is.

A couple of years ago, Rick brought a group of miners in to blast a 60-metre-long tunnel 20 metres down into his granite hill. This new, cold, damp barrel cellar has made him even more acutely aware of how a place can stamp its postcode onto what is grown and made there.

'There's something very special about turning the fruit from the soil above into wine and then taking it deep into the rock below to mature it,' says Rick. 'It's an incredible atmosphere here, and I think it has made the wines taste different. It's very high humidity, probably about 95 per cent, which you just can't create artificially. And because of that humidity, the alcohol in the wine tends to evaporate a little, rather than the water, producing more elegant, finer flavours.'

Thanks to this natural cool dampness Rick no longer needs air-conditioning in his barrel store – an enormous saving of energy and money. This environmental benefit is just one of many eco-initiatives at Giaconda, including the installation of solar power and the move to lighter-weight bottles, specially commissioned from a particularly energy-efficient factory in France.

In 2007, Rick and his nephew, assistant winemaker, Peter Graham, also formed a joint partnership with Rhone Valley winemaker Michel Chapoutier to produce a shiraz called Ergo Sum at the Nantua vineyard, just up the road. While biodynamic practices are yet to be adopted here, Chapoutier's enthusiasm for BD inspired Rick to consult Alex Podolinsky of the Biodynamic Research Institute near Melbourne about converting the original Giaconda vineyard, and Rick has started some trials: 'I'm not just going to jump in without thinking,' he says. 'I want to find out for myself what works and what doesn't.'

Other exciting changes at Giaconda include the addition of a little marsanne to the already awesome, deeply textural, mineral-laced Aeolia Roussanne – 'to tighten up the rich structure a little,' says Rick; the first release of a Giaconda nebbiolo (most of Rick's under-performing pinot noir was grafted over to a selection of four nebbiolo clones in 2007), aged for three years in big, old, 1600-litre casks – 'You have to step back and learn how to make wine again,' he says; an estate-grown shiraz to complement the single-vineyard Warner shiraz; and a new pinot noir made from a blend of Yarra Valley grapes and (what's left of the) Giaconda vineyard fruit.

While all this new development looks like an enormous amount of exhausting hard work, Rick characteristically plays it down. 'I don't want to overextend myself,' he says. 'Yes, there's lots going on, but I'm taking it slowly. I want to make sure I do everything properly.'

Goulburn Terrace/Moon

The newest members of the exclusive club that is the Beechworth winegrowing fraternity are Greta Moon and Mike Boudry. Greta and Mike already have an 8-hectare vineyard – Goulburn Terrace, in Nagambie, central Victoria – and produce some of that region's best wines: subtly honeysuckle-scented, savoury chardonnay; unusual, complex sparkling marsanne; earthy, bramble-fruited shiraz; solid, essencey cabernet; all inspired by the defiantly traditional wines of the 150-year-old Tahbilk vineyard, just across the Goulburn River. Now they also have a property high up in the cool north east of the state, a world away, climatically, from the warm flatlands of Nagambie.

'We've been attracted to Beechworth for many years,' says Mike. 'So when we came across this site for sale, up past Barry [Morey from Sorrenberg's], unirrigated pinot and gamay block, the highest patch of granite sand in the region, we grabbed it. In Nagambie, summer temperatures are often warmer than we'd like, to be honest. It's three degrees cooler up here; in a way it's a form of future proofing in the face of climate change, and allows us to play around with grape varieties a bit more.'

Mike and Greta haven't given up on Nagambie. But they are changing the varietal mix there, also anticipating a warmer future: grafting chardonnay over to marsanne and roussanne, putting in some mourvedre. In Beechworth, initial plantings are a mix of shiraz clones, close-spaced with minimal irrigation. The vineyard will be managed biodynamically, as the Goulburn Terrace vineyard has been for years, with conversion to certified BD status from 2010. In between all this development, Greta – a fabulously passionate woman with a very naughty glint in her eye, like a St Trinian's girl who's never grown up – has gone back to school and trained to be a doctor. ('Most people do it the other way round,' quips Mike. 'They become a doctor first and then plant a vineyard. But that's Greta for you.')

Mike adopts a hands-off approach in the winery. 'I like to play with the timing of doing very little,' he says. 'That's what winemaking's all about: observing carefully, only interfering when you have to, and always at the right moment.'

In this respect he has a lot in common with Phillip Jones, pinot noir guru at Bass Phillip in Gippsland. Coincidentally, Mike and Phillip studied electronics together at uni in the 1960s. Says Mike: 'Who would have thought 40 years later a couple of electro nerds would end up growing grapes biodynamically?'

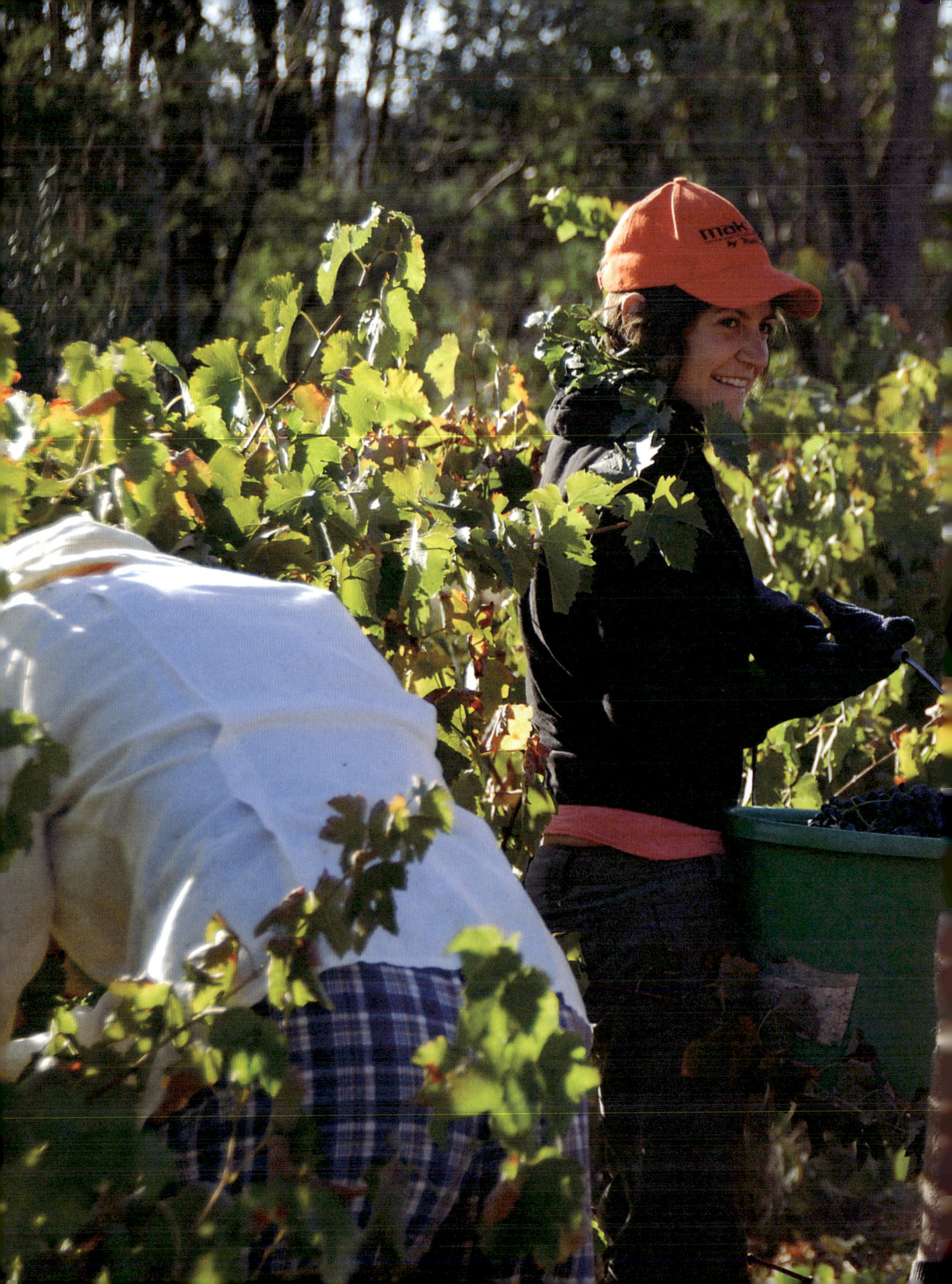

Pennyweight, Beechworth

Pennyweight

Pennyweight was established almost 30 years ago, but the vineyard and the cellar look and feel as though they've been here for well over a century: gnarled, twisted vines poke out of the dirt; barrels are stored on a dirt floor beneath rough timber beams and rusting iron roofs.

When Stephen and Elizabeth Morris (he's from the Rutherglen Morris family) started looking for vineyard land in Beechworth in the late '70s, they were determined to do things the 'old way' – grow grapes without irrigation, make wines simply, without too much buggering around. So they chose a patch of deep red soil surrounded by forest where they planted a whole heap of different varieties including shiraz, cabernet and pinot. Back in the warm heart of Rutherglen, they also planted a couple of hectares of palomino and a little pedro for their superb fortifieds – a pale, savoury flor style, a nutty amontillado and a spicy, complex oloroso – to complement their transparent, soft-textured table wines.

'We were organic from the start because I believed we could do it here in Beechworth,' says Stephen. 'I'd seen the terrible effects of DDT sprays back in the '60s, and I'd been inspired by Masanobu Fukuoka's *One Straw Revolution* books on organic farming. And anyway, organic is pretty much how they operated back home in Rutherglen in the old days. We knew the vineyard had to be dry-grown, too, because that way you get more honest, elegant wines. And when we came here we were told the average rainfall was 36 inches [900 millimetres]: now we're lucky to get 18 [450 millimetres].'

By 2007, after years of crippling drought, the Morrises' faith in farming without irrigation, organically, was wearing thin.

'I felt that organics was missing something,' says Stephen. 'But I'd always been sceptical about biodynamics. Then I visited a neighbour's biodynamic farm at the end of that terribly dry summer and was so impressed that I decided to try it. We were desperate. We felt that if biodynamics could help give us just that little bit of extra soil moisture retention, it could be the difference between surviving and going under.'

It soon became clear from trials that the 500 spray and other BD techniques made a difference to the soil structure and moisture-holding capacity. As a result, the Morrises converted the whole vineyard and are now certified biodynamic.

Sorrenberg

Giaconda may get all the kudos for chardonnay in Beechworth, but other vineyards in the region also produce some stunning wines from the variety. At Sorrenberg, for example, Barry Morey's chardonnay combines lemon syrup intensity with wheatmealy complexity and a chalky, powdery savoury finish.

The chardonnay isn't the only great wine produced at the 25-year-old, 3-hectare Sorrenberg vineyard, there's also a wonderfully complex, finely textured barrel-fermented sauvignon blanc semillon blend; a concentrated and elegant cabernet with a haunting herbal edge to its perfume; and one of Australia's few examples of gamay, here made in a sinewy, earthy style that speaks more of the granitic soil it's grown in than the variety. These are some of Beechworth's very best wines and yet Sorrenberg never attracts the hype that swirls around the region's other vineyards. Then again, once you've met winegrower Barry Morey, the low profile is completely understandable: you couldn't imagine a more humble and down-to-earth winemaker.

Walking onto the vineyard and into the small, cramped cellar, you're struck by how refreshingly unglamorous it all is: barrels squeezed into the space under an old house that feels as though it could have been plucked from Burgundy. Barry would rather be out in the vineyard, or turning his compost pile, or brewing up another compost tea. Or tending the sheep, horses, cows or chooks he runs on the 40 hectares of Beechworth farmland he owns.

Barry's been biodynamic for ages, and recently Demeter-certified, but, unlike many others who have been quick to realise the distinct marketing advantage in letting the world know you have adopted BD, he has kept it extremely quiet. Indeed, Barry had been applying the preparation 500 horn manure to his vineyard for seven years before I discovered he was biodynamic. And that was only because I happened to drop in one day and saw the beautiful piles of black compost.

Rutherglen

Although it's already a warm, dry wine region – well, *because* it's already a warm, dry wine region, really – Rutherglen is extremely well placed to cope with the challenge of climate change.

The traditional wine styles that have built Rutherglen's reputation over the last century and a half – luscious, treacly fortified muscat and muscadelle; 'port', 'sherry' and 'madeira'; heroic, blackstrap reds made from shiraz and durif – are wines born from old, low-yielding, phylloxera-ravaged vines planted in deep, dusty brown clay loams under a baking sun. A bit of global warming shouldn't present too much of a problem, really. But just in case, an enormous variety of alternative grapes have also been planted in recent years – heat-loving cultivars such as vermentino, fiano and zinfandel, and Portuguese reds such as tinta roriz, touriga and tinta cao, good for 'port' but also increasingly being used to make spicy, slurpy reds. Add to this an equally impressive number of underrated warm-climate varieties that have been grown here for decades – blue imperial (cinsault), grenache, even the obscure French white, gouais – and you have a rich diversity of options from which the region's winemakers can choose.

There's a sense of optimism and enthusiasm to be found among both the new generation of old winemaking families, and also among recent newcomers to the region; a heartening mix of respect for heritage and a bold willingness to innovate.

All Saints

All Saints is the best illustration of the new spirit of Rutherglen. Run by fourth-generation members of the Brown family – Eliza, Angela and Nick – the vineyard and the imposing, castellated winery building date back to the 1860s. Young (ish), British-born winemaker Dan Crane is producing some of the region's finest table wines, as well as settling in comfortably to his role as latest custodian of the extraordinary stocks of ancient fortified wines stashed away behind the castle walls – fortified wines that are packaged in innovative, Vino-Lok glass-stoppered bottles. And Dan and Nick are leading the way in the All Saints vineyards by adopting organic practices: the whole 40-hectare property is now herbicide-free, and biodynamic field sprays are being applied on most of the blocks.

'We started down this path of really working on our soils in 2006,' says Dan. 'A lot of the vineyard was severely compacted and pretty much sterile from 30-odd years of herbicide use. According to soil analysis, our carbon levels were not dissimilar to that found on the moon. So, we ripped, composted, mulched, put in cover crops, threw away the herbicide unit, bought a Tournesol undervine cultivator and watched as the place came to life again.'

It hasn't always been easy: weeds continue to be a big problem in a vineyard of this size, and Dan believes frosts have been more of a problem due to the extra ground cover; unlike the old days of scorched-earth, where the bare soil was able to build up some heat.

'On balance, though, the shift towards BD has been really worthwhile. One very obvious change is that we see far less water stress in the hot weather. I'm sure this is down to improved water holding capacity in the soil since we used compost and cover crops. When I try to explain what we are trying to achieve to some of the more traditional local vignerons, I end up saying that we are looking after the vines from the ground down, just as much as from the ground up.'

Dan is producing delicious non-mainstream blends at All Saints such as a lively, lemony white combo of chardonnay and viognier, and an earthy, grippy sangiovese cabernet. Newly grafted (onto old ruby cabernet vines) grenache, mataro and cinsault, or blue imperial, sourced as cuttings from old Morris vineyards, will increase the blending options.

The wines that really impress me, though, are the Family Cellar marsanne and durif, the top-of-the-range table wines from All Saints.

The marsanne is picked by hand from 50-year-old vines (planted with cuttings from Tahbilk in central Victoria), the fruit is hand-sorted and the juice undergoes spontaneous fermentation in barrel, where it remains for 18 months before bottling. With a mouthfilling texture of honey and cream, the wine is balanced by spices, a hint of floral perfume and a lingering, nutty dryness.

The Family Cellar durif is the finest expression of the variety in Rutherglen. The wine is given three weeks of post-ferment maceration before basket-pressing into a mix of old and new, French and American barrels. Despite all this treatment, and despite durif's famously burly natural tannins, the wine is elegant, refined, supple and not in the slightest bit dominated by oak characters: sure, it's pitch-black, and crammed with wild bramble and blood plum fruit, but the structure is round, velvety and persuasive without being forceful, the finish is generous without being hot, and the balance is perfect.

Valhalla Wines

You don't come across too many true outsiders in the Rutherglen wine community. Most of the winemakers and vineyard owners here are locals, born and bred: third-, fourth-, fifth-generation descendents from the English and Scottish settlers that flocked here after the gold rush in the mid-19th century. That's why names like Campbell, Morris, Chambers and Buller pepper the region. And that's how you can be fairly sure, without even asking, that Anton Therkildsen and Antoinette Del Popolo aren't, as they say, from 'round these parts.

Anton came to Rutherglen in 1997 to work in the winery at Campbells. He met (and married) Antoinette, a Sydney-born local doctor, and they decided to settle in the region. They found a good 25-hectare block next door to All Saints and decided to plant a vineyard. It was when Anton had to clamber into a full body suit before spraying his first block of vines in 2003 – on the advice of the chemical company who'd sold him the spray – that the couple decided there had to be a better way.

Just a few years and less than a handful of vintages later, Valhalla has become a model of eco-conscious sustainable winegrowing in Rutherglen. The vineyard is managed with a minimum of soft chemicals – mainly one or two herbicide sprays a year; the winery was constructed out of rendered straw bales; wine boxes, bags, labels and stationery are all produced from recycled materials; the cellar door and toilet wastewater goes through a worm farm before being used to irrigate a copse of trees nearby; and the winery wastewater is used to irrigate a larger patch of native trees.

The wines are good, too. Anton's marsanne is a particulary lovely, spicy, creamy expression of the grape, showing leesy complexity and great richness; and the grenache shiraz mourvedre blend captures the spirit of place beautifully in its red soil–dusted bramble fruit aromas and powdery tannic finish.

Warrabilla

One of the recurring themes of this book is the move away from late-picked, massively alcoholic, blockbuster reds to wines with more restraint, poise and refreshment. An increasing number of Australian winemakers are trying very hard to tone down the head-banging brute force and turn up the elegance. And overall I think this is a fantastic development: on the whole, finer, more restrained, moderately alcoholic reds are better with food. But sometimes, when I'm sitting down to a midwinter plate of slow-cooked lamb shanks, say, braised for hours in red wine with bay, juniper and pepper, I lust after the biggest shiraz or durif I can get my hands on. Something that sucks light into its black-purple heart, that floods the mouth with flavour, that grips the back of the tongue and refuses to let go until it has another bite of sweet meat to wrestle with. It's at moments like these that I reach for

Straw bale winery, Valhalla, Rutherglen

a bottle of Warrabilla; because Warrabilla wines are big – *very* big (16, even 17 per cent alcohol is not uncommon) – but they're usually also *balanced*.

Warrabilla winemaker Andrew Sutherland Smith is fifth-generation Rutherglen: his family established All Saints in the 1860s. He 'broke the umbilical cord of a daily wage' in 1997 after working for a number of local wineries, and with his wife Carol established his own winery out on the western edge of the regional boundary.

The couple have two vineyards: 5 hectares in lighter, sandier soils at the winery, and 12 hectares in richer, red loam over clay a few kilometres to the west. These two sites contribute most of the fruit to Warrabilla wines – the former, says Andrew, is more perfumed, the latter has more body and tannin, thanks to the differing soil types; but the Smiths also source grapes from further afield, including, on rare but spectacular occasions, a dry-grown, organic-by-default (aka woefully neglected) vineyard in granite soils at Walla Walla to the north, just over the Murray in New South Wales.

What I like most about these wines is that they are made not to appeal to a wine critic's palate but because Andrew Sutherland Smith *loves* big reds. Tasting his wines with him you can see the unbridled passion twinkling in his eyes.

I also like Andrew's refusal to follow the herd, and his distinct lack of political correctness.

'People often criticise our wines for not being ageworthy,' he says. 'I reckon that they're over-cellaring them. Why should the wines have to age when they taste so good young? Ageworthiness is just a marketing angle sometimes, I reckon: you look at a lot of so-called ageworthy reds when they're ten, fifteen years old and they're stuffed. But nobody's willing to admit that.'

He also has a sneaking suspicion that many of his critics are just jealous of the concentration and volume of flavour he can squeeze into his wines thanks to his understanding of the region and its terroirs. 'Let's face it, most new Australian wines are over-cropped, gutless and lack varietal definition, because they're planted in shit soils in shit spots.'

It's always refreshing to meet a winemaker who's not afraid to speak his mind.

Back from the brink
Rescuing Australia's great fortified wine tradition

It doesn't take much. Just a sip of Pennyweight's stunning Woody's amontillado, or a glass of Stanton and Killeen's deep purple Vintage Fortified, or a refreshing mouthful of Eric Semmler's elegant Riverland fino and I come over all patriotic and proud of this country's fabulous fortified winemaking tradition. And sad – sad that the amazing history of producing great wines like these is in danger of being forgotten. The few wineries who persist in making fortifieds are collective custodians of ancient knowledge, stubbornly refusing to let a noble tradition die out. But they're a threatened group.

After enjoying pre-eminence in Australia for much of the 20th century, sales of fortified wines have been on a steep decline for years, discarded in favour of fresh young sauvignon blanc and succulent pinot noir. There are exceptions: Rutherglen's winemakers have managed to buck the downward trend by pricing their top wines – the Grand, Rare and Museum muscats – at appropriately awe-inspiring levels ($1000 a bottle, anyone?), and with their hefty new price tags the wines now demand a lot more respect. Another glaring exception is the 160-year-old Seppeltsfield in the Barossa: the new owners (the heritage-listed winery was sold by Foster's in 2007) have injected plenty of energy and cash into selling the best of the best of the extraordinary stocks of ancient fortified wines, and released some unbelievably brilliant, sturdily priced 'oloroso' sherry, well-deep muscat, spectacularly complex brandy and more under the new, exclusive Paramount Collection label. (Joseph Seppelt's original 1850s vision of a thriving, self-sufficient community has also been revived: the Seppeltsfield village now boasts a cooperage, tours, and sales of beers and legendary raspberry cordial as well as those amazing fortified wines.)

Most other attempts to revive the category, though – modern, funky packaging, youth-oriented marketing campaigns, etc. – have been singularly unsuccessful.

The latest push to save fortifieds has come in the form of some bold new names. One of the many problems with the promotion of fortified wines in this country is the fact that, as part of the same trade agreement with the EU that led to the registering of this country's Geographical Indications, winemakers also agreed to stop using protected European names such as sherry, fino, amontillado, oloroso, port and tokay, all of which have been fixtures on Australian fortifieds for decades.

It was hard enough to get people to buy these wines as it was, without being forced to dream up new names, but in late 2007, realising they needed to tackle the issue head-on (the phase-out date for 'sherry' on Australian labels was the end of 2009), a group of winemakers – including Rutherglen's Colin Campbell and Chris Pfeiffer and Seppeltsfield's James Godfrey – rustled up $1 million from the federal government and industry to invent and register some alternatives.

Port is relatively easy to replace: the word tawny is still okay to use, and as most of the port drunk in this country is in the tawny style, producers will simply drop the word port from the label. And because muscat is the name of a grape variety, that can stay, too. But sherry and tokay proved trickier to reinvent.

After more than a year of discussions, focus groups, market research and trademark checks, in early 2009 the group launched the new names: instead of sherry, we now have apera, in dry, medium-dry, medium-sweet, sweet and cream styles. And in place of tokay: topaque.

I don't particularly like most of these new names. I'm not sure even how to *pronounce* apera. (*App*-era? A-*peer*-a? A-*perr*-a? Apparently it's the latter, as in *aperitif*.) But I will enthusiastically promote them, because the grand tradition of Australian fortified wine deserves the new lease of life that these names might provide.

The Grampians and Great Western

Shiraz is king in Western Victoria's Grampians region. A staggering two-thirds of the region's vineyard area is planted to the grape; some wineries only produce shiraz, and the Grampian's fascinating sub-regions have long been widely acknowledged for their ability to produce different styles of shiraz.

The first sub-region to be given full, official GI status, in early 2007, was Great Western, the historic heart of the Grampians and the location of most of its wineries. The oldest vineyards here, some planted in the mid-19th century, produce classic Australian red wines such as Best's Bin 0 shiraz and Seppelt's St Peter's shiraz, all of which express the terroir found around Concongella and Great Western: complex sandy loams shot through with bits of quartzy and ferruginous gravel over deep clay.

There are clear differences between the shiraz produced around Rhymney, where the land is a little more elevated and has a little more quartz gravel running through it (producing more fragrant wines), and Moyston, which is flatter and has some ironstone gravel in the soil (more brambly wines). Over at Mafeking, on the edge of the Grampians-Gariwerd national park, the imposing mountain range that holds rich cultural significance for the Jardwadjali and Djab wurrung peoples, the land is different again, formed by granite and sandstone, and the wines are firmer, bolder. And to the east, past Ararat, the cooler, granite country around Langi Ghiran produces a quite different style of shiraz again, with less density, more juiciness, and more pepper and spice.

Dan Buckle, from the 45-year-old Mount Langi Ghiran winery, has made a number of single-vineyard shiraz wines, each with a clear sense of place. The Gap shiraz, for example, from a vineyard over in the west of the region, right next to the national park, is lush, round, firm; Nowhere Creek shiraz, from a vineyard right on the cool, eastern border of the Grampians and Pyrenees regions, has more dried herb and slinky juiciness; and Robinson shiraz, from a certified organic vineyard near Moyston, has typically sweeter bramble fruit and tangy tannin.

And Rory Lane specialises in the Grampians with his label, The Story. Rory buys a few tonnes of shiraz each vintage from some of the top vineyards in the region, then trucks the fruit to the space he's renting at the Crittenden Estate winery in Melbourne's south-eastern suburbs. It's small-batch, hands-on winemaking here: often some stalks are included in the ferment to emphasise that spicy, undergrowthy character typical to Grampians (particularly Great Western) shiraz, and the wines are bottled without fining or filtration. They are excellent examples of the textural, medium-bodied regional style.

Simon Clayfield
Clayfield Wines

Simon Clayfield is sceptical of many of the current fascinations that keep other winemakers and foodies (and green-tinged wine writers) occupied.

He hasn't got a lot of time for the 'natural' winemaking trend – wild yeast ferments, etc. – and is quite happy adding reliable, consistent cultured yeast to his grape juice; he thinks the locavore movement and the 100-mile diet is little more than 'pathetic, unpractical, touchy-feely stuff'; and he gets stuck into me whenever he can for crapping on about the 'airy fairy' aspects of biodynamics.

He's particularly sceptical of the wine industry's rush to claim green credentials.

'Winemaking's not a lot different to other chemical engineering factories,' he says. 'Things go in one end and come out the other. We cut down a lot of trees to make barrels, cardboard cartons, labels, pallets. We bottle the wine in glass made in huge furnaces. Practically every drop of wine is pumped, sucked, squeezed, squashed, sometimes several times, each time requiring more energy. Wine industry turning green? Don't make me laugh. The only green thing is the vine leaf.'

Not that Simon is a big supporter of conventional, chemically dependent winegrowing, mind you. 'Don't get me wrong,' he says. 'I'm really concerned with the sustainability of vineyards, and in particular our soil. But I think there's a reasonable balance you can strike.'

So the 2-hectare vineyard is run along virtually organic lines, plenty of composting using manure from his own horses, mulching, a little sulphur and copper when necessary. He has leanings towards permaculture practices, too, hence the figs, cherries, oaks and olives also planted on the property. And he keeps wine additions to a minimum; certainly no tannin is allowed anywhere near the ferments, despite it being a common practice in other wineries, because he feels that Grampians-grown shiraz simply doesn't need that kind of boost.

Simon is a Grampians veteran of sorts, having worked at Best's for ten years before planting his own vineyard at Moyston in 1997. He clearly feels a very strong connection to the place: his Massif label is a tribute to Tom Wills, one of the major figures in the development of Australian Rules Football, who grew up in Moyston in the 1840s playing the Aboriginal ball game called marn grook. He's also an excellent winemaker: his black label Grampians shiraz has heaps of opulent blackberry/bramble fruit richness over a typical regional gravelly background, while his Massif shiraz is a more medium-bodied, spicy, toasty-oak, drink-now style.

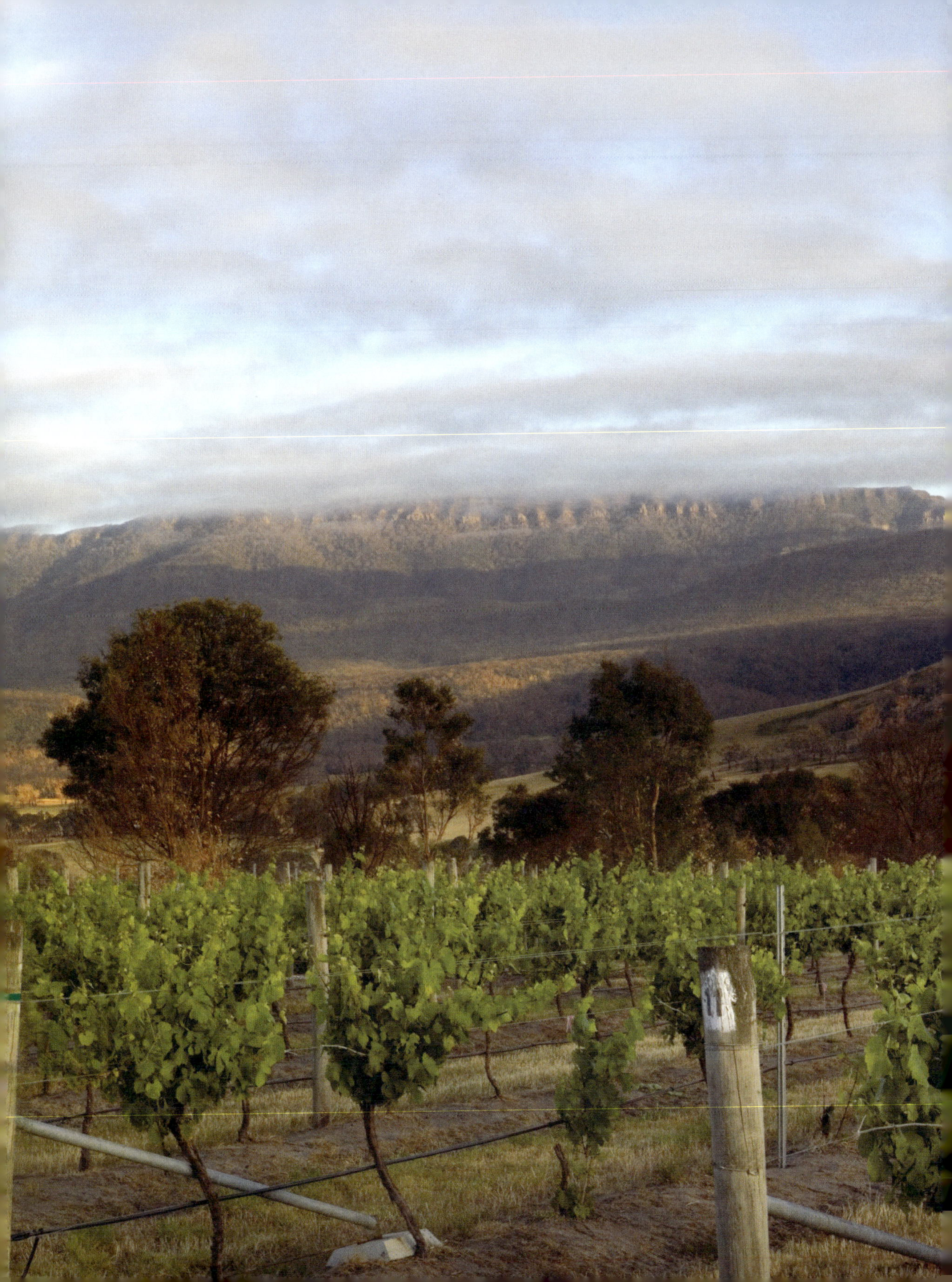

The Grampians

Sparkling shiraz
A lament for a Grampians classic

Emma Wood and the team at the 145-year-old, Foster's-owned, Seppelt Great Western winery at the heart of the Grampians region, produce some of the most fantastic wines in the big brewer's entire portfolio, including brilliant regionally specific shirazes from Heathcote (the old Mt Ida vineyard next door to Jasper Hill), Bendigo and Great Western itself. The St Peter's vineyard shiraz, sourced from the oldest estate vineyard, is a model of multi-layered, savoury/spicy, medium-bodied Grampians shiraz, a wine with great poise and elegance but also with the capacity to age and develop in the bottle for decades. It is unequivocally one of this country's greatest red wines.

Seppelt produce another classic, if underrated Australian red, a style arguably 'invented' at Great Western in the 1890s, that also beautifully expresses the complexity of its terroir. Sparkling shiraz polarises people: some consider it an aberration, a waste of perfectly good grapes, a gastronomic joke, an embarrassment even, while others love the stuff, revelling in its iconoclastic irreverence, and gaining deep satisfaction from drinking it with the right kind of food.

I'm one of the lovers. I think the deep bramble fruit and spice undertow found in Great Western/Grampians shiraz can be enhanced by secondary, fizz-producing fermentation, lees-ageing, extended bottle-maturation and a little sweetening liqueur (the 'recipe', if you like, for the Seppelt Show Sparkling Shiraz). And I think the resulting gentle purple foaming ambrosia is far and away the best thing you could possibly drink with Australian game, such as seared kangaroo fillets or roast emu.

But I'm in a minority. Sparkling shiraz sells well at cellar door wherever it's made, in the Grampians as well as other regions, but it isn't taken seriously by many sommeliers or chefs or even many wine hacks. I think this is a huge wasted opportunity: some of my most treasured Australian wine-drinking memories are of well-cellared bottles of old Seppelt sparkling shiraz, full of a sense of place, history and culture. I think the style deserves to be given a central role in the future of this country's gastronomy.

Pyrenees

The distinctive twang of eucalypt can be found in red wines across Australia, from the Granite Belt to the Great Southern. It's like a background hiss of static: sometimes so faint you simply don't hear it, sometimes so loud that it intrudes on the melody, even drowns out the song. Different people have different thresholds: some love a little gum leaf in their cabernet, some can't stand even the slightest suggestion of a dusty bush path at midday. There's even some debate as to how the eucalypt scent ends up in the wines in the first place: we know that the unmistakable smell is caused by a compound called cineole (otherwise known as eucalyptol), but while some researchers believe cineole occurs naturally in grape skins, as it does in other plants such as basil and sage and bay, and fruits such as blackcurrant, others believe it is transferred from gum trees near vineyards through the air or even through decomposing eucalypt vegetation in the soil.

Either way, you find plenty of cineole in the red wines of central and western Victoria, particularly in the wines of the Pyrenees. You can even smell it on the breeze and see the gum mist hanging in the air when you travel through the place: the eucalypt-cloaked hills that fringe the region (and give it its incongruously European name) are often daubed with a vivid shade of aquamarine, thanks to the oily sky. The Pyrenees soils also stamp a strong sense of place on the wines made here: the lean and bony gravels, sand and quartz that crop up across the region, and the slightly acidic clay subsoils tend to produce low yields and plentiful tannins. But the best Pyrenees winemakers, like those mentioned below, manage to tame these powerful environmental influences and turn them into well-balanced complex elements in their wines.

Mount Avoca

Three 2007 vintage red wines from Mount Avoca vineyard are sitting on the table in front of me. A shiraz, a cabernet and a merlot. And I can't quite believe what I'm tasting. These wines are so much better than the last few vintages. They exude a clear and confident sense of place, of varietal expression, of quality. The shiraz has that distinctive edge of dusty eucalypt that immediately conjures an image of the gum-covered hills that surround the Pyrenees vineyards; the merlot is fleshy to start, but with a gentle hug of tannin on the finish, full of the warmth of the region; the cabernet is fine, dusty, serious but elegant, like the tough, lean soils that characterise the place.

Established by John and Arda Barry in 1970, Mount Avoca was one of the pioneering wineries in the Pyrenees. The estate made some of the region's best wines in the 1980s and '90s, but lost its way in the early years of this century when it was swallowed up by the short-lived Barrington Estates winery syndicate (which also included Yarraman in the Hunter and Hayshed Hill in Margaret River). Matt Barry, son of the founders, bought back the farm when Barrington collapsed, and started the slow and difficult process of re-establishing the winery's reputation. The 2007 reds were the first glimpse of what a good job he's doing.

'It was like turning the Titanic,' says Barry. 'But I suppose every overnight success has years of hard work leading up to it.'

The first thing Barry did when he took over was get rid of the old oak in the winery, and shorten the amount of time the wines were spending in wood. He also hired John Harris, ex-Domaine Chandon in the Yarra Valley, as winemaker. While the changes in the winery are important, though, the key to the quality of the Mount Avoca wines lies in the vineyard.

'By 2007,' says Matt Barry, 'the vineyard had been run along organic lines for 12 years – plenty of composting, lots of mulch. Our soil really is crap gravel and clay in most places, but you can find a lovely rich layer of humus and worm castings under the mulch. I really think this made a difference: during the incredible heat in February, the vines held up beautifully and we picked good, healthy fruit, not dimpled and puckered berries. We picked grapes, not mini plum puddings.'

As well as composting and mulching, Barry has also taken away herbicides, uses sheep to graze down the weeds during winter, and aims to achieve full organic certification in the next couple of years. The family have also built eco-friendly tourist accommodation on the property in an attempt to spread the holistic message.

Few other Pyrenees vineyards have headed down a similar sustainable path. The Robb family's Sally's Paddock property is one: the 36-year-old, dry-grown vineyard is managed along organic lines, and the top wine, a wild yeast-fermented blend of cabernet sauvignon, shiraz, cabernet franc and merlot, is the benchmark for Pyrenees reds, a reliably stunning combination of deeply concentrated black fruit, sturdy tannin and a sprinkling of crushed gum leaf perfume. Allen and Andrea Hart's Dog Rock is also justifiably proud of its environmental credentials: using wind and solar power, minimising or eliminating sprays in the vineyard and using recycled packaging. The Harts have, like Matt Barry, planted tempranillo, and produced some very convincing, fleshy, chewy dry red from it, as well as a brilliant sparkling red of tempranillo, shiraz and cabernet with bold flavours of wild bramble berries, dark chocolate and moist earth. But these vineyards are exceptional: indeed, when Matt Barry organised a seminar on converting to organics at Mount Avoca in early 2009, only a couple of people from Pyrenees wineries turned up.

'A lot of people still think we're a bunch of radical greenies,' says Matt Barry. 'But it's not radical: it's good business. We have chosen to go down the organic path because we think it's the right thing to do. We're not going to sell more wine because it's certified or labelled organic. We'll sell more wine because the wines will be better.'

Henty

This is remote, widescreen country down here in the south-west of Victoria. Cold, windswept farmland, broken by rows of old pines and low, crumbling drystone walls. Some of the soil is black, thick. Some is thinner, redder, full of granulated buckshot. Some lies over old limestone seabeds. It's traditionally spud country, sheep country, cattle country. And now, it's vine country, but only in a scattered way. Henty is a vast GI, stretching from the far western corner up through Hamilton to the edge of the Grampians and east to Warrnambool, and only a few brave souls have been mad enough to plant vineyards here – a couple, tentatively, in the 1960s and '70s, then a handful more in the '90s and 2000s – but what they produce is so good that the reputation of the region far outweighs its total production.

The Thomson family of Crawford River proved soon after they established their vineyard in 1975 that Henty can produce some of the country's best rieslings: highly perfumed, steely, incisive, exceptionally long-lived. In recent years, though, it's the vineyards a little further north, near Hamilton, that have sent waves of excitement rippling out from these volcanic plains.

John Nagorcka
Hochkirch Wines

. . . .

The Nagorcka family have been farming biodynamically on their Hochkirch property in Victoria's western district for a decade. Hochkirch comes very close to the biodynamic ideal of a self-sufficient, closed-unit farm: as well as White Suffolk sheep (the best lamb I have ever eaten), Large Black pigs (which feed on acorns and produce the most amazing homemade ham) and cereal crops, the Nagorckas have an 8-hectare vineyard producing riesling, pinot noir and shiraz.

'The thing about BD soil is that it's in balance,' says John Nagorcka, digging up a handful of rich, dark earth from under the vine. The weathered basalt soil looks like moist chocolate cake: deep black-brown, sweet-smelling, with a remarkable, friable structure. 'All the nutrients are locked up in these crumbs of humus, waiting to be unlocked by the vine. So the vines take what they need, when they need. They grow as they want to grow rather than as they're forced to grow.'

Tongue in cheek, I suggest this sounds awfully close to ascribing some kind of consciousness to the vine.

'No,' he answers, seriously. 'I'm ascribing to plants a partnership with everything else in nature.'

It's a very biodynamic answer. And it's delivered with the kind of fierce conviction I find in other long-time BD growers. In John Nagorcka's case it's backed up by ten years of experience and observation, watching the soil change, seeing how the vines have responded, tasting the effects in the fermenting vat and the glass. Digging my hands into the chocolate cake soil, it's hard not to share that conviction.

John grew up here: his family have been farming the 700-acre farm just outside Hamilton for generations. His father was suspicious of modern agriculture's reliance on chemicals, so the farm has been essentially organic for many years and the move to BD in the late-'90s was a natural progression.

A radiologist by profession, John has also had a lifelong interest in fermenting things: he remembers making 'champagne' out of sweetwater grapes when he was 12. So the decision to plant the vineyard in the early-'90s was also a natural one. 'And besides,' he adds, 'when you have a mixed farm like ours, growing grapes and making wine is one of few things you can do where you have control over every stage of what you produce.'

There is, he argues, a huge environmental advantage, too, in building rich humus through biodynamics: it sequesters carbon and increases soil moisture retention. He points out that while most Australian soils contain less than 0.5 per cent carbon, after about seven or eight years, biodynamic soil carbon can reach between 3 and 7 per cent.

Improving the soil structure also

allows him to cultivate under the vines to keep the weeds down, something many 'conventional' growers, whose undervine soil is often stripped of life and structure by repeated weedicide use, wouldn't dream of doing. 'I've been cultivating undervine for eight years now,' he says. 'And I've never seen the soil look better. Even after the last few dry years.'

And then there's the flavour. Because of the balanced soils and vines, says John, the grapes need very little, if any, manipulation in the winery. 'I think BD gives you a better balance of sweet fruit and ripe acid in the fruit,' he says. 'Alex Podolinsky [whose Bio-Dynamic Research Institute provides Demeter certification for Hochkirch] describes it as a noble acidity, and I can see what he's talking about.'

The Henty region has established a great reputation for riesling, thanks to the stunning, long-lived wines from Crawford River, further south towards Portland. The Hochkirch riesling lives up to this reputation: depending on the vintage, it can be a terrifically taut, steely wine with an incredible line of minerals running right along the middle of the palate (cooler years), or a pretty, lemon-pithy wine, with suggestions of sherbetty sweetness teasing the edges of your tongue (warmer years). In both cases, and true to the Henty tradition, they are rieslings that develop well in the cellar.

Pinot noir from Hochkirch can be a difficult beast: made with up to 30 per cent whole bunch inclusion, it can smell and taste stemmy, earthy, even muddy in its youth and when first opened. But give it time – a thorough decant, say – and the focus tightens to reveal exquisite red berry hedgerow fruit and that ripe acidity John talks about.

The Hochkirch shiraz, labelled, appropriately, syrah, can also be elusive. On some occasions it falls on the green-peppercorn side of spicy, reflecting the cool conditions of this windy, frost-prone part of the world; but sometimes that spiciness is rich, gamey, sweet, more like black pepper and juniper and blackberries. Again, I find that time and air are beneficial.

The cabernet sauvignon is perhaps the least controversial – or the easiest to pin down – of all the Hochkirch wines: dark in colour, it exudes shiny blackcurrants and dark tannins and a lick of cedary, herbal complexity.

It's worth noting that all the Hochkirch wines remain fresh, and can even improve markedly in fruit flavour and vibrancy, for days after being opened, certainly for longer than most 'conventionally' made wines, perhaps as a result of that 'noble' acidity in the grapes and the wine. And this is a trait common to many well-made biodynamic wines,

John's sister, Dianne Nagorcka, has a vineyard up the road called Tarrington. In mid-2008, following the sudden departure of Tarrington winemaker Tamara Irish (to set up a new vineyard called Enigma Variations just outside Dunkeld), John and his wife Jennifer Nagorcka became partners in Tarrington. The 2-hectare vineyard has produced some absolutely stunning chardonnay over the last few years, wines with as much flinty, mineral cut as great chablis.

It will be fascinating to see what effect John Nagorcka's BD methods have on this undeniably special landscape and how it is expressed in the glass.

domaine lucc

merlot

2009

13% ALC/VOL MINIMAL SULPHITES ADDED APPROX 8.2 STD DRINKS
UNFILTERED NATURAL FERMENT ESTATE BOTTLED UNFINED
750 ML

www.domainelucci.com

BASKET RANGE · ADELAIDE HILLS · SOUTH AUSTRALIA

8 South Australia

Adelaide

Adelaide is full of people thinking very hard about the future of Australian wine. As well as all the boys and girls at the Australian Wine and Brandy Corporation (*when* are they going to drop 'and brandy' from this long-winded moniker?) and the Winemakers' Federation of Australia (*love* a good apostrophe, properly used), hunkered down in boardrooms, scribbling on whiteboards, churning out spreadsheets, desperately trying to come up with solutions to the grape glut, the drought, falling exports and an angry jostling crowd of other problems, down in the sleepy suburb of Urrbrae, the scientists at the Australian Wine Research Institute are playing with all the shiny toys in their brand spanking new laboratories in the $30 million Wine Innovation Cluster building.

The AWRI's main job is responding to the wine industry's immediate needs – dealing with smoke taint in grape juice from fire-affected areas, say, or helping winemakers respond to *Brettanomyces* spoilage yeast in their wineries. But the Institute is also very interested in 'unlocking the secrets' of vines, grapes and wines by breaking everything down into its smallest components. For example, the Institute recently succeeded in pinpointing the chemical compounds that produce the characteristic pepper smell in shiraz. And in 2008 the AWRI became the first organisation in the world to sequence the wine yeast genome.

The next bold frontier is metabolomics, or chemical fingerprinting. When I visited the Cluster just after it had opened, AWRI managing director Sakkie Pretorius was keen to show off the most expensive of his new toys, the million-dollar metabolomic measuring machine, which is crucial to this emerging area of research.

'Every wine is the unique sum of its grapes, yeast, bacteria, oak, etc.,' he explains. 'Each of those components – each metabolome – leaves a chemical record in the wine. Say you want to know what the difference is between a $10 wine and a $50 wine. Tasting them tells you there *are* differences, but it is an imprecise technique. And analysis of the two may be virtually identical: alcohol, acid, etc. With metabolomics, we can get a detailed chemical fingerprint of each wine. We can find out what makes the $50 wine different, and then we can use that knowledge to add value to the $10 bottle.'

It's all impressive stuff. But I can't help feeling it's mostly about developing commercially attractive quick-fix solutions rather than addressing the root causes of the problems. For example, the AWRI has genetically engineered a wine yeast that produces less alcohol, and using that knowledge is now developing, through selective pressure techniques, a 'naturally' occurring strain that can do the same thing. This is useful for growers caught in a hot season with over-ripe grapes. But wouldn't it be better to step back, take a broad view, and change where, how and which grapes are grown in the first place?

Something resembling a more holistic approach is being taken by the Wine 2030 project at Adelaide University. It brings together researchers and thinkers from various disciplines to look at big picture issues such as viticulture in a changing climate, greening the distribution chain, coping with water scarcity and understanding Australia's unique terroirs.

For winemaker Brian Croser, one of the instigators of the project and a co-chair of its advisory committee, this last area of research is the most important.

'The [global] market is asking for more and more fine wine,' he said at the launch of Wine 2030 in late 2008. 'Fine wine is expected to be natural. As natural as possible. A pure and unadulterated reflection of its provenance, its terroir…Australia has the potential to supply more fine wine, but to do that it needs to scientifically understand how to optimise its terroir opportunities and use that knowledge to explain their uniqueness to the fine wine world – to compete with the terroir legends of Europe as well as competing on pure quality.'

Peter Gago Penfolds

Since the mid-1990s, starting with the purchase of Mildara Blass, the publicly listed brewing behemoth Foster's has been slowly scooping up famous Australia wine companies, culminating in 2005 with the takeover of the then-troubled Southcorp. This gave Foster's the most remarkable portfolio of wine brands – from big names like Penfolds, Rosemount, Wolf Blass and Wynns to smaller, elite wineries like Coldstream Hills and T'Gallant – and created a wine company of gargantuan proportions.

There is little to get excited about at the commercial end of the Foster's wine pyramid. I think the wines are often depressingly interchangeable, it's hard to tell the difference sometimes between a cheap Wolf Blass red or Lindemans red, Rosemount red or a cheap Penfolds red. And some of the crass attempts to attract new, younger wine drinkers with brands like the low-calorie Early Harvest and Rosemount's O (best served over ice, apparently) rankle with this grumpy old neo-traditionalist.

But it is possible to find some stunning wines in the Foster's portfolio, most of them made in distant outposts of the Foster's empire: regional wineries such as Seppelt, T'Gallant and Coldstream Hills. And then there's Penfolds, whose spiritual heart lies – and where glimpses of its future can be seen – at Magill vineyard winery and cellars, on Adelaide's fringe. Where Dr Penfold settled in the 1840s, where Max Schubert developed Grange in the 1950s, and where Peter Gago and his team are making the best Penfolds red wines today.

Magill is like an autonomous sovereign state, a principality within the Foster's empire. And Peter Gago is the prince, not quite Machiavellian, perhaps, but certainly resourceful and charming enough to convince the powers that be to let him have his head when it comes to Penfolds' top wines. Then again, with Grange selling for $600 a bottle, and annual Grange production reportedly around the 5000–10,000 case mark, there's probably nothing the Foster's management would refuse him.

Peter is very much the right person for the job of Penfolds chief winemaker. His passion for the heritage and culture of the company is palpable. But there's a sparkle of irreverence, a glimmer of iconoclasm shining under the necessarily cautious and conservative surface. There's also, refreshingly, a strong egalitarian streak, an awareness of the loyalty among everyday Penfolds drinkers, and a feeling that this loyalty has been stretched in recent times.

A couple of years ago, Peter developed a wine as a tribute to the first vintage of Koonunga Hill 'claret', the 1976 – a brand that has been stretched and diluted under Foster's rule. This limited-release, retro-labelled bottling captured the soul of this famous brand, and made the 'standard' Koonunga Hill shiraz cabernet taste rather bland and boring by comparison.

'I truly, truly want to get Kooonunga Hill back to where it was,' Peter told me, adding, in barely disguised contempt for his own company's marketing decisions: 'Hopefully one day there'll be just one red in the Koonunga Hill range, and it'll be as good as this.'

It's this willingness to challenge conventions that led to my favourite Penfolds red wine, the Cellar Reserve sangiovese.

The Penfolds 'rule book' is quite clear about the traditional house style for the company's red wines: multi-vineyard, multi-regional sourcing; plenty of tannin (natural or added); acidification to balance the ripe fruit; barrel fermentation; lots of new wood, preferably American. The sangiovese deliciously breaks almost all of these rules.

The wine was developed as part of the Gago-driven experimental winemaking program that has also brought us some fabulous wild yeast, slinky Adelaide Hills pinot, vibrant Eden Valley gewurz and sub-regional single-vineyard Barossa Grenache. All released under the Cellar Reserve label in relatively small quantities. The sangiovese was first made in the early 1990s using grapes planted in a corner of the Kalimna vineyard in the Barossa in 1982. Recent vintages have also included fruit from sangiovese vines planted in the mid-'90s by Penfolds' grower liaison manager, Paul Georgiadis, in his vineyard at Dorrien, and younger vine Marananga fruit.

The wine is made at Magill with no additions except a little sulphur at bottling. No yeast, no acid, no enzymes, no tannin. Nothing. Just naturally fermented in big open pots and matured in old barriques for almost a year before bottling, unfined and unfiltered.

The result is, simply, a brilliant glass of red wine. Savoury, grippy, tart enough to be unmistakably varietal sangiovese. Earthy, dusty, warm enough to be unmistakably Barossa. And bold, big, generous enough to be unmistakably Penfolds.

'It's the antithesis of Penfolds,' says Peter, excitedly. 'It's nothing except crushed grapes. I love showing it to people and being able to say this is 100 per cent, this is real.'

But as much as I adore this wine, it also frustrates me. Every time I taste it I can't help thinking how fantastic it would be to see a similar, hands-off, 'natural' approach taken with some of the other awesome fruit that trundles in through the doors of the Magill winery. Imagine it: unadulterated Block 42 cabernet from those precious 120-year-old vines at Kalimna; Magill Estate shiraz without all that new oak. Wouldn't it be great to taste the essence of these special places in the glass, without the distraction of too much winemaking?

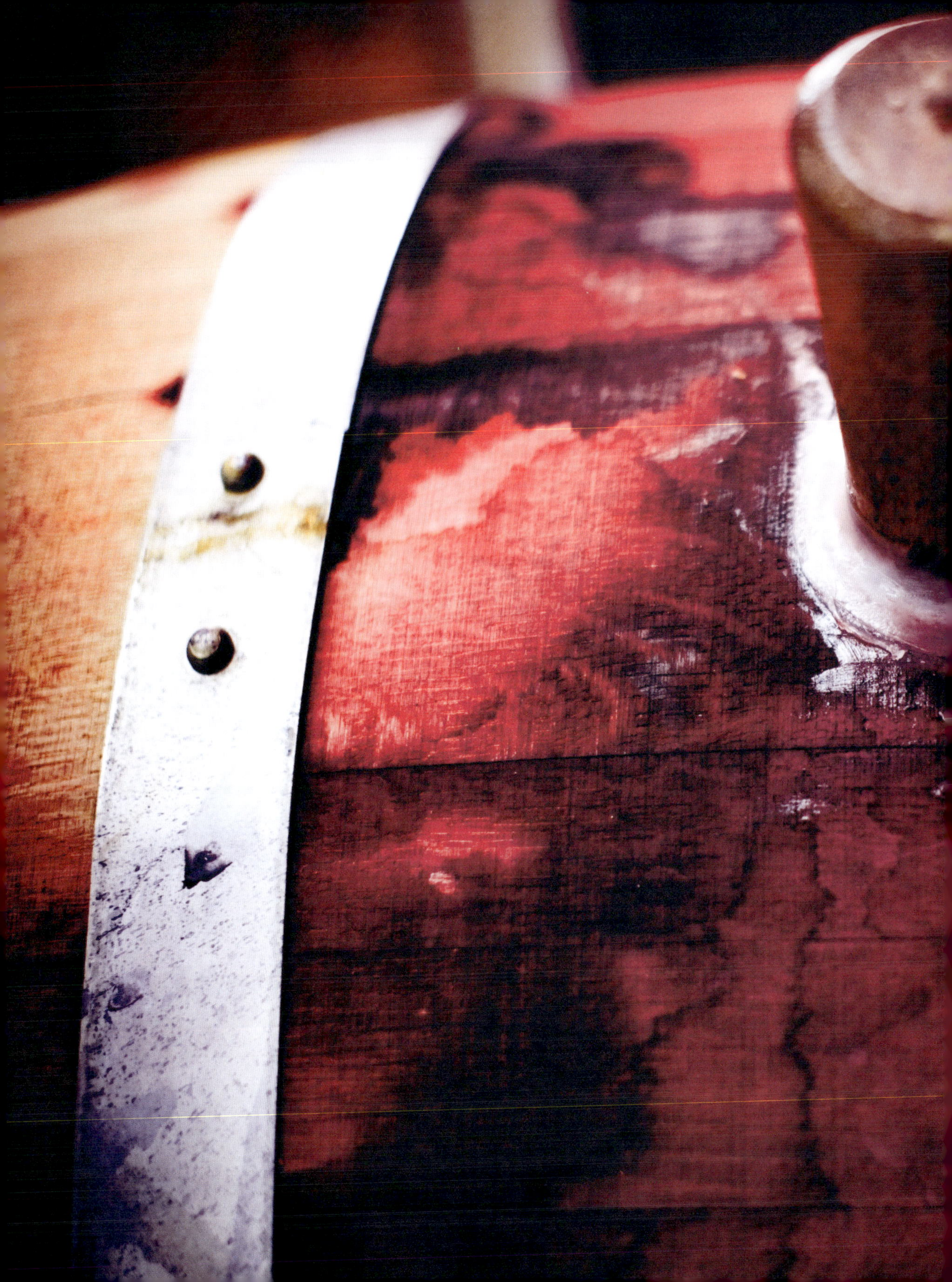

Penfolds Magill Estate, Adelaide

Hewitson

Stepping into the Hewitson wine cellars at Mile End, just outside Adelaide's CBD, is like stepping into a bizarre and intricate installation by some obscure German conceptual artist. The cellars were built as a dairy cold store in the late 19th century and are a warren of cork-lined rooms, many with vault-like heavy doors. The place is slightly dilapidated and humming with a sense of history; the perfect setting, really, for Hewitson's wines, some of which are sourced from very old vineyards indeed.

Dean Hewitson himself comes across a bit like a mad conceptual artist too, with his throaty laugh, slightly wild, Tim Minchin–like dark-ringed eyes and bubbling enthusiasm.

Dean worked in the old Hardys cellars near here in Mile End early in his career, before moving on to stints at the vats in a number of places (including an extended stay at Petaluma) and finally setting up his own, eponymous label in the late 1990s.

As Dean points out, walking into an urban wine cellar just feels right, somehow: grapes need to come from a bucolic landscape of vineyards and rolling hills, but wine is inescapably manufactured and the industrial setting of the old warehouse reinforces this image. It's also a nod to Adelaide's rich heritage as a wine-producing city: at one time, there were vineyards and plenty of wine cellars like this one surrounding the city, before suburbia strangled the life out of them.

Dean makes very good wines from a number of regions around Adelaide including a boisterously brilliant Barossa GSM called Miss Harry; a painfully austere Eden Valley riesling called (appropriately) Gun Metal; an unctuous McLaren Vale shiraz called Mad Hatter; a juicy, pleasantly sharp-edged Fleurieu tempranillo called Private Cellar; and a straightforward Adelaide Hills sav blanc called Lu Lu (this last wine replaced a much more adventurous and interesting dry white called Mermaids, made from muscadelle and only 9.5 per cent alcohol, which never really caught on, unfortunately).

Dean's best wine, though, is the extraordinary Old Garden mourvedre. Made from a single block of dry-grown bush vines planted in the 1850s in the deep red sands of Rowland Flat in the southern Barossa, this is a stunning amalgam of spice, flowers and dusty aromas leading onto a mouthful of macerated plums dusted with bitter chocolate. What I love most about this wine is its poise and elegance: yes, it's a big, strong drink with heaps of flavour, structure and – most of all – length, but it's not heavy, ponderous and overbearing. It has balance, class and, yes, finesse. It is one of Australia's greatest red wines.

First Drop

Minchia. It's an Italian word. Quite rude, too, apparently. Which is why no Italian-speaking person I know will tell me what it means. But they blush when they see the word on the label of First Drop's delicious Adelaide Hills–grown montepulciano. So I googled it. And now I understand.

Using blue Italian slang typifies the bold, brash, quirky approach taken by the First Drop partnership of Matt Gant and John Retsas. They're soldiers of fortune, these two: sourcing grapes from regions circling Adelaide – the Hills, the Barossa, McLaren Vale – stamping them with funky names and labels. The fact that their wines are also bloody good sets this venture apart: there are quite a few new-wave wine ventures out there now with eye-catching designs, punchy names and marketing campaigns aimed at the YouTube generation, but none of them are quite as adventurous with what's inside the bottle as what's on the outside.

Gant and Restas met when they were both working for St Hallett as winemaker and cellar door manager, respectively, in the early years of this century. Their backgrounds were quite different: Gant is an Essex boy who fell in love with wine while studying geography in London; Retsas is a South Australian son of European migrants, who made their own wine and sausages in the backyard. But the pair share an attitude of serious fun when it came to drinking, whether the drink in question happens to be vodka Red Bulls in the Tanunda Hotel or the finest wines available to humanity in some flash restaurant in New York. And they've channelled all these influences – street smarts, a serious respect for wine's traditions, a rude desire to have as much fun as possible – into what they do at First Drop.

Both were deeply immersed in Barossa culture at St Hallett through dealing with many of the region's old growers, and this immersion course has resulted in First Drop's top wines, single-vineyard expressions of shiraz from various sub-regions, collectively called the Fat of the Land: the Ebenezer, from vines planted in the red clay in the north of the valley has juicy squashed red fruit, purple jube flavours and svelte tannins; the Greenock, from the ironstone soils of this increasingly desirable sub-region has more generous, wild bramble berry fruit and furry tannin; while the Seppeltsfield, from red clay loam over limestone to the west has more concentration, greater extract and grippy, dark-chocolatey tannins.

Matt and John's immersion course in *drinking* Barossa shiraz at the Tanunda Hotel has also inspired a few particularly slurpy expressions of the style: one, called Mother's Milk, is all purple velvet and blackberry jam, while another, 2 Per Cent, uses a smidgen of savagnin to give life and lift to the sheer darkness of the shiraz fruit.

Matt's grape-treading experience working in Portugal, Spain and Italy comes to the fore in wines like Bella Coppia (a crunchy pear-textured arneis), Lush (a crisp and tangy rosé made from the Iberian red grape, trincadeira – aka tinta amarela), a plush but tight JR Gantos cabernet touriga blend from McLaren Vale, and the throbbing heart of purple fruit and firm but juicy tannin in that cheeky little montepulciano called Minchia.

Google it.

S.C. Pannell Wines

Steve Pannell is a very busy boy. Since leaving his high-powered job as senior winemaker at Hardys in the early years of this century, he has scored gigs consulting to a number of companies from Argentina to Spain, from Shaw and Smith and Foster's in Australia to Liberty Wines in the UK, for whom he makes some own-label wines. And somehow, in the middle of it all, he manages to produce some great gear under his own label, sourced from vineyards in McLaren Vale and the Adelaide Hills.

When he was at Hardys Tintara winery in the 1990s, Steve made a name for himself by producing red wines that managed to express a deeply savoury tannic side as well as the usual core of voluptuous sweet purple McLaren Vale fruit, thanks to careful management of the skins during fermentation and the use of gentle basket presses. He's continued this approach with his own reds: the S.C. Pannell shiraz shows exceptional depth and concentration. It's laden with ripe black fruits but you can feel on your tongue that there's plenty of *stuff* held back in reserve, waiting to unfurl as the wine ages in bottle. The grenache, made from a 70-year-old dry-grown patch of bush vines, is similarly layered and complex: there's plenty of seductive rich black fruit, but also a sprinkling of subtle spice and satisfying, earthy, lingering tannin.

Steve's international experience has given him a new perspective on what grapes should be grown and how wines should be made in Australia. For a start, he says, we're growing the wrong varieties in many of our regions: 'We should have more lagrein, with its beautiful natural acidity so we don't have to add any in the winery, and aglianico, with those great savoury tannins so we don't need to add any of those either. And carignan. Look at how important carignan is in the hot south of France. Keep the yields down and it can make bloody good wine, cheaply, reliably, great as part of a blend. And it's sustainable, too: it doesn't need water. We need to get with the gig.'

He's concerned about the increasing alcohol content of many Australian red wines. But he doesn't think the solution is technological. 'I'm convinced viticulture is the key to knocking back alcohol,' he says. 'We've got to learn not to plant vineyards according to how wide your tractor is, but according to how the vines want to grow. Plant them closer together and they'll ripen the fruit earlier, with better balance of flavour and sugar.'

Steve believes it's time for Australia to emerge from its decades long 'Francophile period', where Claret and Burgundy were held up as the ultimate expressions of fine wine, into an era where a greater diversity of European wine styles should be embraced and emulated.

'For years, Australian winemakers were seduced by the French and lulled into the false idea that we live in a country whose climate is like Bordeuax or Burgundy,' says Pannell. 'The older generation were totally obsessed with so-called classic French varieties, planted them in the most inappropriate places, and convinced themselves that the wines were pretty good.' Worse, he says, was that Australian winemakers often ignored the fact that other countries with warmer climates similar to ours could grow and make wine every bit as good as those French 'classics'.

Practising what he preaches, Steve's bistro wines, called Pronto, are inspired by the new-wave fresh whites and slurpy young reds coming out of the Mediterranean. The Pronto white is mostly Adelaide Hills sauvignon blanc, blended with a little riesling and pinot gris to cut the obvious perfume and add some textural interest; the red is unwooded McLaren Vale grenache and mourvedre (aka monastrell) blended with a dash of shiraz and the Portuguese red grape touriga – it's full of fleshy purple berries, but finishes snappy and dry.

'We should be making heaps of this stuff in Australia,' he says, 'rather than the heavy, oaky, sweet wines that most people associate with commercial Australian reds. There's no reason at all we can't make more of this style of wine. People love it, especially younger drinkers.'

Younger drinkers, 'people under 35', have also responded very favourably to Steve's brilliant, authentically difficult and deeply savoury nebbiolo, made using grapes grown (from 2009, biodynamically) by Frank Baldasso at Protero in the Adelaide Hills, not far from the Arrivo nebbiolo vineyard.

'I thought no-one but me and a few other hardcore neb-heads would want to drink it, so I only made 100 cases in the first year,' he says. 'But I've been really surprised by how people have jumped at the opportunity to drink something with real dryness and tannin and grip. I reckon it's part of a mini-shift in the tastes of Australian wine drinkers towards elegance and restraint.'

Adelaide Hills

The Adelaide Hills wine region isn't as cool as you might think. Sure, at its core, up around and above the 500-metre mark, in the sub-regions of Piccadilly and Lenswood, the vineyards draped over sharp crests and plunging gullies are indeed the coldest and among the wettest in the state: similar, climatically, to the Macedon Ranges, or Tasmania. But on the eastern slopes of the Hills, down around Macclesfield, and the western slopes at Kersbrook, the country is lower, drier, milder: climatically more like some parts of central Victoria.

There are also big differences in soil types across the region, from loose loams over sandstone and clay with varying amounts of shale and ironstone scattered through the heart of the Hills to rocky, sandy soils glinting with micaceous schist around places such as Mount Barker.

In other words, there's much more to the Adelaide Hills (and, indeed, to life) than sauvignon blanc, chardonnay and pinot. Don't get me wrong: all three grapes make exceptional wine here, especially in the cooler spots. But there are other grapes that might, eventually, prove to be even better suited to the region.

The 'Alsace' duo of riesling and pinot gris, for example, often excite me more than savvy up here. Take Henschke's pinot gris, from David and Annette Innes' vineyard at Littlehampton: a consistently superb example of the multi-layered, textural, ripe and exotic later-harvested gris style and, I think, much more satisfying and characterful than most Hills sav blanc. Or take Kanta, a joint venture between legendary Mosel winemaker Egon Muller and Adelaide retailer Michael Andrewartha, with winemaking contribution from Steve Pannell, to produce a riesling each year from a Hills vineyard at Balhannah. The wine is fermented at Shaw and Smith using indigenous yeasts, is aged for a while on its lees and released a little later than most other Australian rieslings: it is a stunning expression of place and grape, with a green apple bite and a ravishing interplay of chalky dryness and subtle grapey sweetness.

As you'll read, Italian and Spanish red varieties are flourishing here, and the warmer parts of the Hills are home to some of the most exciting medium-bodied new-wave shirazes in the country. Some winemakers persist with cabernet but very few succeed: although much of the region is warmer than you might imagine, it's still a cool place to grow the late-ripening cabernet. Paul and Kathy Drogemuller's sheltered, sun-trap Paracombe vineyard is an exception: their cabernet franc is a succulent, gluggable wine that perfectly balances herbal purple-berry characters with snappy grip, while the cabernet sauvignon can be a tightly coiled ball of dusty tannin and intense black fruit. These wines remind the well-informed taster, perhaps, that Max Schubert sought grapes from a vineyard in the Paracombe district for his first, experimental Granges in the early 1950s.

Janet and Erinn Klein
Ngeringa

Of all the Australian winemakers adopting biodynamic techniques in their vineyards, Erinn Klein has perhaps the most appropriate background. Born in Germany, where his parents were members of an Anthroposophical circle, Erinn went to Steiner school, grew vegies and made compost as a kid before moving with his family to Australia, where they established the Jurlique skincare business, growing biodynamic herbs and flowers for various potions and tinctures in the Adelaide Hills.

In 2001, after working as a flying winemaker for the UK organic wine specialist, Bottle Green, in Europe, and a disillusioning stint at a conventional winery in Victoria, Erinn and his wife Janet planted the Ngeringa vineyard on a sandy loam hill near Mount Barker. A year later they planted another, closer-spaced vineyard in the micaceous schist soils a few kilometres away at Nairne, hanging onto the eastern edge of the Hills. Each vineyard has quite a different personality, apparent as soon as you walk through the vine rows.

The Kleins take their biodynamics very seriously: both vineyards are certified BD by NASAA; the couple run Highland cattle on the property to make their own compost; they are involved in BD preparation-making at Paris Creek; and even used biodynamic straw from the Barossa to construct the strawbale winery.

Like his friend Anton van Klopper, Erinn adopts a very minimal approach in the winery: all the varieties – chardonnay, viognier, pinot noir, shiraz (rightly called, here, syrah) – are wild-fermented in barrel or open vat; the reds are foot-crushed and all malo is spontaneous.

The Kleins produce two tiers of wine. The JE label is for non-varietal estate-grown wines as well as wines made from fruit grown elsewhere, one-offs such as a terrific McLaren Vale shiraz, and the vin santo-like Altus made from pink semillon. Initially, the estate-grown chardonnay and pinot noir were only released as JE wines, which shows admirable integrity: both were good, but they weren't a patch on the wines released under the Ngeringa label. There is also a seriously savoury, complex JE rosé which I think is fantastic, but, because it's only a pink wine, it probably can only ever exist in the more accessibly priced, second-label territory.

The Ngeringa viognier is a wonderful wine, with stunning depth of texture and a heart of honey-dipped hazelnuts, reflecting both the careful viticulture and hands-off winemaking. The Ngeringa pinot noir is tight and nervy at first, then relaxes into a stunning juicy fresh mouthful of wild red berry fruit. But the star here is the Ngeringa syrah, the core of which comes from the Nairne vineyard: bright and brittle scents of purple berries and crackling undergrowth lead on to a juicy, sappy mouthful of elegant red, with lean black tannins and plenty of room to build in the bottle. It's a triumph for both Erin– and Janet Klein, and the Adelaide Hills in general.

Arrivo

Not many people plant vineyards with a crystal clear idea in their minds of the kind of wine they want to produce. Peter Godden did.

Almost two decades ago, when he was studying winemaking at Roseworthy, Peter worked at Joe Grilli's Primo Estate and was introduced to some Barolos and other Italian nebbiolos. And he fell head over heels in love with the grape.

'When I left Roseworthy,' he recalls, 'I drank an Aldo Conterno '82 Barolo. I was just this fledgling, heading out into the world, but I remember thinking: *That's* what I want to make.'

Peter's nebbiophilia quickly become an obsession. By 1992 he had registered the name Arrivo ('I came across this description of nebbiolo in a book on Italy by Burton Anderson: it means "a wine you arrive at after tasting other things"'), and in 1996 he worked at Vietti, one of the best wineries in Piedmont, before joining the Australian Wine Research Institute in 1997 and going on to become one of its principal scientists.

With partner and fellow nebb-nut, wine importer, Sally McGill, Peter planted in 1998 a small block of nebbiolo vines at the bottom of a slope in Gumeracha, in the northern Adelaide Hills, and, characteristically, put the baby vines through rigorous, painstaking trials.

'For the first two years we weighed every bunch,' he says, revelling in his geekiness. 'We did micro-ferments of just 5, 20 kilos of grapes. I amassed enough data to write at least two peer-reviewed papers.'

In 2001, Peter and Sally graduated the vineyard up the steep hill and planted a hectare of seven clones of high-trellised, straw-mulched nebbiolo vines. The mix of clones is important, one of the disadvantages of being a small estate producer is the lack of blending options, Peter says: 'You have to create them yourself, so the more clones you have, the more small ferments you can do, the more complexity in the finished wine.'

The first Arrivo nebbiolo – the 2004 vintage – appeared in 2006 and took the variety to a new level of quality and sophistication in Australia. As well as typical Adelaide Hills pristine red cherry and wild strawberry fruit and an echo of rosemary and gum mist, it was the extraordinary finesse and persistence of the classic tongue-hugging nebbiolo tannins that really impressed.

'Get the structure right first and the fruit will come,' says Peter, sounding for all the world like a Piedmontese. 'That's what I learned in Italy. And not to bottle until the tannins have melted like candle wax in the mouth.'

Italy also inspired two subsequent wines from the vineyard: a deeply coloured, tangy, stunning rosato that spends two weeks in contact with skins and then plenty of time on lees, and a 'lunga macerazione' nebbiolo that spends more than two months on skins before pressing.

'Alfredo Currado [from Vietti] gave me the confidence to do it,' says Peter. 'He told me there's no point in attempting the classic long maceration style unless you go the whole hog. And he said don't taste it until it's been on skins for at least a month because it'll taste shocking and scare you off.'

So he resisted the temptation, and the result is glorious: a wine with deep, resounding, rolling tannins that build and build on the tongue, leaving you craving another plateful of slow-braised beef.

Arrivo is not only one of the most impressive new wine labels in the Adelaide Hills, it's one of the most exciting in Australia.

Hahndorf Hill Winery

'Look,' says Larry Jacobs, standing at the top of the Hahndorf Hill vineyard. He points through a gap in the trees at the bottom of the gully, towards houses and street signs. 'That's the town of Hahndorf, right there. This proximity forces us to farm responsibly. It's a given.'

Because of its proximity to Adelaide, its importance as a tourist area, and because all the region's horticultural businesses tend to be piled on top of each other – orchards hug vineyards nestled between bush reserves behind houses – Adelaide Hills residents are a bit touchy about environmental issues. New wineries open very infrequently, and have to comply with strict guidelines involving pollution and water issues: Petaluma's planned new winery at Woodside (due to be built in time for the 2011 vintage) will incorporate solar power and passive cooling and cutting-edge waste management technology, to ensure that no water leaves the property at all.

Because of this green awareness, in early 2009, the Adelaide Hills became the first wine region in South Australia to have a fully functioning and Government-endorsed environmental management system (EMS) available to members of the winegrowers' association. The EMS was first trialled by 12 vineyards in the region, including Hahndorf Hill, before being adopted by others.

There is also a thriving alternative eco-culture in the Hills – tree-changers who have quit the city life. One of the country's leading sustainable viticulture consultancies, TM Organics, is based here at Stirling; and there is an active community of biodynamic farmers in the region, including the influential Ulli and Helmut Spranz of the wonderful Paris Creek biodynamic dairy farm. This alternative culture is beginning to rub off on the local grape growers, with more and more, like Larry and Marc, taking steps towards adopting organic and biodynamic practices in their own vineyards.

When they bought the cellar door in 2002, Larry (who once ran a wine estate in Stellenbosch, South Africa) and his partner Marc Dobson began the slow process of rejuvenating the run-down 4-hectare vineyard by green manuring and mulching under-vine. They soon stopped using chemicals in the vineyard and began applying biodynamic preparations in autumn 2007. Marc embarked on a course in BD and Larry became one of the early adopters and biggest advocates of the Hills' pilot Environmental Management Scheme.

For Marc, the environmental focus and particularly the holistic approach of biodynamics at Hahndorf Hill is about education and connecting to the wider community. 'Because we're a tourism winery, it's important to engage everyone at cellar door,' he says. 'While the initial concern was making sure we don't affect the neighbourhood with what we do, doing things in a more environmentally sensible way also has a ripple effect. If you take an action with conviction, like a pebble thrown in a pond it will hopefully influence other people.'

Like many in the region, Hahndorf Hill produces a good sauvignon, in a very lean, powdery, crisp style that expresses the slate and ironstone running through the vineyard's loamy soils, as well as pinot grigio, chardonnay and shiraz.

But the vineyard is unusual in that it also boasts the German varieties trollinger and lemberger, red grapes blended together to make a fantastically delicate, faintly herbal, bone-dry rosé.

Lemberger is known in Austria as blaufrankisch, and this connection has inspired Larry and Marc to import three clones of the great Austrian grape, gruner veltliner, with the first vintage – grown from scratch using biodynamic techniques – in 2010.

La Linea

Peter Leske has been keeping himself very busy since stepping down as Nepenthe winemaker a few years ago. He's been consulting to various wineries, and working with various acronyms: sitting on the Technical Advisory Committee of the AWBC, for example, and helping to develop a climate change response kit with the South Australian Wine Industry Association that wine regions can use to help address the issues they face in a warmer, drier world.

He has also developed a wine label with David LeMire MW (ex-Negociants imported wine manager), to produce a red and a rosé tempranillo, and a 'Germanic' style riesling called Vertigo, all from Adelaide Hills fruit. He's also looking at planting mencia on a high, stoney, granitic ridge.

Two quite different vineyards have supplied fruit for the tempranillos: in 2007 the rosé came from a cool site near Echunga, and reflected the vineyard's terroir in its ethereal,

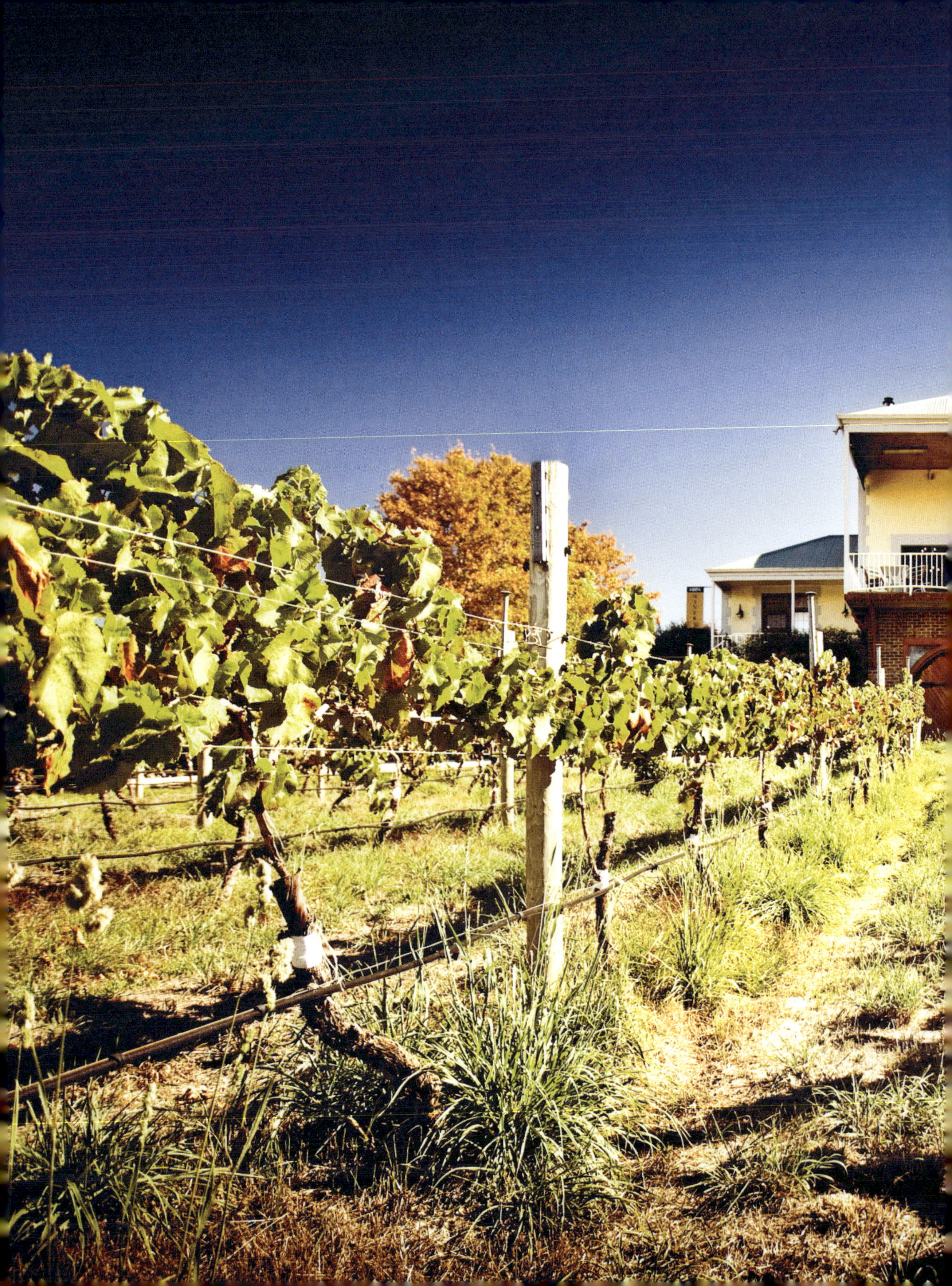

Hahndorf Hill Winery, Adelaide Hills

floral perfume, while the red came from a warmer vineyard at Kersbrook and had dark, rich, chocolatey texture. In 2008, the cooler Echunga vineyard was the source for both wines, and the dry red was particularly successful, with its fine red fruit, spicy overlay and transparent but firm tannins. The riesling is sourced from the even chillier Lenswood sub-region. All the wines demonstrate that these two varieties – tempranillo and riesling – are as comfortable in the Hills as the more ubiquitous pinot noir and sauvignon blanc.

Peter Leske is a careful, thoughtful winemaker, and applies a clear analytical mind to everything he does. Unlike some winemakers with a scientific background (he used to work at the AWRI, with Peter Godden), Peter is not completely dismissive of 'natural' winemaking and chemical-free viticulture but chooses to adopt conventional techniques such as cultured yeast fermentation in temperature-controlled stainless steel, not because that's what he was taught but because he's thought about it carefully and wants, at least initially, to make wines that express a fruit purity.

'I'm not afraid to add yeast and acid,' he says, fully aware that it's much trendier to claim the opposite. Peter and I have spoken many times about minimal intervention winemaking and biodynamics and my other hobbyhorses. But – again, unlike so many of his colleagues – Leske has always been ruthlessly honest and candid in his opinions.

'I think it's a bit of a myth that there is a perfect place in the world where you can make wine totally naturally,' he says. 'Acid is just cold weather in a bag; something we've needed in the last few vintages, let's face it.'

Lucy Margaux/Domaine Lucci

Anton van Klopper, his wife Sally and daughter Lucy live in a small hilltop house in the steep-sided Basket Range. They have 4 hectares of pinot noir vines planted up the hills and down the gullies of their little slice of this secluded bit of the Hills, and have recently bought more land next door and are planting another 4 hectares. They grow and sell their own vegies, which they farm, like their vines, with no additions other than biodynamic compost preparations.

In the winery, Anton adopts a similar minimal approach. Other than a small amount (maybe 20, maybe 50 ppm) of sulphur at bottling, nothing is added to the grape juice. As well as being a firm belief that this is the best way to make wine that expresses an authentic sense of place in the glass, for Anton, making unadulterated wine is an ongoing intellectual and aesthetic challenge: 'If you don't add anything during the winemaking process, what do you do to make sure the wine is as good as it can be?' he asks. To keep challenging himself, he makes wine from other vineyards in the Hills (which he puts out under the Domaine Lucci label) as well as his own vineyard.

As I discovered when I visited Lucy Margaux, the low-tech, slow-food, biodynamic philosophy is lived to the fullest here. We listened to Isaac Hayes and French jazz pianist Jacques Loussier (on vinyl, of course) as Anton kneaded fresh pasta for dinner, tossed with garden herbs and local olive oil. And the wines we drank were labelled with images painted by Lucy, some printed on handmade paper.

To a cynical observer, this might all sound just a bit too warm and fuzzy for words. But it's no airy, romantic hippy lifestyle. Anton has arrived at this point after many years' experience in the conventional food and wine worlds: after an early career in restaurants, he studied winemaking at Adelaide Uni in the late 1990s, and worked at a number of places such as Leasingham in Clare, Domaine Serene in Oregon and Lingenfelder in the Pfalz before establishing Lucy Margaux.

What's more, although much can (and obviously I think should) be made of Anton's hardcore biodynamic practice and 'natural' winemaking philosophy, it would all ring hollow if the wines weren't good. But they are. Really quite exceptional, in fact. And while they're made in painfully small quantities (a barrel of this, a barrel of that), they are truly amazing and well worth tracking down.

The Domaine Lucci Saignée Rosé, made using juice bled from a number of the other wines, is an extraordinarily satisfying and complete pink wine with lovely cherry tomato fruit sweetness/tartness and a soft dry finish – and an exquisite hand-drawn label. A sangiovese made from fruit grown near Balhannah is quite brilliant, with little wild purple currants reined in by graphite, walnut shells, five spice and cloves. The Domaine Lucci Red ('a blend of Burgundy and Bordeaux grapes' is all Anton will say, smiling cryptically) is a soft, gluggable house red with plump forest berry character. And three single-vineyard pinots are simply stunning: Monomeith, from a small vineyard near Ashton, is elegant, redolent of light pink flowers; Little Creek, from Norton Summit, is dry but supple, like kid leather; and the estate-grown Lucy Margaux is all dense ripe black cherry.

Together they make one of the most convincing arguments in favour of 'natural' winemaking I have ever tasted.

Celebrate the grape
Festivals, symposia and workshops dedicated to single varieties

Things are getting out of hand. I've lost count of the number of events held in Australia each year that focus on promoting single-grape varieties. As well as the annual public tastings that take place at wineries – the Cullen Chardonnay Tasting, the Cape Mentelle Cabernet Tasting, the Millbrook Viognier Tasting – where local examples of each variety are sampled alongside international benchmark examples, similar public events are also sponsored by wine companies in capital cities: the Frankland Estate International Riesling Tasting, the Stonier International Pinot Tasting, etc.

Some wine regions have gone out of their way to align themselves with certain grape varieties, in order to promote that unique regional/varietal combination as part of how they tell their story to the world. Rutherglen, for example, has set itself up as a champion of the robust red grape, durif, and in 2008 celebrated the centenary of the variety's arrival in the region; the Riverina has staked a similar claim for its luscious botrytis-affected semillons with the annual Sweet Wine Challenge; Coonawarra has its annual cabernet barrel auction, where a peer-selected line-up of the region's best cabernets from the previous year are sold off at a well-attended charity auction; and McLaren Vale has its Cadenzia project, where different winemakers each release a special wine under the collaborative Cadenzia label – the only proviso being that the wine must contain some grenache.

But as important as these public promotions and celebrations are to the maturing of Australia's wine culture, it's the industry-focused seminars, workshops and tastings, where new ideas are exchanged, issues debated and wines put under the collective microscope, that have more profound influence on the development of viticulture, winemaking and style. Pinot noir has more than its fair share of these events: the biennial Mornington Peninsula Pinot Celebration, for example, is nominally a public event, but ends up being attended mostly by growers, winemakers, media and trade; Tasmanian vignerons have a similar annual Pinot Noir Forum; and Victorian pinot noir winemakers regularly get together for an in-house, closed-door workshop.

Every year since 2006, because of my special interest in tempranillo, I have been invited to moderate a similar day-long workshop organised by South Australian growers and makers of the red Spanish grape. Each winemaker brings barrel samples of their latest vintage tempranillo and as much technical information about the growing and production as possible. The wines are all tasted blind by the group of around 30 people, frank and fearless comments are exchanged, the wines' identities are revealed and each winemaker is then invited to respond.

It never ceases to amaze me how willing these winemakers are to have their wines criticised by their peers, who are also their competitors in a very crowded marketplace. This, I think, is one of the keys to understanding Australia's past success as a wine-producing nation, and is the key to its future success: each winemaker realises that, through this kind of open collaboration, everyone will benefit from an overall improvement in wine quality, diversity, individuality and interest. Crucially, I have witnessed – tasted – the tangible effects of this collaboration: South Australia's tempranillos are, on the whole, much better now than they were four years ago, and I put much of this down to the free flow of opinions that takes place in the annual workshop.

Barossa Valley

Handing on is something the Barossa does particularly well, whether it's a new generation of grape growers inheriting the precious, century-old vines planted by their forebears, or a new generation of grape-treaders inheriting the spirit of all those who have worked the vats before them.

This is one of the reasons there is such a dynamic community of young, small-scale winemakers here: they are part of a rebellious lineage that goes back through Dave Powell at Torbreck in the late '90s to Rockford and Peter Lehmann in the mid-'80s. Renegades determined to save the old Barossa vineyards and the people who tend them from the uncaring corporate wine factories that dominate the region. Most of the members of the Artisans of Barossa group of small wine producers, as well as the growing legion of quality-minded young winemakers have emerged from this Lehmann/Rockford tradition of individuality, pride and dissent. When you hear Kym Teusner, for example, who established his wine label in 2002, talking about 'rescuing' precious shiraz grapes from the Riebke brothers' 130-year-old vines in Ebenezer in 2006 because they'd been turned away by 'the big machine', it sounds very much like Peter Lehmann dramatically quitting Saltram 30 years ago and setting up his own winery to support the growers who'd been left high and dry by the big company.

'I was brought up to believe that knowledge needs to be given back,' says Rockford's philosopher founder, Robert O'Callaghan. 'I'm excited about the fact I've enthused a lot of other people to get on board.'

So am I. I just wish that more of the Rockford protégés had followed O'Callaghan's approach to traditional Barossa winemaking – slowly, by hand, using old, wooden technology, searching for savoury subtlety – rather than following Rockford's famous former winemaker, Chris Ringland, in the rush for powerful, alcoholic, pitch-black wines that win Parker points.

'Power should be hidden in a wine, not obvious,' says Robert O'Callaghan. 'The easiest thing in the world is to make a 17 baumé wine that tastes like it's a 17 baumé wine. The hard thing is to take powerfully flavoured grapes and make complex, discreet wine.'

This, it seems to me, is the big challenge facing the Barossa: making complex, discreet wines rather than trophy-hunting blockbusters. The best of the region's growers and grape-treaders are responding to this challenge by exploring sub-regionality and the individual charms of single-vineyard wines (discussed in detail earlier in this book), and by using grapes other than shiraz – either previously unfashionable grapes such as grenache and mourvedre/mataro, or newer alternatives from the Mediterranean such as tempranillo.

Troy Kalleske
Kalleske Wines

The smell of smoked meat and vinegar comes wafting out of the open front door of the Kalleske house, a low-slung, wide-verandahed, typically Barossan residence on the family's 200-hectare farm near Greenock. It's dark and cool inside, a sanctuary from the harsh Barossa summer sun. I have arrived at lunchtime, but John and Lorraine Kalleske weren't expecting me: they're still finishing their quick meal of mettwurst and pickled vegetables before heading back out to the vineyard, and they're not quite sure what to do with this journalist from the city who has turned up on their doorstep. The Kalleskes are old-fashioned Barossa grape growers at heart; they haven't quite come to terms with all the attention that's been thrust upon them since they emerged a few years ago as one of the most exciting of all the region's new wine producers. Even Troy Kalleske, John and Lorraine's young winemaker son, who has worked the vats at Penfolds and Kendall Jackson in California and was named Winemaker of the Year in 2008 by the Barons of the Barossa, still comes across as a shy, humble soul who'd rather not be standing in the headlights of publicity, thanks very much.

The hype might be new, but the Kalleske family's connection to country stretches back over seven generations. Johann Georg Kalleske arrived in South Australia in 1838 and started growing grapes near the tiny Barossa village of Greenock in 1853. The shiraz vines that now produce the $100-a-bottle wine named in his honour were planted in 1875. For the next century and a bit, Kalleske after Kalleske tended what has now become a 50-hectare vineyard, selling the highly regarded grapes to grateful wineries such as Penfolds. It wasn't until Troy decided to become a professional grape-treader in the 1990s and move back home in 2002 to turn some of the family's grapes into wine that the name Kalleske first appeared on a label.

Troy's wines are simply superb. The Clarry's red, a cheeky, vibrant, spicy blend of shiraz and grenache, offers exceptional value for less than $20; the Greenock shiraz is saturated with the qualities typically found in red wines from this ironstone-rich district, deep black fruit astride an undercarriage of meaty, earthy tannins; and the Old Vine grenache has a glorious perfume of glossy ripe purple plums and crushed dried herbs, filling the mouth with rich squashed black berries and leathery tannin.

As well as this traditional line-up of Barossa styles, Troy also plays with new techniques, varieties and styles. His Florentine barrel-fermented chenin blanc vies with Christian Canute's as one of the most characterful, textural whites in the region; the Pirathon shiraz, made using non-estate fruit, grown by neighbours and friends, is a bold, forceful expression of the new-wave Barossa style; and the Moppa shiraz, while generous and rich, in the Kalleske mould, has a tightness of tannin and perfume lift thanks to the inclusion of a little petit verdot. The Kalleskes have also planted some non-traditional varieties in recent years: it will be fascinating to see what Troy can do with Greenock-grown viognier, durif, tempranillo and zinfandel.

At the same time as they launched their own label, the Kalleske family converted their vineyards to organic viticulture, driven by John Kalleske's desire to revert to older, less intrusive farming techniques. The now-certified organic vines also receive some of the biodynamic field sprays such as preparation 500 horn manure and Troy has become a passionate (if quietly spoken) advocate of BD.

Kalleske is a model for the future of the Barossa: there is a deep respect for the seven generations of history, but it is combined with a willingness to try new things; the wines display exceptional quality and unique personality, across all price points; and the vineyards are farmed in a truly sustainable way. Not a bad recipe for success, really.

Burge Family Winemakers

'Every now and then I have a dream,' says Rick Burge, his eyes widening, his grey curls bouncing enthusiastically. 'I'm back in the Barossa in the 1950s, and I'm making wine from grapes grown the old way, before the whole place became mechanised and people started relying on chemicals in their vineyards. Wouldn't it be fantastic to taste that fruit? To taste the old Barossa?'

Rick is an emotional bloke with a strong sense of his region's heritage and a passionate belief in a back-to-the-future approach to growing grapes and making wine. The Burge name has been connected with the Barossa since 1855; Rick's cousin is Grant Burge and their grandfather, Percival, established what is now the Burge Family wine business in 1928.

Unlike his cousin, Rick has kept his business small and concentrated on making wines from just 10 hectares of vines on two properties, Olive Hill and Draycott. The vines are managed using organic and some biodynamic practices; Rick was inspired to throw away the vineyard chemicals and adopt BD by Julian Castagna, the leading advocate of biodynamics, who'd taken shiraz cuttings from Draycott to plant his own vineyard in Beechworth in the mid-'90s. The emphasis at Olive Hill and Draycott is on gentle farming, low yields, concentrated fruit, intense flavour; Rick can become quite forlorn when he talks of vineyards near him in Lyndoch still chasing huge yields and employing a scorched-earth policy for eradicating weeds.

He tries to keep additions in the winery to a minimum. 'I'd like to see a new category in wine shows for natural wines. 'Wines made with no tannin, no reverse osmosis, no yeast, no acid additions – like they used to be made here.'

In many ways, Rick Burge reminds me of legendary Hunter Valley winemaker Maurice O'Shea. Like O'Shea, he releases some stand-alone wines under different, cryptically coded labels each year that are driven by the peculiarity of the season rather than conforming to a pre-determined marketing plan. So, as well as perennials like the tangy-lemony, ageworthy Olive Hill semillon (one of the Barossa's best examples of the grape); the floral, dense, chewy old-vine grenache he chooses to call Garnacha; and the magnificent, rich and deep but savoury Draycott shiraz, Rick might bottle a one-off combination of shiraz and souzao, or any number of different permutations of the grenache blend: the bright, berryish, Rhone-like Clochemerle; the riper, denser D&OH shiraz grenache; or a wine called G3, a superb, slinky Barossa blend of shiraz, mourvedre and grenache from the disastrously low 2007 vintage, which was the only premium red he made that year.

Rick used to run a small independent music label, and recorded a number of roots musicians including Jeff Lang. The Burge Family wines are like live acoustic albums: full of individuality, soul and an evocative sense of time and place.

Deisen Landscape

Barrels are laid out across the driveway waiting to be racked. A few more are hiding under the shade of a tree. Sabine Deisen is shooing her hens back into the protection of their coop. I feel like I've walked into the bucolic chaos of a small, traditional family wine estate somewhere in southern Europe, not a vineyard near Marananga, in the heart of the Barossa.

Sabine Deisen was born in Dusseldorf to musical parents; her mother was an opera singer, her father a folk musician. Looking for a life more connected to nature, the family arrived in the Barossa Valley in 1968, buying a 16-hectare block of old shiraz and riesling bush vines. Tragically, in the mid-1980s, at the time of the state government–sponsored vine-pull scheme, the family decided to rip the vines out, even though the fruit they produced was highly regarded by a number of local winemakers.

'They never told us the vines were any good at the time though, did they, the buggers?' asks Sabine in her soft German lilt. 'Back then [in the '70s and '80s], the big guys ruled the region like a serfdom: they wouldn't tell you what they really thought of your grapes, or you might ask for more money. But then, in the mid-'90s, Robert O'Callaghan from Rockford told us he remembered how good our old vines were, and John Vickery gave us a bottle of wine he'd made using grapes from this block in the '60s, and it was marvellous.'

Encouraged, Sabine and her partner Les Fensom decided to re-plant 10 hectares of dry-grown shiraz, mataro and grenache – some as bush vines – using cuttings from good old Barossa vineyards. Today, grapes from the Deisen vineyard find their way into top labels such as Rockford and John Duval, and since 2001 Sabine and Les have also made a few hundred cases of their own wine each vintage.

Sabine is a painter and has an artist's sensibility. Strolling around the property I'm struck by the calm harmony of the place. 'We have a little bit of bush, some heritage roses, grapes and grow a little wheat for the chooks,' says Sabine. 'It's our life, we work here. We want to be happy where we live and work.'

The wines are harmonious and warm-hearted, too: a true reflection of place and maker. Sabine Deisen's best wine, her mataro, has immense concentration, weight and earthy complexity, but also has a disarmingly pretty, floral, anise-like perfume floating above dark, glossy black fruit.

Rusden Wines

Christian Canute's calling card is the massive, dark-hearted shiraz he calls Black Guts. This is the wine that earned him his reputation when he started treading the grapes from his family's Rusden vineyard in 1998, after a stint at Rockford. But as impressively uncompromising as the Black Guts might be, the two wines from the Rusden stable that fascinate me most are made from non-mainstream Barossa varieties, chenin blanc and zinfandel.

The chenin, simply called Christian, is picked ripe (as all Rusden wines are) and barrel-fermented in snazzy French oak. The resulting aromatic but highly textural wine shows how well suited the high-acid chenin variety is to the warm climate of the Barossa. There's heaps of flavour, of bruised apple and pulpy lychee and lemon pith, and plenty of richness from both the grape and the barrel, but just enough zest and cut to stop the wine teetering over into blowsiness.

The Chookshed zinfandel is a wild wine indeed, a reflection of Christian's single-minded passion for producing wines with heaps of character and interest. In typical zin fashion, ultra-ripe flavours of sun-drenched hedgerow berries and blood plums are offset by spiky green flavours of pepper and spice, lifted by a touch of renegade acidity, finishing thick and meaty. It's not a wine for tasting and analysing; it looks terrible in a wine show line-up. It's a wine for full-throated enjoyment, alongside a big steaming pot of cassoulet or tagine.

Some people are put off by the wild, confronting nature of Rusden's wines; others are aghast at the prices (the zin is $70, the shiraz $80). But Christian is unapologetic: 'When I started making booze, not one of the top producers in the Barossa was making wine under $20. They were all charging serious money – and getting it. Then they got bigger, started to chase that cheaper market and lost the plot. We shouldn't be doing that, you know? It's like the best winemakers in Burgundy or the Rhone, we should just be aiming to make top booze. We should be proud of that. And we should charge what we think the wines are worth.'

Shobbrook Wines

Shobbrook is one of the Barossa's brightest new winemaking stars. Tom Shobbrook spent six years at Riecine, a leading biodynamic wine estate in Tuscany, before returning to the Barossa in 2007 to start making his own wine. His parents have a 10-hectare vineyard in the Seppeltsfield area; he and his partner, Emma, grow vegies on a small property in Ebenezer to sell at the farmer's market. Inspired by his time at Riecine, Tom is in the process of converting both properties to biodynamic farming. In the meantime, he's gaining valuable experience working for Ngeringa, the exciting new certified biodynamic winery in the Adelaide Hills.

What makes old vines so special?

The heart and soul of the Barossa's rich wine culture is its amazing library of old vines, some of which have produced grapes continuously since the 1840s. It's the authenticity of this viticultural heritage that makes the Barossa story so compelling and keeps attracting the interest of generation after generation of winemakers.

Rob Gibson knows more than most about what makes old vines tick. Before establishing his own eponymous winery and vineyard business in the late-'90s, he spent over 20 years working as a winemaker and viticulturist for Penfolds, gaining an intimate knowledge of the great old vine resource scattered across the Barossa.

'What you need to understand,' says Rob, 'is that the surviving population of old vines here – what I call the original gardens – are very strong vines. The average useful lifespan of a grapevine is about 33 years; after that, productivity begins to decrease and the vine becomes uneconomical. For the vine to survive beyond that, it has to have special attributes: it must be able to continue to produce.'

In other words, old vines aren't good because they're old, they're old because they're good: they've survived because they've proved to be the fittest, the ones that prove to be the best fit for their environment. But what is it that makes them so strong? Rob Gibson points underground.

'The older the vine gets, the bigger the root mass, the deeper the roots go,' he says. 'The more you get away from the 30 to 50 centimetres of topsoil, the better the vine expression. That top layer is a relatively fertile environment, and that's what the vine expresses when the roots are that deep: varietal flavour but not great character. Once the roots go deeper, move out of that luxury zone, it not only checks the vigour of the vine above ground, but also adds another dimension – of finesse – to the flavour of the grapes.'

Rob doesn't dismiss the idea that the roots (or, rather, the mycchorizal fungi associated with the fine root hairs) are able to extract minerals from the soil and rock and transfer them to the vine. But he suspects it has more to do with the fact that the larger root mass of the older vine acts as a survival mechanism – 'it produces a vine insulated from stress' – allowing moisture to be drawn from the soil at a steady and consistent rate, producing fully flavoured, even-structured, characterful grapes.

Because this old vine story is so compelling, many winemakers and marketers have exploited it, ever since Robert O'Callaghan first developed the Old Block shiraz label when he was at St Hallett in the early-'80s. But there has never been any official agreement, and certainly no legal definition, of what age a vine has to be before it can be called old; there is nothing stopping unscrupulous winemakers bottling wine from shiraz planted in the last decade and putting old vine on the label.

That is now changing. In 2006, veteran Eden Valley winemaker James Irvine proposed a voluntary code that could be adopted by people wishing to indicate how old their vines were. He proposed 'junior' as a description of vineyards that have been bearing fruit for 10 to 15 years; 'adolescent' for those vines that have seen 16 to 20 seasons; 'mature' from 21 to 50, 'aged' 51 to 70; 'ancient' for 71 to 100 and 'methuselah' for vineyards with more than 100 vintages under their craggy belts.

This was followed in 2007 by Yalumba, who announced that their wines would from then on comply with an Old Vine Charter. The proposed terms were: Old Vine (vines more than 35 years old), Antique (older than 70), Centenarian (100 years old or more), and Tri-Centenary (a vine whose life has spanned three centuries). The regional winemakers association, Wine Barossa, has now adopted Yalumba's charter (or a version of it) for the whole region. This will ensure a certain level of protection for both winemakers and wine drinkers.

'We're taking it very slowly,' says Tom. 'We have a ten-year plan. Dad was a conventional grower, so I'm gently massaging him over to a BD way of thinking. We've started using a Braun undervine weeder to show him you don't need herbicide, and we've sprayed 500 a few times. But that's not biodynamics. You've really got to get into using all the preps: the fish emulsion, the compost, working with the moon. And you've got to have been doing that for at least two or three years before you can start to make any claims about being biodynamic.'

The idea, says Tom, is to get to a stage where the vines and grapes are so well balanced, nothing is needed in the winery in the way of additions or manipulation. 'The wine should make itself,' he says.

It's a hands-off approach that he's already applied very successfully with his first few wines. They are packed with personality and interest: the riesling, from an old, dry-grown vineyard in the Eden Valley, has the flavour and texture of green apple pulped on limestone; his Salasso rosé, made with no additions at all, is all tangy delicate rose-hips; the Tommy Ruff shiraz mourvedre tastes of pink flowers and raspberries squashed between terracotta; and the Shobbrook shiraz, from his family's ten-year-old vineyard in Seppeltsfield, is svelte black plums skewered on redgum.

Spinifex

It's dark in the big green shed of a winery just off Bethany Road on the eastern side of the Barossa Valley. The ubiquitous winery radio is tuned not to Triple J but Classic FM: a modern Czech string quartet moans quietly out of invisible speakers. Just as I begin to make out the dark shapes of dozens of barrels of wine, quietly maturing, contemplating their fate, the lanky figure of Pete Schell emerges nervously from the gloom, mumbles a greeting and we're off, tasting through the latest vintages of Spinifex wine.

Pete and his partner Magali Gely operate what I think is the best of the new-wave of small-scale Barossa wine companies that emerged at the beginning of the 21st century. Inspired in part by the flurry of Parker-fuelled international interest in Barossa cult wines, a heap of young(ish) grape-treaders from established wineries began to make their own booze around the same time. People like Dan Standish from Torbreck, who launched the Massena label with Jaysen Collins from Turkey Flat; Matt Gant and John Retsas from St Hallett who launched First Drop; Matt Wenk from Two Hands who launched Smidge.

But there was something different about what Pete Schell (also fresh from Turkey Flat) and Magali were doing at Spinifex. These weren't big, blockbuster, showy wines designed to impress. They were wines that managed to take the best of the Barossa's sometimes forgotten varietal traditions and fuse them onto a very European flavour sensibility. (Importantly, perhaps, neither partner is Australian: Pete's a Kiwi, although his grandfather's grandfather was born in the Barossa, with vintage experience in Provence, and Magali is from a wine-growing family near Montpellier.)

Pete loves the idea of blending grapes, especially old-fashioned grapes that have been undervalued in the Barossa for decades, to achieve a complex yet harmonious result. Spinifex's trio of drink-now, bistro wines (released within 12 months of harvest) take this idea to a delicious extreme: the white, called Lola, is a fabulously textural, honeyed, perfumed blend of semillon, marsanne, viognier, ugni blanc, grenache blanc and vermentino; the sensationally savoury, complex, Provençal-style rosé is a blend of grenache, cinsault and mataro; and the slinky, spicy Papillon is a blend of the same three red grapes, sourced, says Schell, from sandier, higher and cooler vineyards to accentuate the bright fruit flavours.

Pete takes inspiration from traditional Barossa, southern Rhone and new-wave Spanish wine styles for his Spinifex reds, and carefully melds the richness of valley-floor-grown fruit with the perfumed lift and grapes from up in the Eden Valley. The Esprit is a bold, spicy, floral, layered blend of grenache, mourvedre, cinsault and carignan; the Spinifex shiraz viognier has uncommonly seductive scent and a disarming, mossy texture; the Indigene mataro shiraz is rich and inky, with the tannic bite of bitter chocolate; and the Taureau, a Priorat-like blend of tempranillo, carignan, cabernet and graciano is fantastically concentrated, sculptural and dense.

As well as sourcing fruit from a number of growers, Pete has also planted a few vines himself, including a small durif 'garden' at Light Pass, which he's farming with biodynamic preparations. He's a big fan of the robust red grape (he uses this fruit to produce his only single-varietal wine), and reckons it should be planted across the valley and used instead of added tannin to improve weaker red blends.

After we've tasted through his wines, Pete takes me for a drive. He doesn't say a lot, doesn't explain what it is I'm meant to be looking at. But as we roll over the undulating Barossa floor and up into the foothills of the ranges, he nods occasionally to a little patch of old vines here, a carefully tended garden there, mostly farmed along old, pre-industrial lines. I realise we're driving across his palette, and these vineyards are his colours. Pete Schell may have only been here for a decade, but he understands the landscapes of the Barossa as well as any old-timer, and he understands how best to put those landscapes together in the bottle.

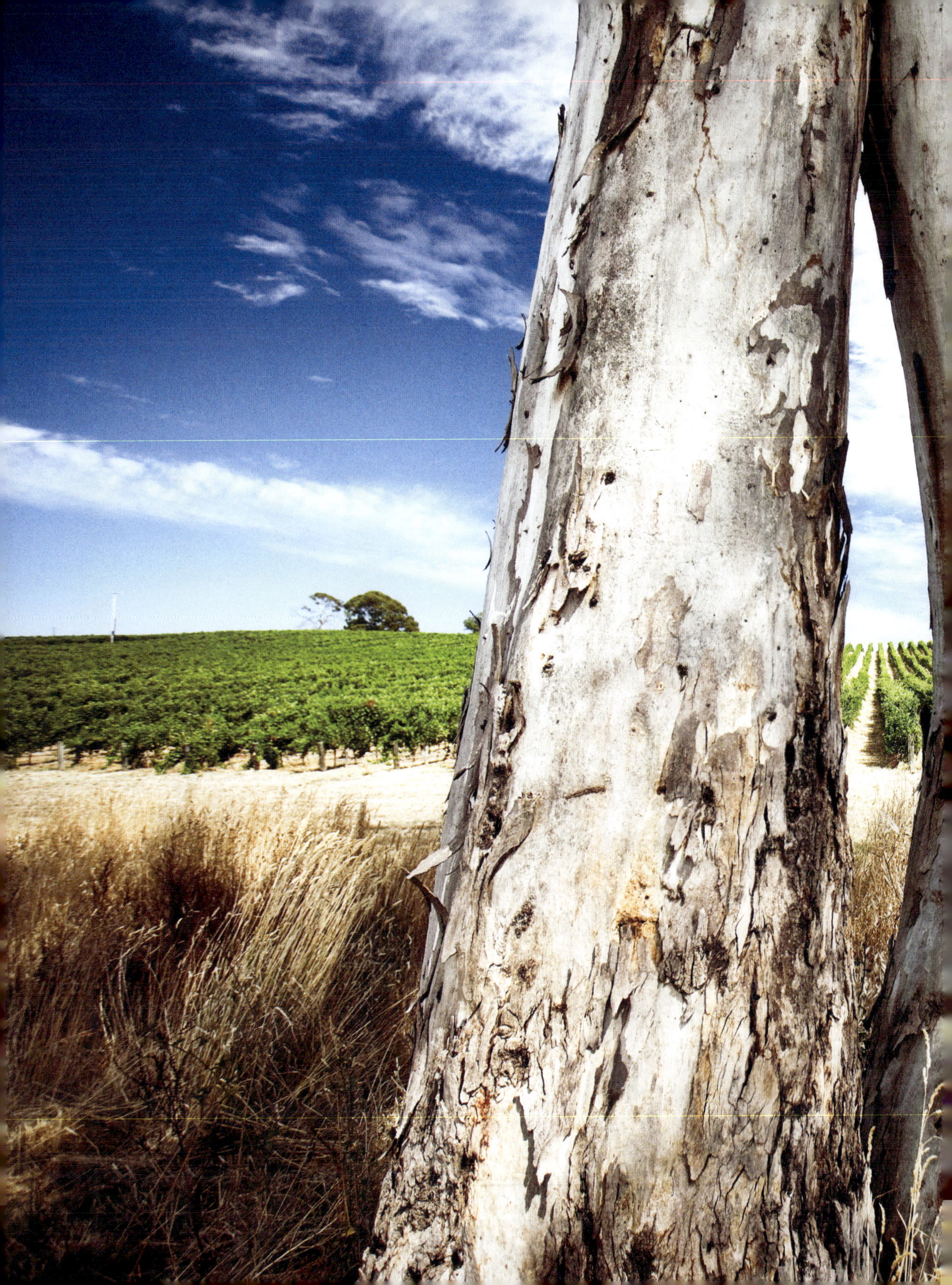

Barossa Valley

Eden Valley

As the realities of climate change begin to bite, Eden Valley's cooler, higher-altitude vineyards may become increasingly important to winemakers on the Barossa Valley floor, who could find that ever-warmer ripening conditions in their own vineyards change the nature and flavour of their grapes beyond what is traditionally perceived to be typical. In other words, thanks to global warming, Eden Valley could begin to resemble the Barossa Valley. To mangle a few biblical images, we may see a mass exodus to Eden.

Since the early days of white settlement, the two neighbouring valleys have seen themselves as halves of one whole: the Silesian Lutheran, rugged Scots and prim English strands that were laid down in both places meshed to form a close-knit community. From very early on, there has been a steady exchange of grapes between the rich brown rolling country of the Barossa Valley floor and the austere, meaner soils of the lofty Eden Valley.

Many Barossa Valley–based wineries source white grapes, particularly Riesling, from the Eden Valley. Eden fruit also finds its way to winemakers further afield, enchanted by the steely austerity of the regional riesling style.

Increasingly, too, the elegance, spice and undergrowthy complexity that Eden Valley's stony, hungry soils give to shiraz are attracting more and more red winemakers from the Barossa Valley, looking for a counterpoint to the plush richness of the shiraz wines they make from the more fertile soils of the valley floor.

There is, however, a big, angry blowfly in the ointment of potential salvation. While Eden Valley's altitude may prove to be a boon in a warmer future, climate change will probably also exacerbate the region's already very dry conditions: as it is, the last few years of drought have put a stop to the development of large new irrigated vineyards in Eden Valley. The drought doesn't appear to have been too much of a problem for many of Eden Valley's old, established, dry-grown riesling and shiraz vineyards – so far. But if the big dry continues, and is followed by more, even deeper droughts, who knows how the vines will cope?

Radford Wines

When Ben and Gill Radford – he a winemaker at Rockford, she a South African–born chef and caterer – bought 30 hectares of land right in the heart of Eden Valley in 2000, one of the main attractions of the property was its small riesling vineyard: a hectare planted in the 1930s, and another planted in the 1970s. The Radfords already knew a lot about the place: it used to belong to friends of Ben's family – he remembers playing here as a kid – and veteran local winemaker Jim Irvine told them that grapes from here used to make their way into the famous Siegersdorf riesling a generation or so ago. So when they arrived, the couple planted a little patch of shiraz, and a couple of rows of viognier, and built a small shed to mature the wines in, initially buying some shiraz from other vineyards while waiting for their own vines to reach the wire.

In 2002, Gill Radford started using undervine mulch to help preserve soil moisture in this often very dry site. In 2006, she stopped using synthetic chemicals such as herbicide on the vines. In winter 2007, she started applying biodynamic preparation 500, the horn manure soil spray, and 501, the horn silica atmospheric spray.

The Radfords have adopted biodynamics because they are trying to let the vineyard speak as clearly as possible through its grapes and its wines.

The rieslings from the Radfords' pale, quartz-strewn, sandy soils are scintillating, full-flavoured examples of the classic Eden Valley style. As well as focused, lean, pebbly citrus fruit, there's a background of textural funk, which partly comes from the fact that a small portion of the riesling is fermented wild in barrel and then back-blended (only 5 per cent or so) into the cleaner, tank-fermented free-run wine; and partly from the fact that the wine spends up to a year in tank, on its lees, to pick up extra richness before bottling. The Radfords have taken the micro-winemaking idea even further and in 2007 added some neutral spirit to one barrel of the wild riesling halfway through ferment, resulting in a fascinating, almost Beaumes-de-Venise-like sweet wine with a spine of unmistakable Eden Valley purity.

Henschke

Such great things, from such quiet people. Stephen and Prue Henschke are softly spoken, charmingly gentle, he with just a twinkle of cheekiness, she seeming slightly surprised at the world around her. They don't look or act anything like the wine megastars that they are. But they are: Stephen and Prue are considered, quite rightly, to be among Australia's top winemakers and viticulturists, respectively.

The wines are well known, legendary, and constantly improving. The whites, particularly the Eden Valley rieslings, are pristine, crystalline, piercing. The line-up of Henschke reds boasts some of this country's very best: the Johann's Garden is the very model of a plush, modern, Barossa grenache shiraz blend; the remarkably well-sculpted, majestic Cyril Henschke cabernet has, over the last few vintages, rocketed into the pantheon of Australia's top cabs; and the Hill of Grace shiraz, with its multi-layered complexity and endless finish, deserves the mantle of Australia's greatest red wine.

As well as producing exceptional wine, though, it's the Henschkes' serious commitment to planning for the future – demonstrated by the fact that Stephen and Prue's grown-up children have started working at the family winery – that sets them apart.

In response to the challenge of climate change, Prue has planted late-ripening, heat-loving red grape varieties such as grenache and mourvedre in some of her Eden Valley vineyards. Something she wouldn't have dreamed of doing ten years ago, because she wouldn't have expected them to ripen sufficiently. She sees it as an insurance policy: if the global warming predictions turn out to be true, even the relatively cool Eden Valley may not be the best place to grow shiraz and cabernet any more. But rather than abandon the terroir that the Henschke family have been custodians of for 140 years, Prue is exploring ways of allowing it to speak through different means.

These different means include the extensive use of organic and biodynamic farming methods. For Prue, biodynamic viticulture is the logical extension of an ongoing conservation process she had already initiated in her oldest, most precious vineyards, Hill of Grace and Mount Edelstone. 'We've been moving towards organics in the vineyards for ages,' says Prue. 'We've been mulching undervine and planting native grasses as a permanent sward between the vine rows. But then I went to a biodynamic workshop and realised that it aligns with the way I think about soil management. The essence of BD is soil health and condition. It's about increasing the fungal life and bacterial activity in the interstitial spaces in that soil, making more nutrients available to the vine's roots.'

The application of biodynamic compost is crucial, says Prue, for two reasons: to increase moisture retention in the soil to help the old unirrigated vines cope with the dry, hot weather, and to hopefully increase the soil's carbon content. This not only helps improve soil and plant health, but also helps to offset carbon emissions.

'Compost is the only way to go,' says Prue. 'It's all part of trying to work out how to sequester carbon through agriculture.'

She argues that implementing these changes in the vineyards isn't just about self-preservation. It's also an opportunity for the wine industry to take a leadership role in the community. 'We can't just wait for the government to address the issues of climate change,' says Prue. 'I think we can help change broader attitudes in society by being a good example ourselves.'

Mountadam

There is truly something special about the Mountadam vineyard. Something about its gaunt, hilly altitude, and the glittering sandstone soils at the peak of the contoured ridge across which it is draped. Indeed, Mountadam is *so* special – an extreme version, if you like, of the terroir that defines the broader Eden Valley – the place has been given its own sub-regional designation: High Eden.

First planted by visionary vigneron David Wynn in the early 1970s, the Mountadam vineyard went through a difficult period in the early years of this millennium, after Adam Wynn, David's son, sold the property to Moet Hennessy, the French multinational which also owns Domaine Chandon and Cape Mentelle in Australia.

The first thing new owner David Brown did when he bought this historic vineyard from Moet Hennessy in 2005 was hire winemaker Con Moshos, who for 20 years had been Brian Croser's right-hand man at Petaluma. Moshos fell passionately in love with the remarkable history and huge promise of this site, and has spent the last couple of years refurbishing the rather neglected vineyard and re-focusing the winery to produce only the best. Out went the bank of cold, unfeeling computers that had been installed to control fermentation, and in came the manual grape-sorting table.

One of the first things Moshos did was commission geologist Doug McKenzie, of the Australian National University, to help explain what made the Mountadam site so distinguished. McKenzie came back with a word picture of how, 500 million years ago, the High Eden ridge was the shoreline of an inland sea; of how that shoreline sank over the ensuing aeons; and how the land was forced up again in tumultuous tectonic shifts, cracking open the sandstone, injecting the fissures with gobs of quartz.

This geological legacy is what you see in the ground as you walk the contours at the top of Mountadam: layers of shining sandstone, interspersed with quartz. This minerality shines in the wines Moshos has made since 2006 as clearly as the grains of mica and feldspar glint in the sandstone rocks. You can taste it in the Mountadam chardonnay, now, under Moshos, a white wine with a pure line of lemon-pith dryness, a restraint and a finesse that was lacking in the previous few vintages. You can taste that minerality

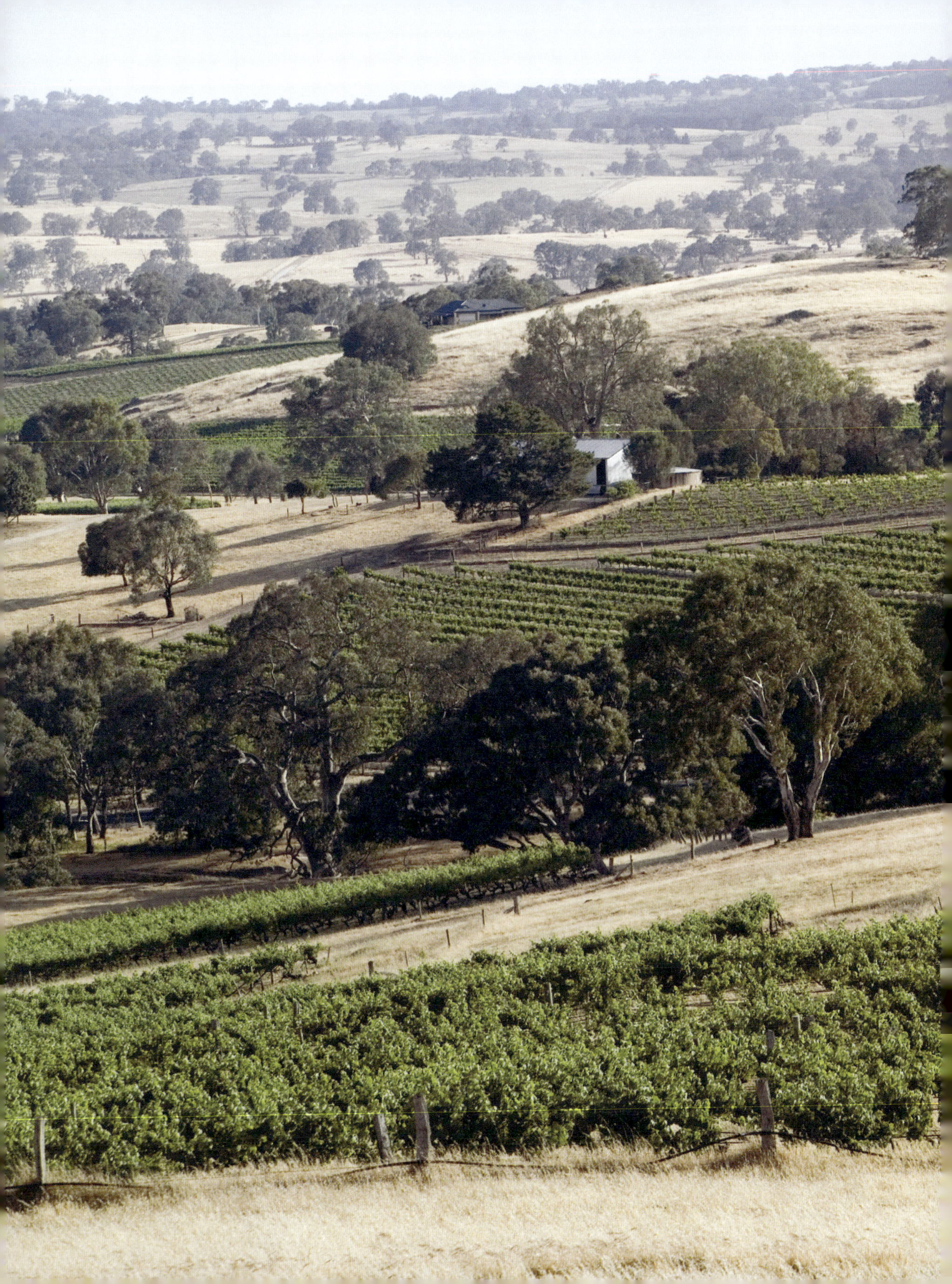

Eden Valley

in the Mountadam shiraz viognier, with its pretty, pepper and rose petal brightness; in the lean and taut Mountadam riesling; and in the Patriarch shiraz (named in honour of David Wynn), a wine which used to be heavy-handed and ponderous but is now vivid and focused.

You can taste the Mountadam minerality most clearly of all, though, in the Marble Hill chardonnay; a new wine from old vines planted on the higher parts of the vineyard.

David Wynn stuck these vines into the glittering soil in 1972. He had propagated them from a cutting taken years before from a chardonnay vine growing in the garden of Marble Hill, the South Australian governor's summer residence in the Adelaide Hills. The garden and the house were almost completely destroyed by bushfires in 1955, and no-one knows precisely where the old chardonnay vine came from, or how it found its way to South Australia. But the story Moshos tells is that the chardonnay vine came from Burgundy and was planted at Marble Hill in the 1860s, making the small patch of old vines at Mountadam not only unique but a living link to ancient wine history.

Whatever the truth, the Marble Hill clone is quite unlike any of the modern clones of chardonnay. 'It flowers later, it sets fruit later, and it ripens later,' says Moshos. And it tastes different: it has a liveliness, a transparency, a purity, and at the same time a density of texture that allows the flavours of ancient sandstone and quartz to dance on the tongue.

Smallfry Wines

Despite the clean, modern label, and quirky name, there's a deep sense of regional history behind Smallfry Wines. Wayne Ahrens and Suzi Hilder run their cellar door operation out of the front room of an old 19th-century bank right in the middle of Angaston's main street. They keep some wine in the old safe, and on the inside of the big, heavy iron door is a typewritten list of every manager of the bank since it was opened.

The Ahrens family date back to the very early years of the Barossa: they settled in the Vine Vale/Bethany district, down the hill from Angaston, in the 1840s. Wayne planted his first vineyard in the Eden Valley, in the southern end of the region, near Irvine and Mountadam, in the mid-1990s. Like many at the time, the intention was to sell fruit, and some big names, including Torbreck, have bought shiraz from this site over the years. But (again, like many), the temptation to make some of that fruit into his own wine became too strong and Smallfry Wines was born.

The sandy loam over gravel soils of this Eden Valley vineyard produce an excellent, classically steely riesling, but Wayne is also very keen on the cabernet he grows here; I prefer the elegant, spicy shiraz, with its almost sangiovese-like, fine, grippy tannins.

Since 2006, Wayne has been applying the biodynamic 500 spray on one block of young viognier and marsanne vines at his Eden Valley vineyard and is very excited by the improvements he's seen in the structure of the soil. His partner Suzi also worked on some biodynamic vineyard trials in the Barossa when she was employed by Foster's.

'One of the things about biodynamics that I really latch on to is the exertion of will and the power of the practitioner,' says Wayne. 'I think this is possibly more important than the influence of the cosmos. Farming biodynamically gives you, the farmer, confidence, and you transmit that confidence in what you do.'

He has also started applying the BD preps on a great old 18-hectare property at Vine Vale in the Barossa Valley he bought in 2008. This magnificently old-fashioned block has shiraz, grenache, cinsault, chenin blanc muscadelle – you name it – planted in between fruit trees, in the classic Barossa 'garden' fashion, alongside a tumbledown wattle and daub, straw-roofed shed. A row of carignan vines runs along the fence line – more carignan vines have been interplanted with semillon – and despite receiving zero irrigation, this variety manages to pump out a healthy crop in even the driest years. Not surprisingly, Wayne has taken cuttings of these old carignan vines and planted them in among some old shiraz and mataro, keeping the old 'fruit salad block' Barossa tradition alive.

Because it's been run 'virtually organically' for over 50 years by the previous owner, Ken Schlieb, Wayne believes he will be able to get this lovely old Barossa garden to a certifiable biodynamic level before long. He's very keen to maximise the distinct spiciness he sees in the grapes grown here in the deep, sandy, old creek-bed soils.

Yalumba

If I had to nominate one company as the leading large family wine business in Australia, it would have to be Yalumba, the lairds of Angaston, on the western edge of the Eden Valley. The company just ticks all the right boxes. It has an amazingly sensitive awareness of its precious 150-year heritage, and builds that depth into the story it tells the world. The company-wide sustainability program, Vitis, pre-dates most other companies' environmental initiatives by several years, and is very impressive in its scope and its commitment to emissions reduction, carbon sequestration and organic viticulture. The leadership the company has shown recently on issues of label integrity by self-imposing a code of conduct regarding the use of slippery terms such as 'old vine' and 'reserve' are commendable. And there's no more vocal proponent of alternative grapes, particularly Eden Valley viognier.

Yalumba's pioneering work with white grapes in Eden Valley goes back decades: they trialled screwcaps on riesling, first in the 1970s, then again in the early 2000s, and developed single vineyard-designated wines (Heggies, Pewsey Vale, Hill-Smith) years before single-vineyard wines were trendy. It's their dogged commitment to viognier that impresses me most, though: the Virgilius viognier, the top-of-the-range white in Yalumba's stable, sourced from now-mature Eden Valley viognier vineyards, is a magnificent expression of both grape and place, with super-exotic honeysuckle syrup and cream crammed in between a latticework of perfectly judged oak and fine acidity. One of chief winemaker Louisa Rose's next projects is the Spanish white grape verdejo, a variety capable of producing aromatic, fresh, sauvignon blanc–like wines in relatively dry, warm conditions. She is also very excited about the potential for southern Italian white grapes such as fiano and vermentino, particularly in Yalumba's Oxford Landing vineyard in the Riverland.

Yalumba lead the industry in the area of environmental performance, and have won many national and international green awards along the way, thanks in large part to Cecil Camilleri, the company's thinker-in-residence. His official title is Senior Technical Manager, Environmental Matters, but that dry description doesn't do justice to the depth and breadth of his work on the ethical and philosophical issues surrounding the sustainable production of grapes and wine. According to Cecil, biodiversity is the key to true sustainability in Yalumba's vineyards. The Vitis Programme of integrated viticultural practice adopted across the company aims to reduce chemical use and maximise environmental awareness, as well as regenerate and protect natural habitats. 'It's a program which recognises the contribution biodiversity makes to mitigating the impact of our emissions and climate change,' says Camilleri.

The revegetation component of Vitis is being put into practice most dramatically up at Oxford Landing in the Riverland. In 2008, Yalumba purchased the neighbouring 600-hectare property, and have embarked on an extensive program of planting native trees and returning old wheat paddocks to bush.

'It's all part of our plan to achieve true carbon zero status,' says Yalumba CEO Robert Hill Smith. 'But we're not stopping in the Riverland. We're looking at buying more land, and converting existing land we own. While it's become fashionable to be talking about it now, we've actually been working on this for many years. Which demonstrates the long-term view of not pushing worries away, waiting to see if they will apply to you one day, but acting on them as soon as they arise.'

Wayne Ahrens, Smallfry Wines, Eden Valley

Clare Valley

In the heart of the Clare Valley lies Wendouree vineyard, one of Australian wine's sacred sites. Visitors stand in awe at the sight of the gnarled and venerable vines; they talk in hushed tones as they wander around the old open fermentation vats and ancient barrels.

I have never been to any winery anywhere in the country as revered by other winemakers as Wendouree. Especially winemakers in Clare: they know how lucky they are to have one of the world's truly great estates in their midst, acting as a touchstone, a talisman, a solace. While all around is change and woe, Wendouree keeps going strong, charting its unbending course.

The wines here are products of their terroir/pangkarra: undulating deep red loam over limestone with surges of slate running through it. The vines are dry-grown, organically farmed ('always have been,' says Tony Brady, typically matter-of-fact), meticulously looked-after. The 11 hectares of old vineyard include cabernet, shiraz, mataro and the best malbec in the country, but regardless of which variety or blend of varieties end up in the six or seven different wines produced here each vintage, all have a remarkable and unmistakable backbone of black licorice and iodine. You find these flavours in many other Clare reds, but seldom as intensely as here. And it's the solid truth of this taste of terroir that continues to make Wendouree such a crucial, inspirational part of the valley's identity.

Another key to that identity, of course, is riesling. Across the region, from the flat lands of Auburn to the south to the bucolic terra rossa tranquillity of Watervale in the middle, the high bumps heading up to Clare itself and the shaley clay of Polish Hill to the east, riesling acts like a lens, projecting all these different landscapes into your glass.

There is also an increasing awareness of the need to look after these great vineyard sites in a more environmentally sensitive fashion, going back, in other words, to the kind of farming that Wendouree has always practised.

When he was a winemaking student in the 1970s, David O'Leary of O'Leary Walker remembers doing work experience in the Clare. Legendary winemaker Mick Knappstein would send him out to sample grapes in old vineyards that he referred to as 'gardens'. Today, O'Leary makes a point of buying much of his fruit from a laconic farmer called Martin Smith, whose vineyard in the Polish Hill River district is the picture of health because, for the last few years, Smith has managed it more like a garden, using careful, sensible organic methods.

Other producers such as KT and the Falcon and Mitchell (see below) have gone even further, taking all synthetic chemicals off their vineyards and employing biodynamic practices.

Jeffrey Grosset,
Grosset Wines

Jeff Grosset tosses the grapes so casually into the middle of the conversation, I almost miss them: '…And I've planted nero d'avola, aglianico and fiano on the shaley bits of the Springvale vineyard at Watervale,' he says, before moving swiftly on to talk about loftier themes such as the moral aspect of terroir.

Hold on a minute. Is this *the* Jeff Grosset, the king of Clare riesling (Springvale and Polish Hill, discussed at length earlier in this book), the guru of Gaia (his high-altitude cabernet vineyard), the prince of pinot from the Adelaide Hills, the svengali of semillon/sauvignon blanc? Talking about planting relatively obscure southern Italian grapes on his prized patch of classic Clare dirt?

It is. And it should come as no surprise, really. Jeff's always been one or two steps ahead of the game, and never afraid to back his instincts: he was told he was mad planting cabernet on a windswept, 570-metre high slope, but that vineyard now produces one of the region's most refined and elegant red wines. The man has a mighty incisive mind inside his gleaming dome, and he's obviously thinking – as all the clever winemakers are – about what might grow best in a hotter, drier Clare Valley. I'm willing to bet that the wines he makes from those three southern Italians will be exceptional, too.

Jeff Grosset once told me that his mother was a dressmaker and his father was an engineer. This explains a lot: the fastidious attention to detail, the precise thinking, the delicate aesthetic sensibility, the focus he brings to the wines. His approach to growing grapes, though, is as much a product of place as it is of parentage.

'When I arrived in Clare old growers talked of their vineyards as gardens,' he says, echoing David O'Leary. 'In the 25 or so years I've been here I've seen that attitude disappear and be replaced by grape growing according to convenience and cost. But the old approach has always stayed with me: the idea that you should manage your garden lightly.'

As a result, Jeff practises what he describes as sensible farming: minimal chemical use, encouraging biodiversity, building organic matter in the soil, careful hand-picking. It's all about maximising the potential of the fruit from each vineyard, so that it can express its true sense of place in the glass.

'It's very important to me that I try to impose as little winemaking on the fruit as possible,' he says. 'It's crucial to understand that the differences between the Springvale and Polish Hill rieslings exist because they're in the grapes, not because of anything I do to the fruit. This is the moral aspect to terroir: it's about honesty. It's about the winemaker not expressing what you *believe* to be there, but the actual *experience* of being there.'

Adelina Wines/Some Young Punks

Of all the new labels to have emerged from the Clare in the last few years, this double-header is, for me, one of the most impressive. What I love about it is the fact that Jennie Gardner and Colin McBryde can pour just as much passion into producing serious wine with a serious label and serious sense of terroir (Adelina) as they do producing a range of fun, everyday drinking wines with gloriously garish pulp fiction labels (the Some Young Punks range of reds, sourced from McLaren Vale, Langhorne Creek and elsewhere – just check out the web site). Not only that, but Colin is also delving into the dark arts of biodynamics, at Adelina, and using bought-in, biodynamically grown fruit from McLaren Vale.

The first Adelina wine that made me sit up and pay attention a few years ago was a grenache. I knew that Clare could produce very good wines from this grape, particularly from the few remaining old grenache gardens scattered around the place, but this wine had something different about it: an extra depth to the heady rose-petal and strawberry fruit flavours, an extra layer of bold tannins.

Then I found out where the vineyard that produced this great red was located and it all clicked: Adelina is next door to Wendouree; on the other side is the Aberfeldy vineyard, from where Tim Adams sources his top shiraz fruit. What's more, the vines are old: the shiraz was planted in 1910, the grenache in 1940 and the cabernet sauvignon in 1978.

The grenache comes from a patch of grey loam over sandstone and is notable for its depth and weight. The shiraz, from red loam over limestone and slate (similar to much of Wendouree's terroir), is inky-rich, pulsing with black fruit and firm but supple tannin. And the cabernet, planted in shaley loam over sandstone, is produced in an amarone-inspired style (where the grapes are allowed to partially desiccate before fermentation) to accentuate that dark, black Clare firmness even more.

Jim Barry

The ever-mischievous Peter Barry has enjoyed great success in the last few years with some brilliantly quirky everyday drinking brands: the Cover Drive cabernet and Silly Mid On savvy blanc blend (both with old Victorian cricketing illustrations on the label), and the Three Little Pigs shiraz cabernet malbec, a classic Clare red blend with butcher's apron–themed packaging.

But there's much more going on behind the scenes at Jim Barry than fun brands. Serious thought is being given to planning for a warmer, drier future in Clare, and the next generation of Barry boys are making their mark on the local wine scene.

'In 2006,' he says, 'I was on holiday on the Greek island of Santorini. My wife and I were eating calamari at a restaurant, drinking this delicious crisp white wine from the local co-op. It was so good, I asked what the grape variety was and they told me it was assyrtiko. Now, it's bloody hot, bloody dry and bloody windy on Santorini, so I thought if that grape works there it will work in Clare.'

He got in touch with leading Greek wine authority Konstantinos Lazarakis who helped source cuttings from the top vineyards on the island, and in early 2008 became the first person to import assyrtiko into Australia. It will take a few years before we get to taste the wine – the vines have to sit in quarantine and go through the slow process of being propagated – but Pete already knows what he's going to do with them.

'I've got some goat country – a west-facing rocky outcrop – where I want to plant them as bush vines, with a fruiting wire 6 inches off the ground.' And then, smiling that cheeky Irish Barry smile: 'You've got to do something that's a bit different, don't you? Keeps things interesting.'

The fact that he's imported assyrtiko is already causing ripples. In Aspen in late 2008 for the annual wine festival, Pete found himself standing at the counter of the Greek stand.

'The winemaker mentioned that he was very excited: he'd heard that an Australian winemaker had taken some assyrtiko cuttings,' says Pete. 'When I explained that winemaker was me, we embraced as only good Greeks can.'

One of the ways that he convinced Lazarakis and others in Greece to help him source some cuttings in the first place was by pouring them glasses of his Florita riesling, sourced from a legendary vineyard in the heart of Watervale. The Barry family bought this vineyard in 1986, but sold off a few acres and the house in one corner to a local artist. In late 2007, this tiny patch, called Clos Clare, was sold again – back to Peter Barry. And his sons, Tom and Sam, have taken it on as their own special project.

The first vintage that the junior Barrys made was a glorious wine, all pristine scintillating lime zest and mineral-water freshness, that fully lived up to the reputation of this classic vineyard site. Clos Clare was already one of the great low-key names in the region: now, with a bit of Barry brio behind it, you'll hear the name mentioned more often.

KT and the Falcon

I visited Kerri Thompson in Clare a couple of years ago, not long after she'd left the corporate winemaking gig at Leasingham and set up her own label with viticulturist Steve Farrugia. It was late in the day when I finally got to Watervale. The drizzle of mid-winter dusk was beginning to settle and it was hard to make out the road signs through the windscreen wipers. I began to wonder if I'd find the KT and the Falcon vineyard block – a small patch of vines they'd been farming biodynamically for a season or two. But when I turned a corner, one property leaped out of the gloom, the grass under the naked vine

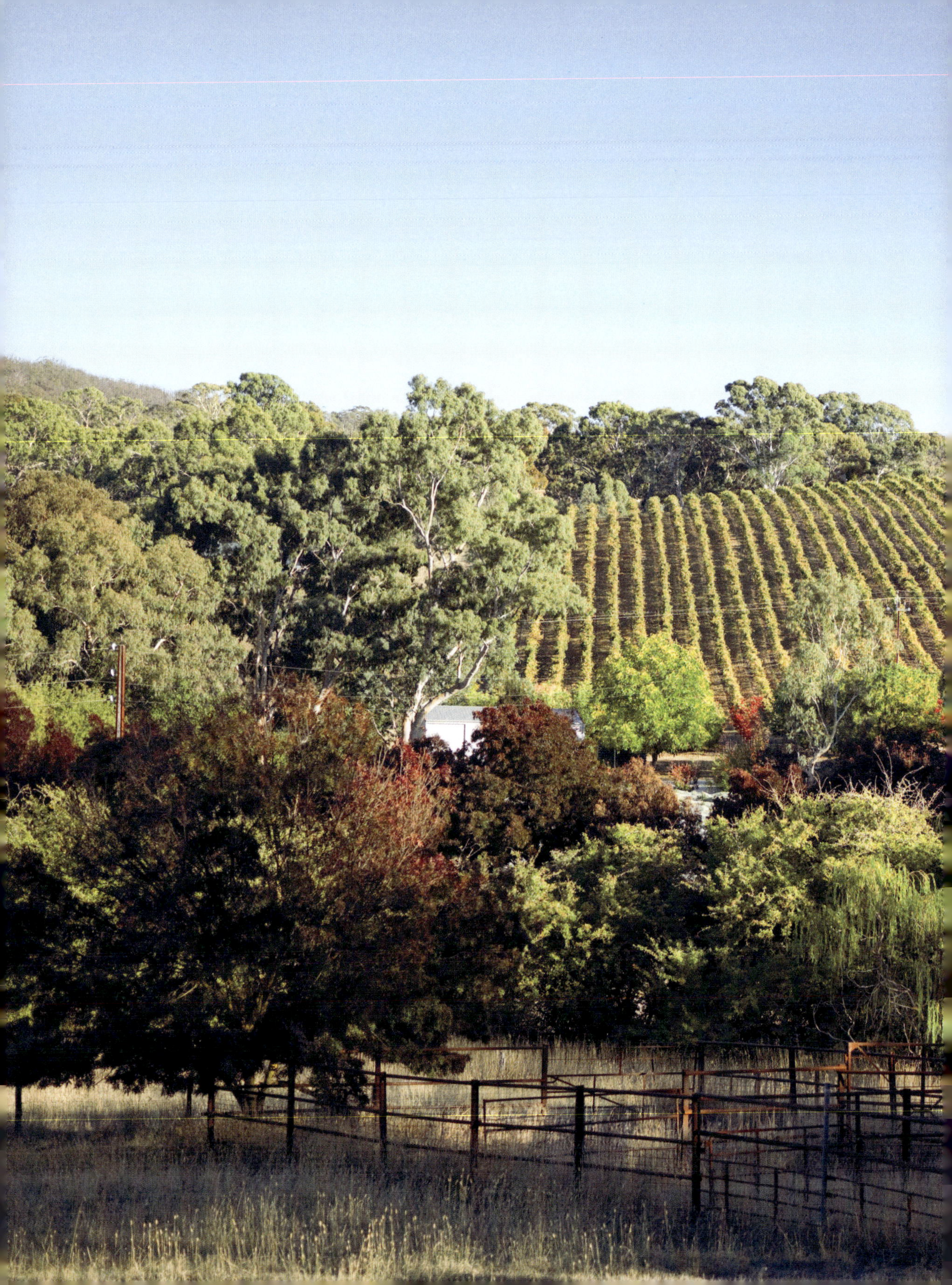

Clare Valley

rows glowing strips of green on grey. Then I heard Johnny Cash blaring out from the house on the edge of the vineyard and knew I had found the right place.

Steve had been a viticulturist for a number of vineyards in McLaren Vale and Clare. Down to earth and pragmatic, he was uncomfortable using chemicals on the vineyards he'd managed and was keen to adopt organic practices on the vineyard that he and KT set up. She is a marvellous mix of serious winemaker, good time girl and shameless hippy. She became friends with Anton van Klopper (see the Adelaide Hills section) when he worked at Leasingham, and although he has been influential, she proudly admits to being 'into stars and nature stuff when I was younger'. Following biodynamics was a natural move for both of them, and it soon made a big difference (apart from just making grass so healthy it glows green in the dusk).

We went for a walk through the nearby Churinga vineyard in the gathering gloom. This old vineyard provides fruit for the KT and the Falcon label, but Steve had been managing it for a long time, back when it was contracted to Leasingham. It's on classic Watervale red loam over limestone soil, with some slate at the top of the ridge, and boasts 50-year-old shiraz, grenache and riesling vines. It had been run 'conventionally' – under-vine herbicide spraying, fungicides, pesticides – for much of its life until Steve took away the chemicals and replaced them with BD compost preps.

'Since we started using these techniques,' says Kerri, 'we have seen so much more microflora activity, earth worms and soil improvements. In terms of balance it is head and shoulders above where it was. I used to take this fruit at Leasingham so I was able to watch the quality of the fruit improve as the BD took hold.'

As well as sourcing grapes from the Churinga grapes and the younger block, Kerri also takes some fruit from Bunny and Yvonne Peglidis' vineyard across the road at Watervale. 'They're hardcore oldies practising traditional Clare viticulture,' she says. 'Just copper and sulphur, a cover crop in winter and a dodge plough for the weeds. And pruning in the driving rain if they have to.'

The wines she's making from these excellent sites are some of the best in the region: the Peglidis vineyard dry riesling is cucumber-cool, pristine and fine; the sweeter Melva riesling (also from the Peglidis vineyard) has lovely soft grapey fruit and an intriguing fennel-like perfume; and the Churinga shiraz is all dark black glossy currants and a sprinkling of aromatic herbs. Since working for Crabtree Wines a couple of years ago, Kerri has also lifted the standard of the already good riesling and tempranillo from that 30-year-old Watervale vineyard.

As well as cementing her reputation as one of Clare's top winemakers, Kerri Thompson has become a high-profile advocate of sustainable viticulture, and is keen to talk about green issues to anyone who'll listen. 'The more I travel the more I realise Australia has such potential to capitalise on our environmental reputation,' she says. 'But only if we look after it properly! If organics and BD can improve the health of our soil, it is a good start.'

Jeanneret Wines

On the back label of each bottle of Jeanneret wine you'll find the following provocative statement: 'None of the fruit used to make this wine has been irrigated with River Murray water.' It's provocative because the majority of Australia's wines *are* made using Murray-, Darling- or Murrumbidgee-irrigated grapes. But why does it apply in Clare?

'It's my quiet little grumble,' says winemaker Ben Jeanneret. 'A few years ago SA Water brought a pipeline from the dying Murray to Mintaro, and sold off allocations to grape growers. That really gave me the shits. In my opinion, it opened up areas to viticulture in the region that just aren't suited to viticulture, and contributed to the oversupply of grapes we've seen ever since.'

Jeanneret says his quiet little grumble gets noticed by people at dinners and tastings, and can inspire some heated debate, but rather than make a big issue out of it he's left it in very small print on the back label.

'It's a bit like us being organic,' he says. 'We're passionate about doing it but don't jump up and down telling the world. Some of our vineyards have achieved ACO Grade-A organic certification, and the winery and bottling line are both certified organic, but we don't make an issue of it, partly because we buy in a lot of fruit, so we can't claim full organic status. And besides, when we started there was a perception that organic was just for cranks, rather than being a way to grow better fruit, so we thought we'd better not turn it into a big deal.'

Jeanneret lets his actions, and his labels, do the talking. A couple of years ago he was the first to commercially release a riesling sealed with the innovative glass Vino-Lok closure. The wine in question was also his first serious, high-priced reserve riesling, but he called it The Doozie. It was, too: an absolute doozie, with classic Clare riesling green apples and limes carving a groove across the tongue. I love the names he gives his other wines, too: Big Fine Girl riesling (a nice Paul Kelly reference and a perfect expression of the relaxed Jeanneret approach), Stumbling Block semillon (because that's what Clare semillon is, for most people, and shouldn't be – oh, and because it's another Paul Kelly song title).

Mitchell

Andrew and Jane Mitchell have been going quietly wild for years. So quietly, in fact, that hardly anyone's noticed. I think it's time to expose them for the old hippies they really are.

'We gave up using herbicides in 2003,' says Andrew. 'We could see that they were doing damage to the soil. And we started using biodynamic preps in 2006. We started

Goodbye glass, goodbye corks
Innovations in wine packaging

One of these days, when he's a bit older, my son will find a corkscrew lurking, unloved, in the kitchen drawer. He'll pull it out, look at it with a puzzled expression on his face and ask: 'Hey, Dad, what's this?' And when I explain what the unfamiliar contraption is for, he'll snort with incredulity: 'You're joking. You mean people used to put a bit of *tree bark* in the top of wine bottles? *Really?*'

The screwcap has become such a familiar sight on almost every bottle of Australian wine you buy it's easy to forget that its near-universal acceptance is barely a decade old. When winemakers in the Clare Valley decided in the year 2000, virtually en masse, to ditch cork in favour of screwcaps, it was seen as a bold and radical move. Winemakers had tried screwcaps before, in the 1970s, and wine drinkers had wholeheartedly rejected the metal seal. This time, however, things were different: drinkers were better informed both about the prevalence of cork taint and the efficiency of the new seal; it helped that the winemakers could drag out bottles of screwcapped rieslings from that first experiment in the 1970s and prove that the wines could age brilliantly.

The screwcap revolution (sorry) that started in Australia soon spread to New Zealand, and then, slowly, to other more cautious, conservative wine countries. I think this dramatic shift to screwcaps has quickened the pace of innovation in other areas of wine packaging: once the almost sacrosanct tradition of the popping cork had been dispensed with, it became easier to challenge other traditional practices, such as bottling wine in glass.

But not all Australian winemakers are equally enthusiastic about these developments. Now that the novelty is beginning to wear off, a more cautious note is being sounded in the ongoing discussion about closures and packaging.

Screwcaps

I am a big fan of screwcaps. The fact that the seal is free of TCA (the compound responsible for cork taint that afflicts one in ten natural corks); the way that screw-capped wines tend to age more slowly, gracefully and reliably than cork-sealed wines; and, yes, the ease of opening that a screwcap offers – for all these reasons, I think that metal is a superior seal to cork. Concerns raised in the early years of screwcap's adoption, mostly to do with the development of unattractive, reductive, sulphide aromas in the wine, have been addressed both by winemakers changing the way they finish their wine before bottling, and by screwcap manufacturers offering seals with varying levels of oxygen permeability. We will definitely continue to see more and more wines sealed this way. But some winemakers don't like the way red wines in particular mature under screwcap, and others are concerned about the larger environmental footprint of aluminium seals, so they have either stuck with cork or moved to Diam.

Corks

Certain winemakers will persist with cork – if the wine has been grown in an organic or biodynamic vineyard (Hochkirch, in western Victoria), or where a winemaker consciously uses 'old-fashioned' techniques (Rockford in the Barossa, or Noon in McLaren Vale) – and while I can understand the philosophical reasons behind wanting to continue with natural cork, I feel corks supposed green credentials are outweighed by the taint-free properties of screwcaps. It's a dilemma, but in this case I prefer the less eco-friendly seal.

Some winemakers, particularly those producing cheaper wines, use budget-priced, so-called 'technical' corks, and I wish they wouldn't. Made from glued together bits of cork shrapnel and topped and tailed with two discs of whole cork, I find these abominations are even more prone to TCA taint and random oxidation than the more upmarket natural corks. A better option is Pro-Cork, which is cork covered at either end by a prophylactic membrane to stop any TCA that may be inside leaching out into the wine. Not very attractive, but quite effective.

Diam

Most winemakers who are fed up with the problems associated with natural cork but are wary of screwcaps have adopted Diam. Marketed by its Portuguese manufacturer, Oeneo Closures, as a taint-free seal, the Diam is made from cork granules that have been treated to a supercritical CO_2 extraction technique to rid them of any trace of TCA, then bound with polymers and moulded into shape. Though I have experienced the odd tainted bottle (despite Oeneo's pledge) and very occasional oxidation in Diam-sealed wines, on the whole it seems to be a good alternative. I still don't like the way it's hard to stick a Diam back in the bottle neck after you've poured yourself a glass – and the manufacturing process *is* extremely energy intensive – but as far as getting the wine to you in good condition is concerned, it's an effective seal.

Glass stoppers

The latest entrant in the closure war is the glass stopper, marketed as Vino-Lok. Similar to the ground glass seals found on bottles in old chemistry labs and pharmacies, the modern version incorporates a ring of the same kind of polymer found inside the screwcap, and fits snugly into the top of the bottle. So far, from Australia I've only tasted a couple of rieslings and one trial red (from Henschke) sealed with Vino-Lok, and have experienced no problems, finding the wines fault-free, fruity and vibrant; similar (if not identical) to wine sealed under screwcap. I have reservations about the unsettling chink of glass on glass when you open and then re-seal the Vino-Lok, but it is – visually at least – by far the most elegant of all the alternatives.

Crown seals

In 2004, Yarra Valley winery Domaine Chandon caused a minor sensation when they launched a new sparkling wine, the ZD blanc de blancs, with a crown seal rather than a cork.

It's remarkable, really, that no-one had done it before. After all, almost every bottle of top-quality sparkling wine you buy has spent 18 months or more under crown seal while it's been resting on its lees in the winery's cellar after the bubble-inducing second fermentation. It's only after the wine is disgorged that the posh-looking, traditional 'champagne' cork is stuffed in the top and wired in place. Why not just put another crown seal on after disgorgement? No risk of cork taint, easier to open – what's not to love?

The loss of tradition, apparently. Very few other sparkling winemakers have followed Chandon's lead, and of the few that do, most are using crown seals only on their sparkling red, itself an iconoclastic style. Even Chandon haven't used the seal on any of their other wines apart from the ZD. Some winemakers remain unconvinced that the crown seal is a better closure: Constellation Wines' sparkling guru Ed Carr, for example, is adamant that his bubbly matures better under cork than under crown, and refuses to switch. The ritual associated with the popping 'champagne' cork is obviously much more stubbornly entrenched than the corkscrew.

Heavy bottles: *so* last century

You will have noticed how wine bottles have become heavier and heavier over the last few years. Especially the top-shelf, top-heavy cult wines from places like the Barossa and McLaren Vale. Positively engorged. It's as though the winemakers want us to think, as we strain our wrists picking up a bottle that weighs more than the wine inside: 'Ooh. Heavy. Must be good.'

With our new eco-hats on, though, it's hard not to look at these bottles and think: 'Ooh. Heavy. Just think of all that embodied energy.' I came across a bottle of Barossa shiraz the other day that weighed almost *2 kilos*. That's just silly. And an environmental disaster.

Glass bottles are not exactly green. Even the recycled ones. Bottles take an enormous amount of energy to produce, and when you've got a few thousand of them stacked up on pallets on a ship bound for the UK, they're heavy, meaning yet more energy is required to transport them. Which is why many wine producers are working hard to come up with eco-alternatives: you will see lightweight glass bottles, plastic bottles, Tetra-Paks and god knows what else being thrust at you as the latest green alternative wine package.

Australian exporters of large volume, branded commercial wine are also playing up the eco-advantages of shipping in bulk (in a big silver bladder in the ship's hold) to be bottled at the final destination. But while this is undoubtedly a greener option (and while it undoubtedly saves the exporter a whole heap of cash), there are concerns over quality. Bulk-shipped wine – and, for that matter, wine bottled in plastic or cardboard – neither tastes as good, nor lasts as long as wine bottled in glass.

Which again raises the dilemma facing those who want to make ethical wine choices. It's a trade-off between quality and conscience: how far are you prepared to compromise enjoyment for the sake of the planet?

composting all the marc from the winery and putting it out on the vineyard. And we've even got four beautiful little cows here now. Scottish Highlanders. They're like big dogs. I love it. I am a child of the '60s, after all.'

We're not talking about a small, warm and fuzzy operation here. The Mitchells have close to 100 hectares of vines: around the winery itself at Sevenhill, at the evocatively named Alcatraz vineyard at Watervale and down at Auburn. This is one of the region's best-known medium-sized wineries – which makes the move to organic/biodynamic viticulture all the more impressive (and might explain Andrew Mitchell's reluctance to publicise it too widely).

Also very impressive – given the commercial importance of the wine in the Mitchell portfolio – are the (relatively) wild techniques used to make the Watervale riesling. Spontaneous ferments and a couple of months' yeast lees contact contribute gorgeous layers of texture and savoury complexity to the core of bright lime zesty fruit. The Mitchells' other best wine, the tangy, lemon- and vanilla-scented semillon, has been totally wild-yeast and barrel-fermented since 2002, in 100 per cent new oak.

McLaren Vale

Thanks to the deep, generous soils on McLaren Vale flatlands and the benevolent Mediterranean climate, it is easy to produce easy wines here – loud, ripe wines with oodles of fruit and no hard edges. These wines have found an eager audience, too, both at the bargain bottom of the price pyramid and at the top, where high-pointed, high-octane, high-price cult bottles have been paraded around the world as the epitome of Aussie shiraz.

McLaren Vale can do better than that. The region can produce much more rewarding, complex and delicious wines that tell a more interesting story in the glass about the country where they're from. Luckily, an increasing number of growers and makers in McLaren Vale are trying to prove just that: focusing on various attributes of single vineyards; changing their viticultural practices to allow the soil to speak more clearly; and planting new grape varieties that might better express what the soil has to say.

As in the Barossa, the slow process of building awareness of McLaren Vale's distinct sub-regions is underway.

'There's a big fault at the base of the Willunga escarpment,' says Toby Bekkers from Paxton Vineyards, pointing at the range of hills that mark the eastern and southern boundary of the Vale. 'Millions of years ago this valley we're in slipped down from those hills. The sea has flowed in and out over the millennia, depositing sand each time, forming this patchwork of rises and gullies and flats with an amazing diversity of soil types and aspects.'

On the gentle rolling country around the McLaren Vale township, down through Willunga and the Sellicks Foothills, you walk across a mixture of black cracking clays, some limestone-based soils, some quite rocky, some red-brown loams, some pure sand. It's warmer down here on the flats, the tannins in the red wines are softer, the fruit flavours richer, more generous. Up in the north-east of the region, past Seaview and around Blewitt Springs, the country rises, and paler-coloured sandier soils predominate, reflecting sunlight back into the canopy, resulting in thicker, more flavoursome skins and more spicy fruit flavours. And up again towards Clarendon, around 200 metres or more above sea level, almost into the southern end of the Adelaide Hills, the soils on the slopes and gullies tend to be more substantial, with red clay, ironstone, some shale; it's cooler here, grapes ripen later, have more perfume and fresh acidity.

While there is great value and heritage stored up in the gnarled trunks of McLaren Vale's old shiraz, grenache and cabernet vines, there is also great potential flowing through the young canes and green shoots of a whole host of new grape varieties, introduced to the region in the last decade or so. McLaren Vale is home to a strong Italian community – growers, orchardists, farmers – and Primo Estate and Coriole, both pioneers of Italian varieties in South Australia, so it's no surprise to find a burgeoning interest in Italian grapes, many of which thrive in this olive and almond-fringed Mediterranean landscape.

These various viticultural streams, ancient and modern, French, Italian and Iberian, converge in a particularly characterful and delicious manner at d'Arenberg, where Chester Osborn is clearly just as at home with old vine grenache as he is with very young vine tempranillo and sagrantino.

Jock Harvey, maker of good sangiovese and barbera at Chalk Hill vineyards, believes this region-wide interest in varietal innovation is a reflection of the strength of the Vale's collaborative spirit and the enthusiasm of its Vine Improvement Society.

'Since the mid-'90s, people like Chester have been championing alternative varieties,' says Jock. 'And now you'll find a lot of sangiovese, barbera, albarino and tempranillo in the district. We're also doing a lot of work on rootstocks and planting density and making sure we share that information with everybody. McLaren Vale has always been a very co-operative region. People are prepared to spill their guts about their own experiences with everyone else. We know that we all need to keep finding ways to grow better fruit and make better wine.'

Paxton

Toby Bekkers plunges his spade into the soil under a row of shiraz vines in the Gateway vineyard, one of many McLaren Vale properties he looks after as viticulturist and general manager at Paxton. He digs up a generous clod of earth and deposits it at the end of the row. Then he walks a little way up the gentle slope, ducks down a vine row and returns a few seconds later holding another clod of soil, which he places next to the first.

Although they were dug from the same vineyard, the two lumps of ground look, feel and smell different. The first is paler, sandier, looser, and has a slightly sharp aroma. The second, dug from under vines just ten rows away, is darker, has good, sticky, humus-rich structure, and smells sweetly earthy, fungal and composty.

The difference between the two bits of the one vineyard is this: the first is still being managed 'conventionally', with chemical fertiliser and herbicide, the second has been managed biodynamically since 2006: no chemicals, just a few sprays of horn manure 500 and horn silica 501.

It's a very convincing demonstration of the efficacy of biodynamics. But there's more 'proof'. Toby and winemaker Michael Paxton have also fermented the shiraz fruit from each block separately; I've tasted the two wines, and the difference is just as clear, with the biodynamic shiraz displaying more life, flavour and vibrancy in the mouth.

It all feels like a long way from the 2004 Biodynamic Wine Forum in Beechworth, where the Paxton crew – Toby, Michael and his father David, one of the wine industry's best-known, hardest-nosed professional grape growers

– along with 100 other curious growers and makers, were dropped in the deep end of the wackier, anthroposophical aspects of BD.

As Nicolas Joly, France's most outspoken proponent of biodynamic viticulture, told the audience about stainless steel tanks receiving negative energy from radio broadcasts, and the dangers of putting a barcode on your wine label because the numbers, somehow, add up to 666, you could see David Paxton bridle. 'I came here wanting to learn about viticulture,' he whispered. 'But then I hear stuff like that and I start squirming in my seat.'

A turning point came at the end of the Forum when the Paxton crew tasted the extraordinary quality of the 70 international BD wines assembled for the event. Inspired by what was tasted, they immediately started trials back in McLaren Vale and, so impressed by the differences they could see the biodynamics had on the soil and the plants, they rolled the methods out across most of their 60-plus hectares of vineyards.

Since then, Toby Bekkers has become one of this country's most passionate, articulate yet level-headed advocates of BD. He talks of increasing the diversity of herbage in the mid-row – by cutting out the herbicide and sowing seeds – as running a monoculture as though it were a forest; he makes his own barrel compost and weed teas and buries his own horns, using manure from the Paxton's Scottish Highland cattle; he loves nothing more than bouncing on his newly spongy soils, and digging his hands into a big pile of rotting mulch under the old shiraz vines, to show you some amazing fungus – right next to the latest soil moisture-monitoring technology.

For me, the most exciting aspect of Paxton vineyards' adoption of biodynamic techniques has been a discernible increase in not only the quality but also the *distinctiveness* of the wines. The Quandong Farm shiraz, for example, from the first vineyard to receive the BD preps in 2004, displays a remarkably similar character each year, regardless of vintage: a fine, tight line of spice running through sumptuous purple fruit. The terroir shines in the wine.

For Toby Bekkers, this is the most important aspect of adopting biodynamics (and other biological and sustainable farming practices), because Paxton is primarily a commercial grape-growing business. 'We hope BD will intensify the attributes of each of our six vineyard sites,' he says. 'We sell lots of small parcels of fruit to different winemakers, parcels as small as 2 or 3 tonnes, and the more individual each of those parcels is, the better. We're even working on tailor-making compost to suit each block of vines. I see it as trying to de-commoditise a commodity product.'

Battle of Bosworth

Joch Bosworth is one of the most important organic winemakers in Australia because he subverts most people's preconceptions of what an organic winemaker should be. For a start, he's not an old, bearded hippy banging on about saving the planet; he looks and acts like one of the mob of youngish, enthusiastic growers and winemakers transforming McLaren Vale at the moment – and having heaps of fun while they're doing it. This is most apparent in the cheeky use of the familiar yellow soursob (oxalis) as the winery's logo: most people see oxalis as an annoying weed, but Joch welcomes it undervine to out-compete other weeds in winter, and uses it as a mulch when it dies off in summer.

He doesn't produce dodgy wines, either (there is still a lingering prejudice among many in the industry that organic equals faulty); the Battle of Bosworth bottles sit right in the normal, modern, fruit-driven, commercially desirable Vale groove: tropical-tasting savvy blanc, bouncy rosé, rich and exotic shiraz viognier, intensely blackcurrant cabernet sauvignon.

It's precisely *because* he is so normal that he has been so influential. I have heard many growers and winemakers say they've been far more willing to consider adopting organics since people like Joch – one of *them* – started doing it.

Joch began converting his parents' vineyard to organic viticulture in 1995, after working for a number of wineries in cooler climates such as Oregon and Sunbury. The Battlers are now fully certified (by ACO) and have 75 hectares of vines. As well as the Battle of Bosworth range, Joch has recently introduced another line-up of very attractive, ripe varietals under the Spring Seed Wine Co., originally developed for the US market, but also now (thanks in part to the global financial crisis) being sold at home.

Joch was one of the first in the region to inject some interest and life into his chardonnay (seldom an outstanding variety in McLaren Vale) by picking the grapes a little early, fermenting in stainless steel and then blending in some barrel-fermented viognier: the result is a wonderfully tangy white, with the former variety's generous ripe melon fruit balanced by the latter's savoury honeysuckle perfume.

For the reds, Joch builds in a little depth and structure by cutting the canes of some of the shiraz and cabernet at full ripeness, and allowing the bunches to hang on the fruiting wire for a couple of weeks to partially desiccate. One of his wines, called White Boar, is made solely from this dried fruit but I don't think it quite works: it's just *too* coarse, *too* dense, chewy and unyielding. But a little of the cordon-cut fruit does wonders blended into the shiraz, shiraz viognier and cabernet, adding a great lick of licorice-like depth and tannin to the wines.

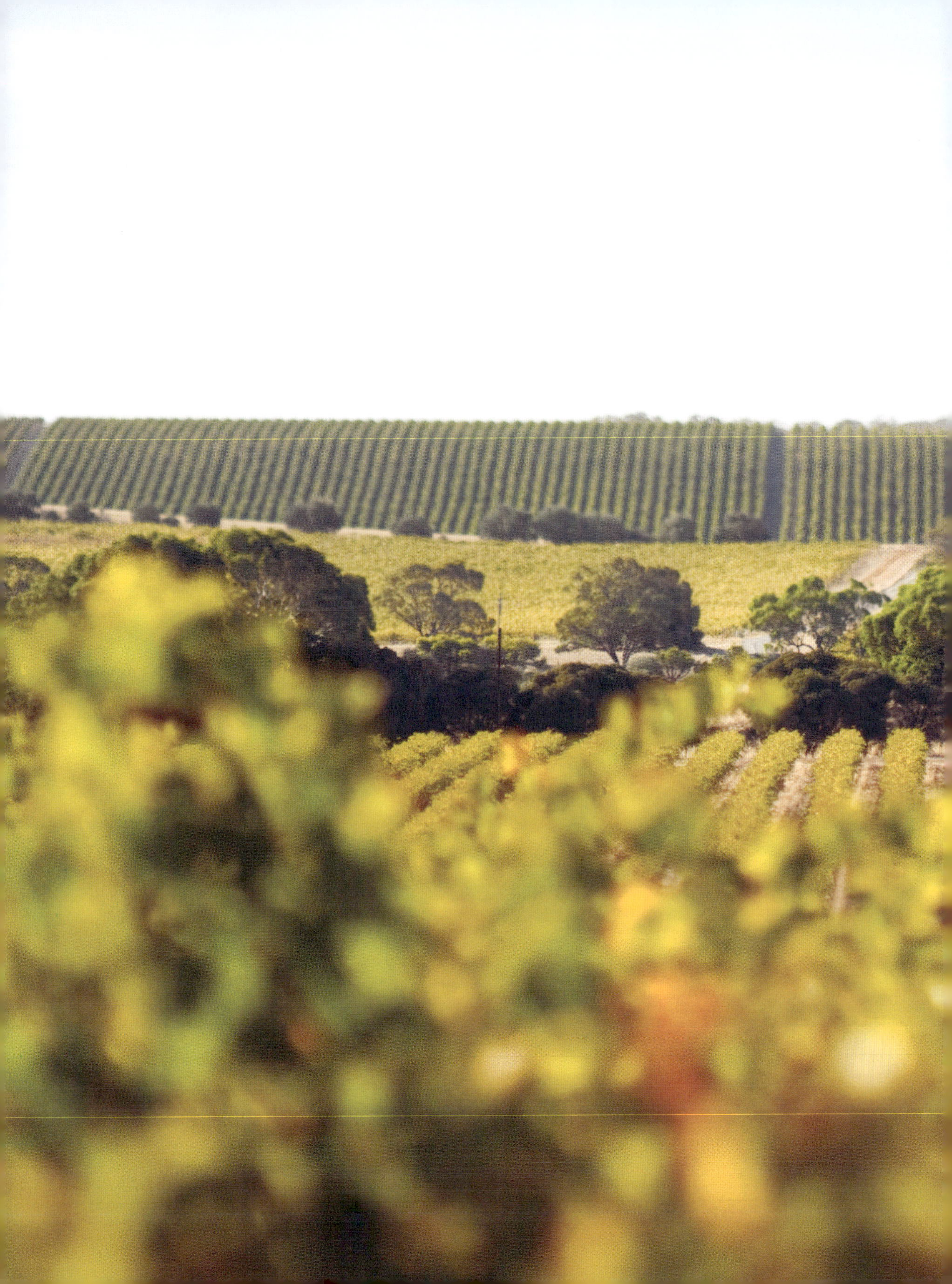

McLaren Vale

Cascabel

Winemakers are a generous lot. Especially towards wine writers. Some might call it bribery. Some might call it perks of the job. Either way, wine hacks are often sent away from a winery visit with a gift or two. In most cases, this gift is a bottle of wine.

When I leave Cascabel, Susana Fernandez and Duncan Ferguson give me a sausage: a spicy chorizo, made by a little guy Susana has come across in the hills above McLaren Vale. 'It's not bad,' she says, her voice still thick with her native Spanish accent, despite more than a decade spent living in Australia. 'The best I have found since I have been here.'

'Here' is a small vineyard and winery shed on Rogers Road at the quiet southern end of the Vale, a couple of kilometres inland from Sellicks Beach. It's where the winemaking couple produce a small range of wines including reds made from tempranillo, graciano and monastrell (the Spanish name they have chosen to use instead of mourvedre or mataro), planted in 1998 because of Susana's winemaking heritage and because they are well suited to this part of the world – better suited perhaps than cabernet and shiraz.

Although it might not sound like it, Susana's praise for the chorizo is high indeed: when it comes to Spanish food and wine, she is extremely single-minded, and has little time for what she sees as half-arsed local attempts to emulate her country's classic, traditional products. Most of her opinions of the local tempranillos she has tried are unprintable; neither she nor Duncan are fans of the conventional, technically correct, squeaky-clean Australian approach to viticulture and winemaking. The couple keep pretty much to themselves: they're not members of the regional association, seldom appear at wine tastings, and don't have a proper cellar door (visits by appointment). As a result, they're not as well known by Australian wine drinkers as they should be: 'We export more than 60 per cent of our wine,' says Duncan. 'We kind of hopped over the locals to the world.'

A hands-off approach in the 12-year-old vineyard and winery makes this place feel less like Australia and more, funnily enough, like somewhere in Spain.

'We're not afraid of grass,' says Duncan, looking out over the refreshingly wild-looking vineyard. 'We're virtually organic; we only really spray the vines with a little bit of sulphur when we need to. And they get no water.'

Cascabel's wines have more in common with Europe, too; the exception being an ultra-fine, taut and minerally riesling from a 4-hectare dry-grown vineyard up in the cool Eden Valley. A co-fermented blend of roussanne and viognier, by contrast, is gorgeously rich and satisfying, with the abundant flavours of honeyed nuts and creamy texture showing why these two white Rhone grapes are so perfect for the warm McLaren Vale flatland vineyards.

Is McLaren Vale Australia's greenest wine region?

The large-scale conversion of Battle of Bosworth, Paxton and Gemtree to organics and biodynamics is impressive. But what's happening in the rest of McLaren Vale is even more profound.

In the mid-'90s, a group of local growers formed the Willunga Basin Water Company and built a $20 million pipeline to pump water from Christie's Beach residential treatment plant, 10 kilometres to the north of McLaren Vale, down to the vineyards for irrigation. This B-class 'waste' water was previously flushed into the sea but now it's used to grow grapes in more than 50 per cent of the region's vineyards.

A similar proportion of McLaren Vale's vineyards are now managed using sustainable, organic or biodynamic practices. And the Vale growers' association recently launched an eco-accreditation scheme called Generational Farming, a points-based system that promotes green viticulture (i.e., the greener you are, the higher you 'score' in the scheme).

'McLaren Vale is fast-becoming a world-leading region for organic wine production,' says organic agricultural consultant Tim Marshall. 'The potential is really vast. For a start you have the natural advantage of the daytime sea breezes and the night-time breezes that blow down off the Willunga escarpment, both of which keep the air constantly flowing, reducing the pressure of diseases in the vines. But I also see a more receptive attitude here: compared to a traditional, conservative region like the Barossa, there are a lot of non-traditional people who own land in the Vale, doctors, lawyers, etc., and a lot of enthusiastic younger people, and they are more open to adopting new ideas.'

Richard Leask, viticulturist at Pertaringa is typical. He's good mates with Toby Bekkers, and after a trip to Burgundy together in 2005, visiting a number of biodynamic vineyards, he started spraying 500 and 501 on his own vines.

'What attracted me was the return to old-style farming,' he says. 'We were told that modern agriculture was going to make things easier, but you look at so-called conventional methods, with their reliance on chemicals and you think: That can't be right, it can't be sustainable. Then you pick up big clods of biodynamic soil with white hyphae running through it and you realise what you're missing in your own ground. I've become involved with Toby and the guys from Gemtree burying the horns and making the other preps, and there's definitely a zaniness to the whole thing. But it's great fun, too.'

In the last couple of years, a number of well-known McLaren Vale producers have also started adopting biodynamic techniques such as spraying the preparation 500 horn manure and the horn silica 501. At Chapel Hill, the motivation for using the BD preps is primarily to improve vine health and resilience: fermented equisetum 508 and valerian are used, for example, as an atmospheric spray to prevent frost damage in lower lying areas of the 45-hectare vineyard. At Kangarilla Road, Kevin O'Brien says he is interested in biodynamics as a way of improving moisture retention and water conservation, and bringing some structure (and earthworms) back into the soils he's flogged with herbicide for ten years. At Wirra Wirra, 24 hectares of winery vineyards have been managed biodynamically by viticulturist Richard Wellsmore since autumn 2007; and both Tapestry Wines and Yangarra are also converting to biodynamics.

Walter Clappis runs his 32-hectare Hedonist vineyard near Willunga biodynamically. 'Whatever's taken up by the roots is going to have an effect on the drink,' says Walter. 'If you can get a purity in the vineyard, then that'll carry through to the winery. We feel much happier doing it, too; the block we bought in 1995 will be in much better nick when we eventually hand it on.'

None of the Cascabel reds are modern, purple, plush numbers. Instead, they tend to be more blood-red in appearance, and often have spicy, gamey characters and an umami-rich, deeply savoury quality. The grenache/shiraz/monastrell blend called Tipico is succulent, supple and slurpy, but finishes dry, as a well-priced basic red blend should; the Rioja-inspired blend of tempranillo and graciano drapes black plumskin tannins across the back of your tongue; and the majestically rustic monastrell is a treasure-chest of bitter chocolate, damson, prune and citrus peel.

These aren't wines for judging in the cold light of a wine show. They're not wines you award points to and collect and trade. They're wines for pouring and drinking and raving about over a large table full of food, surrounded by friends, tearing off hunks of crusty bread, chewing on slice after slice of not-bad locally made chorizo.

Gemtree Vineyards

'We're turning into Gemtree farm,' laughs Melissa Brown, rubbing noses with her alpacas. We're walking through one of Gemtree's many vineyards (the family company owns 130 hectares of vines in McLaren Vale) and the alpacas have trotted protectively up to check us out, leaving their charges – a flock of sheep – to carry on munching the grass under the vines.

You won't find many people as enthusiastic about growing grapes in an environmentally friendly way as viticulturist Melissa and her winemaker partner at Gemtree, Mike Brown. As well as replacing herbicide with livestock, the family have won awards for the 10-hectare wetlands regeneration project on their property, and Melissa is on the board of Greening Australia. Since spring 2006, the family have been trialling biodynamic practices on some parts of the vineyard, converting all 130 hectares to BD for the 2009 vintage.

This is a big commitment for Gemtree: most of the grapes they grow they sell to other wineries (although that is changing as their own brand becomes better known), so it could perhaps be seen as a big commercial risk to adopt what many 'conventional' grape growers consider to be a load of voodoo magic nonsense. What's more, the crew at Gemtree are also helping to spread the biodynamic message across the region through their viticultural consultancy business: they are incorporating BD practices on an increasing number of other people's vineyards.

And it's clearly working for them: from the very first season, Melissa and Mike could see that the BD was making a big difference to their soil health and fruit quality. 'In 2007, even though it was a tough year, the tempranillo we harvested was so much better than in previous years that it blew me away,' says Mike. 'And this has given me greater confidence in the winery: I fermented that temp without adding anything, no acid, no yeast, nothing, and it just went through beautifully, without any problems.'

It was – is – a great wine, one of the best tempranillos produced in Australia, and it inspired Mike to be a braver winemaker. His Moonstone savagnin, also fermented without any additions at all other than a little sulphur at bottling, is a truly thrilling wine: slightly cloudy (an absolute no-no for most technically cautious winemakers), slightly grippy (phenolics in white wine? *Verboten*!) but crammed with perfumed flavours of grapefruit and almond and chalk.

Noon

Every year, around October, Drew and Raegan Noon send me their new release wines to try: the latest vintage of High Noon grenache rosé, one of the greatest and most flavoursome savoury pink wines in the country – bold enough to make a bandol blush – plus last year's vintage of the extraordinary Eclipse grenache shiraz with its amazing, swirling depth and richness, and the firm, solid, dense Reserve shiraz and cabernet, each sourced from old low-yielding vineyards in Langhorne Creek.

Every year, I'm blown away by the sheer quality of these wines. And every year I shake my head in disbelief when I look at the numbers: the High Noon can nudge 15 per cent alcohol, the Eclipse 16.5 or 17; how do the Noons manage to get such complexity and interest and balance in such strong wines? And why do they *persist* in charging such reasonable prices? The 2008 rosé was a mere $17; the 2007 reds, from a painfully low-yielding vintage, just $27 each. These are wines that have had a cult following ever since they were fawned over by Robert Parker in the late 1990s. Drew and Raegan could ask for and easily get two or three times as much per bottle. Why don't they?

The answer to the price question is simple: the Noons are in this for the long haul – and they're not greedy. The gnarly, dry-grown grenache bush vines next to the winery on Rifle Range Road and in the paddock behind were planted in the 1930s and '40s. The family moved here in 1967, initially selling the grapes, along with almonds and apricots from old trees on the property. Drew's father, David, started turning some of the grapes into wine under the family label in the 1970s, and built up a fiercely loyal mailing list following. Keeping prices sensible rather than being seduced by the hype and glamour and international attention is a way of rewarding the support of those loyal customers and ensuring continued support during leaner years.

The answer to the question about alcohol – and how to not let it mask complex flavours – lies in the soil and the climate. The grenache vines around the winery grow in deep sandy loam over a thick layer of orange clay. What little moisture is retained in this country is sucked up by the old roots and deposited in small bunches of tiny berries.

'I'm not sure the vines don't better reflect the place they're grown when they're dry-grown,' says Drew with characteristic, measured thoughtfulness as we walk through the low-slung bushes. 'But you need to let them get fully ripe to express that sense of place. And if that means picking at 16 baumé, then so be it.'

This philosophy, of letting the grapes do all the talking, extends to the winery, which is full of wooden fermenting vats and big old *foudres* rather than gleaming stainless steel and new barriques. Here, Drew is careful to keep additions to a bare minimum: 'If I can't make wine without intervention, I can't see the point of it,' he says.

This single-minded focus on maximising the potential of the terroir is also one of the reasons Drew has been spraying his McLaren Vale vineyard with the biodynamic prepared 500 horn manure compost since 1996. He came across biodynamics while working at Cassegrain in New South Wales in the early '90s, and was inspired by the non-chemical, holistic approach to viticulture, especially in Cassegrain's warm, humid climate.

'Biodynamics is like not irrigating,' says Drew. 'It's just one part of farming this block of land in a sustainable and natural way.'

Samuel's Gorge

Justin McNamee is McLaren Vale's mad artist on the hill. The cellar door hideout he's established on a sheer ridgetop overlooking the Onkaparinga River is in a converted 1850s barn; with its low-walled garden, stone floors, ancient olive presses and tiny cramped rooms stuffed with barrels of red wine, it looks and feels like a cross between a remote Scottish croft, Cretan shepherd's hut and Burgundian cellar.

Justin is surrounded by an eclectic mix of the old and the new: outside sit huge slate fermenting vats rescued from an overgrown paddock; inside are classic bentwood French bistro chairs and a huge, chunky espresso machine plonked right in the middle of the tasting counter, from which the alchemist-philosopher dispenses shots of energy and wisdom.

'In the last few years all we've read about and heard about is the doom and gloom of the wine industry,' he says, knocking back another short black. 'But that's not what I see here, among my winemaker friends. In McLaren Vale there's been an explosion of young people saying: Things are tough, but how are we going to deal with it? What do we need to do to change things around? And then just doing it. It's fucking *brilliant*, I reckon.'

When Justin spotted this amazing little outpost of Vale history one day in 2002 and pestered the owners of the property to let him set up shop in their run-down old barn, he wasn't looking for a vineyard, just a place to make and sell his own wine. During his time at the vats at Tatachilla, before it was bought by Lion Nathan, he had made friends with plenty of growers around the district, and figured he could source top grapes without needing his own vines. But then he found that the Samuel's Gorge vineyard included some tempranillo on the highest bluff and he fell in love. He now makes one of the region's best examples of the variety: dark, dense, brooding and deep, it needs a couple of years in the cellar before it reveals all the sumptuous black cherry fruit lurking behind tongue-hugging, persuasive tannins.

'It's all about texture,' he says. 'Getting good grainy texture to counter McLaren Vale's natural juiciness. Take the grenache. It has big berries, low acid, high alcohol. So I throw a bit of muscadelle in the ferment to give it more complex perfume, and pull a bit of structure together with extended skin and lees contact. I take my time, in other words. It's the Slow Food philosophy applied to wine. No rush.'

He introduces layers to his shiraz by sourcing fruit from all over the Vale: luscious tar from the seaside vines, spice from his own south-facing hillside vines, chunky fruit from Joch Bosworth's black, black clays.

'It's *hard* to make great shiraz here,' he says. 'There's a lot of apathetic winemaking in Australia, because we get the sunshine, we get the sweet fruit. But there's more to it than that. Or there should be. Mid-palate opulence is easy. Complexity's the hard part. There is better shiraz to be made in this country.'

Hot, hot, hot
The continuing problem of high-alcohol wines

You feel it as a warm glow at the back of your throat. Alcohol. Too much alcohol. Hanging there like a hot afternoon, crowding out the memory of any flavour or fruit or freshness there might have been in the wine you've just swallowed.

Fourteen and a half per cent alcohol by volume. That's considered normal these days in most Australian red wines. When I started working in bottle shops in the late 1980s, most reds were 12.5 per cent or 13.5. Now, 15 per cent is common.

What's going on? Why have Australian reds become so much more alcoholic than they used to be? And what are winemakers doing about it?

Some blame global warming: harvest dates are creeping forward into hotter parts of the year, grapes are ripening too fast and sugar levels are going up, resulting in stronger wines.

But in my opinion, Australian red wines have become more alcoholic primarily because winemakers are making them that way *on purpose*. Just look at white wines: whites have become *less* alcoholic in recent years. Why? Because winemakers are picking the grapes earlier, chasing more elegant styles.

But, thanks in part to the influence of US wine critic Robert Parker, many winemakers think they need to pursue a big, alcoholic red wine style to win points and impress the punters. This isn't always the case, though. In fact, it's increasingly *not* the case: many wine drinkers are growing weary of overly alcoholic wines, and are asking for restraint.

Winemakers can employ a few methods to bring overly alcoholic wines back into balance. One is adding water. There is a long tradition in Australia of the 'black snake' (winery slang for a hose). Old winemakers tell stories of grapes routinely being picked at high ripeness – when the flavours are softer and more lush – and then given a bit of 'black snake treatment' (watered down) to bring the wine's finished alcohol down to 13 or so.

According to the Food Standards Code, wine is allowed to contain up to 7 per cent added water. Strictly speaking this rule is intended to account for the water used to flush out pumps and lines and accidentally get into the wine. But 7 per cent's a fairly significant margin: add 7 per cent water to a 15 per cent alcohol wine and you end up with a 14 per cent alcohol wine; very useful if you want the riper flavours, but don't want the alcoholic burn.

Another way of reducing alcohol is to put the wine through a reverse osmosis machine, and this method has been in high demand following the recent spate of very hot vintages. Personally, I'd rather drink wine that's been 'corrected' with a bit of rainwater than wine that's had its 'ideal' alcohol level dialled up on a machine.

Southern Fleurieu

Australian viticultural elder John Gladstones pointed at this region way back in 1992. In his masterwork, *Viticulture and Environment*, a painstaking analysis of the climates of all Australia's wine regions, Gladstones said that the then-unplanted Fleurieu Peninsula had 'arguably the best conditions of all in mainland South Australia for table wine production.'

A big call, but Gladstones was adamant. 'I believe this to be a region with exciting potential for viticulture,' he wrote. 'The temperature and sunshine data point to a wide range of table wine styles, from full-bodied Bordeaux and Rhone styles at low altitudes to classical cool-climate styles from about 200m up.'

At the time, few people paid any attention to Gladstones' prediction. Back in the early '90s, it used to *rain* in cooler parts of South Australia, even in summer (remember?). Growers must have looked at the cold, wet Fleurieu and wondered if old John had taken leave of his faculties. A few brave souls did plant, though, and although it's taken a few years — almost 20, in fact — it looks like his prediction is finally coming true. Just not quite in the way he expected.

The first wines from the region started dribbling out in the mid-'90s. Winemakers in other, warmer regions, particularly in McLaren Vale, soon twigged to the advantage of buying grapes from down here: even the flatter, Mediterranean-ish bits of the northern peninsula are just that little bit cooler than much of the Vale, producing reds — shiraz, tempranillo and zinfandel — with a nice sprinkling of spice. Which chimes nicely, of course, with the 'Rhone style' characters that Gladstones envisioned.

For me, though, the two vineyards that validate the old viticulturist's vision are located at extreme points of the region, and they both grow *Burgundian* grapes: Brian Croser's close-planted pinot noir 350 metres up on the crest of a hill at Parawa, and John Edwards' chardonnay down on the sandy coast at Victor Harbor.

Tapanappa Foggy Hill Vineyard

At the height of summer, the vines of Foggy Hill look like a huddle of green fairy penguins, crowding together to protect themselves from the elements. The close-planted 4-hectare vineyard is perched on one of the last steep north-facing slopes on the Fleurieu Peninsula. It's fairly extreme viticulture down here: on the other side of the hill, there's nothing but wild ocean until you hit Antarctica, and southerly winds constantly whip across the top of the cowering vines.

Foggy Hill is Brian Croser's newest South Australian vineyard venture: he and his partners in the Tapanappa wine business – Champagne Bollinger and the Cazes family of Bordeaux – also have the Whalebone vineyard at Wrattonbully (cabernet, merlot and some young, close-planted sauvignon blanc) and the Tiers chardonnay vineyard at Piccadilly in the Adelaide Hills.

Croser bought 'the best farm on the Peninsula' in 2003 after losing his precious Petaluma wine company to brewer Lion Nathan, attracted both by Gladstones' prediction and his own study of the climate. On paper (heat degree-day summations, mean January temperature, rainfall, etc.) it's cooler here than Piccadilly. Cooler and wetter. But in reality there is an extra complexing factor in the form of mild nights during the growing season, allowing the grapes to continue metabolising for 24 hours a day. As a result, the pinot ripens here a good two weeks earlier than the Adelaide Hills, and produces lighter-coloured, more delicately flavoured, but more tannic grapes.

'It looked obvious to me that this was a pinot noir climate,' says Croser with his customary iron-clad self-belief. 'And probably an exceptional pinot noir climate at that.'

The geology of the site fascinated him, too. The hill he chose to plant on is covered with a layer of sandy loam over orange cracking clay, atop ironstone originally formed from highly weathered Cambrian sandstone. It's a complex, multi-layered terroir shot through with gravelly bits of that ironstone. Lots of stuff for the vine roots to explore.

To build even more complexity into the finished wine, Croser has three clones of pinot noir at Foggy Hill: 114, 115, 777. The vines are planted 1.5 metres by 1.5 metres, and are low-trained, too: the grapes hang just 50 centimetres from the ground, which is back-breaking work for the pickers and pruners, but helps shelter the fruit from the wind.

The proof of the pinot, of course, is in the drinking, and the first vintage, the 2007, was indeed a knockout wine: it had gorgeous, ethereal, charming red fruit purity, and an arresting, finely tannic, long, silky finish. The 2008 was, if anything, even better. And this, remember, is from four- and five-year-old vines.

Looks like Croser – and Gladstones – were right. Again.

I'm not so sure, though, about the house Croser has built down on the beach – and I mean literally right on the beach – a few kilometres from Foggy Hill. He says that the pinot noir vineyard is 'buffered from the effects of climate change' because it is in such a marginal position. Quite possibly. But if the sea levels rise, as most climate scientists predict, nobody will be able to stop this house being swept away. Not even Brian Croser.

Mt Billy

It's a familiar story. Wine-loving dentist plants a few vines, is bitten by the winemaking bug, buys some grapes from other vineyards and – whoops – he's producing 2000 cases of wine a year. Suddenly, the passion has become a business.

The dentist in question is John Edwards. The passion-that-became-a-business is Mt Billy. The just-over-2-hectare vineyard outside Victor Harbor started, as vineyards do, as an early 1990s wine-fuelled dream. 'We were having a barbecue and someone said: Why don't you plant some vines,' remembers John. 'So I did.'

The flyaway sandy soil that his young chardonnay and pinot meunier were planted in turned out to be so poor that it took five years before the vines squeezed out a crop. In the meantime, John was seduced by the prospect of making red wine from some old Barossa shiraz, grenache and mourvedre vines. So he dabbled in a bit of that.

John soon suffered more than his fair share of setbacks – problems with corks that turned out to be tainted, and export deals falling through – but there's obviously plenty of resilience behind the mild-mannered exterior, because he kept going. The Victor Harbor vineyard eventually started producing, and suddenly he found himself with heaps of wine to sell: a few Barossa reds, and elegant chardonnay and dry rosé from a region very few had heard of.

Luckily, the wines are excellent. Pete Schell from Spinifex makes the wines from John's Victor Harbor vineyard, and they are truly superb: the chardonnay is absolutely beautiful, floral and wheatmealy, while the pinot meunier rosé is seriously savoury, spicy and satisfying.

John Edwards is constantly re-evaluating how he can better manage his Victor Harbor vineyard. 'When we started,' he says, 'we were, according to Gladstones, a cool climate. We're now a moderate maritime climate.'

In an effort to give his poor soils a fighting chance, he's taken away the vineyard chemicals and started applying compost. He's also planted and grafted some shiraz, malbec, sangiovese, durif and even the late-ripening mataro. Given the quality of the wines produced so far from this site, it'll be fascinating to see how these varieties perform as the climate becomes even warmer and drier.

Mt Billy, Southern Fleurieu

Langhorne Creek

Langhorne Creek is a grape factory. It's flat, making large-scale viticulture easy and cost-effective. It's warm enough to ripen cabernet and shiraz effortlessly yet cool enough (thanks to the sea breezes that roll in over Lake Alexandrina) to produce wines with generous fruit flavours. The region's 6500 hectares of vines are still managing to churn out around 65,000 tonnes of grapes each year – about 4 million cases of booze, most of it blended with wine from other regions and destined for South Eastern Australia GI labels such as Jacob's Creek and Wolf Blass. But it's a region on the cusp of catastrophe.

Due to its location at the end of the Murray Darling system, Langhorne Creek has been more acutely affected by prolonged drought and river mismanagement than just about any other region in Australia. The abundant water that once allowed irrigators in the district to literally flood their vineyards is running out, and much of what is left is too salty to irrigate vines.

Desperate short-term solutions include a $70 million pipeline to a point further up the Murray River, and plans for an even more expensive pipeline extension of the reclaimed water scheme used to irrigate much of McLaren Vale. But in the long term, Langhorne Creek's better vignerons are trying to re-imagine their region by moving away from large-volume, low-cost wine to smaller-volume, higher-quality wines. A microcosm, if you like, of the industry as a whole.

Briony and Tony Hoare's new Beach Road label features some deeply convincing examples of how well-suited fiano, greco di tufo and primitivo are to this warm part of the world. And Rebecca and Lucy Willson project a convincing image of new generation enthusiasm at Bremerton, where there's a welcome lightness of touch to the wines, a certain finesse behind the full-throated fruit that so often typifies the Langhorne Creek style.

An increasingly precarious relationship with the environment has inspired many of the region's growers and winemakers to embrace a suite of eco-sensitive initiatives, including winery waste-water recycling, extensive revegetation programs, carbon-reduction policies and undervine mulching. The region's wine community is also actively involved in developing an Environmental Management System, and has adopted the Angas Bremer Water Management Committee's mandatory requirement that 2 hectares of deep-rooted perennial plants be established for every 100 megalitres of irrigation water used.

But unless the long-term water issues bedevilling this part of the world are resolved – either by biblical rains or political solutions – all the large-scale environmentally friendly initiatives you care to name will be pointless, and Langhorne Creek will have no other option but to return to small-scale, dryland grape growing.

Casa Freschi

Because of the flamboyant Italian flavour of the names he's given his red wines – La Signora, Profondo – you expect David Freschi to be a gregarious showman revelling in his cultural heritage. So it's a surprise to find a softly spoken, calm and humble winemaker pottering around in the tiny barrel cellar at Casa Freschi. There's no showiness here at all.

David's parents, Attilio and Rosa, came to Australia from the Veneto in 1954. They moved from their market garden in Adelaide to Langhorne Creek in the 1960s, settling on the current property where they planted a small, 2-hectare vineyard to cabernet, shiraz and malbec, in 1972. Attilio Freschi brought an Italian perspective to growing vines and making wine that must have seemed a little strange to others in the region at the time. Sourcing his cuttings from the oldest vines on the Potts family vineyard, he was one of the first to plant away from the river, where water was less reliable (and less important to someone chasing quality rather than excess tonnage), and he dedicated the worst, the hardest soil to the vineyard, so the plants could struggle a bit. And although the Freschis sold most of their fruit to Penfolds and Seppelt, Attilio was much more interested in making red wine for family and friends in the little cellar he built under the shed.

The young David Freschi was working at Corbans winery in New Zealand in the late-'90s when his father died, and he decided to move back home and establish a new label from the estate-grown fruit. Vintage experience in Italy also inspired David to plant that most capricious and stubborn of red grapes, nebbiolo; so from 1999 onwards another 2 hectares comprising 10 clones of the variety have been established.

David's approach to growing grapes differs from his dad's: Attilio would aim for around 3 to 4 tonnes per acre (the regional average was around six) whereas his son is happy with one. And while the original 1972 vines are planted in sandy soils over deep clay and limestone gravel on traditional wide-spacing of 1600 vines per hectare, the newer nebbiolo vines are 4000 vines per hectare.

Not surprisingly, given the soils, vine density and yields, David Freschi's reds – La Signora (the nebbiolo-based wine) and Profondo (made from the older cabernet and shiraz vines) – are tightly structured, intensely flavoured and deeply savoury, in many ways unlike the soft, generous, open reds you might find elsewhere in Langhorne Creek. But they still have that lifted whiff of mint and dried herbs so characteristic of the region.

In 2004, David established a 4-hectare, dry-grown white wine vineyard 560 metres up in the Adelaide Hills near Mount Lofty. On the rubbly quartz, shale and sandstone slope, he's close-planted (at 8000 vines per hectare) 13 clones of chardonnay, pinot gris, gewurztraminer and riesling, and like the Langhorne Creek property he manages the vineyard virtually organically, without any synthetic fertiliser, pesticide or fungicide.

The winemaking philosophy with the whites is similar to the reds: do as little as possible, and let the fruit speak for itself. The result is two sensational wines: La Signorina blends the pinot grigio, chardonnay, riesling and gewurztraminer grapes to produce a really pretty white, with lifted citrus perfume and a rich, grapey-sweet, pineapple tang on the tongue; while the Altezza chardonnay (whole-bunch-pressed straight into barrel, wild yeast ferment, 18 months on lees, no fining, no filtration) is a fabulously textural white, with savoury, nutty, creamy complexity.

They make a perfect pair to balance the two Langhorne reds.

Temple Bruer

David Bruer doesn't care about making enemies. Never has. Ever since he and his wife Barbara established their vineyard in Langhorne Creek in the 1970s, the former head of Roseworthy's winemaking course has spoken his mind freely to anyone who'll listen on a wide range of controversial topics from organic farming (Temple Bruer was one of the first certified organic wineries in South Australia) to the Green Party, genetic engineering and environmental mismanagement.

'Lake Alexandrina is now so salty it has been declared unfit for human consumption, for god's sake,' says David, staring at me sadly over his spectacles. 'We've been a bunch of fuckwits with how we manage water. Grape growers, winemakers: we've just been so stupid.'

This kind of cantankerous talk might not go down well in the Australian wine industry, renowned for its she'll-be-right, don't-mention-the-war attitude. 'I'm not at *all* liked in the district,' confesses Bruer, but it makes for some thought-provoking conversation and some innovative winemaking.

One of his favourite topics is alcohol creep – the increasing strength of many Australian red wines, whether as a result of warmer seasons or deliberate winemaking decisions to pick later. He believes that winemakers have a 'duty of care to our customers', and 'no wine should be over 13.5 per cent alcohol, for health and safety reasons'. As a result, he uses reverse osmosis technology to reduce the alcohol in his wines, a technique that many other advocates of organic and 'natural' winemaking (myself included) abhor.

Even more surprisingly, given his organic status, for many years David also supported the use of genetic modification to develop yeast strains that could produce lower alcohol levels and benefit the industry in other ways.

'Yes, GM might be unethical, and Monsanto – Monsatan as I call them – might be evil,' he used to say. 'But you ignore the technology at your peril. Just imagine the environmental benefits if they do manage to splice a mildew-resistant gene into grape vines. You'd not only wipe out the need for all those fungicide sprays, but you'd dramatically reduce the number of tractor passes though the vineyard, reducing compaction, saving energy. The list goes on.' It was a position that made him many enemies in hardline anti-GM organic circles.

That was before the Victorian and New South Wales state governments lifted their bans of GM crops, and before farmers started planting Roundup Ready canola – genetically modified by Monsanto to be resistant to a herbicide produced by…Monsanto. Now, he has, reluctantly, changed his position, and is totally opposed to GM.

'There's no room for nuance in this debate any more,' says David, exasperated, angry. 'The agrochemical companies and their lobby groups are growing so strong, I feel I need to take a stand. Even a nine-year-old can see how fucking stupid Roundup Ready canola is. If the wine industry adopted GM it would be extremely damaging for Australia's image around the world. We can't let it happen.'

To the casual observer, Temple Bruer could reinforce any prejudice about organics: David looks like a ragged academic, the winery is cluttered and the vineyard dishevelled. But outward appearances belie the deep level of thought and commitment here – and any lingering doubts are completely overturned by the often excellent quality of the wines.

The 20-hectare vineyard is surrounded by extensive re-vegetation projects that exceed the local water management committee's guidelines; these projects include the planting of an endangered native daisy that provides a habitat for the natural predator of light brown apple moth, one of the grape-grower's least-favorite pests. The winery has achieved both ISO 9001 and HACCP accreditation, is certified organic (by BFA) and will soon be carbon neutral.

The Bruer mind is constantly ticking, and he employs people with a similar spirit of enquiry. He has experimented using vinegar as a natural herbicide for couch grass; he has a secret plan to use a grape variety that's resistant to oxidation as the base for a preservative-free sparkling wine; and winemaker Vanessa Altmann has successfully trialled the production of vegan (i.e., manure-free) compost.

This constant innovation and willingness to adopt new ideas has led to what I consider Temple Bruer's greatest contribution to Australia's wine life: reliable, high-quality, no-added-preservative wines that still provide enjoyable drinking a few years after they're released.

A combination of organically grown fruit, careful winemaking and fastidious attention to detail at bottling – under screwcap – have produced a verdelho that I'm happy to drink (which is an achievement in itself, as I normally can't bear the grape), a firm and robust cabernet merlot and a rich, purple-fruited shiraz malbec.

Coonawarra and the Limestone Coast

When was the last time you bought, drank and really enjoyed a bottle of Coonawarra cabernet? It's a question I like to put to trendy sommeliers, eager young winemakers and fellow reptiles of the press, the kind of people who rave about Grand Cru burgundy, artisan Barossa grenache and Austrian gruner veltliner. Unfortunately, the answer, often, is: can't remember. Or, worse: Coonawarra cabernet? Why bother?

Coonawarra suffers from a bit of an image problem. Plenty of people still buy red wine from the region, but they seem to be older, more conservative wine drinkers. Perhaps it's because the region is so remote; perhaps it's because it's dominated by the large corporate wineries; perhaps it's because cabernet sauvignon, wherever it's from, is far from being the most popular red grape in Australia right now. Whatever the reason, Coonawarra doesn't have the same youthful energy crackling through it that you can see – and taste – so clearly in regions like the Barossa, the Yarra or the Hunter. In those other places, networks of young, enthusiastic winemakers are reviving and revitalising regional wine styles, establishing their own artisan labels. Not in Coonawarra.

This is partly, I believe, because the region is dominated by big, publicly listed companies such as Foster's and Pernod Ricard. During the '80s and '90s, these companies standardised the use of broadacre, chemically dependent viticultural techniques such as machine (or minimal) pruning, machine picking and scorched-earth undervine herbicide regimes. This viticultural approach reduced the potential quality of the fruit and, by extension, the capacity for that fruit, and wine made from it, to reflect the true flavour of the terra rossa terroir.

At the same time, many of Coonawarra's best-known producers today seem hell-bent on extracting every last drop of colour and flavour from their cabernet and shiraz, lavishing their pitch-purple wines with oodles of oak, in an attempt, perhaps, to emulate the warmer South Australian regions further north. These modern Coonawarra reds are powerful, impressive and deservedly popular, and they can be a joy to drink. Well, maybe I'm just getting old, and reverting to my old claret-loving ways, developed during the early days in the UK wine trade, but, increasingly, when I have a hankering for Coonawarra, I'm drawn instead to the finesse of Bowen Estate, the elegance that Sue Hodder has introduced to the top wines from Wynns, the lean, savoury qualities of Redman, and the beautiful, rustic, salami-loving edge of Zema Estate's reds. Most of all, though, I reach for the transparent flavours, natural grape tannins and subtle oak of the reds from Highbank.

Highbank

Highbank is one of the least-known of all Coonawarra's vineyards, and yet it produces what I think are some of the region's most refined, elegant and ageworthy wines. Tasting the Highbank Coonawarra red (a blend of cabernet sauvignon, merlot and cabernet franc) after a few years in the cellar have imbued it with a gentle perfume of cedar and cassis, you're reminded that fine, elegant, ageworthy wines like this were once considered the truest expression of the cool region's legendary terroir of terra rossa red soil over limestone. And what makes these wines different is the viticulture: in stark contrast to every other vineyard in Coonawarra, the Highbank vineyard is run using organic principles.

Dennis and Bonnie Vice, by contrast, have farmed their 4-hectare vineyard right in the heart of that terra rossa strip organically since they established the place in the mid-1980s. Dennis's soft Californian accent is familiar to many grape growers and winemakers through his time as a viticulture lecturer in Adelaide in the early-1990s. He is also a well-known face in the organic field from his time as a certification officer for NASAA. He says that while he and Bonnie's approach to growing grapes has been viewed with some suspicion by the neighbours for most of the last quarter century, there are some signs that Coonawarra might be turning a little green. Rymill, for example, have adopted a sustainable viticulture program that aims to reduce chemical inputs and replace them with softer, biological sprays where possible; and Patrick T viticulturist Rex Hutchison has adopted a number of biological, organic and even biodynamic techniques such as making and spreading compost, planting permanent grass swards between the vine rows to out-compete the weeds, spraying beneficial microbes onto the vines, and even putting out biodynamic preparation 500 through the undervine dripper lines.

Until a few years ago, the Highbank wines were made under the supervision of Trevor Mast at Mount Langi Ghiran in the Grampians, a few hours' drive east, across the Victorian border. Now, they're made at Paracombe in the Adelaide Hills, where Dennis is also involved in the new label, Protero, whose wines are made by Paracombe's Paul Drogemuller and the peripatetic Steve Pannell.

While the winemaking location might have changed, the winemaking philosophy for Highbank stays the same: low-yielding fruit from hand-pruned vines, hand-picked and fermented gently, with minimal additions (certainly no tannin), a short, ten-month stay in French oak, and then bottling with relatively low SO_2. All the better to let the land do all the talking in the glass.

Bellwether

Now that she has cut herself loose from corporate life, Sue Bell looks set to establish herself not only as one of the Limestone Coast's top independent winemakers but also as a leader in the Australian wine industry.

In 2008, after leaving the Constellation-owned Stonehaven winery, where she made some excellent, lithe reds and beautifully aromatic whites, Sue travelled extensively: to India with the Australian Rural Leadership Program, and on through Bordeaux and Burgundy. And then she returned to Coonawarra and set up her own label, Bellwether.

'My dream,' says Sue, 'was to make a top-notch head-turning Coonawarra cabernet. I've already got a few parcels I made while I was still working for Stonehaven tucked away in barrel and bottle. Then in 2009, I sourced grapes from Mike Wetherall, whose vineyard is on a ridge across the road from Penley Estate. I know it's definitely a ridge, and you don't get many of those in Coonawarra, as my car rolled down it one day into a strainer post. The concept for the cabernet is simple, but not exactly what you'd call traditional Coonawarra: hand-picked fruit, fermented in open-top fermenters, indigenous fermentation, basket-pressed [much to the amusement of Bruce and Mal Redman, whose winery space she was using] and subtle use of good French oak.'

The first release, in late 2009, of the 2006 Bellwether Cabernet was seriously impressive and did indeed turn heads: intense, wonderfully complex and multilayered (licorice, dried herbs, cassis), it had firm but superbly elegant tannin length and should mature beautifully in bottle.

With the help of Tasmanian winemaker friends Fran Austin (Constellation's Bay of Fires), Shane Holloway (Delamere) and Jeremy Dinneen (Josef Cromy), Bell has also sourced some chardonnay from Relbia, south of Launceston: again, the emphasis is on artisan winemaking, chasing extreme quality – free-run juice, indigenous ferment in barrel, etc.

For Sue, making wines that are a true expression of where they're from is not just about producing a delicious or distinctive drink, but is also about engaging with questions of cultural identity.

'The wine industry needs to make much more effort to truly embrace regionality, not just pay lip service to the concept of regionality,' she says. 'Winemakers need to assist in the rediscovery of who and what our regions are, who they represent, the climate, the people, the history. And we can't limit ourselves to cabernet, shiraz and chardonnay [to do this]; we need alternative varieties. To match the mosaic of climates, people and regions of the Australian continent we need many more styles and varieties – many we haven't even yet heard of.

'I firmly believe that an industry that respects regional expression has a huge ethical

Cape Jaffa Wines, Coonawarra

role to play in the future. While we make wine just as a commodity we are pushing a drug and should be taxed accordingly and suffer public wrath. But when we grow, make and sell wine ethically and sustainably with respect for culture, we are getting back to what it is all about: a substance that enhances life and society, doesn't damage and strangle it. We as alcohol producers have a major role to play in leading Australia out of the gutter that is the current drinking culture.'

Cape Jaffa Wines

Coonawarra isn't the only region within the larger Limestone Coast GI where large-scale, conservative, chemically assisted viticulture predominates. Wrattonbully to the north, Padthaway to the north again, Bordertown beyond that, Robe and Mount Benson over on the coast itself – in all the places where the rich soils over ancient seabed limestone outcrops have attracted grape growers, it is rare to find anybody adopting green techniques in their vineyards. And if they are, they're likely to be using controlled, unthreatening biological principles rather than organic or biodynamic methods.

Greg Koch, for example, with advice from biological farming consultancy Lawrie Co, has adopted the biological approach on 7 hectares of his Redden Bridge vineyard in Wrattonbully, applying specially formulated beneficial bacteria and fungi to his vines and soil. Koch has noticed a marked improvement in the richness and quality of the grapes he grows, and has managed to eliminate sulphur and copper from his spray regime. Despite these impressive results, other growers across the wider region are only now beginning to follow his lead.

I'm telling you all this to point out how unusual it is for Cape Jaffa (which is where Greg Koch has his Redden Bridge wines made) to decide to become certified biodynamic; indeed, it is one of only two certified BD wineries in the whole of South Australia (the other being Ngeringa in the Adelaide Hills).

The Hooper family established the 25-hectare vineyard and winery at Cape Jaffa Wines in the early 1990s, and quickly built up a suite of sustainable viticultural techniques: controlling weeds through cultivation and grazing sheep; using biological sprays rather than systemic chemicals for pests; using milk and compost tea as fungicides. In 1998 they started applying biodynamic preparations and following the astro calendar, both in the vineyard and the winery, timing operations such as racking and bottling to cosmic rythms. Cape Jaffa began the conversion to certified biodynamics in 2006 and became fully certified in 2008.

The wines have always been good, particularly the savoury, spicy shiraz and the restrained, faintly European semillon sauvignon blanc, but because some grapes are bought from other vineyards in the region for use in the wines sold under the Cape Jaffa label, these wines are not labelled as biodynamic (even though most of the fruit is BD). So in 2008, the Hoopers released a new label called La Lune, made solely from estate-grown, 100 per cent BD grapes. I find that these wines have more character than the 'standard' Cape Jaffa wines – not always a character I particularly like, but a unique, identifiable character nonetheless.

The La Lune semillon sauvignon, for example, is a fantastic expression of the barrel-aged, lees-contact sem sav style, with piercing notes of citron and hay, and an almost chewy richness to it, but finishing with a tang as refreshing as the wind racing in from the Great Southern Ocean. The La Lune cabernet is also a superb expression of grape and place: taut, herbal aromas, with tight little blackcurrants wedged in between tense, grippy tannins. But the La Lune shiraz is too dense, dark and oaky for my taste, although others like it a lot.

'We're getting more and more excited about biodynamics every year,' says Derek Hooper. 'What we're finding is that we've amplified the climatic flavours and regional character in the grapes and wine. And following a philosophy of minimal intervention in the vineyard has influenced the winemaking: we've really backed off on the manipulation, we're using less new oak, we're really letting the fruit do the talking.'

Hooper says that he is slowly turning some of the locals on to the benefits of BD – not necessarily the vineyard owners, but certainly the Cape Jaffa staff and their social networks. He has established a community garden and vegie patch on the property, and holds planting days for family and friends, days that also include some horn-burying and compost-making.

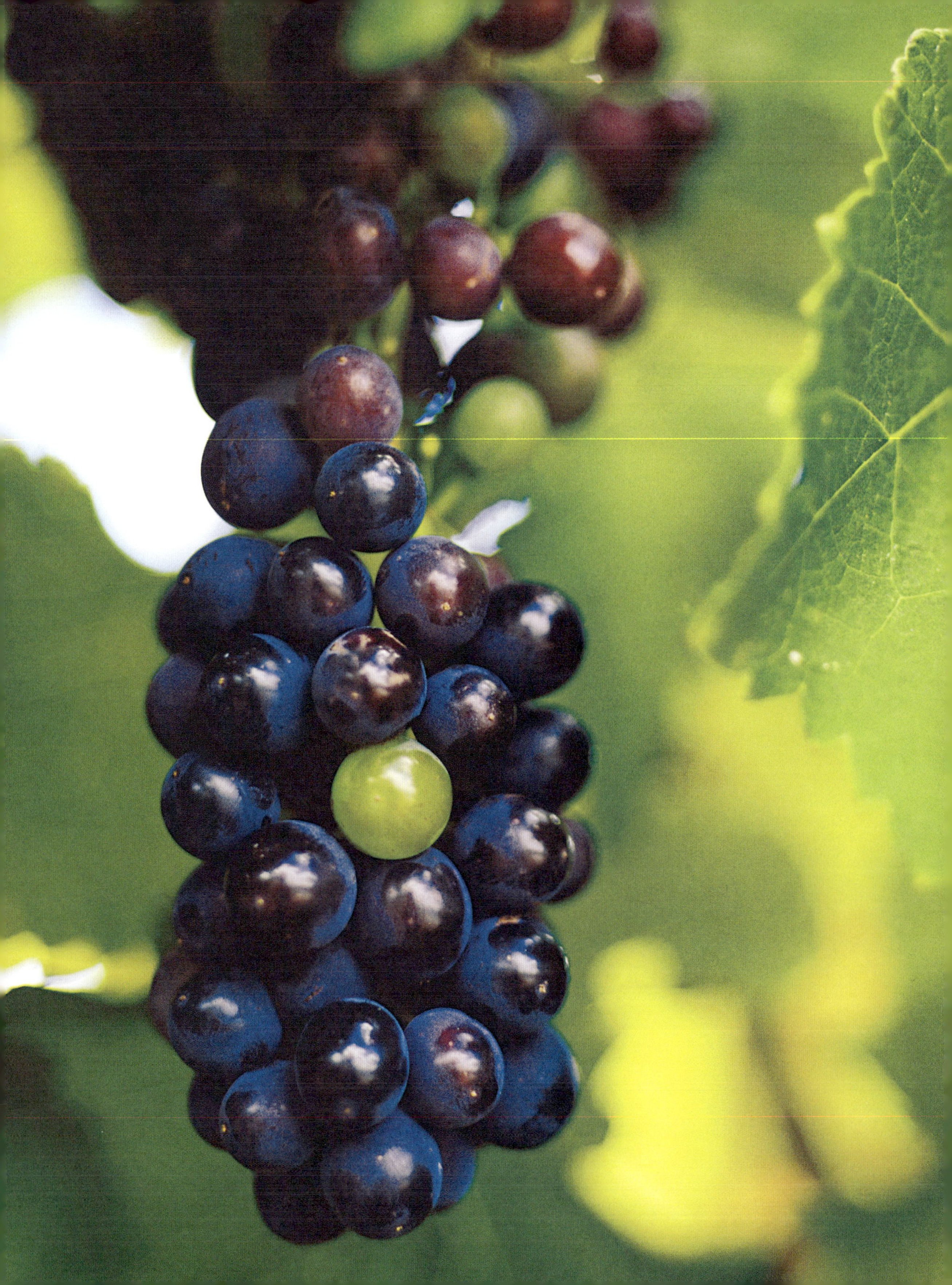

9 New South Wales

Hunter Valley

Just before he died in 2006, I interviewed the legendary wine judge, writer and raconteur, Len Evans, at his Hunter Valley home, Loggerheads.

Evans was frail, but characteristically scathing of the Australian wine industry's complacency, its failure to show enough of this country's great wines to the rest of the world. He was confident, though, about the future of the Hunter, the region that he and other ebullient pioneers such as Max Lake and Murray Tyrrell had helped bring to life in the 1960s and '70s. The region was safe, he said, in the hands of the young generation of winemakers.

'Hunter wine has improved out of sight in the last ten years,' Evans told me. 'And it's thanks to the new ones. There's a fantastic cadre of young people up here, swapping information, looking at each other's wines, being very critical of each other.'

But the 'young ones' are faced with a big challenge. 'I think the Hunter is definitely on the horns of a dilemma,' he said. 'I think it's lost its singularity as a wine district. It's become a lung of Sydney. As it becomes more prosperous, the land becomes more expensive, and the ones who want to stay in the wine business need to make their wines as well as they possibly can. You just can't now thump out a nice semillon with a she'll-do-mate kind of attitude any more, I mean you really can't.'

In Evans' heyday, the Hunter was widely respected as one of Australia's top regions; its ageworthy semillons and earthy reds rightly regarded as distinguished wines of terroir.

'At the end of the '60s,' said Evans, 'Grange was the same price as Tulloch's Private Bin [a classic Hunter red]. Now, Tulloch's Private Bin doesn't exist any more [it has, since this interview, been revived]. And Grange is several hundred dollars a bottle. Why? What's gone wrong? What went wrong, of course, was that the Hunter became a bottle department [hotel wine shop]. Now, you can't have a fine wine area and a bottle department in the same place. The Burgundians realised this a long time ago. So now that's what we're fighting to do: to become an established fine wine area again.'

One of the ways the Hunter is aiming to prove its bona fides to the world is by focusing on what it's calling its Heritage Vineyards. The region is home to quite a few plots of old vines, tucked up back roads, on gentle hillsides, along old creek beds: places like the Howard family's 1960s Somerset vineyard on the rolling red country out along Marrowbone Road, Tyrrell's precious 100-year-old HVD chardonnay vineyard, and the extraordinary 1880s planting of shiraz up on the hill behind the winery at Mount Pleasant. The regional growers' association has identified all these blocks of pre-1968 vineyards and put them on its Heritage register; pre-1968 because they were planted in those days using cuttings from other, established, proven Hunter vineyards rather than cuttings from commercial nurseries, keeping alive a viticultural lineage that stretches back to James Busby and the vines he brought to Australia from pre-phylloxera France in the early 19th century.

Of course, long before this register was finalised, the new generation of younger winemakers had already learned where these best blocks are, and now fight to get their hands on small parcels of very special fruit.

Krinklewood

Krinklewood is the most exciting new Hunter Valley wine label to have emerged in the last five years. The quality of the wine alone is enough to justify this rather big call, but the fact that Krinklewood is also a glowing example of biodynamic viticulture in action obviously also gets my juices flowing even more.

Rod Windrim and his family established their 20-hectare vineyard in the Broke Fordwich sub-region of the Hunter in 1997. Rod is a builder by trade, a builder who appears to have done quite well for himself: as well as the country vineyard property in the Hunter, there's also a house in Sydney's affluent northern beaches. Indeed, at first glance, Krinklewood looks like yet another Sydney treechange vigneron's Hunter dream-come-true (and there are plenty of them scattered across the region) – all glitz and no guts: there's the Provençal aesthetic of the cellar door and vineyard house; the manicured lawns and topiary; the shed full of expensive brand-new undervine weeders and other vineyard toys; the paddock full of beautiful Limousin cattle that Rod's been breeding for 20 years.

But then Rod starts talking about studying the work of Rudolf Steiner and how uplifting he found it, like nothing else he's ever felt in his life; about how, since adopting biodynamics in the vineyard in 2002, his whole philosophy of life has changed; and about how, when he's feeling stressed, he comes down to the paddock and sits with his cows to chill out and absorb some of the big animals' calm.

Rod will probably hate that I even mentioned that. But I think it's important: he passionately believes that biodynamics is the best way to run a vineyard; even in the Hunter, a region traditionally characterised by high humidity and rainfall towards the end of the growing season, both of which can be a huge headache for grape growers.

There is a burgeoning biodynamic movement in the Hunter in the field of general agriculture and the region is home to one of the most inspirational BD farmers, John Priestley. But very few vineyard owners in the traditionally conservative Hunter wine community have adopted biodynamic techniques, let alone converted to organic farming. Indeed, the only other certified biodynamic vineyard in the region is Macquariedale, whose ageworthy semillons and intensely regional red wines – plum-compote-like merlot and deeply earthy shiraz – should be enough proof that the methods can work.

'Sometimes I can't believe how winemakers and growers here can just sit back and carry on with business as usual,' says Macquariedale's Ross McDonald. 'What with climate change and how we're poisoning the river system, everything points to the fact that we've all got to have a softer approach with farming. But still people are sceptical that we can grow grapes in healthy vineyards just by using the biodynamic preps.'

I saw for myself what a huge difference biodynamics can make when I visited Rod at Krinklewood a couple of months after the disastrously wet 2008 vintage.

Rod had picked his whites and some mourvedre for his rosé, but then the rains came – and didn't stop. The natural resilience of the biodynamically grown vines, and some careful concoctions of BD sprays, put off the onslaught of mildew and rot for a week or two, but eventually the vineyard succumbed and Rod lost his red grapes.

Rod told me this story as we walked through the vineyard. The soil was spongy underfoot (as healthy BD soils so often are); an amazing diversity of grasses and, yes, weeds, flourished under the vines; birds and insects trilled and buzzed through the canopy; the place was humming with life, despite experiencing what many in the region described as the worst vintage in living memory.

Then I walked through a conventionally managed vineyard just down the road. Like Krinklewood, this vineyard had lost its entire 2008 red crop to the moisture and mould. But unlike Krinklewood, the owner had spent tens of thousands of dollars on hard-core chemical sprays trying to keep the mildew at bay. The soil was hard and crunchy. The undervine strip was bare and dusty. And it was silent. Nothing flew, nothing crawled, nothing scuttled. It was lifeless.

The Krinklewood vineyard is mostly planted to the Hunter classic grapes – shiraz, semillon, chardonnay and verdelho – and his winemakers, Jim Chatto at Pepper Tree and Liz Jackson at First Creek, do a superb job of turning those grapes into appropriately classic Hunter wines. The semillon is taut and chalky in youth, picking up hay and cheese savoury characters as it sits in bottle; the verdelho is one of the country's best, with grapefruit-pith leanness and mineral cut; the chardonnay is intense, mealy, with a pineapple-rind tang; and the shiraz is fabulously regional, with soil-dusted wild bramble berries squashed between iodine-soaked wooden slats.

But Rod has also planted a smattering of alternative grapes, including mourvedre and tempranillo. While some Hunter winemakers are increasingly interested in grapes other than semillon, chardonnay and shiraz, good examples of alternative varieties are not overly common in the region. David Hook produces a properly crisp, bone-dry pinot grigio from early picked grapes and a very good, juicy, fleshy barbera; and a few winemakers have found viognier well adapted to the heat, but these are exceptions.

'My dream was to make an iconic, Provence-style rosé,' Rod told me once. And it's a dream come true: Krinklewood's sensational, subtle, entrancing, savoury and tangy mourvedre rosé is one of Australia's best dry pink wines.

The innovation doesn't stop there. Krinklewood also produce a fantastic wild yeast white called Spider Run from chardonnay, semillon and verdelho, co-fermented in barrel to produce a wine with gorgeous grape-pulpy richness, creamy texture and powdery acidity. And in 2005, full of the holistic enthusiasm of new biodynamic converts, Rod and his family picked some shiraz themselves and, rather than sending it off to the contract winemaker, made it in the shed behind the cellar door. 'I was right in there in my board shorts,' grins Rod energetically. 'I made that wine with the help of my brother, my son, and four slabs of stubbies.'

Meerea Park

Meerea Park have gone further than perhaps anyone in making the most of the region's old vineyards, and turning them into ultra-traditional Hunter style wines.

Meerea Park winemaker Rhys Eather produces no fewer than four different semillons and four shirazes from single-vineyard fruit. Each is an accurate expression of where it was grown, augmented by sensitive handling in the winery and, in some cases, judicious bottle maturation before release.

The Epoch semillon is sourced from 40-year-old vines planted in the old water courses of sandy soil over yellow clay that run through the russet mounds of the Somerset vineyard, and is released as a young, crisp, apple-crunchy wine. The Hell Hole semillon, also released young, is sourced from the flatter sands of the Braemore vineyard and is both more intense and more austere. The Terracotta semillon comes from the red soils of Somerset, not classic semillon country, but perfect for producing an early maturing white that will fill the mouth with lemony richness at about five years old, which is when this wine is released. Rhys also makes four different shirazes: Alexander Munro sourced from the Ivanhoe vineyard; Terracotta, co-fermented with a dash of viognier; and two wines from the Howards' Somerset vines – Hell Hole, which is matured only in French oak and tastes more like dark velvet, and The Aunts, which is matured in American oak and tastes grainier, dustier.

'Howard shiraz has a character all its own,' says Rhys. 'Part of that has to do with the vines themselves, I think. The Howards got their cuttings from Stevens, an old vineyard in the area which was originally planted with shiraz from the Busby collection [dating back to the early 19th century]. The wine from that red soil tastes like nowhere else in the Hunter.'

Rhys Eather was one of the first in the Hunter to experiment with co-fermenting shiraz and viognier. In 2007, he tried something new again, and fermented half of the Somerset shiraz destined for Hell Hole as whole bunches, stalks included. The result was so different – spicy, perfumed and exciting – and such a clear demonstration of the quality of the fruit and of the site, that the small batch was bottled separately and sold under the Meerea Park XYZ label. It was a very convincing experiment, and will lead to more innovative winemaking with the other single-vineyard wines.

The Eather brothers are acutely aware of how special these mature vineyards are. 'In 2008,' says Garth, 'even though most of the crop was a write-off thanks to the rain, we still bought red grapes from our best growers. We paid half of what we normally pay for that old vine Howard fruit, but at least we paid something, so that we could ensure we'd get it next year. A lot of growers were badly let down by the wineries in that year. But we felt we have a moral obligation in this industry as well as a commercial one. We're in it for the long term.'

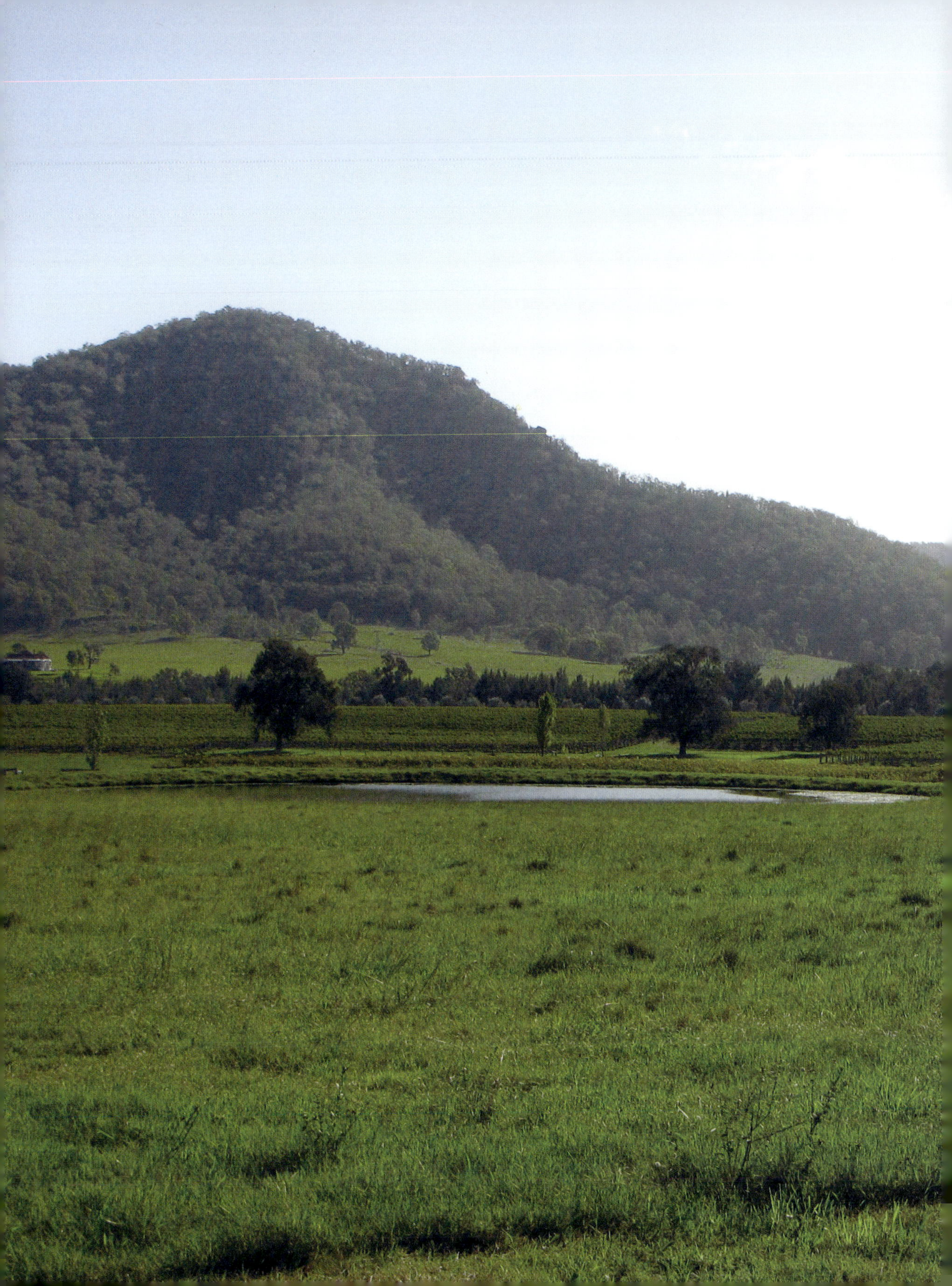

Krinklewood, Hunter Valley

The Hunter Valley new wave

Hunter pioneers such as the late Len Evans, Murray Tyrrell and Max Lake must loom like creator spirits above the new generation of Hunter winemakers, watching their every move, making sure they don't stray from the path of regional righteousness.

Young(ish) grape-treaders like P.J. Charteris at Brokenwood are passionately committed to making wines that are not only a true reflection of their terroir, but are also part of a grand regional tradition that stretches back well over a century. Classic Hunter styles such as early picked semillon that is fresh, light and chalky in youth but evolves in the bottle into a honeyed, toasty national treasure, and shiraz that can be plush and purple and oaky when young, but soon succumbs to the entrancing, earthy, hard-to-describe characters that make the Hunter unique.

One of the best evocations of the elusive classic Hunter shiraz flavour I've ever heard came from P.J. Charteris, despite (perhaps because of) the fact that he's a Kiwi: 'When I was a kid growing up, every autumn Mum would take Black Doris plums from big old trees out the back and cook them up with quills of cinnamon and other spices. The plums would go into preserving jars and be stored under the house. And whenever we'd drag one out, open it, warm the plums and pour it over ice-cream, we'd be reminded of autumn. And when I got to the Hunter and tasted some of the great old Graveyard shirazes at Brokenwood, there it was coming out of the glass: the smell of spices and plums. The smell of autumn.'

The flowering of renewed pride in the Hunter's past is obvious at the 115-year-old Tulloch winery, back now in family hands after a brief spell languishing in the portfolio of Australia's largest corporate wine company. One of the first things that young Christina Tulloch did when the family took control was reintroduce the old Pokolbin Dry Red label for the winery's shiraz, and the much-loved Private Bin label for the top shiraz. The bottles – and the deliciously brambly red wine inside – are like a vote of confidence for the region's rich heritage.

It's also a fascinating and rewarding exercise to drink the Meerea Park single-vineyard semillons next to the single-vineyard semillons produced by Andrew Thomas. While Thomas's winemaking is cleaner and more protective than Rhys Eather's, and the resulting wines can be a little too austere in their extreme youth, the underlying terroir differences shine through just as clearly. The O.C., from a loamier patch of sandy soil in the heart of the Pokolbin sub-region, is fuller-flavoured, with juicier, more immediate lemon zest characters, while the Braemore, from a vineyard planted on the sandier, alluvial flatlands up towards Belford, is leaner, more austere, and more ageworthy.

Mudgee

Mudgee is a beautiful, bustling nest of organic and biodynamic wine producers. The relatively small region boasts an unusually high number of certified organic vineyards, including Botobolar, Lowe Family (both featured below), Broombee, Martins Hill and Thistle Hill.

In early 2009, Thistle Hill was bought by neighbouring winery, Erudgere, and, symbolically, the new owners are now in the process of converting their own vineyard to certified organic practices.

'This is such a good demonstration of how organics has evolved in this region,' says Thistle Hill founder Lesley Robertson. 'Erudgere's owners, Rob and Mary Loughan, are American, and the reason they wanted to merge with our vineyard is that they need more organic wine, because so many customers are asking for it in the US. When we first certified, years ago, being organic was seen as a negative: people thought you were just a hippy, and that they'd have to strain the wine through their teeth. Now they realise that it's possible to have organic wines that are also high quality.'

There is a strong green collaborative streak among Mudgee winemakers, too, and a broader engagement with the environmental issues facing the wider farming community. Lowe Family Wines, in partnership with Ed Turner of nearby Frog Rock vineyard, has purchased a state-of-the-art compost-turning machine (like the one at De Bortoli in the Yarra Valley) to produce hundreds of tonnes of compost from a variety of sources including the local council's green waste.

Lowe Family's Jane Wilson spends a lot of time speaking to both grape growers and farmers about the importance of adopting more sensitive practices in the New South Wales central west.

'It's all about lifting your resource and increasing your soil's capacity to bounce back,' she says. 'If you have healthy biology in the soil, you have a buffer to help you even out extreme events like drought and wet years. But I'm not a zealot. I don't want everyone to convert to certified organics overnight. I just think that talking about organics, showing people how it can work, can help drag everyone towards greater sustainability. If we can just get them to start to think about what's below the ground and realise that it's a resilient system but it can't be flogged to death, then that's a huge positive step across the catchment. It's much better that 90 per cent of the farmers are travelling just under the full organic level than not.'

Lowe Family Wine Co.

When David Lowe and Jane Wilson established their 11-hectare vineyard at Mudgee in the mid-1990s they modelled it on the great old vineyards they knew from time working in the Hunter Valley. 'We wanted to plant a young vineyard that would give us a wine with the flavour identity of a 50-year-old vineyard,' says Jane. 'So we planted without irrigation, with each vine trained to a single stake, the old-fashioned way.'

As far as chemicals were concerned, they established the vineyard conventionally, albeit with minimal herbicide and fungicide application, but soon found that something was lacking in the fruit and the wine.

'We were chasing that elusive balance of flavour,' says Jane. 'But we felt when we were growing conventionally that the grapes were fading just before picking; not much, but still the difference between, say, a $30 and a $50 bottle of wine. And when we looked at our soil biology, we found things were good but not complex enough to give full nutrient support to the vine.'

So they started to adopt biological practices inspired by the Soil Food Web Institute such as compost tea and beneficial microbe foliar and soil sprays. This led to more organic techniques and the adoption of some biodynamic practices – making compost with the BD preps added to it; spraying preparation 500 in spring and autumn – and, eventually, organic certification.

It hasn't always been easy: in late 2007, they decided to go the whole way and take sulphur and copper (both of which are allowable as fungicide sprays under an organic regime) out of the equation and use 'competitive biology' (compost teas, etc.) instead. The timing couldn't have been worse: the 2008 vintage was the wettest anyone could remember, and that year's crop was virtually wiped out. Undeterred, Jane Wilson still believes that the more biological activity you can encourage under the ground, the more raw materials the vine has to work with, then the more complex and individual the resulting wine.

'No other agricultural product captures a picture of where it was grown as well as wine,' says David Lowe. 'Everything you do, everything that happens to the plant over 12 months, is captured in the solvent nature of ethanol. And because of the organic and biodynamic methods, we began to see even more obvious differences from one block of vines to the next.'

'Our two main shiraz blocks were originally planted according to soil type,' says Jane. 'We recognised some differences between the blocks very early on but we couldn't be sure they weren't just fermentation or vintage variation. From 2003 onwards, though, the blocks were so distinctly different that we now benchmark Block 8 (which is clay and sand) against traditional Aussie shiraz and Block 5 (more stone and shale in the soil) against Cote Rotie, or similar, new-wave Australian styles. We love chasing that terroir.'

I think there's a noticeable improvement in the other reds, too: they are certainly tasting more distinctive, more sure of themselves, as each vintage progresses (2008 notwithstanding). The merlot, for example, expresses both its warm climate and red clay origins and its varietal identity in the form of rustic, open-textured, wild plum fruit, Pomerol-like coffee and chocolate richness, and raggedy, torn-silk tannins. The zinfandel, for me, is the other standout: a brooding, sumptuous wine, with more wild black fruit, the classic sweet/sour hit of rhubarb compote richness, and a complex finish like layers of damp leaf litter in a forest at dusk.

Botobolar

I've told this story before, in my book, *Crush*, published a decade ago. But it's worth repeating because it's even more relevant now than it was then.

It's 1991. I'm sitting in a small flat in Brighton, England, sharing a bottle of Australian red wine with some friends. The wine is black, rich, sweet-composty, like liquid soil. It has such an immediate sense of itself, of where it's from, bound up in its pitch-black depths. It's a shiraz from Botobolar, the pioneer organic vineyard in the warm New South Wales region of Mudgee.

The amazing, evocative taste of that wine stayed with me for a long time; it was one of the reasons I chose to explore Australian wine further and why I moved to the country a year later. The fact that the wine was organic was important, too: I realise now that it set an early course for the path my wine-writing has ended up on over the last few years. In other words, me buying that bottle of Botobolar in Brighton back then is directly connected to you reading these words right now.

I eventually made the pilgrimage to where that bottle came from just after the 2008 vintage. From the fabulous rain goddess sculpture at the front gate – with her stern warning sign: 'Trespassers will be composted' – to the flock of surprised quail flying out from a thick cover of St Barnaby thistle and wildflowers as I drove past, Botobolar vineyard lived up to 17 years of expectation. The place looks and feels like an organic vineyard – in the best ways, of course – and it's still producing bloody good wine.

Botobolar was established by journalist Gil Wahlquist in 1971, long before the concept of organic farming (as a deliberate response to chemically assisted farming) was widely known or used. Gil was ahead of his time in many ways: he also planted a small olive grove (long before that became trendy) in the '70s, and started using biodynamic methods around 1990 (ditto). He also established what he called a small 'survival vineyard': a permaculture-like collection of different grape varieties, interspersed with mulberry trees, isolated from the rest of the 20-hectare vineyard and never sprayed with anything (not even copper or sulphur) to see if it was possible for vines to survive that way.

The present owners, Kevin and Trina Karstrom, took over from Gil in 1994, having given up promising but ultimately dull careers in investment wanking (their phrase). Kevin had picked up vintage experience working for various Mudgee wineries before taking over, but Botobolar was still quite a shock to the Karstroms when they arrived.

'At first the learning curve with organics was so steep it almost pushed you over,' says Trina. 'But the more we learned about organics and our relationship with the earth, the more committed we became to it.'

As well as the ubiquitous Mudgee grapes, chardonnay, shiraz and cabernet, Botobolar also boasts a fruit-salad mix of the surprisingly inappropriate (pinot noir – not really all that well suited to Mudgee's warm climate), the old-fashioned (crouchen – almost extinct elsewhere), the Germanic (riesling and traminer) and the thoroughly appropriate (marsanne and mataro). The Karstroms also source grapes from other certified organic vineyards such as Thistle Hill and Rosnay in Cowra.

The use of sulphur dioxide is kept to a bare minimum here, and Botobolar also produces some of the best no-added-preservative wines in Australia: fleshy, juicy reds that can still drink well two years or more after vintage. I am particularly attracted (and not just in a sentimental, nostalgic way) to the budget-priced Rain Goddess white, a wine featuring crouchen and a varying (depending on the vintage) supporting cast of other white grapes such as riesling and traminer: aromas of white flowers and flint, grapey mouth-perfume and crisp finish.

The Botobolar shiraz is still the star, though. The first thing you notice is the impenetrable black colour, common to the reds of the region. Mudgee winemaker David Lowe puts this regional character down to the sunlight – Mudgee gets more than the Hunter, say, over the hills to the east – and the radiant heat that bounces under the vines off the red earth. Being inland, Mudgee is also cooler and drier than the Hunter, and the reds often have higher alcohols but retain better acidity.

There's a density to this wine, too, a supple solidity in the mouth, a deeply satisfying savoury quality. The Japanese describe this 'savoury in the sweet spot' sensation as 'umami' – the fifth taste – and it's the same kind of experience you get from eating soy sauce, Reggiano cheese and really ripe tomatoes (all of which are high in the amino acid, glutamate). And blood: cooked blood, like black pudding.

It's a solid, chewy expression of the heavy red clay soil and the Mudgee sun, full of the smells of sweet, damp compost and black, black fruit. Full circle.

Di Lusso

Italian grape varieties are nothing new in Mudgee. Winemaker Carlo Corino first planted sangiovese (followed by barbera and nebbiolo) at the Montrose vineyard in the early 1970s; 50 years before, Sydney surgeon-cum-vigneron Dr Thomas Fiaschi had planted the musky, spicy Italian red grape, aleatico, at his vineyard, close to the present-day site of Di Lusso wines.

Ex-banker Rob Fairall fell in love with Italian wines while travelling around the world with his career in the 1980s and 1990s. As these grapes started to appear in more and more Australian vineyards throughout that decade, he became inspired to establish his own vineyard, olive grove and fig orchard, in Mudgee, and opened an Italian restaurant in Sydney, supplied by the produce of the vineyard.

'What particularly attracted me to the red Italian varieties in particular is their savoury, food-friendly quality,' says Rob. 'I much preferred them to the dead-fruit, heavy characters I was finding in so many Australian red wines in the 1990s.'

So Rob planted sangiovese, nebbiolo, lagrein and barbera, plus the white grape picolit and some aleatico. He also buys grapes from other vineyards including, over the last few years, the Chalmers collection down on the Murray River. Di Lusso viticulturist and winemaker Julia Page clearly has an affinity with these grapes: the rosato (made from lagrein) is properly savoury, snappy and crisp; the vermentino (from Chalmers fruit), is all chalky dryness, with hay and nut aromas, crying out for salt cod fritters; the aleatico makes a pretty, pink, rose-scented sweet wine, delicious wth perfumed Italian biscotti or cakes and a small cup of extra-strong espresso; and a deeply earthy 2006 aglianico (also made from Chalmers fruit) is still one of the best Australian examples of this grape I've tasted.

While all these grape varieties are perfectly well suited to their warm, dry environment, the most compelling Italian–Australian moment comes when I walk into a small shed out the back of the Di Lusso winery. Here, laid out on racks stacked high to the ceiling, are slowly drying bunches of chardonnay and picolit grapes. The desiccation is part of the appassimento process, an ancient Italian method of making intensely flavoured, lusciously sweet wines. As the bold, bright Mudgee sun beats down outside, here in the shade the heady scent emanating from these grapes, particularly the aromatic picolit, seems like an extract of place, a distillation of the region's hot air and rich soil.

TRESPASSERS WILL BE COMPOSTED

Botobolar, Mudgee

Orange

One of the criticisms I continue to hear from ill-informed European or American winemakers, journos and sommeliers is that all Australian wines are heavy, over-ripe and tricked-up (over-acidified, full of enzymes or aromatic cultured yeasts, etc.). Still, amazingly, the perception from afar is that Australia's vineyards must all be planted on a vast plain of flat red soil under clear blue skies, churning out a surging ocean of cheap wine, created to a recipe in refinery-like grape-processing facilities.

Whenever I come across such blatant viticultural prejudice, I feel a bursting urge to be Scotty on the Enterprise, able to beam these wrong-headed bigots slap-bang into the heart of Orange, preferably in autumn, as the last grapes are being picked off the vines. At this time of year, with its extensive plantings of russet- and gold-painted European trees and plunging gullies and fine, brisk, delicate wines, you couldn't imagine a region further in character from the ocker, sun-baked Aussie stereotype.

It's cold mountain country up here: the regional boundary of the Orange GI is the 600-metre contour line; some of its vineyards are perched on hillsides up to 1000 metres above sea level. As it does in other high-altitude regions (Macedon, Adelaide Hills, Granite Belt), this relative proximity to the sky makes a big difference to the quality of the fruit grown here. Terroir isn't just about the ground, the soil in which the vines are rooted; it's also about the air and the atmosphere above the plants. Here in Orange, the light has a great clarity – an intensity of UV radiation – that accumulates as layers of flavour in the grapes. This complexity is in turn captured and preserved by the beautiful, translucent natural acidity that you find in regions with long, cool, slow growing seasons.

You struggle to find heavy, flabby, tricked-up wines here. Preconceptions are constantly confounded.

Bloodwood

Stephen and Rhonda Doyle were doing things outside the mainstream at Bloodwood way before the mainstream winemaking community in Orange was even established. In many ways, this gloriously iconoclastic estate is the model for all the other iconoclasts featured in this book: for a while there I was even going to steal Bloodwood's tag line – The New Tradition – and use it as a subtitle.

The Doyles were pioneers when they founded their vineyard high up on Griffin Road, just outside town, in 1983. When they arrived there were two trees on the property, now there are well over 10,000; a feat of revegetation that was achieved without even a whisper about carbon offsets or eco-credentials. They have always followed organic principles in the vineyard whenever possible but have never made a big noise about it. 'We only ever spray with copper and sulphur, and only then if we have to,' says Stephen. 'We like to use human beings for all the vineyard activities, too: I've not yet met a machine harvester with a nose.'

The Doyle sense of humour is classically dry and laconic, with the irony knob turned up to nine and a half. But it's a laid-back approach informed by serious thought and intent. So on one hand Stephen Doyle displays a deep understanding of what lies beneath the 8 hectares of hillside vineyard ('low-vigour soils of calcareous laminated silt stone, greywake and limestone breccia overlying a friable red clay base and a deeply fissured Middle Ordovician volcanoclastic parent material'…apparently), and Rhonda Doyle talks passionately about the importance of developing a thriving local food culture (she was a co-founder of the very successful Food of the Orange District festival). And on the other hand, the Doyles have created some of the slyest, funniest wine labels in the country.

Incensed by the French nuclear tests on Mururoa Atoll in the early 1990s, for example, Stephen christened the Bloodwood sparkling wine Chirac: 'The biggest fizz in the Pacific'. And, egged on by a number of his most ardent fans (including your correspondent) in the late 1990s, he took the bold step of putting his in-house, pet name for the Bloodwood Rosé – Big Men in Tights – on the front label. It's been Big Men in Tights ever since, and it boasts one of the best back label descriptions anywhere – 2007's, released just after the third Telstra share offer, was a cracker: 'About as red hot as a T3 tranche on special, at least this frankly full dividend in your future pink drinking sureties will yield a very palatable return, replete with Turkish delight and spice, into an otherwise bland portfolio awash with colourless saccharin imitation offers. And yes, there is enough bitter dark chocolate and raspberry jujube in this lolly jar to appease every last amigo's mum. So keep the dastards honest, stick this in the fridge, splash it in a glass and remind yourself once more: all this will pass!' My favourite Doyle-ism, though, came just after the introduction of mandatory allergen labelling a few years ago: in small print, just under the words Big Men in Tights, appeared the phrase: 'may contain traces of nuts'.

It's not all fun and games at the Doyle winery, though. Stephen also produces some seriously good examples of what the Orange region can do so well, thanks to its complex soils and clear, crisp, high-altitude light and air. The Bloodwood riesling is a tightly wound, lean and limey thing when it's young, but that lime morphs into tangerine peel and richness with five or ten years in the cellar. The chardonnay is also seriously savoury, with wheatmeal dust and mineral powder sprinkled over white peach skins and lemon pith. The Big Men in Tights, usually fashioned on juice bled away from malbec skins, has – as the label suggests – plenty of rosewater and violets and a perfectly balanced hint of sweetness. And the Maurice cabernet (named after legendary Hunter winemaker and fellow iconoclast, Maurice O'Shea) displays bordeaux-like cedar and grainy berries, and is one of a surprising number of Orange cabernets that, contrary to expectation, appear to like it up here in the cool, 800 metres above sea level.

Having been at it now for over a quarter of a century, the Doyles have a philosophical view of the sustainability of vineyards – and farming in general – in rural areas like Orange.

'In the next 20 years,' says Stephen, momentarily serious, 'Orange has to establish itself as a cool, environmentally friendly area.' And then that wicked twinkle, 'This will be really important for when we are forced, in the future, to transport our wine by bicycle. Or horse and cart.'

Tamburlaine

Tamburlaine is one of those Hunter Valley stalwart wineries that seems like it's been around forever. The original vineyard and winery, on McDonalds Road in Pokolbin, was established in 1966, at the beginning of the boutique boom; its managing director and chief winemaker, Mark Davidson, has been there for a quarter of a century; and most of the wine is sold to a loyal, long-term direct mail client base.

And yet Tamburlaine also happens to be right at the cutting edge of sustainable Australian viticulture. As well as 12 hectares of certified organic vineyard in the Hunter, the winery also has a 93-hectare vineyard at Borenore in Orange which from 2009 was certified biodynamic, making it one of the largest single BD vineyards in the world.

Mark Davidson has been painting Tamburlaine an ever-deeper shade of green for the last decade. In 2000, he developed an in-house program called Sustainable Quality Viticulture, which led, in turn, to organics, and finally to biodynamics. Tamburlaine have also developed an organic wine brand called Wild Mountain in conjunction with UK importers, Stratfords Wine Agencies.

The wines emerging from Tamburlaine's Orange vineyard have improved steadily over the last few years: the riesling has that clarity common to the best rieslings in Orange – a kind of purity that can take your breath away, like an accidental squirt of orange zest in the eye; and the shiraz (labelled syrah) hums with prickly pepper and spice, and fine-grained tannins, like sucking on plum skins.

'We're not a bunch of tree-huggers who became winemakers,' Mark Davidson points out in his typical, direct, no-bullshit manner. 'We're winemakers who became tree-huggers. But we've never sold the conversion to our long-term customers, our wine club members – many of whom are quite a conservative bunch – along environmental lines. We've always said, and we believe, that growing grapes organically is better for quality.'

Tamburlaine's Orange vineyard is run by charismatic local vigneron, Justin Jarrett, whose own property is also managed organically. Like Davidson, Jarrett believes there is a direct correlation between organic and biodynamic farming methods and improved quality in the grapes.

'We're employing all these techniques such as biodynamic field sprays and compost teas and rock phosphate because we want our deep basalt soils to reach that magic 6 per cent carbon content figure,' says Jarrett. 'Most Australian vineyards' soils are lucky to have 1.5 to 3 per cent carbon, and this is one reason, I think, why they consistently produce grapes with ripe flavours only at higher baumés. This doesn't happen in Europe so much. There you get perfectly ripe flavours at lower baumé. Why? What's the difference? I think it's because the European soils have often got more carbon in them. If we improve our carbon content, we could get better flavours at lower baumé.'

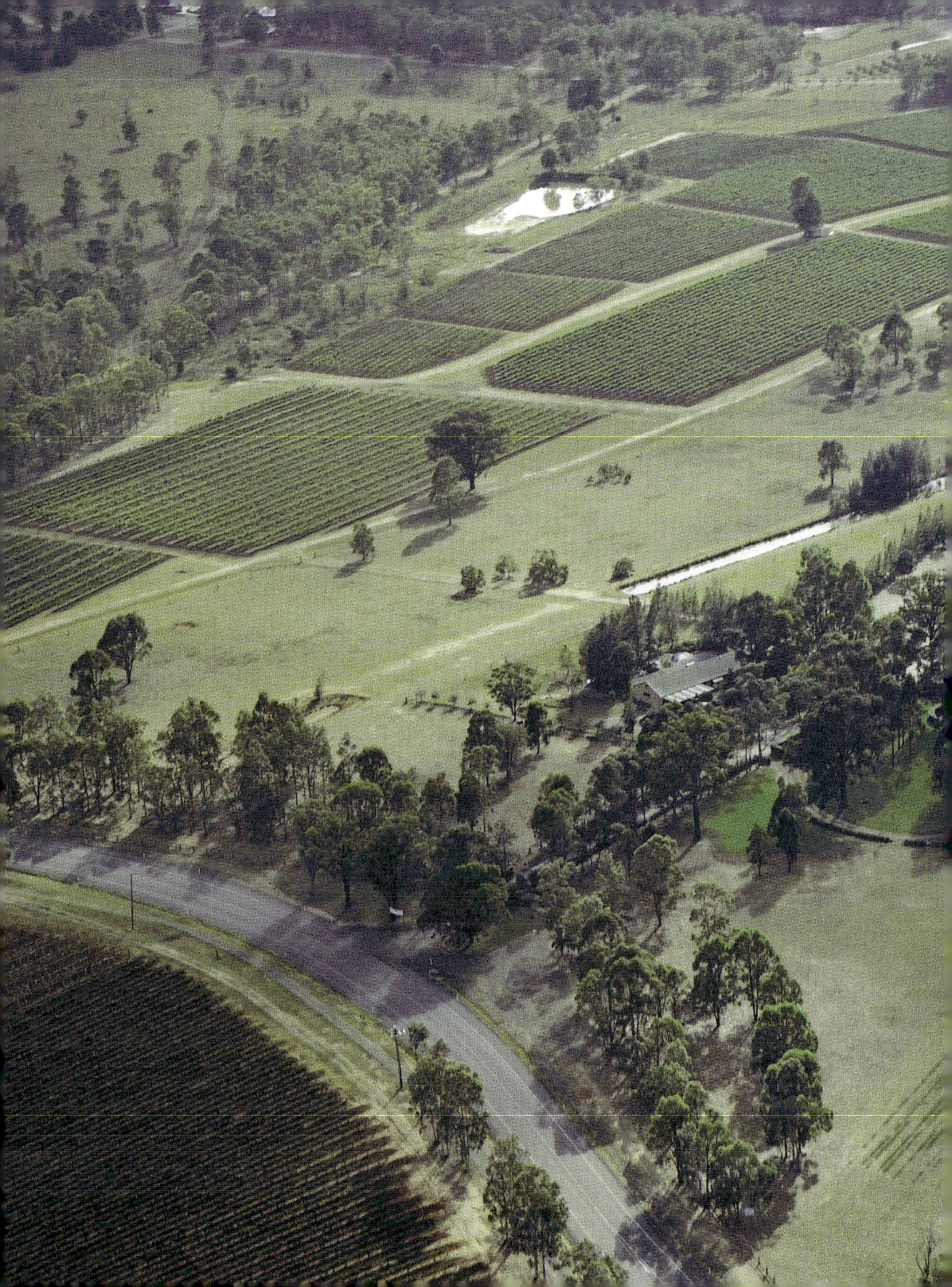

Tamburlaine, Orange

The fact that a vineyard the size of Tamburlaine's at Orange has converted to certified biodynamic practice should inspire others in the region to explore alternative viticulture and winemaking: there were certainly plenty of interested growers and grape-treaders at an organic field day I went to at Tamburlaine during the 2009 vintage.

Cumulus Wines at Molong, on the fringe of the Orange region, has converted some blocks on its vast, 500-hectare vineyard to biodynamics, and assistant winemaker Andrew Bilenkji has installed an egg-shaped concrete fermenter like the one at Sutton Grange winery in Victoria. And a little further afield the New South Wales Department of Primary Industry has established an organically managed vineyard at Bathurst as part of a broader, significant investment into organic agricultural research.

It looks like Stephen Doyle of Bloodwood's wish that Orange should become truly green in the next two decades may well come true.

Wallace Lane/Ross Hill

Winemaker Phil Kerney is sliding from barrel to barrel, tank to tank, drawing samples of the wines he's made from his first vintage here in Orange. The vintage isn't over yet: it's late-April 2009, and some cabernet sauvignon is still bubbling away in a large vat in the corner. But, already, enough of Phil's baby wines tastes good enough to make me very excited indeed.

Phil Kerney moved up to Orange in late-2008 from Victoria's Mornington Peninsula, where he had established a creditable reputation for the wines he made at Willow Creek. He started work here at Wallace Lane, a new winery established as a joint venture between the Robson family of Ross Hill Wines in Orange and Greg Jones, chair of the New South Wales government's Wine Advisory Board.

The winery is housed in an old converted apple-packing shed. Apples have been a very important crop in the high country around Orange since the 1850s. Third-generation apple – and now grape – grower Borry Gartrell has more than 150 different types of heritage table and cider apples at Borrodell on the Mount, and he supplies both cider apples and perry pears to the excellent Victorian cidery, Henry of Harcourt. Orange also boasts its own very good cidery at Small Acres and one of the country's leading cider experts, David Pickering, of the Department of Primary Industry, whose own private collection of cider apple varieties runs to over 50.

This apple-growing heritage means that large cool-rooms abound. Those at Wallace Lane, now all used to store barrels, allow inventive winemakers like Phil Kerney plenty of flexibility: he can bring each of the four rooms at the winery down to whatever temperature he wants, to slow ferments, speed malos, preserve flavour, etc.

Phil plunges a wine thief into a barrel of chardonnay and squirts the cloudy straw-coloured liquid into my glass. It's a chardonnay that's been fermented with plenty of solids, no additions (no yeast or acid), and has superb depth, texture and weight.

A wild ferment pinot gris is next. We taste the pretty, floral free-run juice component and then the pressings, with amazing pear-skin graininess and funky aromatics – the latter portion, muses Phil, might be judiciously blended back with the lighter component to increase the interest and deliciousness of the finished wine.

He shows me a super-lean and precise riesling from the quartz-infested brow of a hill at over 1000 metres above sea level; taut and nervy pinot noir and spicy shiraz (after so many years on the Mornington Peninsula, it's no surprise that he's learned how to coax the best from these two varieties in these styles); and some excellent cabernet, glowing purple, so full of life and cassis perfume, straight out of that still-fermenting vat. The most memorable young wine of all, though, is a cabernet franc from a north-east-facing stony block of ground at Ross Hill vineyard. A light purple red in colour, the wine dances on the tongue, a riot of cranberries, sappy twigs, cinnamon and allspice. It's chock-a-block with a sense of place and time.

'I'm not, perhaps, what you'd call a normal winemaker,' says Phil. 'I've had people say to me when they've found out what I'm doing: Oh, you're *brave*. When what they mean is: don't you know that's not what we *do* here? But I believe the time is right for this kind of winemaking in Orange.'

Although it's true, I think, that many of the region's wines can err a little towards the safe side, Phil Kerney's techniques aren't exactly revolutionary. Philip Shaw, for example, has always wild-fermented the eponymously labelled wines he makes from his 20-year-old Koomooloo vineyard at Borenore, west of Orange. He's also careful to pick whites early, to preserve that spine-tingling natural acidity and pure mountain flavour, and works hard on introducing texture into the sauvignon blanc through lees-contact and judicious barrel-ageing; it's easy to capture the immediately appealing, herbaceous characters of sav blanc grown up here, it's much harder to make serious, tangy, multi-dimensional wine out of it.

But Phil Kerney has shown that his approach to winemaking is emphatically well suited to the region's distinctive purity, transparency and focus. In his new employees, the Robson and Jones families, he may have found people who are prepared to let him take Orange wines to an even higher level.

Cowra

Cowra, stuck geographically between the cold mountain heights of Orange and the hot flatlands of the Riverina, is sloughing off its 40-year reputation as a warm, reliable grape factory, and is emerging as a home for quality-minded, unusually eco-conscious wine producers, thanks to the formation of the Cowra Sustainable Wine Partnership.

This comprehensive program of benchmarking is aimed at reducing chemical use in the vineyards, building soil health, encouraging winter grazing of livestock in the vineyards and increasing the use of renewable energy sources, and has been adopted by many of the region's vineyards.

And at Wallington Wines, Margaret Wallington has built a straw bale winery that keeps a constant temperature of 18°C throughout the year and needs no air conditioning or heating. She also recycles all the winery waste water for use on the vineyard, composts her grape marc, is working towards carbon neutral status and is converting the 400-hectare property to organic and biodynamic farming practices.

'There's a critical mass of growers in the area going this way,' says Margaret. 'We can all feed off each other's experience.'

'The lack of rain over the last few years really united everybody,' says Tom Ward of Swinging Bridge Estate, fellow instigator of the CSWP. 'It encouraged us to group together to try and do something about it. It's also led to other partnerships, like a mulching project with Cowra council.'

For years now, the Cowra council have been stockpiling a massive amount of mulched trees and lawn clippings and sundry organic matter. In 2007, the region's vineyard owners twigged to this brilliant resource sitting literally in their own backyard, and started talking to the council about taking the composted mulch off their hands. For a fee, of course, but a very reasonable one. There's enough material here – 12,000 cubic metres – to mulch the ground under every hectare of grapevines in the region.

A couple of the local vineyards took part in a trial looking at the effects of undervine mulch on crop yield and grape and wine quality – important considerations in this warm and dry region. At Rosnay, two rows of merlot were chosen: one row had a wide layer of composted mulch spread under it and the other had none. I tasted wines made from each row and the difference was clear: the un-mulched vines produced a wine that was lighter, simpler, red-fruity, while the mulched-vine wine was slightly fuller-bodied, with richer fruit flavour, and firmer tannin. As a result of the trial, many vineyards in the region are now using the council's composted mulching as a matter of course, and reaping the benefits in increased quality.

Rosnay Organic Wines

Sam Statham hands me a metre-long piece of stiff fencing wire with a sly grin on his face. 'Here you go,' he says. 'Your very own penetrometer.'

Golly. I had no idea I needed – let alone wanted – a penetrometer. But now I've got one, I'm inexplicably keen to use it. Starting right now, in the Rosnay vineyard at Canowindra, north of Cowra in the warm New South Wales central west.

I stick the wire into the grass-covered ground under a row of shiraz vines and it's like slicing through butter with a warm knife: the makeshift penetrometer easily finds passage deep into the beautifully friable soil.

'There you go,' says Sam. 'Look at that. That's what a decade of biodynamic farming will give you. Healthy soil. It's pretty simple.'

To prove his point, we hop into his car and drive to a nearby vineyard: large, conventionally run, with bare, herbicided strips of terracotta earth under the vine rows baking in the midday sun. 'They flog this place,' says Sam. 'Pile on the chemicals and the water. Chase large crops. Try your penetrometer in that.'

I try. Nothing. Tough as rock. Just scratching at the dusty surface. So I try again, pushing harder until the stiff wire begins to bend under the strain. The difference is remarkably stark.

Sam grew up on his family's sheep farm at Barraba in northern New South Wales. He finished a degree in geography in 1996, and like most graduates went travelling to France, Africa and New Zealand. In a pub in Christchurch one night, he got chatting to a stranger, who told him there was work available on a nearby biodynamic farm.

Sam had read about biodynamics in a book his grandfather owned, and while sceptical of the theory, what he saw in practice impressed him deeply. It struck a chord with the polycultural European and African farming methods he'd studied at uni and seen on his journey, and seemed like a truly sustainable alternative to the chemical-dependent farming methods he'd witnessed during brief stints working in 'conventional' vineyards.

'In 1995, my parents had sold their farm at Barraba and purchased a small farm with better soil and water here in Canowindra,' says Sam. 'The aim was to join in the wine boom with an investor, but the investor dropped out in 1996, leaving them with a good farm but not enough capital to develop it as planned.'

So, encouraged by what he'd seen on his travels, he moved back to the family property and helped develop what is now known as Rivers Road Organic Farms.

'We copied local vineyard developments using community title as an investment structure,' he says. 'But with a difference. Ours is a community title farm that is polycultural and all certified organic, which provides for people to build and live on the farm in a cluster of house blocks in the middle of the farm blocks.'

It's a truly remarkable place to visit: a very old-fashioned utopian ideal that appears to be working in reality. As well as two vineyards, the Stathams' biodynamically managed Rosnay vineyard and Herb and Jenni Gardner's organic Gardners Ground vineyard, and some pretty spectacular straw-bale houses, there are four other agricultural operations at Rivers Road, including certified organic sheep (which graze right across the property, helping to manage weeds under the vines), a large-scale organic vegie grower, plus olives, figs and cereal crops such as spelt.

The Rosnay wines are made at Windowrie Estate and can be very good indeed: I particularly like the tangy, waxy, lemon-scented semillon, and a fabulous, pale, savoury mourvedre rosé Sam produced in 2008. Windowrie's Jason O'Dea also produces vibrant cabernet and shiraz from his own 6-hectare biodynamic vineyard, Pig in the House. In both cases, the wines are a vast improvement on the heavy and cooked characters that have often been found in this really quite warm region.

For the Statham family at Rosnay, greener viticulture is not just a personal choice, but also something they would like to see adopted across the region, state and country. Sam has sat on the vignerons committee of Biological Farmers Australia and the Australian and New Zealand Organic Wine Show, is a highly vocal campaigner against genetically modified organisms, and was one of the instigators of the Cowra Sustainable Wine Partnership.

Canberra

When the Hardy Wine Company built its flash Kamberra winery and cellar door in 2000 right next to the racecourse in downtown Canberra it was seen as a huge vote of confidence for the region. Small winemakers such as the visionary Edgar Riek at Lake George, the Kirks at Clonakilla and the Carpenters at Lark Hill had done a good job of building a name for Canberra's boutique wines since the 1970s, but investment by a major national company signalled to the world that here was a serious winemaking area to watch.

So when Hardys sold Kamberra in 2006 and walked away from making wine in the region, it could have been seen as a disaster, especially for those growers who had planted vineyards especially to service the needs of the big company. But it wasn't a disaster. Instead, the multinational's departure provided a series of great opportunities to the smarter growers and winemakers, and has spawned some terrific new wines, including some superb, taut, spicy, medium-bodied shiraz produced under the Collector label by ex-Kamberra winemaker Alex McKay.

The timing of the Kamberra sale also turned out to be particularly fortuitous: the building was flogged off just before disastrous frosts descended on the region, dramatically reducing the crop in many vineyards. This meant that winemakers such as Clonakilla's Tim Kirk, who lost 90 per cent of the fruit on his own estate, were luckily able to source grapes from a number of ex-Hardys growers and make wonderful regional shiraz that year, establishing beneficial relationships that have continued in subsequent years.

It's no surprise, perhaps, that shiraz has emerged as the leading grape in this region. There are many similarities between the high (350 to 800 metre) rolling country here and the hills of Beechworth, in north-east Victoria further down the Great Dividing Range: both feature granite outcrops and boast some good patches of granite-sand soils as well as brown volcanic and shaley loams. Climatically the two regions are almost identical (although Canberra has drier summers). And they share a similar story: while our wine-drinking attention was initially drawn by chardonnay and pinot noir in the 1980s and early '90s, recent wines indicate that the future lies more emphatically in Rhone varieties – shiraz, viognier, roussanne – and Mediterranean reds such as tempranillo and sangiovese.

Canberra's other strong grape, of course, is riesling: the classic white variety likes the meaner, stonier soil sites, and is able to tolerate the summer warmth and drier conditions in the flatter, lower country, producing wines with a good, steely backbone and ability to age well. Appropriately, one of the region's more outspoken winemakers, Ken Helm, has established a successful tasting competition in Canberra called the International Riesling Challenge, which has done a lot to build a noble connection between grape and place.

Lark Hill

Since adopting biodynamic principles in 2003 and becoming fully certified in 2008, the Carpenter family's Lark Hill vineyard has never looked healthier. Oh, and the wines are better, too. It's as simple as that. The words proof and pudding spring to mind. But you want more detail, I'm sure.

'We've had droughts here before,' says Chris Carpenter as we drive up the bumpy 800-metre hill at Bungendore, east of Canberra. 'My parents have been here since 1978; 1988 and 1998 were both pretty dry times, but not as dry as now. This is the longest drought we've ever experienced, and yet the vineyard is in the best condition it's ever been in.'

It certainly is: I'm here at the end of another hot summer and while the hills all around – and many of the vineyards – are showing the browning effect of fierce sun and scorching winds, the vine leaves here are still a vibrant green, and the soil under them has a soft, spongy texture.

Chris puts much of the vine health and resilience down to the heavy layer of moisture-retaining composted mulch laid in strips under the vines. His parents, Sue and David, are also convinced that applying the biodynamic preparations, spraying the horn manure 500, and following lunar rhythms have played just as important a part.

These people aren't – to use their own tongue-in-cheek expression – loincloth wearers. Well, not all the time: Sue does dabble in a little water divining every now and then. The Carpenters came from a science/academia background and Chris has studied biochemistry at the Australian National University. So they are highly articulate, scientific, even, in their appreciation and explanation of biodynamics.

'We measure everything,' says Sue. 'And we have found higher amounts of nutrients available to the yeasts in the juice of our biodynamically grown grapes than we found in the juice of grapes grown conventionally. Low nutrients in the juice can lead to difficult ferments, with yeasts struggling to convert all the sugar and taking undesirable metabolic pathways such as producing hydrogen sulphide. Good juice nutrition leads to clean ferments with healthy yeast cell division. It's one of the reasons why we feel comfortable fermenting all our wines spontaneously now.'

And how do the BD preps, particularly 500, increase soil and vine health?

'Mycorrhizal soil fungi form a permanent relationship with plant root cells by penetrating the cell wall with their hyphae,' she explains. 'They exchange nutrients for sugars produced by the plant and stored in the root. These soil fungi connect to form huge networks: the underground threads of one fungi organism may cover a whole vineyard block and help to share the nutrients around to all the vines. Using herbicide can kill off these fungi, and change how the vine takes up nutrients.

'Now to biodynamics. The cow has more stomachs than other ruminants: horses have one, goats and sheep and kangas two, cows three. There are seven types of stomach bacteria in cows, five in most other ruminants. Hence composting cow manure for preparation 500 is more effective than other manures. The 500 is a starter for building up a good healthy dose of this bacteria; stirring it in warm oxygenated water builds up the bacteria colony; and this bacteria in turn stimulates growth of the soil fungi involved in nutrient exchange.'

But proof, pudding…

'We had a group of local growers from the viticultural society visit us the other day,' says David. 'We were expecting a group of disbelievers. We've certainly experienced a fair bit of suspicion from conventional vineyard people over the last few years. But these people turned up, saw how good the vineyard looks, thought about how theirs were faring in this drought, and immediately started asking questions. They wanted to know where to buy the lunar calendar, how to make nettle tea, how to stir the preps. We couldn't get rid of them.'

And then there are the wines. From the 2006 vintage, the quality of Lark Hill's wines has improved significantly – and they were already very good. The riesling is now especially delicious, both in its dry form – lean, searing acidity framing intensely grapey, perfectly poised citrus fruit – and its late-picked, 'auslese' form. And the pinot noir is arguably Canberra's finest, with sappy undergrowth, dried herb tannin and red berry juiciness.

The Lark Hill wine that excites me the most, though, is the gruner. In chapter five, New Tastes, New Flavours, I introduced you to the 800 young gruner veltliner vines clinging to the top of the Carpenters' shaley hill. Established from scratch along biodynamic lines, these vines have grown up beautifully in trying conditions, producing their first proper crop in 2009: a magnificent wine with a savoury smell of chalk and hay and a gorgeously mouth-filling, slightly oily texture.

In October 2004, I stood on this windy hilltop when it was just a bare paddock. Sue closed her eyes and said she could feel the energy of the place, feel its calmness, feel how well suited it could be for gruner. She asked me whether I could feel the calmness too. And you know what? I think I could.

The proof of the pudding, though…

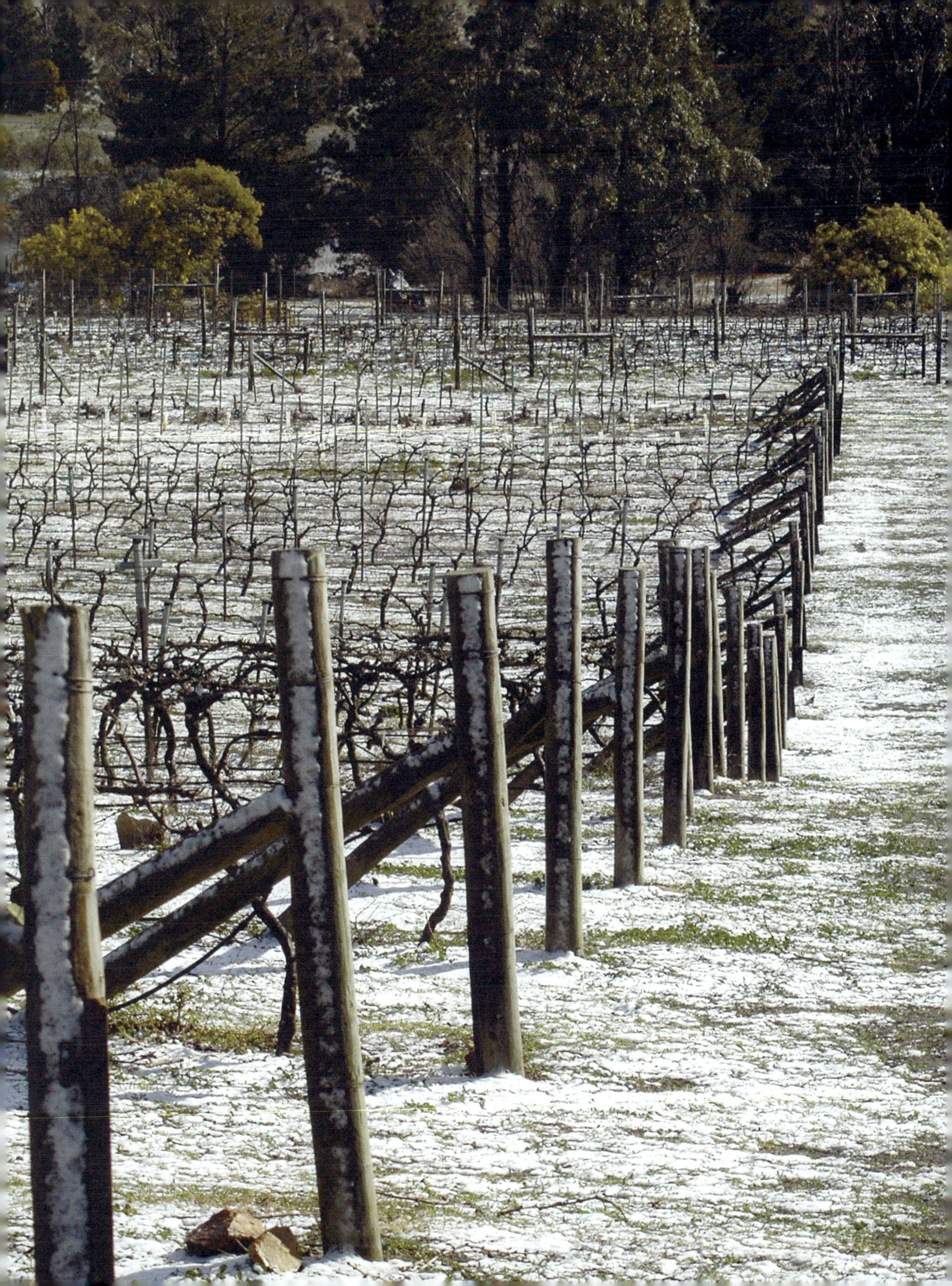

Lark Hill, Canberra

Clonakilla

Tim Kirk refers to his religious faith a lot in conversation, or when he's addressing a room full of wine drinkers or other winemakers. And even though he always does so with a glint in his eye and the hint of an ironic smile on his lips, so as not to alienate the atheists, you know there's serious intent and belief there.

He describes himself as an enthusiastically practising Catholic. He talks – as I've mentioned elsewhere in this book – of God creating the universe out of love and revealing Himself in transformative acts such as the fermentation of grape juice, and how it's the job of the winemaker to capture that love. And now that he's started making and spreading compost on his vineyards, he's full of wonder at this other act of transformation: how marc from the winery can be piled onto a paddock, where cows piss and shit on it and it becomes perfect organic fertiliser. God's love revealed again.

Crucially, Tim describes a 1991 visit to the Northern Rhone and a taste of Guigal's sublime Cote-Rotie – shiraz blended with a little viognier – as an epiphany: 'It was a revelatory moment,' he says. 'The wine met you at a level that was deeper than just fermented fruit. It was a thing of beauty, a thing of dignity. I thought that if I could ever achieve that for our humble vineyard, I'd be a happy man.'

His father, Clonakilla's founder John Kirk, had coincidentally already planted a little viognier in their Murrumbateman vineyard; so in 1992 Tim co-fermented some of the white grapes with the shiraz – and the rest is history. Clonakilla shiraz viognier is now one of the best red wines in the country, an exceptionally fine, complex and beautiful drink; as emblematic of the new, 21st-century Australian wine sensibility as Penfolds Grange is an icon of the last millennium.

Tim Kirk and assistant winemaker Bryan Martin simply don't know how to produce a bad wine. The Clonakilla whites are among the best in the region: steely, lime-juicy riesling and deeply textural viognier that, unusually for this grape in Australia, can improve in bottle for a few years, quite Condrieu-like in its savoury undertow. The Hilltops shiraz, first made in 2000 using grapes from vineyards that had been abandoned by Southcorp (now Foster's), is one of the most reliable, best-value reds in Australia: layered, plummy fruit with a spicy meatiness that's reminiscent, to continue the Rhone analogy, of St Joseph. The Rhone analogy is handy, actually (and entirely appropriate, given Tim's love of, and regular visits to, that region). From 2007, Kirk and Martin have made a shiraz called O'Riada using fruit sourced from other Canberra vineyards around Murrumbateman and Hall; this is more Hermitage-like, with its rather luscious, slippery, spicy bramble/berry fruit and fine tannins. And whereas the new-classic shiraz viognier, which includes around 6 per cent of the white variety and 20 per cent whole bunches in the ferment, can taste uncannily like a top Cote-Rotie, the new Clonakilla syrah (no viognier, no stalks but whole berries, spontaneous ferment, month-long maceration) is all Cornas: wild, gamey, garrigue-like dried herb scents, a flood of spicy black fruit and firm, robust, chewy tannin.

As well as being an integral part of the Clonakilla story, Bryan Martin also produces excellent wines under his own label, Ravensworth, from grapes grown on the Rosehill vineyard just up the road and around the hill in Murrumbateman. Bryan makes a rich and exotic viognier but my pick of his whites is the marsanne: a fabulously textural, stone-fruity wine with honey and wholemeal bread characters accentuated by wild-barrel ferment, lees stirring and minimal filtration. His shiraz viognier is superb, with more exaggerated and forceful perfume and fruit than the Clonakilla. And the Ravensworth sangiovese can be stunningly intense, with morello cherry fruit and very fine, powdery tannins.

Bryan has also worked and taught as a chef, and finds time to write about food for the *Canberra Times*, all of which will stand him in good stead when the Clonakilla Dining Room opens. Tim and Bryan were excitedly making plans for this latest addition to the farm when I visited in late 2009: sheep, pigs, goats and a vegie patch will join the vines and olives, and provide raw materials for small-scale private meals and cooking classes in a new, purpose-built space on-site.

'I've always loved the idea of gardening, of self-sufficiency,' says Tim. 'There's something fundamentally human, something psychologically and spiritually correct about growing your own food and eating it. And when we begin to talk about the meals we'll have in our own place, well, it all begins to sound like a pretty rewarding lifestyle really, doesn't it?'

Mount Majura

Canberra wine pioneer Edgar Riek identified this beautiful east-facing slope at the foot of Mount Majura as good potential vineyard country many years before it was first planted in 1988. The soil here is a lovely complex mix of iron-rich, red volcanic loams full of chunks of rhyolite and ancient limestone. It's a combination that produces grapes with exceptional structure, perhaps even a little *too* much grip in the mouth at times.

Winemaker Frank van de Loo made the Mount Majura wines over at Brindabella Hills in the east of the region for a few years before his own winery was built on-site in 2007. Frank learned very quickly about the differences between grapes grown in the eastern granite soils and the central and western red soils.

'Roger [Harris, Brindabella winemaker] always complained about his wines being too fruity and not savoury enough,' says Frank. 'Whereas, even though we were making my wines in a very similar way at first, I had to fight against too much tannin, too much savoury character in the wines from Majura. The difference was in where they were grown. So now, learning how to best express this site has become what we're all about.'

This means painstakingly trialling a number of different grapes. The vineyard was planted initially to cabernets, merlot and franc, riesling, shiraz, chardonnay and some pinot noir. Frank has introduced newer grapes such as pinot gris, tempranillo (a mixture of clones) and graciano. Next to be planted are touriga and mondeuse.

As is the case with so many other vineyards across the region, both riesling and shiraz do very well here; the former in a typically fresh and citrusy style, the latter showing lots of black pepper and mid-palate plummy suppleness, balanced by those fine but firm tannins Frank talks about.

More exciting in the long run, though, are the Iberian grapes. The graciano here is a thrillingly spicy, juicy red wine, with even more pronounced spiky pepper than the shiraz. And the tempranillo has pure red/purple berry fruit, and the variety's trademark soft but persuasive tannins, lifted by a lick of eucalyptus. Frank blames the gum trees next to the tempranillo block. 'They're as much a part of the terroir as the soil,' he says.

A trial blend of the three red grapes in 2008 indicated that, eventually, this combination could produce a truly awesome wine that will best express this lovely site: the fleshiness of the shiraz lends a great counterweight to the spice of the graciano and the savoury quality of the tempranillo.

But while all this experimentation might be fun for the winemaker, that wine still has to sell. Frank is confident. 'You've got to try to make the best damn wine you can,' he says. 'I really believe that if you do, people will buy it.'

New South Wales High Country

The emerging high country regions clustered within the Southern New South Wales and South Coast Zones are studded with vinous gems: growers and winemakers taking their vines and their vats on really unusual and exciting journeys.

Tony Cosgriff has crafted some very convincing tempranillos from Centenniel Vineyards near Bowral, both in serious, brooding dry red and crisp, fragrant dry rosé form. Celine Rousseau makes consistently refined, savoury wines at Chalkers Crossing, excelling with whites such as a Hunter-thrashing semillon and piercingly citrusy chardonnay from Tumbarumba, unequivocally the most exciting source of pristine cool-climate chardonnay in the state. Tertini produce a stunningly rich, multi-layered, gorgeously textural arneis from their vineyard near Berrima in the Southern Highlands. And Nick Bulleid, consultant, writer, Master of Wine, is in the process of adopting biodynamics on his 1-hectare Hatherleigh pinot noir vineyard at Crookwell, 900 metres up in the high country north of Goulburn.

The Hilltops region gets my vote for most exciting emerging region, though, thanks to the truly thrilling new wines emerging from vineyards such as the 20-year-old Grove Estate, with its vibrant, forest-fruity zinfandel and sumptuous nebbiolo (both made with winemaking assistance from Tim Kirk at Clonakilla in Canberra), and the particularly adventurous Freeman vineyard.

Freeman

Brian Freeman's wines, made in homage to the reds of the Italian Veneto region and the whites of Friuli, have received great critical acclaim, but nothing I've so far read or heard does justice to how truly exciting, innovative and inspirational they are.

Brian was head of the wine science course at Charles Sturt University in Wagga Wagga in the early 1990s when he first came across a comprehensive range of Valpolicella and Amarone wines at a tasting held for the students. He was blown away by the completely different flavour profile of the rondinella and corvina grapes these wines were made from, and their savoury tannin structure, derived from the fact that the grapes were partially dried – the appassimento method – before fermentation.

So, in classic can-do Australian winemaker fashion, Brian sourced six cuttings of rondinella and corvina from the CSIRO collection at Merbein, propogated them, bought a site in the Hilltops region and planted a vineyard.

The vines thrived. In fact, they love being in the deep, red, decomposed granite soils so much they tend to spread a large canopy and throw out plenty of bunches: crop-thinning has been necessary for most of the last six or seven vintages.

Brian was determined to see how these brand new grapes would taste when grown in Australian soils and put through the Italian appassimento process. But, after visiting the Amarone producers around Verona, he thought the traditional drying method of laying bunches out on racks in draughty lofts took too long, and ran too high a risk of mould infections. So he scratched his head for an alternative – and realised the answer was literally just up the road.

The Freeman vineyard is at Prunevale, right in the heart of the Hilltops region. For well over a century, this part of the world has been famous for its stone fruit: cherries in particular (also a very important crop in the hills around Verona, as it happens), but also plums and their dried cousins, prunes. 'The place was set up to keep the British Empire regular,' says Brian, with the straightest face.

It didn't take long to find a solar-powered dehydrator that could dry his grapes to exactly the required amount of desiccation in a matter of days rather than months or weeks; a brilliant example of a wine being the product of the cultural elements of terroir just as it is the product of the country and the climate.

'Originally we dried about 10 per cent of the rondinella and corvina crop completely, until they became almost like raisins, then added them to the freshly picked grapes and fermented them together,' says Brian. 'This completely changed the tannin structure of the wine, the seeds become brittle and this component brought just what I was looking for to the wine. In the last couple of years, though, we've been drying the dehydrated portion out less, and also experimenting with ripasso – first fermenting the wine from the fresh fruit, then macerating that finished wine with the dried fruit. It gives us silkier tannins, and that sweet mushroom Amarone aroma that I thought was coming from a little botrytis infection in the Italian versions I tried.'

In 2004, Brian bought the neighbouring 30-hectare vineyard. Established in the 1970s, this new property included a remarkably mixed bag of grapes, including the aromatic traminer and red, muscatty aleatico.

'I was looking for a white partner to the rondinella corvina,' he says. 'And I was inspired by these grapes to go for a field blend like the ones you find in Fruili. So in 2006 we released the first Fortuna: a blend of riesling for acidity, barrel-fermented chardonnay for weight, sauvignon to give the wine zest, pinot gris for its savoury character, and a splash of aleatico for aroma and natural grape tannin.'

That whisper of tannin has shocked a lot of other winemakers. Tannin? In white wine? Never! 'Some winemakers find the Fortuna style challenging,' admits Freeman. 'Some have even told me they think it's downright faulty.'

For me, though, a little phenolic grip, an element of minerality to balance the creaminess and perfume of the other grapes, is what makes Fortuna a particularly successful and delicious full-bodied white wine. The perfect counterpoint to the rondinella corvina with its hint of dried grape bitterness.

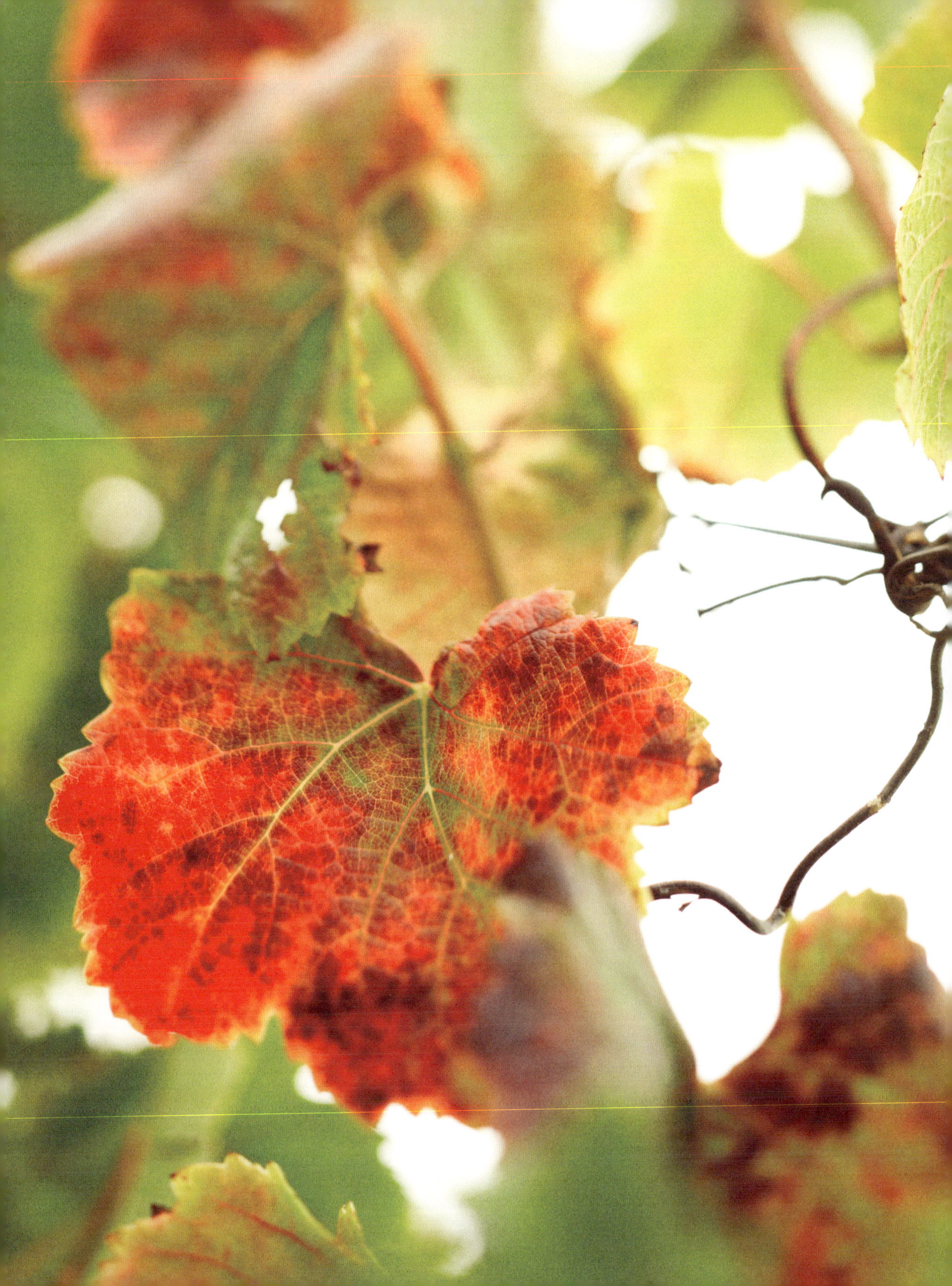

10 Western Australia

Perth and Surrounds: Swan Valley and the Hills

The capital city of Western Australia is surrounded by wine. As well as the old Swan Valley vineyards, planted in hot red soils on the city's northern doorstep, there are vineyards planted in deep white tuart sands to the north and south of the city, and more vineyards scattered up throughout the gravelly loams of the cooler Perth Hills to the east. All these regions are under pressure from the rapacious urban development that has characterised life in and around WA's capital over the last decade or so: drive out from the city centre in any direction and you have to travel a long, long way before you can escape the feeling you're crawling through one enormous building site.

Between all the earth-movers and the land sale signs and the cement mixers and the cranes in the hinterland, you can still find signs of the very early bucolic years of Perth's viticultural development hidden on hillsides and down back streets. Remnants of little forgotten home vineyards poking through overgrown grass; a vine-trained pergola with chooks scratching beneath the shady canopy; reminders of the old Croatian settlers who made new lives here after the First World War by planting fruit trees, vegies and vines.

Some of this old-fashioned garden spirit lives on in two biodynamic vineyards just outside Perth. Judy and Gerry Gauntlett's 1-hectare Gilead Estate vineyard north of the city produces only about 400 cases of wine a year, including a spicy, gamey shiraz that totally belies its origins, tasting for all the world like it comes from somewhere much cooler. 'We get virtually no summer rain and the soil's pure sand,' says Gerry. 'We need all the help we can get in these conditions. So we converted to biodynamics in 2002. And since then we've improved the organic matter and tilth of that sandy soil no end. Even the postman has told us he's noticed that the place looks different now.'

And at Wandering, south of Perth, Leonard Bruin and Wouter Denig have been running their Hotham Ridge vineyard biodynamically since 2006, as part of a farm that also includes an olive grove, orchard, vegie patch and plenty of native vegetation. There's a distinct southern Italian feel here, both in the wild rusticity of the zinfandel and other reds, and in the range of products Bruin and Denig release under the Cheetaning Park label, including verjuice, red wine vinegar, olive oil and a vincotto made according to an old nonna recipe given to them by a couple of Sardinian backpackers.

Talijancich and the Swan Valley tradition

One of the most extraordinary wines in the Talijancich cellar in the Swan Valley is the 1965 Solera Pedro Ximenez, a profoundly raisined treacle that would compete with the best Spanish 'black sherries'. I first tasted this unctuous fluid in a wine show in Perth and was compelled, moth-like, to visit the winery where it was made, drawn by the dark amber light emanating from the glass.

When I got there, James Talijancich drew a barrel sample of pedro from last year's vintage to compare: from the same, gnarled centenarian vines that squeezed out that amazing '65, this bright burning golden syrup tasted like the essence of Swan Valley sunshine.

'Young people come through and taste these wines and they love them,' says James. 'They recognise the history and the precious heritage.'

Despite being an entrenched part of the Swan Valley establishment – Talijancich was established in 1932 and James is third-generation winemaker – this is also one of the region's, Western Australia's, most progressive wineries.

James makes some very good whites: a floral verdelho and an intensely appley, taut chenin blanc (one of the region's better grapes thanks to its naturally high acidity). Both benefit from extended lees contact – ten months in the case of the verdelho – and have a good, lean, savoury finish.

He's also shown that Spanish red varieties are well suited to the area: a tempranillo, made using grapes from a vineyard in the Perth Hills a few minutes' drive to the north, is full of red cherry fruit and fine, firm tannin, while the estate-grown graciano is a fabulously wild red, with solid, chewy bramble fruit and coal-dusty grip.

'Graciano's a great grape for this area,' he says. 'You can pick it at 14 baumé and still not need to add any acid.'

Since 2002, the 6-hectare Talijancich vineyard has been farmed biodynamically, using the prepared 500 horn manure spray from Alex Podolinsky in Victoria, and this is one of the reasons, I think, why that graciano has such an assertive personality. The only other producer in this fairly conservative region to have gone down a similar green path is the certified organic Harris Organic Wines winery. So what made James convert?

'It's not so much a matter of converting,' he says. 'We've never used herbicides. The old way of farming here was to strip-dig. But a few years ago we noticed our sandy soil wasn't as rich as it used to be. We were going to use more organic methods, green manuring, that kind of thing, but we were particularly impressed by seeing the changes to a farm in Waneroo that had gone biodynamic: the top layer of sand had turned into humus. So we gave that a go.'

James saw the differences after a couple of years. 'The vine leaves weren't that deep blue-green you see in vineyards fertilised with NPK. They were a glowing lime green. And the original plantings, those 1932 shiraz vines, have never looked better.

'My grandfather always told me: don't ever think you own the vineyard. You own the title but not the land. You need to treat it with respect and pass it on.'

At every winery and cellar door I visit in the Swan Valley, people keep telling me how popular their fortified wines are becoming again. Not only that, but it's the young people, apparently, who are driving this resurgence of interest in muscat, port and pedro – young winemakers as well as young wine drinkers.

When I arrive at Lamont's, winemaker Digby Leddin is arranging the bottles for that night's Young Vintners tasting group. When gen-X and gen-Y winemakers get together in most other Australian regions, they usually bring along crisp young whites, or modern, terroir-driven reds. Leddin and his mates in the Swan and other regions surrounding Perth make these, too: Lamont's, for example, produce exceptional riesling and long-lived malbec from a vineyard down at Frankland. But the wines that'll be discussed at tonight's Young Vintners tasting are all fortified: classic old Hardys ports, venerable vintages from Portugal, special sherries from Spain, and extraordinary bottles of ancient alcoholic raisin juice from the Swan.

I find this back-to-the-future passion quite moving. Strong, concentrated tawny tinctures have been produced on the Swan Valley's baking flatlands for over a hundred years. You can still find ancient vineyards here – such as the patch of thick, gnarly old pedro ximenez bushes just off the main driveway leading into Houghton's cellar door, which is where James Talijancich sources his fruit from – that rival any revered vine gardens in the Barossa or Rutherglen for their sheer sense of history.

At John Kosovich Wines, Arch Kosovich is another young one keeping the fortified flame alive: he jumps from barrel to dusty barrel, drawing out samples of what look and taste like melted chocolate and liquidised prunes: old liqueur muscat, infinite in complexity. Drinkers hardly know about these wines let alone get to taste them in the eastern states, so it's wonderful to see them being maintained and appreciated by a whole new generation.

Faber Vineyard

John Griffiths shoves a glass of white wine in my hand as soon as I walk though the door of his Faber winery in the Swan Valley.

'You don't like verdelho,' he says in characteristically blunt fashion. 'I know that. You keep bagging it in your articles. So try this.'

'This' is golden, honeyed, toasty, rich but dry, delicious. It has a perfume I can't quite place. I take another sniff. And another.

'Over-ripe nectarine, sitting in a fruitbowl, just on the edge, before it starts to rot,' he says, reading my mind and filling in the blanks. He's smiling. He can see he's made his point. And he underlines it by revealing the bottle: a 1994 verdelho he made when he was at Houghton. Then he opens the verdelhos he's made in the last couple of years from his own 6-hectare vineyard here at Baskerville. And they're delicious, too: bursting with freshness and life, not a trace of the flabbiness I find so often in wines made from this grape.

John Griffiths is one of Western Australia's best winemakers, intelligent and forthright, a champion of new and unusual varieties (his petit verdot is a gorgeously plummy, glossy red), regionality (his Margaret River chardonnay, made from bought-in grapes, is elegant, wafery and citrusy) and the heritage and potential of the region he's chosen to settle in.

'I like warm regions,' he says. 'I know that's not fashionable. But I've never been caught up in the hoopla and glamour of this industry. I try not to follow trends. I liked fortifieds when everyone was drinking red. I liked reds when everyone was drinking whites. And now I like this warm region even though everyone's talking about cool regions.'

John believes in the ability of the Swan to produce generous, soft, open-hearted reds from shiraz, grenache and mataro, and practises what he preaches. 'These wines have *drinkability*,' he says. 'They may not be technically correct and squeaky clean, but they're bloody drinkable.'

But what about climate change, global warming? The Swan is already Australia's hottest winegrowing region. How will it cope with a few extra degrees on top – and even less rainfall?

'Oh we'll cope,' he says. 'Climate change isn't a problem. The wine industry is constantly changing. The future will make us.'

He reckons urban sprawl poses a greater risk to the Swan than global warming.

'Take the old bloke across the road. He's 80, and he's got 30 acres of grenache. He's lucky if he's getting $500 a tonne for it, but he's sitting on a million-dollar property. When he dies, maybe even before, it'll be sold and that'll be another old vineyard that disappears.'

Millbrook Winery

Because of roadworks from Jarrahdale to Millbrook up in the southern Perth Hills, I had to drive in the back way, through a brand new housing estate that looked like it had been lifted from the suburbs and plonked here in the hills, just over a rise from the winery and its 8 hectares of vines.

It was a stark reminder of the development pressure encroaching on the Perth Hills. The high country that snakes along the east of the city is full of pockets of urban fringe dwellers, attracted here by the same milder conditions that attract the grape growers and winemakers. Even though it's only a 20-minute drive down the hill from Millbrook to the sandy coastal region of Peel, it's much cooler up here during the summer, particularly during the night, and that can make all the difference between broad and delicate flavours in the wines.

Millbrook founder Peter Fogarty, who also owns Lakes Folly in the Hunter Valley in New South Wales, planted viognier at Jarrahdale in 1996 after a trip to the Rhone Valley. At the time, viognier was just emerging as a trendy variety, but was yet to establish itself in the Western Australian winemaking psyche.

Since then, as Millbrook's business has grown, winemaker Damien Hutton has bought grapes from all over Western Australia: I tasted some stunning Margaret River malbec from barrel at the winery, as well as some ripe but intense chardonnay from the emerging Fergusson Valley region east of Bunbury.

But the best wines are the three tiers of viognier, all of which come from the Perth Hills: Millbrook's own estate-grown grapes and other vineyards, right up to Chittering. The 'standard' Millbrook viognier, matured on lees in tank, is deliciously creamy, with mouthcoating honeyed texture. The estate viognier, wild-fermented on solids in barrel, has remarkable apricot kernel intensity. And the Limited Release, another wild-yeast fermented wine, made using hand-picked fruit, is impressively rich and weighty.

John Gladstones compared this region climatically to the Douro Valley in Portugal. Tasting Millbrook's viogniers, it feels more akin to the Northern Rhone.

Myattsfield

Then again, taste the brilliant touriga-based 'vintage port' produced by young winemakers Josh Davenport and Rachael Robinson – spicy, vibrant, lively and thrillingly intense – and you're straight back in the Douro.

Josh and Rachel are big fans of fortified wines and robust table wines, and are members of the Swan Valley Young Vintners group, but planted their vineyard and built a winery here at Carmel, near Kalamunda, because of the cooler nights in the hills and the little bit of extra finesse this brings the wines.

The pair make good whites from conventional grapes – leesy, textural chardonnay, subtly complex barrel-fermented semillon – but the dry reds made from alternative Mediterranean varieties are terrific. Their estate-grown mourvedre is packed with both bright red fruit and earthiness, and their tempranillo (made with grapes sourced once again from the McCusker vineyard in the north of the Perth Hills), while grippy and oaky, has a core of dark, fleshy fruit. Josh and Rachel were also the first in Western Australia to plant durif.

The cellar door here is bright, modern, clean. But when we walk out back, up the hill, past the vineyard and the chooks and the vegie patch, to the small shed where they store their barrels of fortified wine, a solera of PX, some muscat, suddenly it feels like we're slipping back through time, back to when those old Croatian settlers tried to recreate little snippets of the old country around Perth by planting and growing and picking and making…and drinking.

Margaret River

Margaret River isn't all glitz and glamour and showpiece wineries and package tours. Sure, from a distance it looks like there's little more than an endless stream of formulaic new labels flowing out from Western Australia's most famous region; and when you're there it feels like there's little more than an endless stream of tourists flowing in. But behind all the hype and the flamboyance, away from the main drag, in quiet vineyards and thoughtful cellars, many of Margaret River's better growers and makers are focusing on what the region does best, and trying to do it better.

Some of the most exciting new developments are coming from the oldest estates. The sons and daughters of the first wave of Margaret River pioneers, the generation that's grown up immersed in the wine culture of the region, have developed a great pride in the distinct terroir and sub-regional differences of their vineyards, and are trying very hard to express that identity in the glass.

Ed Tomlinson of Lenton Brae, for example, celebrated the 21st vintage of his vineyard's groundbreaking semillon sauvignon blend in 2007 by producing a magnificently textural, complex barrel-fermented version of the wine simply labelled Wilyabrup, after the sub-regional location of his family's property; it was nowhere near as commercially acceptable a style as the 'normal' wine, but it was a whole lot more distinctive. And second-generation winemaker Stuart Watson has helped to take his family's 35-year-old Woodlands vineyard at Cowaramup from relatively shadowy obscurity, known and appreciated mainly by Perth cognoscenti, to the bright lights of national and international critical acclaim. The gorgeously complex, concentrated, elegant red wines produced here add considerable weight to the assertion that Wilyabrup/Cowaramup is the best sub-region of Margaret River, thanks to its unique combination of terroir (the soils of the district are particularly rich in gravel), clone (most of the original cabernet vineyards here were planted with cuttings taken from the best Houghton vines in the 1960s) vine age and proximity to the sea (to take full advantage of the afternoon breezes).

The Watsons are acutely aware of how special their vineyard site is, and are taking steps to ensure its sustainability through undervine mulching, throwing away the herbicides and pesticides, applying biodynamic compost to the soil and following the lunar calendar whenever possible. The vineyard and winery have also been registered as carbon neutral with the Carbon Reduction Institute.

Thanks to the high-profile environmental efforts of Woodlands, Cullen and others, more and more Margaret River vineyards are heading down the green path, many assisted by local biological agriculture company, ERA Farming.

'We make 3000 tonnes of compost at a time with the biodynamic preps in it,' says Anthony Quinlan, ERA's viticultural consultant. 'We don't necessarily tell people it's BD compost, though. We say that it's compost with "microbial inoculants" included.'

Over the last few years more than 20 vineyards in the Margaret River have spread the ERA compost out under the vines and in the mid-row. One of those vineyards is the Reynolds family's 17-hectare Cowaramup Wines, which sells most of its grapes, but also makes some wine under the Clown Fish label.

Russ Reynolds is the last bloke you'd expect to hear talking about spraying homeopathic doses of cow poo on his soil when the moon is 'opposition Saturn'. He's a big man with a big handshake and no-bullshit manner, and you feel he should be driving a giant mining truck not burying cow horns. But here he is, making big piles of biodynamic compost to spread over his property and talking about how, compared to 'conventional' viticulture, this is a much nicer way to farm.

'You've got to continually supply organic matter to the soil,' says Reynolds. 'That way, you build up the soil biology so that the vine can access the nutrients it needs.' Since he's started using the compost and other biodynamic practices, he says, not only has he reduced his water usage by 30 to 40 per cent, but he's also seen an improvement in the grading of the grapes from the wineries that he sells to.

With down-to-earth people like Russ Reynolds getting such good results from biodynamics, the movement is bound to spread even further across Margaret River.

Cullen

One of the biggest debates about biodynamics is whether it's the practices themselves that make a difference – spraying special compost according to lunar cycles and cosmic rhythms, etc. – or whether it's simply that the practitioners are out in the vineyard more often *paying the vines more attention* that can result in better grapes and better wine. Similarly with the great wines coming out of Australia's best biodynamic vineyards: are they so delicious *because* they're biodynamic, or are they so delicious because the kind of thoughtful, creative, romantic people who make great winemakers are also the kind of people likely to be *attracted* to biodynamics?

This is the kind of chicken-and-egg conundrum you contemplate over lunch at Cullen's sublime in-house restaurant. The food – all organic or biodynamic, much of it grown just behind the winery, in a lush, abundant kitchen garden – is carefully matched to the wines grown in the vineyards surrounding you. It's a self-contained, sustainable, holistic approach to gastronomy that in many ways is about as close to the biodynamic farming ideal as envisioned by Rudolf Steiner as you can get.

But it's an approach that is also informed by Vanya Cullen's Buddhist view of the world, and the Cullen family's philosophy of 'quality, integrity and sustainability', both of which pre-date the adoption of biodynamics at this vineyard at the turn of this century.

So has biodynamics helped nurture excellence here, or did a quest for excellence lead Cullen to biodynamics?

One of the main reasons Vanya started converting the vineyard to organics in the 1990s and BD the following decade was a concern for the diminishing health of the soil and the old vines. The conversion has undoubtedly improved soil and vine health, but it has also changed the quality of the grapes: I think you could taste a clear improvement in the (already superb) Cullen wines from around 2004, when the vineyard became fully certified biodynamic. I think the wines are finer now, quieter, more assured and elegant. The Diana Madeline cabernet merlot in particular has greater complexity, more depth and layers, and the Mangan red (a blend of merlot, malbec and petit verdot) has more precision, focus and intensity.

This increased assuredness in the fruit, this clearer sense of identity revealed through taste, has also led to the development of new wines. Until 2007, Vanya had blended the semillon and sauvignon blanc grapes grown on the Cullen vineyard and the neighbouring Mangan vineyard – the former featuring slightly more gravelly soils than the latter. But that year the grapes from each vineyard tasted so different that Vanya decided to bottle them as two separate sem/sav blends. The effect was so startling that she repeated the exercise in 2008, and once again each vineyard's personality shone in the glass: the Cullen is more intense, has greater nettley cut and glistening green fruit, the Mangan is leaner, more chalky, less fruity but more refreshing.

Biodynamics enhancing the terroir? Or just a winemaker paying attention to detail? Who cares? As long as it continues to produce better wine.

Burnside Organic Farm

Lara and Jamie McCall run a fabulous 15-hectare mixed farm and accommodation business in the heart of Margaret River. The place is humming with life: chooks, avocados, pigs, olives, capers, macadamias, guinea pigs and just less than a hectare of young, dry-grown zinfandel vines. A very small winery was built in 2008. The whole lot is certified biodynamic, and is the model of a sustainable farming business, complete with garage winemaking operation.

The property is managed using permaculture principles: water is 'harvested' across the farm by swaling, an ancient technique that involves digging a shallow trench along the contours of a gentle slope to direct rainfall to where it is needed; the chooks play an important role keeping weeds and weevils at bay under the fruit trees and the vines; and as much of the family's food as possible, including stunning homemade prosciutto, comes from the farm.

The McCalls have a strong connection to both the old community and the new green movement in Margaret River: Jamie's father worked on the Busselton Medical Study with Kevin Cullen, and his cousins are Anthony and Tim Quinlan.

The adoption of biodynamics at Cullen was one of the reasons the McCalls headed down a similar path. Witnessing a number of old Cullen vines – some irrigated, some not – being pulled out a few years ago also reinforced the McCalls' decision not to water their zinfandel vines: 'The roots of those vines that had been irrigated had bunched up near the surface of the soil,' says Jamie. 'But the roots of the dry-grown vines had stretched out deep into the ground, looking for moisture. We thought that encouraging the vine to explore its environment by not irrigating was probably a better way to produce a more interesting wine.'

Dry-farming also means it takes longer for the vines to become established, and can lead to stress, especially in extreme seasons like the cold 2006 and hot 2007. As a result, the quality of the Burnside zinfandel has been patchy, but glimpses of the variety's edgy, exotic spicy perfume in the first vintage, 2005, and the fact that the McCalls have also sought winemaking advice from Peter Stanlake (who consults to several other companies including the biodynamic Hotham Ridge vineyard south of Perth), make me think this is definitely a vineyard to watch.

Cape Mentelle

Rob Mann has only been Cape Mentelle winemaker since the end of the 2005 vintage, but it seems like a lot longer. He even has a similar laconic, lanky air to Cape Mentelle founder David Hohnen (see McHenry Hohnen). Then again, young Rob has Western Australian wine flowing through his veins, and a strong family connection to this vineyard and winery on Wallcliffe Road: he's the grandson of the legendary Houghton philosopher-winemaker, Jack Mann, and nephew of Dorham Mann, who advised the Hohnen brothers to plant Cape Mentelle in the late 1960s.

Halfway through my visit, Rob proudly shows me a couple of hams he'd made from David Hohnen's pigs, hanging in a dark corner of the cabernet sauvignon barrel cellar (making your own prosciutto is a popular pastime among Australia's new-wave winemakers). He clearly feels completely at home.

Since arriving, Rob has introduced quite a few changes to the Cape Mentelle vineyards and winery. 'One of the main focuses has been on resurrecting the old vineyards through increased organic mulching, some biodynamic techniques, and different pruning,' he says. 'The cabernet vines in particular were struggling a bit, and used to produce small berries with tough seeds. We've halved the number of bunches with our pruning, and got double the berry size. We're still picking the same low yield – maybe 5 tonnes to the hectare – but we've got healthier bunches, and riper tannins.'

There's also a new vibrating sorting table and air knife to sort fruit and eliminate unwanted leaves, stalks and other material from the grapes before crushing. 'It's amazing how much green crap is left at the end, after the grapes have been through,' he says. 'And having cleaner fruit means we can leave reds on skins for longer, extract more ripe grape tannin, and reduce the amount of new oak from 75 per cent to 40 per cent.'

The results are clear in the glass. Cape Mentelle's wines were already very good, and occasionally excellent, but they have extra brightness and fruit definition now. The chardonnay, for example, has shifted gear from being a ripe, mouthfilling 14.5 per cent alcohol style to a more restrained, subtle and complex 13.5 per cent alcohol wine. 'Suddenly when you don't have that extra percentage of alcohol there's a whole range of fruit flavours you can appreciate,' he says. And the barrel-fermented semillon sauvignon, Wallcliffe, is an even more layered and textural and interesting wine than it was before.

'Wallcliffe is the best wine to make,' he says, almost breaking into a smile. 'You press the juice into barrel, come back in nine months, and bottle it. It's truly expressive of its site. The best wines I reckon are the ones you do least to.'

He's beginning to sound just a little bit like his grandfather.

McHenry Hohnen

Before he takes me to see his new and rather impressive winery, David Hohnen insists on showing me his real pride and joy: the pigs. As we rattle and bounce around in his beaten-up old ute across his 24-hectare vineyard near Witchcliffe, south of the Margaret River township, he explains his approach to growing grapes, the foundations of what he calls his grandpa farming methods.

'I reckon compost is the key,' he says. 'The vines we grow in Australia came originally from countries where the soil is defined by deciduous trees; trees that lose leaves in winter, building *up* carbon. Our acidic Australian soils have been formed by eucalypts, which shed in summer, leading to carbon *loss*. So building carbon in your soil becomes the most important thing if you want to grow good grapes: if we can assume that healthy soil makes more elements available to the vine, then healthy soil also makes more distinctive wine.'

David had introduced many organic practices at Cape Mentelle before leaving in 2003 to concentrate on this new venture. But he's taken the grandpa farming even further here. As well as composting, minimising (or eliminating) chemical sprays and growing a permanent grass sward undervine to keep soil temperatures down, he also lets sheep run through the vines in winter to graze ('and crap; they're an essential link in the nitrogen cycle'), and he has a precious stand of French oak trees that he hopes one day will produce a crop of truffles.

Oh, and then there's the pigs. A dozen big black sows, and their little black piglets, snuffling noisily around the property. He calls them the rotary hoes of the farm and makes some of them into sensational snags: his Jarrahdene sausages have developed a cult local following.

As well as the Margaret River staple grapes – semillon, sauvignon, chardonnay, cabernet – David has also planted an array of Mediterranean varieties: roussanne, marsanne, grenache, mataro, tempranillo, zinfandel.

'I could see climate change on the horizon back at Cape Mentelle,' he says. 'We started looking further south in Margaret River for possible vineyard sites in the 1990s. That's why we've come down here and planted these crazy grapes. Right now, we're usually a week, ten days later ripening here than they are up around Margaret River township, but in the future our ripening patterns could resemble those vineyards further north.'

Eventually we get to the new winery and I'm slightly surprised to see it has a grand sense of scale to it: the large fermentation cellar and the barrel hall sit either side of a spacious, European-style courtyard. Despite its modern appearance, though, because the young winemakers here are predisposed to natural techniques (Freya Hohnen, David's daughter, is a Buddhist with a strong interest in permaculture; Ryan Walsh's parents have

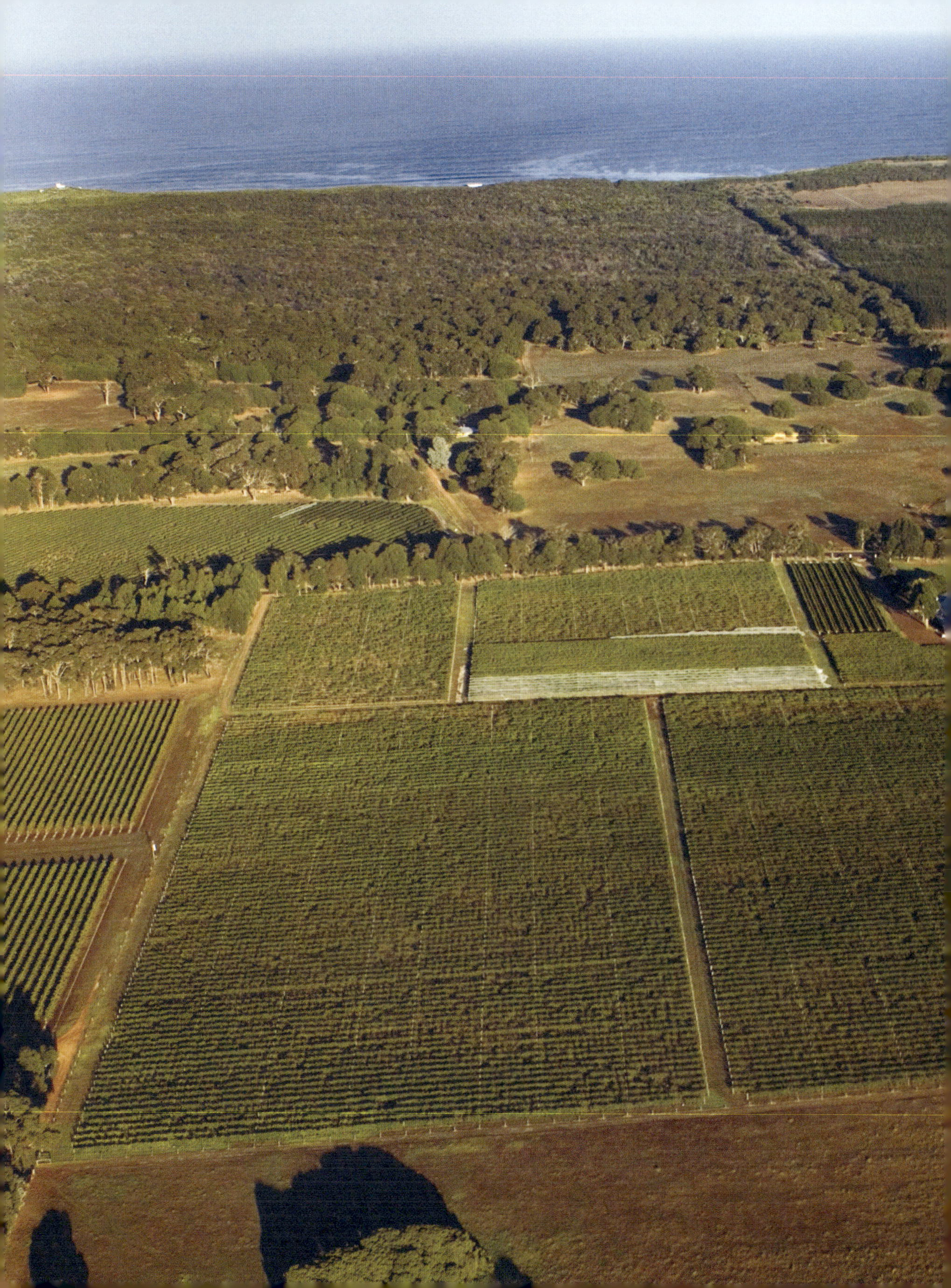

Cullen Winery, Margaret River

an 8-hectare biodynamic vineyard) the winemaking follows a similar grandpa philosophy to the farming. Ferments are wild, additions are kept to a minimum – acid only when necessary, tannins never ('adding is the easy way,' says Walsh) – and maturation is in mostly older oak. The result is some of Margaret River's most characterful, flavoursome and well-named wines.

The 3 Amigos white, a blend of marsanne, chardonnay and roussanne, is fabulously honeyed, textural and spicy; the 3 Amigos red, a shiraz, grenache and mataro blend, is slinky, earthy, dense; and McHenry Hohnen's most intriguing red, called Tiger Country, is a flexible blend of all sorts of grapes.

Ryan Walsh clambers up some barrels and treats me to a tasting of the components that will end up in the next Tiger Country. A splash of purple cabernet in my outstretched glass is concentrated, grippy and fine; a slurp of petit verdot is plump and fleshy; he squirts some tempranillo next, to stain my teeth with its black cherry sweetness; and finally, a slug of deeply wild, spicy, tannic graciano.

'It's the tiger in the country,' says Walsh, grinning darkly.

Marri Wood Park

Julian Wright has seen the light. In the early 1990s he was working as an investment advisor in Perth, and, like many other cashed-up city-dwellers, he bought a block of land to plant grapes in Margaret River.

'Initially I managed the vineyard from a distance,' says Julian. 'But I had an awakening when I was down here one day and saw the contractor put a chemical hazard helmet on and lock himself into the cab of the tractor before turning the spray unit on and heading out into the vines. I thought, Christ, that stuff must be powerful. So I resolved to stop using harmful chemicals.'

He also started thinking harder about the damage that growing grapes could do to the wider environment: 'I realised that many vineyards in Margaret River ran the risk of destroying the soil as the wheat farmers had done in other parts of WA. A vineyard, if it's heavily watered and fertilised, is going to go the same way, it'll just take longer. And the root cause in both cases is chasing yield.'

After attending a biodynamic workshop at Cullen in 2004, he decided to try the techniques: 'I thought it was all a bit hocus pocus at first, but it wasn't going to cost me anything to give it a go.' A dramatic effect on vine health and soil structure was soon apparent: the country at Yallingup, in the north of the Margaret River region, is more sandy, less gravelly than further south, and yet after a couple of years of spraying the 500 horn manure, Wright noticed more earthworms, a darker colour and better organic content in the top soil.

He has now fully embraced the practices, making and spraying weed teas, skim milk (to combat mildew), casuarina and horsetail and fish emulsion. He has also embraced the philosophy. 'I'm going to get some guinea fowl and geese and kill our own meat and plant a vegie patch and really turn this into a self-contained farm,' he says, full of optimism. Marri Wood Park was certified Demeter biodynamic (in conversion) in 2008.

As a result of the shift to BD, Julian began to ask himself what kind of wine he really wanted to produce on his vineyard. The answer was – of all things – chenin blanc. 'I had a dream of a bone-dry, barrel-fermented, ageworthy chenin that could make me famous, even if it takes ten or fifteen years.'

So he approached Bob Cartwright, the legendary ex-Leeuwin Estate winemaker to give him a hand and the result is terrific, a wine that shows signs of one day making Wright's dream come true. Fantastically lean and taut, full of the flavour of green apple skin laced with minerals, it's one of the region's best new whites.

Pemberton and Manjimup

Bloody hell, what's *that*? I'm driving through the tall marri gum forests just outside the town of Manjimup, heading down to Pemberton, when I whizz past a dam so full it's overflowing. It's been such a long time since I've seen a dam even remotely close to capacity that I don't recognise it at first. All that water, lapping over the brim. It's an almost obscenely luxurious sight to this eastern stater.

It's also a vivid reminder that, traditionally, this part of the world is one of the dampest in Western Australia; even with the long-term threat of reduced rainfall thanks to the changing climate, it will still be decidedly moister than regions further south. Early settlers learned that wherever the giant marri and karri trees grew it was probably wet enough, at least 35 inches of rain a year, to support European crops, from apples to cherries. Early vineyard pioneers in the 1980s also found that the gravelly hilltops, 200 metres up in the cleared bits of forest, were also particularly well suited to viticulture. The only thing that today's vignerons can't agree on is which grape varieties grow best in those vineyards.

Actually, that's not quite true. The winemakers in this part of the world have a rather ignoble tradition of disagreeing with each other. It took a long time for them to decide on whether Pemby and Manji should be considered two distinct regions, or whether it made more sense to lump them together as one GI. Eventually they went for the former option, but I think the latter would have made more sense: although the country to the north around Manjimup is a little warmer and drier than the country around Pemberton, there is far more unity in the topography, climate and spirit of place than you find in other large, single regions such as the Great Southern. The reason *why* they chose the two separate regions option all boils down to an old rivalry between the Manji and Pemby footy teams apparently, or so I've been told.

Anyway, back to the which-grape-goes-best-where debate. The Pannell family at Picardy are still backing pinot noir and chardonnay as the region's (or at least their own vineyard's) leading varieties, and while the chardonnay is superbly tangy and savoury, thanks in part to Burgundian clones in the vineyard and Burgundian barrels in the cellar, the pinot for me seldom lives up to expectations. Far more successful, I think, is the Picardy shiraz, a gloriously spicy, undergrowthy expression of grape and place which neither Bill (founding father) nor Dan (winemaker son) Pannell rate as their top wine.

For most people, sauvignon blanc has emerged as the region's top white grape, both commercially and critically: the best wines have a nettle-like cut and lemon-pith texture that sets them apart. Other aromatic white grapes seem to like it here, too. And merlot performs particularly well. But I have also tasted glimpses of greatness in sangiovese I've drunk from Manjimup and Pemberton, and believe that, once better clones become available in Western Australia, this variety could excel.

Herriot Wines

John and Yvonne Herriot's certified biodynamic vineyard and farm is one of the most exciting little domaines in Manjimup. As well as 10 hectares of vines – a real fruit salad block, with everything from zinfandel to cabernet to malbec and sauvignon blanc – the Herriots have sheep, Belted Galloway cattle and the beginnings of a small orchard of heritage cider apples, inspired in part by the quality of the Tangletoe cider made at nearby organic vineyard, Mountford.

The winery has been carefully designed to minimise energy use: rather than install electric temperature control, for example, John has run pipes from the outside walls of the winery through water tanks to the inside, to cool the air as it enters the cellar.

The vines are planted at the top of the hill in light, orange-pink karri loam over clay, and are not irrigated. The grapes that have performed best over the last few years are sauvignon blanc, riesling and shiraz. 'But if I had my time again,' says John, 'I would just plant riesling and shiraz because they're definitely the ones which look most comfortable here.'

In keeping with the biodynamic philosophy of allowing the farm's unique sense of identity to emerge, John chooses to add as little to the wines as possible, preferring to let them find their own path stylistically. Ferments are spontaneous, no acid, enzymes or tannins are added, and the wines have just a small amount of sulphur dioxide added at bottling. John is also moving away from new, small barrels to older, larger vessels; he's even importing large German oval-shaped wine casks that hold thousands rather than hundreds of litres of wine to mature his rieslings in.

This process of stripping away has led to some distinctive but decidedly non-mainstream wines: the Herriot sauvignon blanc is particularly ripe and grape-pulpy in style, balanced by a lick of crystalline acidity on the finish; the Natascha's off-dry riesling is reminiscent of a later-harvest Alsace riesling, with concentrated flavours of spiced apple; and the Reserve shiraz has plenty of gamey black pepper and macerated plums, with a rich and supple, medium-weight chewiness in the mouth and an earthy, gamey finish.

'What I like most about farming biodynamically,' says John, 'is that it's all about finding out what works for you on your bit of land. It's our farm. It's nobody else's. We've got to find our own way.'

Lillian's Vineyard

I have a very big soft spot for John Brocksopp and the superb wines he makes at his tiny vineyard deep in the forests of southern Pemberton. The former Leeuwin Estate viticulturist has been working in the wine industry for over four decades. He paints watercolours. He writes *letters* – longhand, with a pen, on paper – because he doesn't like email. Which makes him sound like a quaint old Luddite. But there's nothing the slightest bit fusty or conservative about him, his vineyard or his wines.

John and his wife Dinah bought their sleepy hollow in 1983. Originally they thought it would be 'a hobby farm for an old retired grape grower'. They had every intention of planting some cherries. 'But vines are the only thing I know,' says John, so in 1993, 3 hectares went in. Unlike the small, rather Burgundian, close-planted then-10-year-old chardonnay and pinot noir vineyard next door at Lefroy Brook (John now makes the wine from those grapes too), he planted marsanne, roussanne, viognier, shiraz and mourvedre (which, showing his age, he calls mataro), all varieties associated with the Rhone Valley.

This was partly a climatic decision: this sheltered part of Pemberton is very continental, with warmer days but cooler nights than Margaret River, John's old stomping ground. But mostly it was a romantic decision he'd been nurturing for decades. 'I worked at Seppelt's Barooga vineyard in the late 1960s,' he says. 'They had the whole 57 variety thing going on in those days. It was a viticulturist's dream. And I just fell in love with these grapes, particularly marsanne.'

John is fastidious in the vineyard. He uses a modified lyre trellis for good fruit exposure and to allow airflow. He measures everything meticulously – he aims, for example, for his marsanne bunches to be no more than 230 grams each – and achieves great intensity of flavour at moderate alcohols.

The Lillian's viognier is a great example of this: even though the grapes can be picked at remarkably low sugar levels – 10 or 11 baumé – the wine is very concentrated but elegant, with a lovely interplay of sweet/savoury elements in its taste of honey on chalk. The marsanne, blended with a little roussanne, is beautiful, with haunting stone fruit aromas and texture, some flowery herbs and great longevity. And the shiraz mataro has far more complex, garrigue-like meaty scents than you'd expect to find in what is, ostensibly, a cool-climate region.

'When I worked for Sepps,' remembers John, 'they made a very good Great Western red called hermitage esparte; old names for shiraz and mataro, of course. They were lovely, complete models, those wines.'

Which is an apt description for his own wines. Lovely, complete models.

Smithbrook

Some of the most memorable food and drink combinations I've ever indulged in have been both simple and humble. A cold can of VB and some leftover barbecue lamb on a hot Sydney summer's night after stepping off the plane from midwinter London. A hot dog in supermarket white sliced in the vineyard shack at Bannockburn, with some old, undergrowthy pinot noir grown just outside the window. And a glass of Smithbrook Yilgairn Blanc, the vineyard's barrel-fermented tangy, chalky sauvignon blanc semillon, with a sweet, succulent marron caught that morning in the dam.

The Lion Nathan–owned Smithbrook vineyard provides some of the most convincing evidence that the Bordeaux family of grapes – that tangy sauvignon/semillon and juicy, fine-grained merlot in particular – are among the best-suited to Pemberton/Manjimup. The vineyard is right on the border between the two regions – in fact, on a map, the boundary line appears to kink for no other reason than to scoop Smithbrook into Pemberton, the more widely known of the two…funny that.

The vines are draped across a series of round hilltops and shallow gullies, with fertile Karri loam on the lower slopes, rising to gravelly Marri loams and even some finer gravel Blackbutt soils on the top, which tends to be where the finer quality grapes such as those used in the Yilgairn label wines are grown.

Following the 2008 departure of winemaker Mike Symons (who skipped across the continent to take the reins at Lion Nathan's Stonier winery on the Mornington Peninsula), assistant winemaker and viticulturist Ashley Lewkowski was promoted to the top spot. A trained environmental scientist, Ashley has spent the last couple of years converting Smithbrook's 60 hectares of vineyards to organic farming methods, including running a flock of chickens, 1200 guinea fowl and sheep through the vines as natural weed- and pest-control. Smithbrook hopes to be fully certified organic by 2010.

In June 2009, Lion Nathan sold the vineyard to the Fogarty wine group, which also owns Millbrook winery in the Perth Hills. Lion have retained the Smithbrook brand, and Ashley has continued to make and promote the wine, even though, technically, he's now a Fogarty employee. Weird. I'll never quite understand how people who run big businesses think.

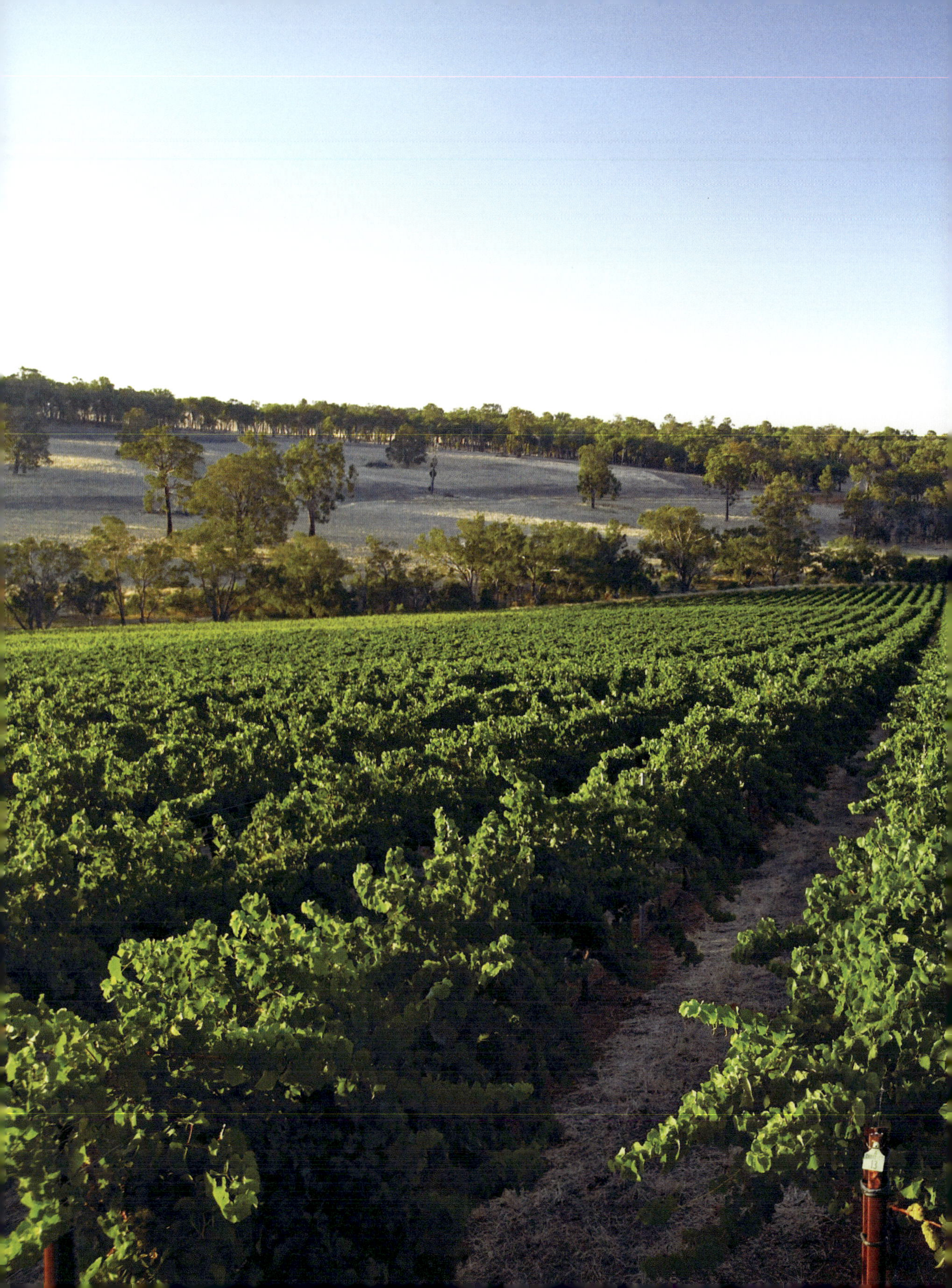

Yard Wine Company, Great Southern

Great Southern

The grape growers and winemakers of Western Australia's vast, sprawling Great Southern region have been exploring the fascinating deliciousness of sub-regional diversity for longer than most other Australian Geographical Indications.

Thanks to the early viticultural identification work of people such as Dr John Gladstones and the sterling, persuasive efforts of Plantagenet Wines' founder, Tony Smith, while other Australian regions were busy bickering about their boundaries in the mid-'90s, the Great Southern winemakers quietly agreed to draw up the broad, warmer landscape of Frankland River, the cooler rocky undulations and steeper hills of Mount Barker and the Porongurups, and the green coastal beauty of Denmark and Albany as sub-regional GIs.

A similar mix of soils exists across the sub-regions, mostly sandy, gravelly karri and marri loams, derived from weathered granite and gneiss, so one of the most important factors in how the vines grow and how the GIs are defined is the proximity to the sea.

'The critical thing during the growing season,' says Gavin Berry from West Cape Howe, 'is how early the sea breeze gets to your vineyard. I'll be standing in Frankland on a warm summer afternoon and there'll be not a whisper of wind. But I'll phone the winery at Denmark and the breeze will be rolling in off the ocean. There can be a ripening difference of at least a couple of weeks between the two sub-regions.'

This early identification of sub-regional identity and viticultural strengths has given the Great Southern an advantage, as winemakers from Western Australia's warmer regions clamour to plant vineyards and/or source grapes from down here. Frankland in particular has been carpet-bombed with vineyards: there are huge tracts of sauvignon blanc and shiraz now, much of it planted by managed investment schemes during the heady days of the late-'90s and early-2000s.

In contrast to the hopeful large-scale plantings, the clever winemakers are going the other way, focusing on smaller and smaller patches of country to make better, more distinctive wines.

Frankland Estate

More than 2500 hectares of vines spread out across the Frankland sub-region, but you can count the number of wineries here on one hand. It's a stark illustration of how this area has developed in the last decade or so: most of the investment has come from outside, with many large wine companies such as Houghton and large managed investment schemes seeing Frankland as the great white and red hope of Western Australian wine, thanks to its cool but not *too* cool climate.

It's easy to understand why so many people have been inspired to plant in this part of the Great Southern: the early wines, particularly the rieslings, from pioneers such as Alkoomi were (and continue to be) stunning, and recently established wineries such as Ferngrove have reinforced the area's suitability to producing deeply coloured, intensely flavoured but medium-bodied reds from shiraz, cabernet and, particularly, malbec. But there is a question mark over the long-term viability of the region because of the water situation: Frankland's groundwater is too salty to irrigate with, and many large-scale commercial vineyards rely on a complex system of rain-harvesting called roaded catchment, where parallel sloping ridges and troughs are carved into the land around each dam to increase run-off. This system has worked quite well until now, but the drop in rainfall predicted as a result of future climate change will put pressure on the vineyards here, particularly on those chasing the yields required to keep investors happy. As a result, the smarter growers such as Frankland Estate are looking for more sustainable, water-wise ways to grow their grapes.

Before I rocked up at the winery I had no idea that Frankland Estate was converting to organic viticulture. But when Hunter and Elizabeth Smith told me they were adopting greener methods on the vineyard their parents, Barrie Smith and Judi Cullam, planted 20 years ago, it seemed like the most natural progression.

Barrie and Judi have always run the vineyard with a low-input philosophy, and have been keen innovators in the winery. The rieslings (Frankland Estate's best wines, in my opinion) have improved markedly with each vintage because more attention has been paid to the unique terroir of the vineyards, and less intrusive techniques such as wild-yeast fermentation in big old *foudres* have been introduced, allowing the purity of the grape to shine. So now that the kids are grown up and are more involved in the day-to-day running of the place, it made sense to go that extra step and aim for organic certification.

'It's all about putting the biomass back into the soil,' says Hunter. 'Mulching the canes, composting the marc, growing green manure crops, allowing guinea fowl under the vines. That's what's going to ensure the continued health of the vineyard. And that's what's going to give you the truth in the bottle at the end of the day.'

Truth in the bottle. It's another thoughtful definition of terroir. And it's something I think you can taste more of now in the red wines of Frankland Estate. In previous years the reds here have sometimes seemed a little hard, earthy, unforgiving, lacking the fruit intensity that burns brightly in the best reds of the region. But recent vintages are glowing: the cabernet has sweet violets, is fine and tightly structured, and the shiraz has more typical Frankland plum and velvet tannin.

The whites have been excellent here for a long time, particularly the sensational trio of single-site rieslings. Each displays the influence of the differing soil types the vines are anchored in: the Isolation Ridge (ironstone-rich loam over clay) is intensely flavoured but restrained, and needs many years in bottle to show its best; the Cooladerah (a vineyard on a gravelly ironstone knoll) is a little floral, but even more taut; and the Poison Hill (white clay) is the most generous of all, with expansive lime and lavender flavours.

Hunter and Elizabeth also show me barrel samples of the various varietal components of Olmo's Reward, their top red, named after the Californian viticultural professor who in the 1950s identified this part of the world as being suitable for grapevines. The malbec is ablaze with more violets, spice, fennel and roast lamb sweetness; the cabernet franc is pure blackcurrants; the merlot has flowers and herbs and liquefied soil; the petit verdot has sweet red berries and candied tobacco leaves. There is plenty of truth in these barrels.

Larry Cherubino

Former Houghton winemaker Larry Cherubino is exploring the finer detail of sub-regional and single-vineyard differences with wines he releases under his eponymous label, sourced from across Western Australia, mostly from Great Southern.

He makes a number of single-site rieslings in The Yard range: Acacia, from a vineyard on top of the hill above Alkoomi in Frankland, is drier, leaner, with lime juice crawling up the sides of your tongue; Kalgan, from a much cooler vineyard south east of the Porongurups is rounder, grapier, lighter, less expressive; and Whispering Hill, from in-between, at Mount Barker, is the most forceful, with plenty of green apple bite (this last vineyard, one of the region's more distinguished sites, was planted by Capel Vale, who Larry consults to, and whose wines have improved dramatically over the last few years). The 'reserve' riesling, released under the Cherubino label, from another vineyard at Mount Barker, is even more intense, with shimmering acidity and great layers of stony texture.

'Texture's one of the things I've learned to strive for,' says Larry. 'With these rieslings, for example, I'm not adding any yeast or sulphur early on in the piece as we always used to at Houghton, and I reckon I'm getting better mouthfeel as well as better aromatics, although the perfume takes longer to appear in the wine after bottling.'

Larry is making some of the best wines in the west right now across all price points. His everyday Ad Hoc label, The Yard single-vineyard offerings and the self-titled reserve label all show great understanding of regional and sub-regional characters. Even the cheap Ad Hoc Straw Man white deftly blends the grassy crispness of sauvignon blanc from Karridale in the cool south of Margaret River with ripe, lemon-dripping semillon from the warmer Wilyabrup area in the region's north.

By doing less to them, Larry is also teasing sensational regional character from his red wines: slinky, spicy Frankland shiraz, taut and polished old-vine Margaret River cabernet. Rather than too much plunging or pumping over during ferment, the cabernet is macerated for longer at higher pH than many Australian winemakers would be comfortable with, to extract richer, riper tannins. The shiraz is not acid-adjusted, and spends ten months in barrel without racking. 'I reckon I've killed more good barrels of red over the years by stuffing them full of acid than anything else,' says Larry.

And there are some great projects lurking in the wings: he is playing with sangiovese and tempranillo from Mount Barker, and bringing new clones of some top Mediterranean grapes into Western Australia, including mencia (from the trendy Spanish region of Bierzo), fiano (from southern Italy) and tempranillo (from Ribera del Duero).

I don't know about you, but the prospect of tasting a Cherubino-made mencia from the gravelly soils of Frankland gives me goosebumps.

Marchand and Burch, Mount Barker and the Porongurups

A spirit of change and renewal is abroad in Mount Barker and the Porongurups. There's new life at the 40-year-old Plantagenet where John Durham, ex-Cape Mentelle winemaker, is teasing limey intensity from the old riesling vines and a succulent juiciness from the old cabernet. Chatsfield, once one of the leading vineyards in the Porongurups and a source of outstanding gewurztraminer, has been bought by talented Geographe-based winemaker Gordon Parker, who is thrilled to be working with some of the oldest aromatic white vines in the state. And Gibraltar Rock, formerly Karrivale, first planted in 1979, is emerging as one of the leading new-old wineries in conversion to biodynamics.

Biodynamics is not new here. John and Jan Pickles' tiny, Jeeleunup Gully vineyard near Mount Barker was one of the first in Australia to be certified biodynamic in 1985. 'In the 1980s, if you were into it, Mount Barker was *the* place in WA for biodynamics,' says local viticulturist, Doug York. 'An old farmer here was making the 500, and people from all over the state were coming down to learn how to do it.'

York, a passionate advocate of biodynamics, uses the techniques on his own 3-hectare vineyard, Larkmead Estate, north of the Mount Barker township. He also runs Clydesdale horses, and uses them to cultivate the vineyards he works for.

'I'm getting more and more people phoning up and asking about the practices, asking if they can hire the horses,' says York. 'Word is getting out about the quality of the fruit. People are seeing that wineries like Howard Park are willing to pay more for the Gibraltar Rock grapes because they're so good. And that inspires them to give biodynamics a go.'

For the last couple of years, Burgundy-based biodynamic winemaker Pascal Marchand has been flying out to Western Australia regularly to consult to Jeff and Amy Burch's Howard Park winery. Brought together by a shared obsession with pinot noir, Marchand made friends with the Burches in Burgundy 12 years ago. In 2007, the two men decided to set up a joint venture, so Marchand selected some chardonnay and pinot noir from Mount Barker and the Porongurups, and some shiraz from Frankland, sourced from the most gravelly blocks on each vineyard, to release under the new label. The wines, made according to biodynamic principles – picked according to the lunar calendar, and with no additions of yeast or acid – are fabulously intense, savoury and focused.

Initially, Marchand and Burch sourced grapes from existing vineyards for their eponymous wines, but eventually the plan is to concentrate on a special pinot noir vineyard planted in 2007 expressly for the joint venture. Established on the highest, stoniest block of Howard Park's Mount Barker vineyard, it's a 1-hectare plot of densely spaced (1.5 metres by 0.8 metre) vines, farmed biodynamically from the beginning.

It's one of the most exciting back-to-the-future vineyard developments in the state.

Oranje Tractor, Albany

Albany, Western Australia's most far-flung wine region, is building a name for itself as a sophisticated gastronomic hub. The population of this historic port is booming and a thriving local food scene has emerged, with many small organic producers taking advantage of the local restaurant and farmers' market scene. Renowned chef Russell Blaikie from the excellent Must Wine Bar in Perth says that Margaret River might have the name but Albany and Great Southern has the produce. He was talking about food, but he could have been talking about drink.

Pam Lincoln and Murray Gomm's beautiful little organic vineyard just outside Albany is a great site for growing classic, mouthwatering riesling. The 2003 won trophies for best aged riesling at both the Qantas Wine Show of Western Australia and the National Wine Show in Canberra. It wasn't a one-off, either: I've tasted a number of vintages of the Oranje Tractor riesling now from young to old, including a Germanic-style, medium-sweet expression called, cheekily, Reverse, and all share a touch of alluring lavender-like perfume, even the bottle-aged wines, among the hints of toast and spice. This fragrant, dried-flower character is something I typically find in rieslings from the Great Southern.

Pam and Murray's dry-grown 8-hectare vineyard was planted in 1999, and the wines are made by Rob Diletti at Castle Rock, one of the leading wineries in the Porongurups. The best grapes on the property – including the riesling – come from the patches of deep marri loams that have the most mashed-up laterite in them, which could account for some of that flavour intensity and cut.

Oranje Tractor has been organic since 2003, but Pam acknowledges it hasn't been easy. 'We get weevils, African black beetles, snails, grasshoppers, you name it. But the guinea fowl and chooks help us keep on top of that. The biggest perceived problem other people have with organics is weeds. But we deal with it by sowing ryegrass right under the vines in spring, which also helps keep in some of the winter moisture. Everybody thinks we're cool and wet down here, but it can get pretty dry in the summer.'

For Pam, converting to organics was a no-brainer: in 2001, she won a Churchill Fellowship to study organic grape and wine production in the USA and Europe, and she was also involved in setting up the local Albany farmers' market with its strong organic, sustainable, regional and seasonal focus. For Murray, who grew up on a dairy farm in Albany, it's about integrity.

'People can visit us here, walk across our farm, they can talk to us and they can see that we're doing things right, in a sustainable way.'

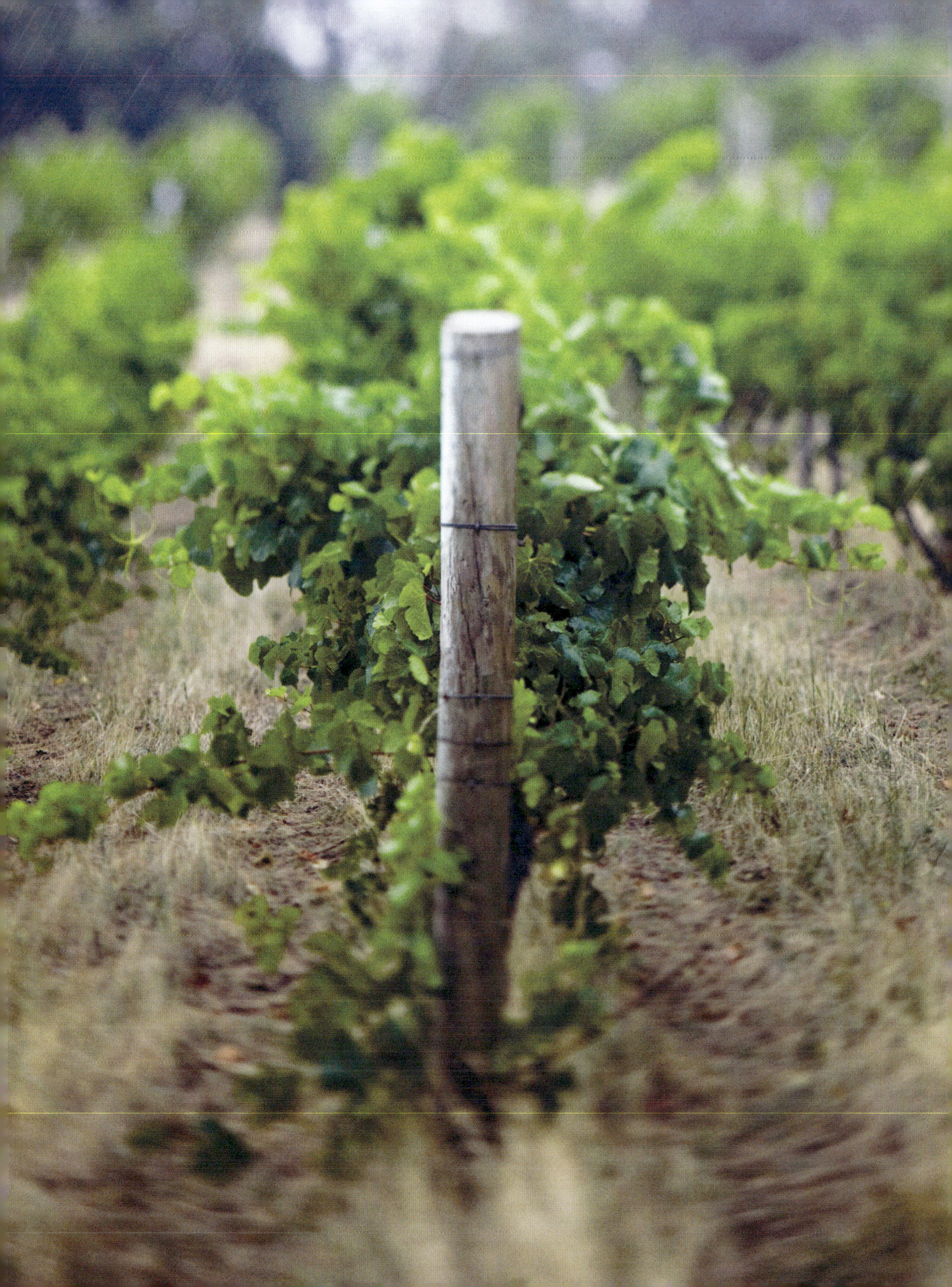

11 Tasmania

Tasmania

Tasmania seduces you. Its wild landscapes entrance. The island state feels like a sanctuary from dry, dusty mainland Australia with its often-despondent rural communities and its overcrowded cities. But scratch Tasmania's idyllic surface and you'll find evidence of a troubled soul.

Just look at the way Tasmania deals with its forests. Tasmania relies on its precious woodlands to project a clean, green image to tourists around the world. But as a visitor it's all too easy to see the effects of the island state's industrial logging policy: you will find yourself driving through truly awe-inspiring country, under soaring canopies of ancient eucalypts, and turn a bend in the road to discover a naked hillside wasteland of chain-sawed destruction. Forests slaughtered for woodchips.

A similar tension between image and reality can be found in Tasmania's wine industry. On paper, and in the minds of many, Tasmanian wine looks refreshingly diverse, boutique and focused on quality, especially compared to the mainland industry. There are 160 licensed wine producers and 250 vineyards covering just 1500 hectares across the island. All the grape varieties planted in Tassie are premium: pinot noir leads the way in reds; chardonnay, sauvignon blanc, riesling and, recently, pinot gris in whites.

But the island's wine industry is not quite the idyllic collection of artisanal vignerons it could be. The reality is that there are only 30 *wineries* on the island; most of the licensed producers, many of them 'lifestyle vignerons', have their wine made for them by a contract winemaker. Indeed, just two of these contract operators – Winemaking Tasmania and Frogmore Creek – have over 70 clients on their books.

Supporters of contract winemaking say that the prevalence of professional winemaking in Tasmania has brought the level of winemaking in the state up to an admirable level. It has, they say, reduced the amount of faulty wine. But, critics ask, at what cost?

According to one former contract maker who has 'seen the light' and is now focusing on just making his own wines, small-scale growers are often ambivalent about the outcomes of their wines and want to have very little input into what the experts do with their fruit.

'The "I'll leave it up to the professionals" attitude generally prevails,' he says. 'This makes for winemaking to a house style or recipe, which is not good for the expression of Tasmanian fruit in general. Sure, competent contract winemaking is, on the whole, better than incompetent amateurs making wine in small batches. But what we *don't* need is too much of a commercial focus, with everything tasting the same. And that could happen if we're not careful. The best of both worlds for our state, I think, would be to have at least another ten to 15 small, good winegrowers raising their fruit *and* making their own wine, taking some winemaking risks with small batches, letting their terroir show through. That's the only way, in my view, that we're going to produce more complex wines that will cellar and create a point of difference.'

Stefano Lubiana Wines

The Derwent Valley, to the north-west of Hobart town, is a little warmer and drier than you might expect, given its southerly latitude of 43 degrees. Most of the region's vineyards are planted on the southern banks of the river, on slopes angled to the sun, and the annual rainfall, much of which falls in winter, seldom exceeds 600 millimetres. Consequently, although the standard cool-climate Tassie grapes dominate the viticultural scene – riesling, chardonnay, pinot noir – and produce wines with great depth and intensity, some growers are also doing well with later-ripening varieties such as merlot. Some, like Steve and Monique Lubiana, have even boldly planted nebbiolo and shiraz; an insurance policy, perhaps, for an even drier, warmer future.

Steve and Monique have been travelling just outside the mainstream of Tasmanian wine ever since they established their 18-hectare vineyard on a steep bend in the river in 1990.

Over the years, Monique has been a highly vocal critic of the Australian wine industry's approach to marketing and taxation. She has long argued that the powers that be – the Winemakers' Federation, the Wine and Brandy Corp – are merely mouthpieces for the big companies, and have done too much to sell Brand Australia in the form of supermarket wines and not enough to sell the diverse, higher-price wines from the smaller producers. She has also been a long-time advocate of Australia moving from an *ad valorem* tax system, where wine is taxed on its value, to a volumetric system, where wine is taxed on the volume of alcohol it contains. The volumetric approach, of course, would make commercial, cask wine more expensive, and premium, boutique-produced wines, like Lubiana's, cheaper. Which is precisely why the industry (dominated by the big producers) is so against the change, and why many in the industry think Monique Lubiana is a troublemaker, and wish she'd go away. I think she's exactly the kind of outspoken, headstrong renegade the industry needs more of.

The industry could also do with a few more winemakers as talented as her husband, Steve. The estate range of Stefano Lubiana wines, grown on the vineyard's gravelly slope, is faultless, and includes superbly steely riesling, varietally correct pinot grigio, firm but supple pinot noir and excellent, complex sparkling. Steve also buys fruit from various spots around the state, and blends it with his own younger vine material to produce excellent, snappy, mostly unwooded wines for his second label, Primavera.

In the last couple of years, quality at Lubiana has shifted up a notch or two, with the release of some pace-setting wines, including a (very) late-disgorged, Prestige sparkling from 1995, which shows just how savoury and multi-faceted

Tasmanian bubbly can be with extended lees age; a super-rich and nutty reserve chardonnay called Collina; and a dark, burly, rather magisterial barrel-selection pinot noir called Sasso. All three are serious minded and seriously priced ($70 to over $100), but Lubiana also has fresh, attractive, affordable new wines such as a floral, gorgeously labelled nebbiolo rosato, and a sweetish riesling called Alfresco: a cross between a Mosel Kabinett and a moscato, he accurately describes this lime-juicy liquid as a 'pre-aperitif'.

Given the Lubianas' restless desire to improve what they do, it's no surprise to learn that they stopped using chemical fertilisers on their vineyard in 2001, and from winter 2008 they stopped using synthetic chemical herbicides and fungicides altogether and started applying the biodynamic soil spray, preparation 500. Steve says he hopes to gain organic/biodynamic certification in a couple of years. If and when he does, it will undoubtedly encourage other growers to consider going down a similar path.

Derwent Valley

Moorilla

Moorilla's owner, elusive millionaire David Walsh, is clearly not in the wine game because he thinks he might make a quick buck. Far from it: the man has invested – is investing – enormous sums to turn the 50-year-old estate into nothing less than the showpiece of the Tasmanian wine industry.

As well as revamping the winery and cellar door buildings and establishing Moorilla's destination restaurant, The Source, Walsh and his team have installed a craft brewery (the Moo Brew beers are among Australia's finest – and most dramatically packaged); hired a promising new young winemaker, Conor van der Reest; completely redesigned the wine range and labels (which now feature moody and rather provocative photographs of writhing naked dancers); and, most symbolically, cut total production back to a limit of 150 tonnes, or around 10,000 cases. Add Walsh's much-hyped, $55 million dollar, Nonda Katsalidis–designed Museum of Old and New Art, with its bold themes of sex and death, and Moorilla has become the complete, very high-profile Tasmanian cultural package.

Other changes at the estate are a little less obvious.

Vineyard manager Pete Mueller is in the process of converting Moorilla's 3-hectare Derwent Valley vineyard to biodynamics. The company's 15-hectare St Mathias vineyard up in the Tamar will continue to be run conventionally for now, but there are plans to establish a new vineyard, east of Hobart at Dunalley, and run that biodynamically from day one.

Pete believes that the BD preps, plus barrel compost he makes on-site, will help bring life and vitality back to a vineyard he says has been 'flogged pretty hard over the decades'.

'Some of these vineyards are 30 years old,' says Pete. 'We dug some deep holes recently and you could see where the chemical fertiliser residues had collected as salt crusts. Makes you realise what damage we've been doing all those years. And yet I've got a couple of rows of gewurztraminer on a shallow, horrible bit of dirt that I've never added anything to, and they always perform brilliantly. Maybe it pays to do less, sometimes.'

Conor van der Reest is producing some exceptional wines from the fruit Mueller grows – the aromatic whites have uncommon precision and concentration of perfume and scintillating acidity – but the wines will get even better once he starts playing with his new, energy-efficient winery. As well as gravity-assisted processing and thermal recycling to heat water (all of which is re-used on the property), the new winery has smaller tanks to limit the size of fermentations, producing a wider variety of blending options to increase quality and complexity in the wines.

The winery's long-term aim, says Conor, is to produce all its own electricity and become carbon negative. 'Eventually,' he says, 'Moorilla, through the vineyard, winery and its other business components, will put back more than it takes. This may take a long time to achieve, but we're not planning on going anywhere.'

Winstead Vineyard

A little further inland from Hobart, near the surprisingly named town of Bagdad, Neil Snare produces savoury, earthy pinot noir and super-aromatic, grapey, slate-dry riesling from his 18-year-old, 3-hectare vineyard. Since the beginning, Neil has adopted a minimal spray regime in the vineyard, and has applied plenty of mulch and chook poo in an effort to build up organic matter in soil that he describes as 'thin duplex over carboniferous shale that had been ploughed, supered, planted and harvested for decades before we bought the place, with nothing going back in.'

The manuring has worked: the soils definitely have better structure and life than before. 'But with the number of dry years we have experienced recently,' says Neil, 'I'm still trying to improve the condition of our soils to improve moisture retention and texture, and looking for ways to improve the microbial action within the soils to help this.'

Which is why Neil has joined the Biodynamics Tasmania association. 'I think BD can help us with our vineyard health and wellbeing,' he says.

Neil was inspired to investigate biodynamics by a neighbouring Bagdad vineyard owner, Graham Roberts, who, in 2008, had his first pinot noir made at Winstead. Graham is on the committee of BD Tasmania, and has been using the biodynamic preps (and, obviously, no synthetic chemicals) on his own 2-hectare vineyard since he planted it five years ago. 'We're on the dolerite, black cracking clays at our place,' he says. 'Already, thanks to the BD, a better soil structure is emerging and there are lots of worms. We're in a pretty dry part of the state, in a bit of a rain shadow, so we need all the help we can get.'

Graham is finding increasing interest in biodynamics among vignerons and farmers in Tasmania. 'Conventional growers receive an agricultural science training,' he says. 'They're taught reductionist thinking rather than being taught to see the big picture of what's really happening. So they take a soil sample in to be tested, it's put under a microscope, and the chemical company gives them a recipe of what to do, how much to add to "fix" things. The poor old farmer's getting done in the bum, I reckon. But it's changing: now you even see articles on soil carbon in the country rag. Finally, the message is getting out there: look *after* your soil, fellas.'

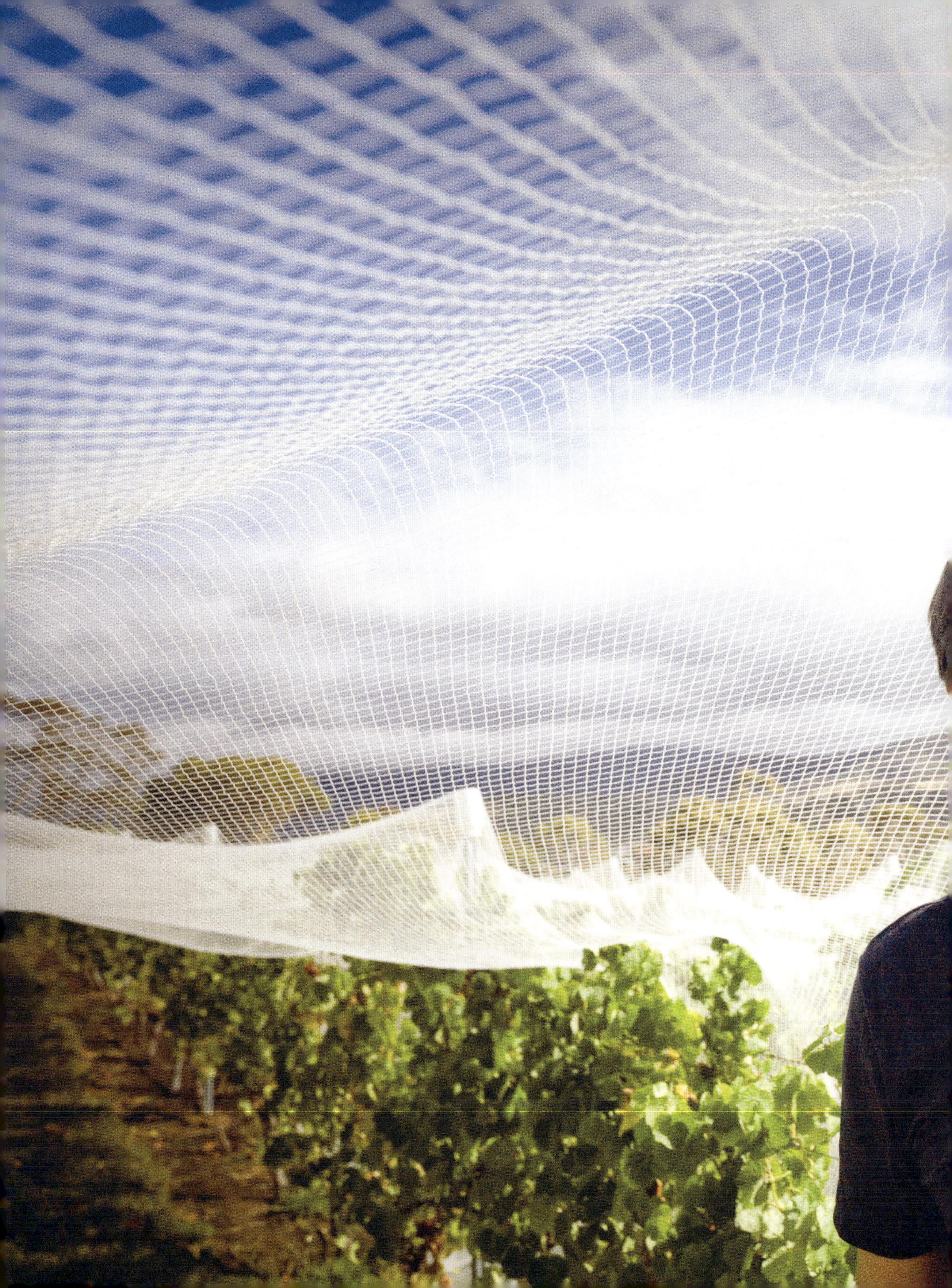

Vineyard Manager Peter Mueller,
Moorilla, Derwent Valley

The terroirs of Tasmania

A couple of years ago, Richard Doyle from the University of Tasmania and Duncan Farquhar, then at the Tasmanian Department of Primary Industries and Water, put together a detailed map of the island's geology and soils and how they relate to the state's wine regions. It is a valiant attempt to chart Tasmania's terroirs that many other Australian wine regions would do well to emulate.

Doyle and Farquhar identified seven Tasmanian winegrowing regions: the emerging North West, spread out between Devonport and the shadow of Cradle Mountain; the Tamar Valley, around Launceston; the North East, around Lebrina and Pipers River; the East Coast; Coal River Valley to the east of Hobart; Derwent Valley to the west of the city; and Huon Valley and d'Entrecasteaux Channel stretching out to the south.

The ocean surrounding the island influences all of Tasmania's vineyards; you seldom get the spikes of heat here during the summer that can afflict mainland regions. It is, perhaps surprisingly, warmer and sunnier in the south, around Hobart, than it is in the north, around Launceston: good cabernet, for example, can be grown in the Coal River and Derwent valleys, when the season is kind. It's drier than you might expect on the East Coast: while vineyards can thrive in the damp North East without irrigation, it is a harder proposition around Swansea or Bicheno, where annual rainfall can be as low as 300 millimetres. Wherever you are, though, Tasmania is unequivocally a cool climate.

The island state has been subjected to a number of major geological influences over the aeons. As Doyle and Farquhar point out, Tasmania lay at a 'hinge point' when the Australian continent tore away from Antarctica around 170 million years ago, forcing magma up as dolerite through the existing ancient sandstones and mudstones that had formed when Tasmania (with New Zealand and Australia) was part of the supercontinent of Gondwana. Subsequent volcanic activity contributed areas of basalt, while basins such as the Coal River Valley formed as the New Zealand subcontinent drifted east. Finally, layers of windblown sand and gravel were deposited during the last ice age, like a thin icing on this complex geological cake.

As a result, Tasmania's vineyard regions enjoy an enormous complexity of soil types. In some areas, one soil dominates: the deep red basalt-derived loams around Pipers River in the North East, for example. But some regions, even some single vineyards, can go from dark black clay loam to pale, bleached sand and all shades between. The majority of the best vineyards, however, tend to be found on brown and orange loamy soils and black cracking clays associated with the dolerite and basalt parent materials.

Coal River Valley
Frogmore Creek and Tony Scherer

For many years, Andrew Hood was one of Tasmania's leading contract winemakers, operating out of a winery at Cambridge, near Hobart. He made wines for many other vineyards, including his own wines under a number of labels, such as Wellington. Then the owners of Frogmore Creek, a vineyard next to the winery, and one of Andrew's clients, bought the contract-making business, retaining him as a partner and winemaker. Today, Andrew Hood has 'retired' (he continues to consult to the business), and while the winery still has many contract clients, it produces its own wines only under the labels Frogmore Creek (from estate-grown fruit) and 42 Degrees South (bought-in fruit).

While they tread a fairly safe path with their contract clients, winemakers Alain Rousseau (who first made his name in Tasmania at Moorilla Estate) and Nick Glaetzer (of the Barossa winemaking family) are prepared to be quite experimental with the Frogmore Creek wines. During my visit, I tasted pinot noir trial wines that had been fermented using a number of techniques: wild yeasts; carbonic maceration; 100 per cent stalks; co-fermentation with a little bit of chardonnay and pinot gris; grapes that had been cane-cut and partially dried (a kind of on-the-vine amarone approach); and even pinot fermented with a sprinkling of tannin derived from Barossa shiraz grape seeds. Not surprisingly, given this open-minded attitude, the Frogmore Creek wines can be exceptionally good: I particularly like the multi-layered and exuberantly flavoursome, partially barrel-fermented sauvignon blanc.

For a few years at the beginning of this century, Frogmore Creek was Tasmania's only certified organic vineyard. Then, in 2006, facing a losing battle against some particularly aggressive weeds, the company's founder and major shareholder, Californian businessman Jack Kidwiler, decided to drop the organic status and use herbicide.

Tony Scherer, also from California and a long-time organic grower, is a partner in Frogmore Creek, and lives on the property. Not surprisingly, Tony wasn't all that happy about the loss of organic certification. But, he says, the company's new vineyard manager, Jen Doyle, who worked on organic and biodynamic conversion trials at Cumulus Vineyard in Orange, New South Wales, is intent on reinstating Frogmore's organic status.

In the meantime, Tony has established a small, very densely planted (9600 vines per hectare) vineyard on a rocky dolerite hill above Frogmore Creek. Not surprisingly, given Tony's background and his close involvement with the Tasmanian Pinot Noir Forum (an annual tasting/seminar/workshop event for growers and makers of pinot), this new vineyard has initially been planted only to pinot noir, but may also include some gamay. And from the outset, it will be run biodynamically, something that is dear to Tony's heart. The fruit will be picked separately and fermented in a small, purpose-built cellar dug into the hill, where the biodynamic calendar will also be followed for picking, racking, bottling, etc.

It's early days, and the first wines are years away from being picked, let alone sold, but Tony is toying with Rockytop as a name for the new venture. File it away for future reference.

Meadowbank Estate

Gerald Ellis understands the importance of bundling wine, art, food and ecological responsibility, and does so with impressive style.

Gerald has been growing grapes for 30 years. He owns 10 hectares of vineyard at Meadowbank, near Frogmore Creek at Cambridge (his wines are made there by Alain Rousseau and the team), as well as 40 hectares at Glenora in the Derwent Valley. He sells fruit – notably to Constellation, where it ends up in the top sparkling, Arras – as well as bottling some himself for sale through the popular cellar door and restaurant at Meadowbank, which focuses on local produce as much as possible, and even lists food miles next to each dish on the menu.

Meadowbank is also home to one of the most remarkable examples of wine-related art in the world. In 2005, Tasmanian writer Graeme Phillips and Czech-turned-Tasmanian artist Tom Samek collaborated on a nonsense-verse account of the island's 185-year-old wine story, illustrated by intricate, quirky wood carvings installed all over an upstairs floor above the cellar door. Called, in typical Samek punning fashion, A Flawed History, it's a cheeky, vivacious, rich work that rewards close contemplation, and acts like a songline for anybody interested in understanding the heart and soul of wine in Tasmania.

Gerald is also involved with Tony Scherer from Frogmore Creek and microbiologist Dean Metcalf from Biocontrol Australia in commercialising a product called Aerated Compost Extract (ACE). This specially formulated compost tea, tested by Tasmanian PhD student Alice Palmer from 2005 to 2007, was found to suppress powdery mildew on the leaves of riesling vines as effectively as a synthetic fungicide. There is, obviously, great interest in ACE among those growers wishing to convert to organic viticulture.

Frogmore Creek, Coal River Valley

East Coast

Apsley Gorge Vineyard

Given the extremely high quality of the wines produced on the East Coast, it's perhaps surprising that more vineyards and wineries haven't been established here. True, it's relatively remote: a two and a half hour drive from either Hobart or Launceston is a long drive by Tasmanian standards; and true, it's relatively dry: annual rainfall can be as low as 300 millimetres. Nevertheless, the few growers and makers who *are* prepared to live in this beautiful isolation and take advantage of the sunshine, moderated by the proximity to the sea, and the diverse soils to make their own wines, are rewarded with some of the island's best grapes.

Brian Franklin is a disarming combination of straight-talking abalone diver and obsessive wine tragic: his legendary cellar door, an old abalone packing shed looking out across the ocean at Bicheno, is only open during the cray fishing season; plus he has worked vintage in Burgundy every year since 2000, and his winemaking techniques are inspired by the legendary Henri Jayer.

In 1989, Brian planted his 5 hectares of pinot noir and chardonnay in a heavy clay site with patches of riverflat loam and some stones a few kilometres inland from Bicheno. Not surprisingly, the winemaking at Apsley Gorge is decidedly modern Burgundian: wild-yeast ferment for both the chardonnay and pinot noir, a fully de-stemmed, whole-berry, long cold soak for the latter before ferment kicks in, minimal additions (no acidification unless absolutely necessary), a year or so in good, new oak, mostly Francois Freres, before bottling and another year resting before sale. He has also recently purchased a vibrating sorting table to help weed out any unwanted green or damaged fruit at harvest.

In many ways, the Apsley Gorge wines are blissfully ignorant of fads and fashions in winemaking. The chardonnay in particular is a big, yellow, creamy example of the grape, all nutty and honeyed, and rather over the top. Similarly, the pinot isn't anything like the fashionable sweet, bright fruit style that might win medals at wine shows, but is instead rather meaty, solid and chewy. And this is precisely why I love them: both wines have character in abundance, reflecting both the bold vision and determination of their maker, as well as the warm clay site they were grown in.

Spring Vale

Spring Vale vineyard is a delicious juxtaposition of old and new. The cellar door is in a renovated stable building constructed by convicts in 1842. You can feel the history hanging in the air, gently prickling your skin. The historical link is reinforced again on the labels: an ancient-looking early engraved map of Van Diemen's Land, as Tasmania used to be known. But the wines here are among the most thoughtful and 'modern' you'll find anywhere on the island.

For the last couple of years, Spring Vale have produced an unwooded chardonnay called Chardonnay Junior, and a pinot noir/pinot meunier blend called Pinot Junior. To emphasise the cuteness of the name, they're sold in half bottles for around ten bucks a pop. The wines themselves are seriously exquisite: the chardonnay has a seam of lemony chablis-esque minerality running through it, while the pinot is all succulent juiciness. But the way they've been named and sold manages what many other producers strive for and seldom achieve: it makes 'fine wine' fun. Those cute half bottles are, needless to say, flying out the door.

The point here is that while the 23-year-old, 6-hectare Spring Vale vineyard, on a gentle slope of well-drained heavy clay over ironstone north of Swansea, produces great grapes, it's the smartness of the family team – founders Rod and Lyn Lyne, son and daughter Tim and Kristen, and Kristen's winemaker husband, David Cush – that sets the wines apart.

The Spring Vale team also produces two of Tasmania's best examples of gewurztraminer and pinot gris, the former showing some oxidative handling in the form of spiced apple richness and a pleasingly phenolic finish, the latter with smoked pear-like complexity. The chardonnay, too, is a rich, textural expression of the grape. But the standout wine is Spring Vale's 'grown-up' pinot noir: regularly up there with Tasmania's best, it has uncommon plummy vinosity and warm, generous spicy aromatics.

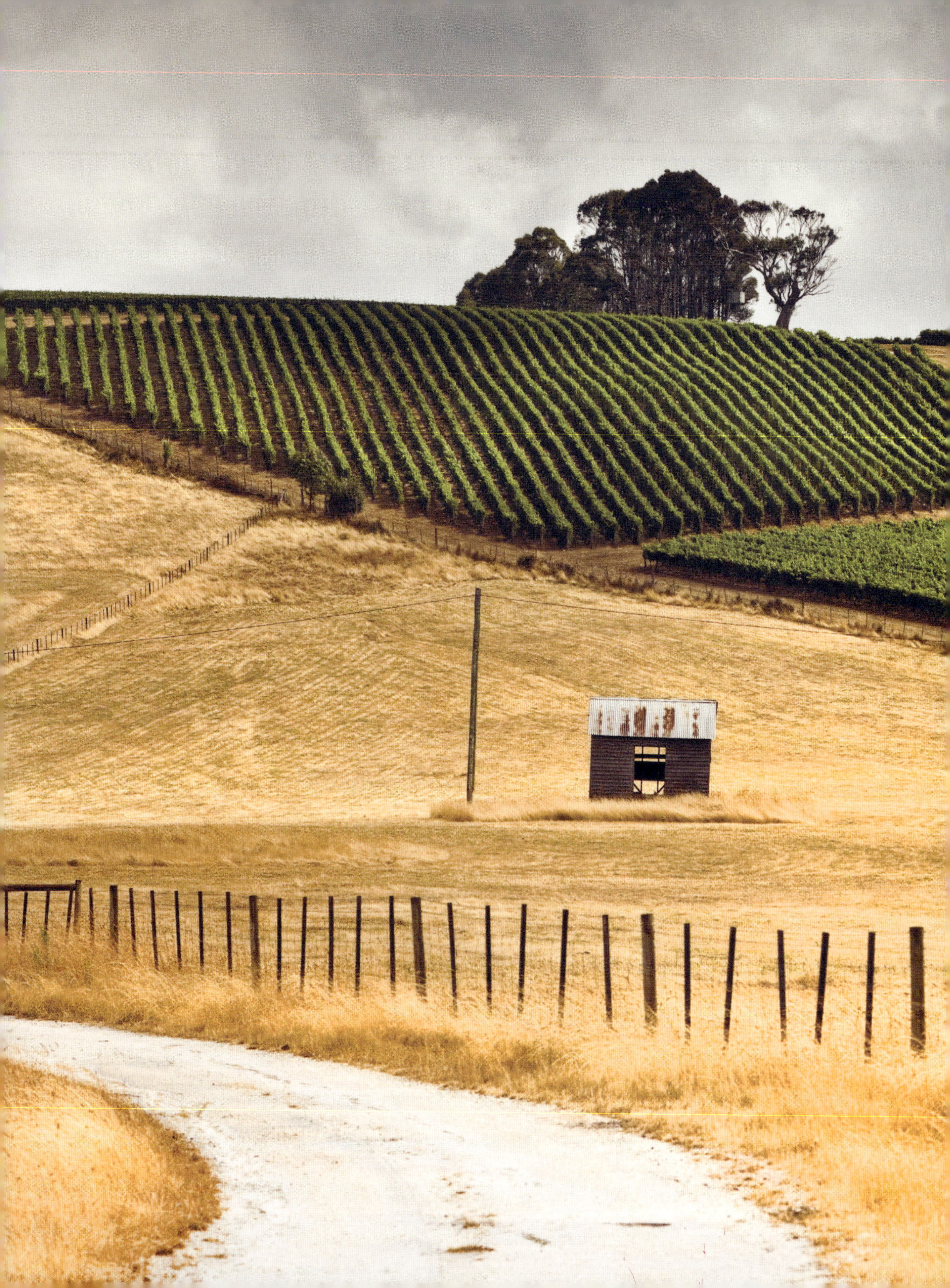

North East

North East

Delamere

In many ways Pipers River in Tasmania's North East is the heartland of the island's modern wine industry. It was here, at Lalla in 1956, that a Frenchman from Provence, Jean Miguet, revived the state's forgotten wine story by planting the first commercial vineyard in 70 years (the vineyard, now appropriately called Providence, still produces exquisite chardonnay and pinot noir). Graham Wiltshire at Heemskerk and Andrew Pirie at Pipers Brook Vineyard then took Tasmanian wine to the world in the 1970s and '80s. And this is the region where the three major mainland wineries with a stake in Tasmania – Yalumba, Taltarni and Constellation – are based. The climate here is cooler than the Tamar Valley to the west, and many of the best vineyards are planted on the distinctive, deep red basalt-derived soils.

Not surprisingly, the North East's reputation has attracted a number of young grape-treaders keen to rejuvenate the island's wine industry. Of this new mob, Shane Holloway is perhaps the most irrepressibly enthusiastic. He needed to be, too: when the 32-year-old Holloway bought the Delamere vineyard, along with its winery, cellar door, house, orchard, chooks and guinea fowl in late 2007, he was subjected to a baptism of fire.

'Mate, we had everything thrown at us during vintage 2008,' he tells me. 'Bushfires, hurricanes, outbreaks of powdery mildew, phones getting cut off for two weeks during harvest. Bloody Telstra. I've got grey pubes, I tell you. But the grapes – the quality is cracking. I couldn't be happier.'

The Delamere name will be familiar to long-time Tasmania watchers. The densely planted (7500 vines per hectare), dry-grown vineyard was established by Richard Richardson in 1982, and has produced some fabulous wines over the last quarter century. The combination of vine maturity, vine density and lack of irrigation can be tasted in the first wines Holloway released under the new, revamped Delamere label: a 1994 Blanc de Blanc sparkling chardonnay (disgorged by Holloway in 2008), was super-stylish, with cracked wheat and wholegrain toast aromas leading onto a mouthful of creamy lemon; and a 2007 pinot noir (again, fermented by Richardson, bottled by Holloway), was classic Pipers River pinot: pale in colour, but packed with sappy flavours of strawberry and undergrowth, it had both deep intensity of savoury flavour and an ethereal sprightliness on the tongue.

As Holloway adopts organic and biodynamic techniques in the vineyard, something he says he intends to do slowly and cautiously, and as he revels in the opportunity to play with his 'cracking' fruit in the winery, his enthusiasm and energy will produce even more delicious wines.

Brook Eden

Sydney-based cinematographer Peter McIntosh always wanted to have his own vineyard. So he did a part-time winemaking course, and initially looked at sites in Orange, west of Sydney. His accountant tried to talk him out of it, so he stopped speaking to his accountant. Then a taste of a Pipers Brook Summit chardonnay drew him to the North East, and in 2004 he bought the 20-year-old, dry-grown Brook Eden vineyard, two-and-a-bit hectares of dry-grown vines on deep red basalt soil. The vineyard contains the usual Tassie mix of chardonnay, pinot and riesling, and in my opinion the latter is the standout grape: really scintillating and fine.

In 2006, Peter stopped using herbicides on the vineyard. In 2007 he stopped using any synthetic chemicals on his riesling vines. And in 2008 he moved to a totally organic regime, and started applying the biodynamic preparations across the vineyard. He is also involved in a trial initiated by Alice Palmer (see Meadowbank), using compost tea instead of sulphur or copper on some of the chardonnay vines.

'In our location we practise viticulture on the edge,' says Peter. 'And I feel that organics and biodynamics can help us get a nudge from Mother Nature. By keeping yields right down and improving soil health, I hope to get stronger plants, and pinot noir grapes with thicker skins, which will help us, particularly in the cooler, wetter years.'

Peter always knew he wanted to run his vineyard organically. He worked at Rosnay Organic Farms in Cowra, New South Wales, planting vines and olives, while looking for his vineyard site. He was inspired to start using biodynamics by the amazing results Hunter Valley BD farmer John Priestley has achieved on his citrus orchard.

'There's a lot more labour involved,' he admits. 'But because you can't rely on chemicals, you have to become a better farmer. Another plus, too, is that once you get to the stage of a John Priestley, with nice balanced soil, biodynamics ends up costing you less than so-called conventional farming. Many dairy farmers in Tasmania's Midlands are heading that way – brewing compost tea, looking at biodynamics – basically because they can't afford fertiliser any more. The irony is that the chemical companies, by putting their prices up so much, are forcing farmers to go organic. It's a self-fulfilling prophecy.'

Pipers Brook Vineyard

The 200-year-old Belgian trading company, Kreglinger, purchased Andrew Pirie's Pipers Brook Vineyard and the Ninth Island brand at the turn of this century. Since then, Kreglinger (who also own the Norfolk Rise vineyard on the Limestone Coast in South Australia) have continued to develop both the reputation that Pirie had built and the winery's position as a leader in the Tasmanian wine scene. Wines under the Pipers Brook label, particularly the single-vineyard wines such as the Summit chardonnay and Lyre pinot noir, are increasingly refined, elegant, complex examples of the North East terroir they are predominantly sourced from; the Ninth Island range of varietals, mostly sourced from Kreglinger's warmer vineyards in the Tamar Valley, offer well-priced expressions of the grape and region; and the ultra-premium Kreglinger sparklings, while not perhaps as refined as the exceptional fizz Pirie used to make here under his eponymous label, are still very good, multi-layered and satisfying wines.

Recently, Kreglinger have quietly begun the process of moving all of their 200 hectares, across seven properties, to organic viticulture. By mainland, even by international, standards, the scale of this would be considered ambitious. In the context of an island wine industry with only 1500 hectares of vines, it is extremely significant.

'We stopped using herbicide on all our seven properties in 2004,' says long-time vineyard manager Bruce McCormack. 'Currently, a couple of those vineyards, covering 40 hectares, are at pre-certification stage. But we're not doing this so we can boast on the label about being certified organic. We're doing it because we honestly believe it's the future of grape growing. It will improve soil health, deliver us better fruit, and help us care more for our land.'

Bruce says that moving to organics in a traditionally cool and wet climate such as the North East required a leap of faith, and he admits it hasn't always been easy. 'We had a bad year in 2007 in one vineyard with powdery mildew,' he says. 'There are definitely problems with how we'll cope with disease. But that event also taught us a lesson: that you have to manage each property differently. It's not like following a chemical spray calendar.'

Bruce, like many other organically minded viticulturists, has learned to love his weeds. 'I don't see them as being completely detrimental to the vineyard,' he says. 'They contribute to soil structure with their root systems.' And the alternative is not worth considering: 'I fundamentally know that herbicide has a detrimental effect on soil health. Some of our vineyards have had herbicide poured on them for 30 years. Since we stopped doing that, soil tests have shown a return of microbial life, of yeasts and bacteria, and that activity increases each year that the soil has a chance to recover.'

A sparkling future

In the mid-1980s, French Champagne house Louis Roederer staked a claim for sparkling in Tassie when it established the Jansz vineyard in collaboration with Heemskerk (the Jansz vineyard and label are now owned by Yalumba), and Victorian winery Taltarni established the Clover Hill vineyard for top-quality bubbly. In the 1990s, Domaine Chandon and Hardys joined the rush to the island, sourcing grapes for their multi-region blends. Towards the end of that decade, other brilliant locally produced bubblies emerged, including Andrew Pirie's eponymous sparkling wine at Pipers Brook (now morphed into the Kreglinger label), and some excellent fizz from smaller producers such as Stefano Lubiana.

Fran Austin, the winemaker at the Constellation-owned Bay of Fires in the Pipers River region, sources fruit from around the country to produce some intensely flavoured table and sparkling wines. She is convinced that the key to the quality in Tasmanian fizz is the fact that the island state is a truly cool climate.

'You get a very different acid structure in the grapes down here,' says Fran. 'A lot of mainland cool-climate regions are cool because they're high up, not because they're down south. In high-altitude wines, the acidity can taste hard. But in cool-latitude wines, you get softer, mouthwatering juicy acidity. And incredible depth of flavour, which means you can work the wines more, let them spend more time on lees before releasing them, producing a more complex end result.'

Not far from Bay of Fires, at Yalumba's Jansz winery, winemaker Natalie Fryar agrees that the latitude and maritime influence are the key to the unique quality of Tassie fruit.

'Bass Strait really mitigates the climate here,' she says. 'We have a truly extended ripening period, meaning we can pick full-flavoured grapes for sparkling at just 11 baumé but with 12 to 14 grams per litre of natural acidity. And because the wines have such astounding flavour and structure, they can take the kind of techniques that are common in Champagne. So we've become a lot more confident with the fruit and are doing things like barrel-fermenting rosé, and lees-stirring and extended ageing before disgorging – without the wines losing their finesse.'

Every year since Nat started at Jansz at the turn of the century, the wines have improved, becoming deeper, more complex, more satisfying. But, as at Bay of Fires, the best is yet to come. 'In my time here I've seen single blocks in the vineyards begin to produce fruit with more defined personality. Some of the vineyards are over 20 years old now, and it really does make a difference when a vine's mature.'

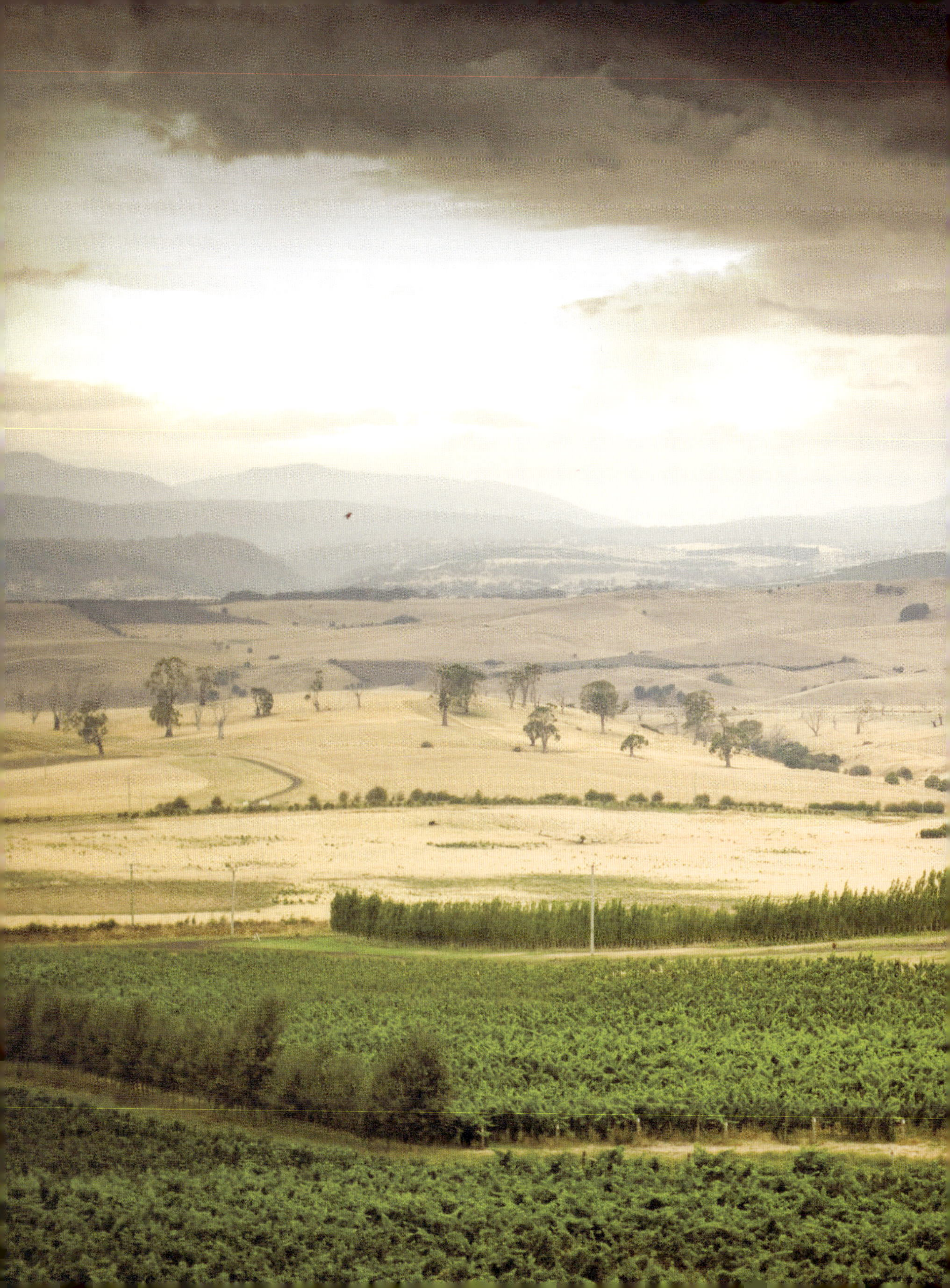

Josef Chromy Wines, Tamar Valley

Tamar Valley

Grey Sands

The wines of Grey Sands stand out from the Tasmanian crowd because they're not pristine, fruit-driven and precisely made but funky, interesting and full of character. The pinot gris is cheesy, chewy and deeply textural, a real mouthful of complexity: lots of skin contact, lees-stirring, barrel work going on in here. The Romanesque red is even more unusual: predominantly shiraz, with a dollop or two of the Portuguese grape touriga and other island rarities such as lagrein thrown into the blend, the wine has a volatile lift and a spicy tartness that would get it thrown out of a wine show but make it a thirst-quenching partner to food.

The vineyard was established in 1988 by Robert and Rita Richter on an elevated patch of grey, gravelly sand over clay a few kilometres west of the Tamar River. Rob clearly relishes going against the grain: 'Back in the 1980s, when I first thought about planting a vineyard, the battle lines were being drawn in the Tamar over whether pinot noir or chardonnay was going to be the grape that would make the region's reputation. I wasn't all that enamoured of chardonnay, but I'd seen some awesome pinot gris when I was in the UK – Zind Humbrecht's Rangen – so I decided to plant that. Which was a bit tricky at the end of the '80s, let me tell you: I ended up getting a couple of clones from the CSIRO at Merbein. They were the only ones who had any.'

Over the years, other weird varieties (weird in a regional context, that is) have followed. As well as the shiraz (taken as cuttings from Meadowbank vineyard down south), the Richters have planted petit verdot ('a cruel variety if you don't have a warm season'), malbec ('I really like what they're doing in New Zealand with merlot malbec blends'), cabernet franc, and that lagrein ('if they can ripen it at 800 metres above sea level in Italy, I don't see why it wouldn't do well in the Tamar').

In recent years, the level of fruit intensity apparent in the Grey Sands wines has deepened. 'As the vines have started to get up to the second decade mark,' says Rob, 'something starts to happen, they seem to come into balance. We don't irrigate, but even though the vines are in pretty silty sand, you don't see them turn a hair with the dry seasons we've had recently.'

It's taken him a while, but in Fran Austin at Bay of Fires, Rob has found a contract winemaker who is willing to take risks and make the wines he sees in his mind when he's working the vines. 'It's hard to find winemakers who are prepared to go out on a limb,' he says. 'I'm really keen on seeing lots of biological things happening in the wines, lots of malo and using indigenous yeasts for ferments, lots of lees ageing. I've been hunting for a winemaker who could relax and let nature take its course, and Fran is able to do just that.'

Josef Chromy Wines

Josef Chromy, OAM, is a force of nature. This, his third – or is it his fourth? – major wine business in Tasmania was established in 2003, when Chromy bought an established vineyard and cellar door at Relbia, south of Launceston, after selling his Tamar Ridge vineyard and winery to Gunns. He was 73 at the time.

In just a few years, with the energy of a man half his age, he's built this latest venture into the very model of a modern, mid-sized Tasmanian wine company: 61 hectares of vineyard, including a picturesque hillside draped in vine rows opposite the compact, bright and welcoming cellar door/restaurant; a new winery run by Jeremy Dineen, one of the state's most talented young winemakers; and a smart range of high-quality, sleekly packaged, well-priced wines. Fittingly, these wines pay homage to Chromy's background as a Czech refugee in the 1950s: the $20 second label (chardonnay and pinot that offer some of the best-value drinking on the island) is called Pepik, the Czech nickname for Josef, and the reserve wines are called Zdar, the name of Chromy's home town.

Jeremy Dineen worked with Andrew Hood (see Frogmore Creek) before starting with Josef Chromy wines, and brought with him a particular love of riesling. Dineen helped Hood develop the FGR (medium-sweet, Germanic style) riesling in the early 2000s, and isn't afraid to work some texture, even a lick of sweetness into the wines he makes now: the Josef Chromy rieslings exhibit a lovely, almost Alsace-like creaminess and richness, while retaining their fresh aromatic quality.

There's texture aplenty in the other wines, too: the Josef Chromy chardonnay displays the effects of full solids ferment and six-month lees contact in the form of great concentration and harmony; even the keenly priced Pepik chardonnay sees some barrel ferment and lees action. And the pinots, while bright, spicy and full of red fruit, finish with a subtle but serious tannic grip, something Dineen attributes to the black cracking clays and slightly warmer climate of the Relbia area.

Stoney Rise

Joe Holyman was working for a winery in the Limestone Coast, South Australia, in 2000 when he first developed his own Stoney Rise range of wines. Named after a surf break at Robe (hence the image of the dreadlocked surfer dude on the label), initially the wines were made from bought-in local fruit and were squarely aimed at a quirky, younger audience. Indeed, Holyman got into legal trouble from the French with his cheeky Cotes du Robe brand.

In 2004, Holyman and his wife Louise decided to get serious and move back to the island (his family already own vineyards in Tasmania), so they bought the 20-year-old Rotherhythe vineyard on the Tamar at Exeter and renamed it Stoney Rise. (There's a lot of succession going on in Tassie at the moment: look too at Delamere, Brook Eden, Kreglinger, Moorilla – all established vineyards being revived by new owners.)

The quirky energy that fuelled Holyman's early venture is still present in his attitude and labelling, but the wines he makes are now a little more grown-up, partly due to the fact that the mature vines at Stoney Rise provide some particularly concentrated, tasty grapes.

For my taste, Holyman subjects his chardonnay to too much new French oak: the wood drowns what I think are quite subtle, citrusy aromatics in the fruit. The pinot noir from this vineyard, by contrast, responds much more favourably to its winemaker's touch. The 'everyday-drinking' Stoney Rise pinot is matured for less than a year in older oak, and displays floral, succulent, snappy red berries: a very 'modern', appealing and fruit-driven wine. The pinot produced under the Holyman label is fermented using indigenous yeasts and a quarter of the wine is matured in new oak; the result is more savoury, boldly structured and ageworthy. Both are among the best new pinots to have emerged from the Tamar Valley in recent years.

Tasmanian Organic Wines

Ian and Caryl Cairns' 1-hectare, certified organic vineyard isn't in the Tamar Valley. It's not in any recognised wine region at all, in fact. It's out on its own, about 40 kilometres southwest of Launceston, 300 metres up on the eastern foothills of the Cluan Tier. Very few Tasmanian vineyards are planted at altitude (it's cool enough down here already), but Ian swears this sheltered, north-east-facing site is surprisingly warm; he also mulches under vine with stones, in an attempt to both keep the weeds down and reflect some heat into the vine canopy.

The Cairns have been farming here since 1991 when they established a small market garden, growing mesclun leaves organically, using biodynamic preparations. In 1999, they planted 400 pinot noir vines in their sandy soil, adding another 1500 or so Burgundy clones of pinot in 2004. The land the vines are planted in has never had any chemicals applied to it: 30 years ago it was bush, and the farmer who cleared it didn't bother with super or any other 'improvement'. The vineyard has been managed biodynamically since it was planted, and produces pinot with a rare delicacy and finesse and straightforward beauty. The 2008 was the first 'commercial' vintage (all 250 cases), and it was gorgeous: pale, transluscent aromas of fine red fruit and a very fine, juicy, ethereal presence in the mouth. It's one of the finest, most elegant, unforced and natural Tassie pinots I've tried.

Trouble in the Tamar

In recent years, Tasmania's wine industry has attracted enormous public attention not only for what it produces, but also because it has been dragged into environmental and political controversy.

The major Tasmanian forestry and woodchipping company, Gunns, bought into the wine game earlier this decade with the purchase of the Coombend, Rosevears and, most importantly, the Tamar Ridge vineyard and winery. The company then hired two of Australia's highest-profile wine men, viticulturist Dr Richard Smart and winemaker/CEO Dr Andrew Pirie (along with the new, eponymous wine brand the latter had established after leaving Pipers Brook Vineyard a couple of years before), and set about dramatically expanding its vineyards and winery capacity to the point where Gunns now processes around half of the state's total grape harvest.

A visit to Tamar Ridge is a very impressive affair. The company is making all the right noises about 'sustainability', with state-of-the-art waste-water recycling systems and undervine mulching in place. Gunns, together with the Federal Government, have also set up an internationally significant $1.8 million wine research program into, among other things, pinot noir clones. And this spirit of innovation and exploration has also led to trial plantings of new (to Tasmania) grapes such as albarino.

But it's impossible to divorce Tamar Ridge from its parent company, Gunns, and its controversial position in Tasmanian society. Whether you believe that Gunns' notorious pulp mill, located not far from the Tamar Ridge winery, is an environmental and social disaster or a great thing for the local economy (and I think you know which side of the argument I'm on), it's hard to ignore or feel comfortable about the worryingly close relationship the company has enjoyed with the state government over the years.

As one winemaker puts it: 'To put it bluntly, it's hard not to see Gunns as just using their wine businesses to launder the image of their forestry business.'

What's more, much of Gunns' vineyard expansion has come about through managed investment schemes, in which tax breaks tend to be a higher priority for most investors than growing low-yielding, high-quality grapes. And with the fruit from these new vineyards, Gunns plan to produce larger quantities of cheaper-priced wine than the state's industry has ever known, something that could potentially damage Tasmania's fine wine reputation.

Not surprisingly, many of the island's top vineyard owners and winemakers are deeply concerned about the woodchip company's involvement in the industry.

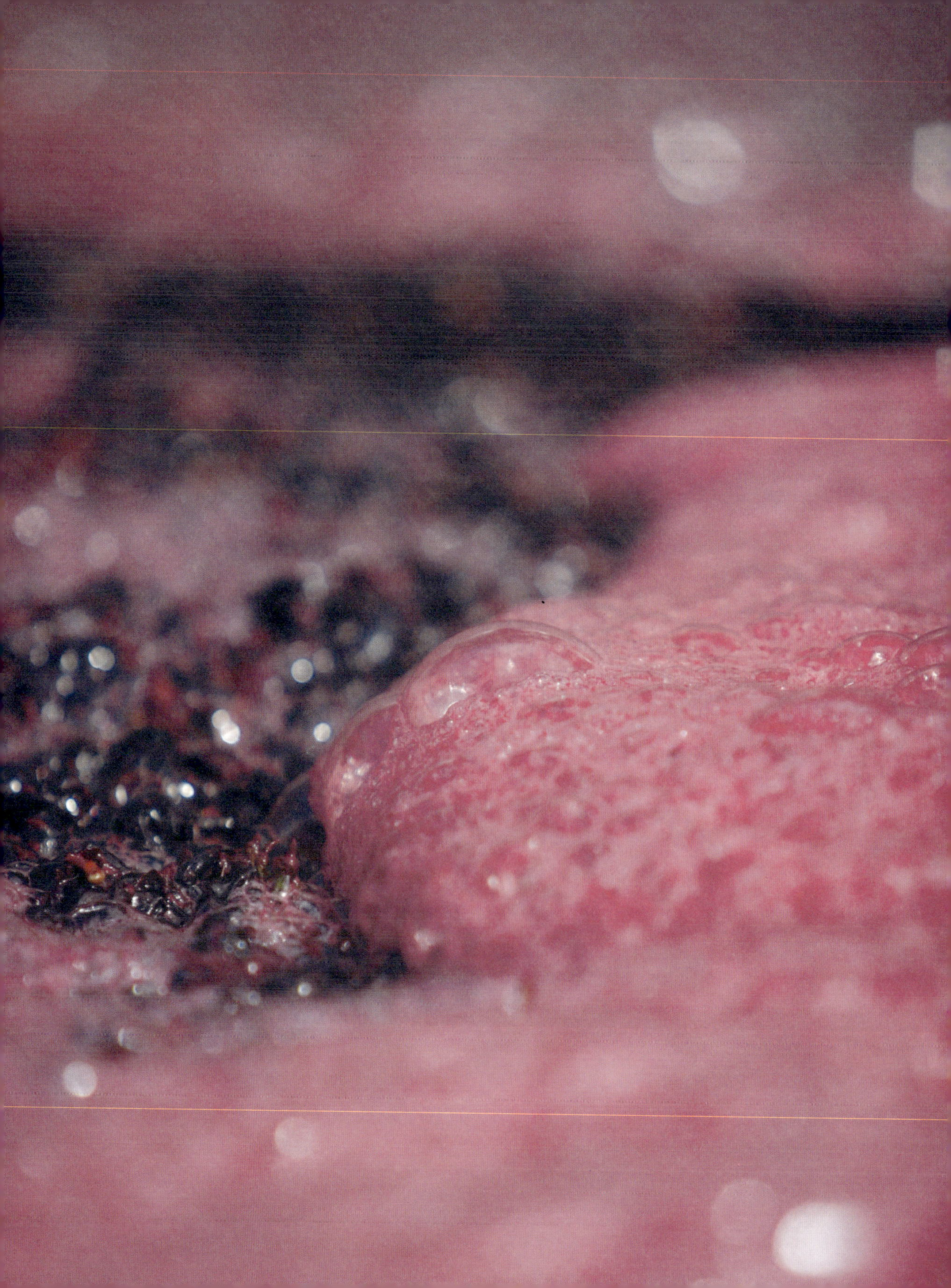

12 Queensland

The Granite Belt

The first time I visited the Granite Belt in far south Queensland, in the late 1990s, I was awestruck by the landscape: scraps of vineyard planted in fine granite sand, tucked in between massive craggy boulders. These granite outcrops were thrust up through older Devonian trap rock as the Australian continental plate collided with the Pacific oceanic plate, 290 million years ago.

This ancient decaying granite sandy soil, combined with the cool nights and clean, clear light that come from being at high altitude (the Granite Belt's vineyards sit between 800 and 1000 metres above sea level), make the place look and feel like no other in Australia I'd been to. And I was far from being the only person to have had such an emotional response to the granite country: for many thousands of years before white settlement, this was special country for the Kambuwal Aboriginal people; early settlers discovered ceremonial sites known as bora rings here, indicating that the place has long held deep spiritual significance.

But on my first visit, very few of the Granite Belt's wines were capturing that unique sense of place in the glass. Yes, several of the region's well-established vineyards such as Ballandean Estate had made some excellent wines over the years, particularly some stunning sweet sylvaner, but most of the dry whites and reds were hard and lacklustre.

The Granite Belt has come a long way. It is now not only home to a host of truly exciting new wineries (two-thirds of the state's vineyards are here) but the region has also, cleverly, created a niche for itself as a champion of non-mainstream grape varieties such as viognier, sangiovese and tempranillo. A niche marketing campaign called Strange Bird was developed in 2007, built around a touring trail focusing on the alternative varieties offered at most of the regions' cellar doors. And while this might sound like nothing more than a slick, contrived marketing gimmick, there is real substance behind the stylish presentation in the form of very good wines. What's more, some of the alternative varieties grown here are beginning to capture the cool, granite-sandy essence of the place.

Like many of the best ideas, the Strange Bird concept was hatched over a beer one evening in the local pub. One of its creators, winemaker Jim Barnes, has been working in the region since 1998.

'The best thing about Strange Bird is it's become a really co-operative thing,' says Jim. 'Everybody in the region has come together and is working together, which is something that's been hard to achieve in the past. People obviously needed a theme everyone can latch on to. And I think it's helping people make better wines, too; wines that are better suited to the place. In the early days, people were trying to mimic McLaren Vale, and that was just wrong. We can't make wines like that here.'

Boireann

The difference, they say, between a good winemaker and a great winemaker is attention to detail. This thought pops into my head halfway through a visit to the tiny Boireann vineyard and winery.

Peter and Therese Stark have no fewer than 14 different grape varieties squeezed into just 1.5 hectares of immaculately tended vineyard in the north of the Granite Belt region – everything from common or garden shiraz and cabernet to barbera, nebbiolo, grenache and tannat. Each variety has its own, carefully hand-painted sign posted at the end of its row. The tiny winery is one of the tidiest, calmest I've ever seen. Little wonder that in less than a decade, Peter Stark has made such a name for himself: the attention to detail here really is extraordinary.

Amazingly, Peter is self-taught. No winemaking lectures at TAFE. No correspondence course at uni. Fifteen years ago the man was working in a bank in Rockhampton. He and Therese bought their secluded rocky treechange property just outside Stanthorpe in 1994 to set up a bed and breakfast business. They planted a few vines and made wine for family and friends, 'But it turned out so well, I thought, well, maybe we'd better do some more,' says Peter.

The wine that forged Peter's reputation a few years ago was an intensely flavoursome shiraz viognier made from estate-grown grapes; critics quite rightly drew comparisons with leading shiraz viognier producer Clonakilla in the Canberra District in New South Wales. The wines that lifted his reputation (and the reputation of the Granite Belt) even higher were the 2007 reds: a brilliantly succulent barbera; a supremely elegant, and unmistakably varietal, merlot; a stunningly deep-tasting cabernet; a fabulously wild and rustic mourvedre; and an intensely spicy shiraz.

What was truly remarkable about these wines is that most of them were made from other people's grapes: frost almost completely destroyed the 2007 crop at Boireann so Peter bought in fruit from other Granite Belt vineyards. And yet they had the same intensity and depth found in wines from his own vineyard – because they'd been lavished with the same passion, the same extraordinary attention to detail.

What floors me, though, standing in the Boireann winery, is an estate-grown wine dragged out of the museum: a 2005 tannat. Just one barrel was made (all Peter Stark's wines are available in painfully limited quantity, just a few hundred bottles of each) from young vines, but to this Madiran lover it tastes so utterly confident of its varietal identity, bold, full, chocolatey, meaty, it could have been plucked from old, gnarly vines in south-west France.

Boireann

Sirromet

Although Sirromet's winery and cellar door are located just outside Brisbane, the company's main vineyards, the source of Sirromet's best wines, are in the Granite Belt. This is a large operation, by Queensland standards: with 144 hectares of vines and an annual crush of 1200 tonnes, Sirromet dwarfs almost every other wine company in the Sunshine State.

Much of Sirromet's energy and drive comes from charismatic general manager and chief winemaker Adam Chapman. One of Adam's favourite phrases, 'Don't Get Comfortable', is taped to the computer screens of the younger winemakers in the office. He's constantly trialling new techniques, and questioning the status quo. For example, Sirromet's Granite Belt vineyards were planted, from 1998 onwards, to no fewer than 21 different grape varieties – to see which would work best. 'It was the classic Aussie sprawl,' says Adam. But in less than a decade, that sprawl has been tightened to just 13 varieties, and not necessarily the obvious ones.

'Shiraz is not performing on that vineyard as well as we'd like,' he says. 'We've got to be realistic about it. Does it really stack up in this region in comparison to McLaren Vale and Barossa? No. But chardonnay and verdelho and viognier are ringing my bells. Nebbiolo I think has huge potential. But sauvignon blanc? All I can say is that we're probably the only winery in Australia pulling sauvignon blanc out at the moment.'

As well as producing some delicious wines – I particularly like the tangy, dry verdelho; the richly textural viognier; the fleshy, properly varietal merlot; the bramble-fruity sparkling red made from petit verdot – Adam has also helped to create a community-minded, eco-aware culture at Sirromet.

The winery offers lab analysis and bottling services, as well as contract tirage and disgorging, and educational tours for local school teachers, encouraging the application of science teaching to a real-world situation. Sirromet has also established a very impressive waste-water treatment and composting facility at its winery and cellar door at Mount Cotton, south of Brisbane: all the grape skins and stalks and seeds are composted along with shredded paper and green waste from the large property in a large and very efficient worm farm before being spread out on the vineyard and soil.

Symphony Hill Wines

The 4-hectare Symphony Hill vineyard stretches up through the 1000 metres-above-sea-level barrier, making it one of Australia's highest patches of vines. The vineyard shot to national prominence when the 2003 reserve shiraz became the first ever Queensland wine to win a gold medal at the Sydney Show, in 2005. I think the quality of that wine has been maintained and surpassed: owner Ewan Macpherson and vineyard manager/winemaker, Mike Hayes, a third-generation Stanthorpe boy, share a passion for new grapes, and their pinot gris, viognier and tempranillo are all pure, flavoursome examples of their respective varieties. Mike, a burgundy tragic, even manages to make a convincing pinot noir, in a region that is really not at all suited to the variety.

As a result of being poisoned by herbicide early in his career, Mike is taking the vineyard towards a low-input regime, and then to organic viticulture: spreading compost and mulching undervine, which will help build up organic matter in the fragile, shallow sandy topsoil, he also applies other biological sprays such as fish emulsion to the vines. This is unusual in the Granite Belt: most vineyard owners are at best ambivalent and at worst downright hostile towards the concept of organics.

Wild Soul

The words of the winemaker I'd just visited were still ringing in my ears as I walked into the small and welcoming cellar door at Wild Soul. 'You'd be mad to grow grapes organically in the Granite Belt,' she'd said, contemptuously. 'And you can't grow good grapes without irrigation. You just can't do it here.'

Really? Try telling Andy and Beth Boullier that. Since they first started planting what is now 1.3 hectares of shiraz, cabernet and merlot in the light, rocky soil of the Wild Soul farm, the Boulliers haven't used any synthetic herbicide, pesticide or fertiliser. Or irrigation. They pull the weeds by hand. And unlike most conventional – and many certified organic – vineyards, the Boulliers don't even use copper, resorting only to sulphur sprays to prevent mildew outbreaks.

The unconventional (by regional standards) viticulture doesn't stop there. Andy Boullier tries wherever possible to follow the lunar and stellar cycles of the biodynamic calendar for the timing of picking, pruning and winemaking activities. The wines are fermented simply, in open pots, without refrigeration, and gently basket-pressed – unfiltered and unfined; sulphur additions at bottling are kept very low; and, most provocative of all, the prices fluctuate each year to reflect the quality of the season, rather than following the industry standard of rising annually regardless of vintage variation.

So, for example, while the 2005 shiraz – an elegant red wine with fine, powdery tannins – was from a good vintage and cost $26, the 2004 – much lighter, but still very pleasant – from a rainy vintage, only cost $14. There is something enormously refreshing and honest about this approach.

The Boulliers run a very low-key cellar door operation, but I think the wines deserve to be better known as they're some of the prettiest and finest in the region. Not only can organic, unirrigated viticulture definitely work in the Granite Belt, but it can also produce delicious wines.

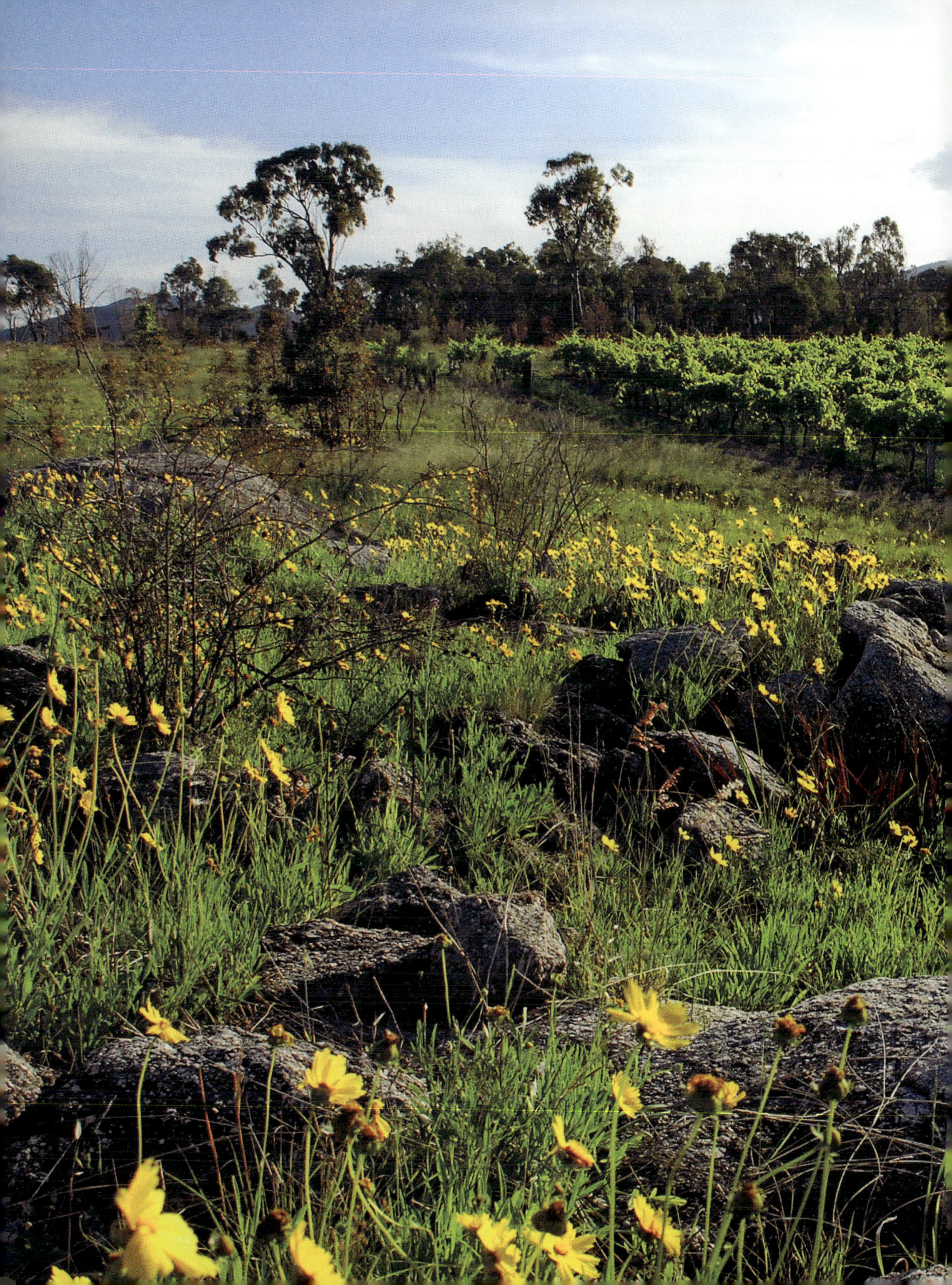

Granite Belt

Picture credits

p. ii: James Boddington; p. vi: James Boddington; p. 1: James Broadway; pp. 6-7: Adrian Lander; p. 8: Adrian Lander; p.13: Maps: courtesy Dr Richard Smart and John Gwalter; p. 16: *Samuel de Pury's Vineyard*, William Barak, c. 1898, copyright Musée d'ethnographie (MEN), Neuchâtel, photo: Alain Germond; p. 21: Paxton Vineyards (www.paxtonvineyards.com); p. 24: Map: Martin Von Wyss, vW Maps; p. 30: James Broadway; p. 39: (clockwise from top left) Max Allen, James Broadway, Max Allen, James Boddington; p. 42: Smallfry Wines (www.smallfrywines.com.au); p. 46: Henschke (www.henschke.com.au); p. 53 Courtesy Australian Alternative Varieties Wine Show; p. 54: Adrian Lander; p. 58: James Boddington; p. 66: Adrian Lander; p. 67: Max Allen; p. 74-75: Max Allen; pp. 90-91: James Broadway; p. 92: Courtesy South Australian Murray-Darling Basin Resource Information Centre (SAMRIC), River Murray Aerial Photography; pp. 102-103: Max Allen; p. 111: Angove Wines (www.angoves.com.au); p. 112: James Boddington; p. 115: Max Allen; p. 116: Max Allen; p. 121: Adrian Lander; p. 124: Adrian Lander; pp. 126-127: Andrew Chapman; p. 130: Max Allen; p. 131 Courtesy South Pack winemakers/ Imbibo; pp. 138-139: Wedgetail Estate (www.wedgetailestate.com.au); p. 141: Max Allen; p. 142: Adrian Lander; pp. 144-145: Adrian Lander; p. 151: Max Allen; p. 155: James Broadway; p. 161: By Farr and Farr Rising (www.byfarr.com.au); p. 165: James Broadway; p. 167: James Broadway; p. 171: James Broadway; p. 173: Max Allen; p. 176: James Broadway; p. 179: Max Allen; p. 185: Vinea Marson (www.vineamarson.com); p. 187: James Broadway; p. 188: Jean Paul's Vineyard (www.jeanpaulsvineyard.com.au); pp. 192-193: Rees Miller Estate (www.reesmiller.com); p. 195: Pizzini Wines (www.pizzini.com.au); p. 199: Adrian Lander; p. 201: Max Allen; p. 202: James Boddington; pp. 206-207: Pennyweight Winery (www.pennyweight.com.au); p. 212: Adrian Lander; p. 214: Construction images courtesy Huff 'n' Puff Strawbale Constructions, Valhalla Wines (www.valhallawines.com.au); p. 217: James Boddington; pp. 220-221: James Boddington; p. 225: James Boddington; p. 229: Max Allen; p. 230: James Broadway; pp. 236-237: Adrian Lander; p. 243: Max Allen; p. 244: Ngeringa Wines (www.ngeringa.com); pp. 248-249: Adrian Lander; p. 253: Max Allen; p. 255: James Boddington; p. 256: Kalleske Wines (www.kalleske.com); p. 261: James Boddington; pp. 264-265: Adrian Lander; p. 267: Max Allen; pp. 270-271: James Boddington; p. 275: Smallfry Wines (www.smallfry.com.au); pp. 280-281: Adrian Lander; pp. 284-286: James Broadway; p. 291: Paxton Vineyards (www.paxtonvineyards.com); pp. 294-295: Adrian Lander; p. 298: The Hedonist (www.hedonistwines.com.au); p. 307: Courtesy Mt Billy Wines, photograph by Kate Elmes (www.mtbillywines.com.au); p. 315: Courtesy Cape Jaffa Wines, photograph by Wild Creative Photography (www.capejaffawines.com.au); p. 318: James Boddington; p. 322: Max Allen; p. 324: Max Allen; pp. 326-327: Courtesy Krinklewood, photograph by Rod Windrim (www.krinklewood.com); p. 330: Max Allen; p. 331 Lowe Family Wine Co. (www.lowewine.com); p. 335: Max Allen; pp. 340-341: Tamburlaine Organic Wines (www.tamburlaine.com.au); p. 346: Rosnay Organic Wines (www.rosnay.com.au); pp. 350-351: James Boddington; p. 357: Freeman Vineyards (www.freemanvineyards.com.au); p. 358: Cherubino Wines (www.larrycherubino.com.au); p. 362: Max Allen; p. 369: Max Allen; p. 370: Courtesy Cullen Wines, photograph by Frances Andrijich Photography (www.cullenwines.com.au); pp. 374-375: Courtesy Cullen Wines, photograph by Frances Andrijich Photography (www.cullenwines.com.au); pp. 382-383: Cherubino Wines (www.larrycherubino.com.au); p. 390: Adrian Lander; p. 395: Stefano Lubiana Wines (www.slw.com.au); pp. 398-399: Adrian Lander; p. 403: Frogmore Creek Wines (www.frogmorecreek.com.au); pp. 406-407: Adrian Lander; pp. 412-413: Adrian Lander; p. 418: James Boddington; p. 423: Courtesy Granite Belt Wine Country; p. 426-427: Courtesy Granite Belt Wine Country.

Index

Bold entries indicate featured producers

A

Adams, Tim 278
Adelina Wines/Some Young Punks, Clare Valley, SA 278
Ahrens, Wayne 272–3
Alcorso, Julian 44
Alkoomi, Frankland River, WA 387
All Saints Estate, Rutherglen, Vic. 211–12
Allies and Garagiste, Mornington Peninsula, Vic. 134
Altezza, Adelaide Hills, SA 33
Amietta, Geelong, Vic. 160
Anderson, David 'Duck' 184
Anderson, Liam 40, 184
Anderson, Stuart 173
Angove, John 14
Angove, Tom 100
Angove Family Winemakers, Riverland, SA 12, 14, 48, 62, 69, **100–1**
Antonini, Alberto 181–2, 195
Apsley Gorge, Tasmania 404
Armstrong, Sue and Bruce 100–1
Arrivo, Adelaide Hills, SA 86, **245–6**
Austin, Fran 314, 411, 414

B

Back Verandah, Riverland, SA 101, 104
Baddaginnie Run, Strathbogie Ranges, Vic. 189–90
Bannockburn Vineyards, Geelong, Vic. 160, 162
Barak, William 29
Barich, Tony and Pam 4–5
Barlow, Professor Snow 10–11, 189–90
Barnes, Jim 421
Barrett, Rod and Sandra 159
Barry, John and Arda 224
Barry, Matt, 224, 225
Barry, Peter 278–9
Bass Phillip, Gippsland Vic. 33, 148, **165–7**
Battle of Bosworth, McLaren Vale, SA 293, 297

Bay of Fires, Tasmania 62, 314, 411, 414
Beach Road, Langhorne Creek, SA 308
Bekkers, Toby 37, 289, 291–2
Bell, Sue 314, 316
Bellwether, Coonawarra, SA 314, 316
Berry, Gavin 384
Best's Great Western, Grampians, Vic. 76, 218
Bicknell, David 122, 128–9
Bilenkji, Andrew 342
Billings, Warwick 12
Bindi, Macedon Ranges, Vic. 151–2
Blanck, Frederick 125
Bloodwood, Orange, NSW 107, **337–8**
Boireann, Granite Belt, Qld 422
Bonfiglioli, Dr Rod 61
Bonic family 105
Bonney, Graham and Ruth 163
Bosward, Reid 43, 135
Bosworth, Joch 293
Botobolar, Mudgee, NSW 42, 68, 329, **332–3**
Boudry, Mike 205
Bowen Estate, Coonawarra, SA 312
Brady, Tony 276
Bremerton, Langhorne Creek, SA 308
Bress, Bendigo, Vic. 174
Bridgeman, Paul 132, 135
Briggs, Aunty Carolyn 18, 28, 40
Brocksopp, John 380
Brokenwood, Hunter Valley, NSW 328
Brook Eden, Tasmania 409, 416
Broombee Organic, Mudgee, NSW 329
Brown, David 269
Brown, Eliza, Angela and Nick 211
Brown, Melissa and Mike 299–300
Brown Brothers, King Valley, Vic. 51, 68, 77, 78, 86, 106, 118, 181, 194, 195, **197–8**
Bruer, David and Barbara 310–11
Bruin, Leonard 360–1
Buckle, Dan 218
Bulleid, Nick 355
Burch, Jeff and Amy 388
Burge, Rick 257
Burge Family Winemakers, Barossa Valley, SA 257
Burnside Organic Farm, Margaret River, WA 371

431

By Farr and Farr Rising, Geelong, Vic. 160, 162

C

Cairns, Ian and Caryl 416
Camilleri, Cecil 274
Campbell, Colin 217
Campbell, Ken and Joy 158
Canute, Christian 259
Cape Jaffa, Mount Benson, SA 316–17
Cape Mentelle, Margaret River, WA 372
Capel Vale, various regions, WA 387
Carlei, Sergio 26, 115–16
Carlei Wines and the Green Vineyards, Beaconsfield, Vic. 115–16
Carmody, Pat 117
Carpenter family 36–7, 56, 347, 348–9
Carrodus, Dr Bailey 132, 135
Cartwright, Bob 377
Casa Freschi, Langhorne Creek, SA 309–10
Cascabel, McLaren Vale, SA 296, 299
Castagna, Julian 80, 201–3
Castagna, Beechworth, Vic. 32, 80, 81, 201–3
Castle Rock, Porongurups, WA 389
Centennial, Southern Highlands, NSW 355
Chalk Hill, McLaren Vale, SA 290
Chalkers Crossing, Hilltops, NSW 355
Chalmers, Bruce and Jenni 61, 97–8
Chalmers Wines, Murray Darling, NSW and Heathcote, Vic. 61, 87, **97–8**, 141
Chapel Hill, McLaren Vale, SA 298
Chapman, Adam 424
Chapman, David 134
Chapoutier, Michel 180, 204
Charteris, P. J. 328
Chatsfield, Porongurups, WA 65, 388
Chatto, Jim 323
Cherubino, Larry 387
Chrismont, King Valley, Vic 196
Chromy, Josef 415
Church, David 136
Clancy, Paul 50
Clappis, Walter 298
Clark, Nicholas 160
Clarke, Andrew 118

Clayfield, Simon 219
Clayfield, Grampians, Vic. 219
Clonakilla, Canberra District, NSW 81, 347, **352–3**
Clown Fish, Margaret River, WA 368
Cobaw Ridge, Macedon Ranges, Vic. 153
Cockbill, Janet 160
Collector, Canberra District, NSW 347
Collins, Jaysen 262
Collis, Maree 37, 158
Cooper, Alan and Nelly 153
Cooper, Joshua 153
Coriole, McLaren Vale, SA 84, 289–90
Cosgriff, Tony 355
Crabtree, Clare Valley, SA 282
Craiglee, Sunbury, Vic. 117
Crane, Dan 211
Crawford River, Henty, Vic. 226
Crittenden, Garry 61, 143
Crittenden, Rollo 143
Crittenden, Mornington Peninsula, Vic. 82, **143**, 146, 148, 218
Croser, Brian 33, 44, 233, 269, 304, 305–6
Cullen, Margaret River, WA 369–70
Cullen, Vanya 38, 369–70
Cumulus, Orange, NSW 32, 342, 401
Curly Flat, Macedon Ranges, Vic. 153–4
Cush, David 405

D

d'Anna, Franco 137
d'Arenberg, McLaren Vale, SA 290
Dal Zotto family 196
Dal Zotto, King Valley, Vic. 196
Davenport, Josh 365–6
David Hook, Hunter Valley, NSW 324
Davidson, Mark 339
Day, Robin 45
De Bortoli, Riverina, NSW and Yarra Valley, Vic. 41, 48, 81, **104–5, 123–4**, 128, 137, 169, 329
De Castella, Damien 187
De Castella, Louis 187, 188
De Castella, Will 187–8
de Pieri, Stefano 61
De Pury family 29, 136

Deisen, Sabine 258
Deisen Landscape, Barossa Valley, SA 258
Del Popolo, Antoinette 213
Delamere, Tasmania 314, 408, 416
Delatite, Upper Goulburn, Vic. 65, 190
Denig, Wouter 360–1
Dhillon, Bill 151, 152
Dhillon, Michael 151–2
Di Lusso, Mudgee, NSW 333–4
Diletti, Rob 389
Dineen, Jeremy 314, 415
Dobson, Marc 246–7
Dog Rock, Pyrenees, Vic. 225
Domaine Chandon, Yarra Valley, Vic. 224, 269, 286, 411
Downie, Bill 42–3, 132, 169–70
Doyle, Richard 400
Doyle, Stephen and Rhonda 107, 337–8, 342
Draper, Paul 133
Dredge, Peter 182–3
Drogemuller, Paul and Kathy 242, 313
Dry, Peter 59
Duncan, Andrew 101, 104
Dunn's Creek, Mornington Peninsula, Vic. 141
Durham, John 388

E

Eather, Rhys and Garth 325, 328
Edwards, John 304, 306
Ellis, Gerald 402
Ellis, John 154, 156
Evans, Len 49–50, 320–1, 328

F

Faber, Swan Valley, WA 364
Fairall, Rob 333–4
Farmer, David 23, 25
Farquhar, Duncan 400
Farr, Gary 80, 160, 162
Farr, Nick 160, 162
Fensom, Les 258
Ferguson, Duncan 296
Fernandez, Susana 296
Ferngrove, Frankland River, WA 385
Fiaschi, Thomas 78, 333

First Drop, Adelaide, SA 239–40
Flanders, Barney 134
Fletcher, Brian 118
Fogarty, Peter 365
Foillard, Jean 42
Forbes, Mac 132, 133–4
Foster, Adam 137
Foxey's Hangout, Mornington Peninsula, Vic. 148
Frankland Estate, Frankland River, WA 385–6
Franklin, Brian 404
Freeman, Brian 356
Freeman, Hilltops, NSW 355, 356–7
Freschi, David 33, 309–10
Frog Rock, Mudgee, NSW 329
Frogmore Creek and Tony Scherer, Tasmania 34, 106–7, 401–2
Fryar, Natalie 411

G

Gago, Peter 58, 234–5
Gant, Matt 239–40, 262
Gardner, Herb and Jenni 278, 346
Gardners Ground, Cowra, NSW 346
Gauntlett, Judy and Gerry 360
Gely, Magali 262–3
Gembrook Hill, Yarra Valley, Vic. 134
Gemtree, McLaren Vale, SA 297, 299–300
Georgiadis, Paul 235
Giaconda, Beechworth, Vic. 204–5
Giant Steps/Innocent Bystander, Yarra Valley, Vic. 106, 129
Gibraltar Rock, Porongurups, WA 388
Gibson, Barossa Valley, SA 260
Gibson, Rob 260
Gilead, Swan District, WA 360
Gladstones, John 304, 305, 365, 384
Glaetzer, Nick 401
Glastonbury, Rob 104–5
Gleave, David 181
Glover, Michael 160, 162
Godden, Peter 245–6, 250
Godfrey, James 217
Gomm, Murray 389
Gordon Parker, Geographe, WA 388

Goulburn Terrace/Moon, Nagambie Lakes and Beechworth, Vic. 205
Graham, Peter 204
Greenstone, Heathcote, Vic. 141, **181–2**, 195
Grey Sands, Tasmania 414
Griffiths, John 364
Grosset Wines, Clare Valley, SA 277
Grosset, Jeffrey 18, 27, 28, 29, 277
Grove Estate, Hilltops, NSW 355
Guard, Andrew 43

H

Hahndorf Hill, Adelaide Hills, SA 246–7
Hanging Rock Winery, Macedon Ranges, Vic. 154, 156
Harris, John 224
Harrop, Matt 119
Hart, Allen and Andrea 225
Harvey, Jock 290
Hatherleigh, Southern New South Wales 355
Hayes, Mike 424–5
Heathcote Winery, Heathcote, Vic. 69
Hedonist, McLaren Vale, SA 298
Helm, Ken 347
Henry, Paul 50, 51
Henschke, Stephen and Prue 268–9
Henschke, Eden Valley, SA 51, **268–9**
Herriot, John and Yvonne 379
Herriot Wines, Manjimup, WA 379
Hewitson, Dean 153, 238
Hewitson, Adelaide, SA 238
Highbank, Coonawarra, SA 313
Hilder, Suzi 272–3
Hill Smith, Robert 51, 274
Hoare, Briony and Tony 308
Hochkirch Wines, Henty, Vic. 227–9
Hodder, Sue 312
Hoddles Creek Estate, Yarra Valley, Vic. 137
Hohnan, David 372, 373
Holloway, Shane 314, 408
Holyman, Joe 415–16
Hood, Andrew 401, 415
Hook, David 324
Hooper family 316–17
Hotham Ridge, Wandering, WA 360–1

Howard Park, Margaret River and Great Southern, WA 388
Hutchison, Rex 313
Hutton, Damien 365
Hyett, Bruce 157

I

Ingham, Elaine 123
Ingle, Tony 100
Innes, David and Annette 242
Irish, Adam 148
Irish, Tamara 228
Irvine, Eden Valley, SA 83
Irvine, James 261

J

Jackson, Liz 323
Jacobs, Larry 245–6
Jamsheed, Yarra Valley, Vic. 65, 133
Jansz, Tasmania 411
Jarrett, Justin 339
Jasper Hill, Heathcote, Vic. 41, **179–80**
Jean Paul's Vineyard, Upper Goulburn, Vic. 187–8
Jeanneret, Ben 283
Jeanneret Wines, Clare Valley, SA 283
Jim Barry, Clare Valley, SA 278–9
Jinks Creek, Tonimbuk, Vic. 118
John Kosovich Wines, Swan Valley, WA 363
Joly, Nicolas 203, 292
Jones, Greg 342
Jones, Phillip 33, 148, 165–7, 205
Josef Chromy, Tasmania 314, **415**
Judy's Farm, Yarra Valley, Vic. 137

K

Kaesler, Barossa Valley, SA 43, 135
Kalleske, Troy 255–6
Kalleske, Barossa Valley, SA 255–6
Kangarilla Road, McLaren Vale, SA 298
Kapolice, Steve 115
Karstrom, Kevin and Trina 332–3
Kelly, Dr Alexander 58, 60
Kerney, Phil 342–3
Kiltynane, Yarra Valley, Vic. 37, **125**, **128**
King River Estate, King Valley, Vic. 198

Kinloch, Upper Goulburn, Vic. 186
Kinzbrunner, Rick 118, 204–5
Kirk, John 352
Kirk, Tim 26, 347, 352–3, 355
Kirkhope, Kate 37, 125, 128
Klein, Janet and Erinn 243–4
Knaggs, Trevor 198
Knappstein, Mick 276
Koch, Greg 316
Kooyong, Mornington Peninsula, Vic. 98, 141–2
Kosovich, John 363
Krinklewood, Hunter Valley, NSW 38, 322–4
Kristen family 405
Krstic, Dr Mark 45
KT and the Falcon, Clare Valley, SA 279, 282–3

L

La Cantina, King Valley, Vic. 196
La Linea, Adelaide Hills, SA 247, 250
Laffer, Phillip 20, 34
Lake, Max 320, 328
Lambert, Luke 132–3
Lamont's, Swan Valley, WA 363
Lamothe, Guy 137
Lance, David and Cathy 135
Lance, James 135–6
Lane, Rory 218
Lapalus, Gilles 32, 173
Lark Hill, Canberra District, NSW 36, 56, 82, 347, **348–9**
Larry Cherubino, various regions, WA 387
Laughton, Ron and Emily 41, 179–80
Leask, Richard 297
Leddin, Digby 363
Lee, Tony 148
Lehmann, Peter 25, 63, 254
Lenton Brae, Margaret River, WA 367
Leske, Peter 247, 250
Lethbridge, Geelong, Vic. 37, 106, **158–9**
Lewkowski, Ashley 380
Lillian's Vineyard, Pemberton, WA 380
Limbic Wines, Pakenham Upper, Vic. 118–19

Lincoln, Pam 389
Lost Valley Winery, Upper Goulburn, Vic. 81, 186
Loughnan, Rob and Mary 329
Louis de Castella, Heathcote, Vic. 187
Lowe, David 330–1, 333
Lowe Family Wine Co., Mudgee, NSW 329, **330–1**
Lubiana, Steve and Monique 394–5
Lucy Margaux/Domaine Lucci, Adelaide Hills, SA 250–1
Luke Lambert, Yarra Valley, Vic. 132

M

Mac Forbes, Yarra Valley, Vic. 106–7
McBryde, Colin 278
McCall, Lara and Jamie 371
McCall, Lindsay 12
McCarthy, Kevin 146, 147
McCaughey, Winsome 189
McCormack, Bruce 410
McDonald, Ross 323
McGill, Sally 245
McHenry Hohnen, Margaret River, WA 373, 376
McIntosh, Peter 409
McIntyre, Rick 141
McIvor Estate, Heathcote, Vic. 183
McKay, Alex 347
McMahon, Dylan 136
McMahon, Peter and Margaret 136
McNamee, Justin 301–2
Macpherson, Ewen 424–5
Macquariedale, Hunter Valley, NSW 323
Maddens Rise, Yarra Valley, Vic. 132
Main Ridge Estate, Mornington Peninsula, Vic. 141
Mann, Dorham 81, 372
Mann, Rob 372
Marchand, Pascal 115–16, 388
Marchand and Burch, Great Southern, WA 388
Marks, Adam 172, 174
Marri Wood Park, Margaret River, WA 376–7
Marson, Mario 183–4
Martin, Bryan 352–3

Index 435

Martins Hill, Mudgee, NSW 329
Massena, Barossa Valley, SA 262
Mast, Trevor 313
Mayer, Timo 132, 134
Meadowbank, Tasmania 107, **402**
Meerea Park, Hunter Valley, NSW 325, 328
Melton, Charlie 107
Metcalf, Dean 402
Middleton, John 122, 201
Millbrook Winery, Perth Hills, WA 365, 381
Miller, David 190–1
Mills, Gary 65, 132, 133
Miranda, Sam 198
Mitchell, Andrew and Jane 283, 288
Mitchell, Colin and Rosa 175, 177
Mitchell, Clare Valley, SA 283, 288
Montrose, Mudgee, NSW 84
Moon, Greta 205
Moondarra, Gippsland, Vic. 168–9
Moorilla, Tasmania 396–7
Moorooduc Estate, Mornington Peninsula, Vic. 141
Moraghan, Phillip 153–4
Morey, Barry 208–9
Morris, Dominic and Kristina 174–5
Morris, Stephen and Elizabeth 208
Mosele, Sandro 98, 141–2, 181
Moshos, Con 44, 269, 272
Mount Avoca, Pyrenees, Vic. 224–5
Mount Benson, Limestone Coast, SA 81
Mt Billy, Southern Fleurieu, SA 306
Mount Horrocks, Clare Valley, SA 107
Mount Langi Ghiran, Grampians, Vic. 218, 313
Mount Majura, Canberra District, ACT 353–4
Mount Mary, Yarra Valley, Vic. 122, 136, 183, 201
Mount Pleasant, Hunter Valley, NSW 321
Mountadam, Eden Valley, SA 44, 269, 272
Mountford, Manjimup, WA 379
Mueller, Pete 396
Muller, Egon 242
Munchenberg, Brett 96
Murphy, Patrick and Anthony 109–10
Myattsfield, Perth Hills, WA 365–6

N

Nadeson, Ray 158–9
Nagorcka, Dianne 228
Nagorcka, John 227–9
Naked Range, Yarra Valley, Vic. 137
Neal, Doug 163
Ngeringa, Adelaide Hills, SA 243–4
919 Wines, Riverland, SA 99
Noon, Drew and Reagan 300–1
Noon, McLaren Vale, SA 300–1
Norris, Rob 119

O

O'Brien, Kevin 298
O'Callaghan, Mark 132
O'Callaghan, Robert 254, 258, 260
O'Donohoe, Michael 108
O'Leary, David 276, 277
O'Leary Walker, Clare Valley, SA 276
O'Shea, Maurice 257, 338
Oakridge, Yarra Valley, Vic. 107, 122, **128–9**
Olssens, Clare Valley, SA 86
Oranje Tractor, Albany, WA 389
Organic One, Riverina, NSW 105, **108**
Osborn, Chester 290
Overnoy, Pierre 42

P

Page, Julia 334
Palmer, Alice 409
Pannell family 378
Pannell, Steve 240–1, 313
Paracombe, Adelaide Hills, SA 242, 313
Paradise IV, Geelong, Vic. 163
Paringa Estate, Mornington Peninsula, Vic. 12
Parker, Gordon 388
Patrick T, Coonawarra and Wrattonbully, SA 313
Paxton, David 291–2
Paxton, Michael 291
Paxton, McLaren Vale, SA 37, 289, **291–2**, 297
Penfolds, Adelaide, SA 58, **234–5**
Pennyfield, Berri, SA 104
Pennyweight, Beechworth, Vic. 208, 215
Pertaringa, McLaren Vale, SA 297

Peter Lehmann, Barossa Valley, SA 25, 63, 254
Pfeiffer, Chris 217
Pfifferling, Eric 42
Philip Shaw, Orange, NSW 49, 343
Phillips, Graeme 402
Picardy, Pemberton, WA 378
Pickering, David 342
Pickles, John and Jan 388
Pig in the House, Cowra, NSW 346
Pipers Brook Vineyard, Tasmania 409–10, 417
Pirie, Andrew 408, 409, 411, 417
Pizzini, Fred 195–6
Pizzini, King Valley, Vic. 86, **195–6**
Plantagenet, Mount Barker, WA 388
Plunkett Fowles, Strathbogie Ranges, Vic. 186
Podolinsky, Alex 36–7, 204, 362
Pondalowie, Bendigo, Vic. 174–5
Port Phillip Estate, Mornington Peninsula, Vic. 141
Powell, Dave 254
Prancing Horse, Mornington Peninsula, Vic. 115
Prentice, Neil 168–9
Pretorius, Sakki 232–3
Priestley, John 322, 409
Primo Estate, McLaren Vale, SA 64, 289–90
Prince Albert Vineyard, Geelong, Vic. 157
Protero, Adelaide Hills, SA 241, 313
Proud, Stuart 132
Providence, Tasmania 408
Pryor, Geoff 114
Pullar, Michael 118–19
Punch, Yarra Valley, Vic. 136

Q

Quealy, Kathleen 81, 146–7
Quealy, Mornington Peninsula, Vic. 146–7
Quinlan, Anthony 368

R

Radford, Ben and Gill 267
Radford Wines, Eden Valley, SA 267
Rathbone, Graeme 136
Rathbone, James and Clarice 136

Ravensworth, Canberra District, NSW 353
Rebenberg, Geelong, Vic. 158, 159
Red Edge, Heathcote, Vic. 182–3
Redden Bridge, Wrattonbully, SA 316
Redesdale Estate, Heathcote, Vic. 183
Redman, Bruce and Mal 314
Redman, Coonawarra, SA 312
Reedman, Phil 61
Rees Miller, Upper Goulburn, Vic. 190–1
Rees, Sylke 190–1
Retsas, John 239–40, 262
Reynolds, Russ 368
Richardson, Richard 408
Richter, Robert and Rita 414
Riek, Edgar 347, 353
Riley, Lincoln 137
Rimfire, Maclagan, Qld 68
Ringland, Chris 170
Rising, St Andrews, Vic. 132
Ritchie, David 190
Robb family 224–5
Roberts, Graham 397
Robertson, Lesley 329
Robinson, Rachel 365–6
Robinvale Organic & Bio-dynamic Wine 78, 82
Robson family 342, 343
Rockford, Barossa Valley, SA 78
Rose, Louisa 60, 274
Rosnay Organic Wines, Cowra, NSW 37, 333, 344, **345–6**, 409
Rousseau, Alain 401, 402
Rousseau, Celine 355
Rusden, Barossa Valley, SA 259
Rymill, Coonawarra, SA 313

S

Sally's Paddock, Pyrenees, Vic. 224–5
Sam Miranda/Symphonia, King Valley, Vic. 198
Samek, Tom 402
Samuel's Gorge, McLaren Vale, SA 301–2
Schell, Pete 262–3, 306
Scherer, Tony 34, 401–2
Schrapel, Geoff 38
Schubert, Max 242

S.C. Pannell Wines, Adelaide, SA 86, **240–1**
Scorpo, Mornington Peninsula, Vic. 141
Semmler, Eric and Jenny 99, 216
Seppelt Great Western, Grampians, Vic. 218, **222**
Seppeltsfield, Barossa Valley, SA 216, 217
Seville Estate, Yarra Valley, Vic. 136
Sexton, Phil 129
Shadowfax Wines, Werribee, Vic. 119–20
Shaw, Philip 49
Shobbrook, Tom 259, 262
Shobbrook, Barossa Valley, SA 259, 262
Sirromet, Granite Belt, Qld 424
Smallfry Wines, Eden Valley, SA 272–3
Smart, Dr Richard 11, 14, 417
Smith, Barrie and Judi 385
Smith, Hunter and Elizabeth 385–6
Smith, Tony 384
Smithbrook, Pemberton, WA 381
Snare, Neil 397
Sorrenberg, Beechworth, Vic. 208–9
South Pack 129–34, 137
Spinifex, Barossa Valley, SA 262–3, 306
Spring Vale, Tasmania 405
Staindl, Paul 148
Staindl, Mornington Peninsula, Vic. 120, 148
Standish, Dan 262
Stanlake, Peter 371
Stanton and Killeen, Rutherglen, Vic. 216
Stark, Peter and Therese 422
Statham, Sam 37, 345–6
Stefano Lubiana Wines, Tasmania 62, **394–5**
Steiner, Rudolf 36, 38, 40, 105, 322, 369
Stevens, Leonie 190
Stocker, Dr John 61
Stoney Rise, Tasmania 415–16
Strachan, Fred 5
Strachan, Stephen 50
Studley Park Vineyard, Melbourne, Vic. 114
Sutherland Smith, Andrew and Carol 215
Sutton Grange, Bendigo, Vic. 32, **173**, 342
Swinging Bridge, Cowra, NSW 344
Symons, Mike 380
Symphony Hill, Granite Belt, Qld 424–5
Syrahmi, Heathcote, Vic. 137, 183

T

T'Gallant, Mornington Peninsula, Vic. 146, 147, 149
Tahbilk, Nagambie Lakes and Beechworth, Vic. 51, 65, 68
Talijancich, James 362–3
Talijancich, Swan Valley, WA 362–3
Tamburlaine, Orange, NSW 339, 342
Tapanappa Foggy Hill Vineyard, Southern Fleurieu, SA 33, 44, **305–6**
Tapestry, McLaren Vale, SA 298
TarraWarra, Yarra Valley, Vic. 125, 128
Tasmanian Organic Wines, Tasmania 416
Temple Bruer, Langhorne Creek, SA 42, **310–11**
Ten Minutes by Tractor, Mornington Peninsula, Vic. 141
Tertini, Southern Highlands, NSW 355
Teusner, Kym 254
Teusner, Barossa Valley, SA 254
Therkildsen, Anton 213
Thistle Hill, Mudgee, NSW 329, 333
Thomas, Andrew 328
Thompson, Kerrie 279, 282–3
Thomson family 226
Tintara, McLaren Vale, SA 58, 60
Tolley, Kym 48
Tolley, Sam 50
Tom's Drop, Riverland, SA 108–9
Tomlinson, Ed 367
Toole, Stephanie 107
Torbreck, Barossa Valley, SA 43, 107
Trentham Estate, Murray Darling, NSW 87, **109–10**
Tulloch, Christina 328
Tulloch, Hunter Valley, NSW 328
Turkey Flat, Barossa Valley, SA 68
Turner, Ed 329
Tyrrell, Murray 320, 328
Tyrrells, Hunter Valley, NSW 41

V

Valhalla, Rutherglen, Vic. 213
van der Loo, Frank 353–4
Van Der Muelen, Graham and Margaret 136
van der Reest, Conor 396–7

van Klopper, Anton 2–3, 243, 250–1, 282
Vice, Dennis and Bonnie 313
Vickery, John 258
Vinea Marson, Heathcote, Vic. 183–4

W

Wahlquist, Gil 332
Wallace Lane/Ross Hill, Orange, NSW 342–3
Wallington, Margaret 344
Wallington Wines, Cowra, NSW 344
Walpole, Mark 181, 182, 195
Walsh, Dave 396–7
Walsh, Ryan 373, 376
Wandin, Professor Joy Murphy 29
Wanted Man, Heathcote, Vic. 181
Ward, Tom 344
Warrabilla, Rutherglen, Vic. 213, 215
Warramate, Yarra Valley, Vic. 136
Watson, Stuart 367
Webb, Leanne 11
Webber, Steve 26, 123–4, 137
Wedgetail Estate, Yarra Valley, Vic. 137
Wellsmore, Richard 298
Wenk, Matt 262
Wetherell, Mike 314
Whetton, Penny 11
Whistling Eagle, Heathcote, Vic. 181
White, Phillip 108–9
White, Robert 20
Wild Duck Creek, Heathcote, Vic. 40, 184
Wild Soul, Granite Belt, Qld 425
Wildcroft, Mornington Peninsula, Vic. 148
William Downie, Gippsland, Vic. 169–70
Williams, Bob 36
Willson, Rebecca and Lucy 308
Wilson, Jane 329, 330–1
Wiltshire, Graham 408
Windowrie, Cowra, NSW 348
Windrim, Rod 38, 322–4
Winstead, Tasmania 397
Wirra Wirra, McLaren Vale, SA 298
Wood, Emma 222
Woodlands, Margaret River, WA 367
Wright, Julian 377–8
Wynn, David 269, 272
Wynns, Coonawarra, SA 234, 312

Y

Yalumba, Eden Valley, SA 48, 51, 60, 80, 261, **273–4**
Yandoit Hill, Bendigo, Vic. 175, 177
Yangarra, McLaren Vale, SA 298
Yarra Yering, Yarra Valley, Vic. 132, 135
YarraLoch, Yarra Valley, Vic. 129
Yates, David 157
Yeringberg, Yarra Valley, Vic. 136
York, Doug 388

Z

Zema Estate, Coonawarra, SA 312